Public enterprise in less-developed countries

Public enterprise in less-developed countries

EDITED BY LEROY P. JONES

Associate Professor of Economics
Director, Program in Economics and Management of Public Enterprise
Boston University

WITH RICHARD D. MALLON, EDWARD S. MASON,
PAUL N. ROSENSTEIN-RODAN, AND RAYMOND VERNON

CAMBRIDGE UNIVERSITY PRESS

CAMBRIDGE

LONDON   NEW YORK   NEW ROCHELLE
MELBOURNE   SYDNEY

CAMBRIDGE UNIVERSITY PRESS
Cambridge, New York, Melbourne, Madrid, Cape Town, Singapore, São Paulo, Delhi

Cambridge University Press
The Edinburgh Building, Cambridge CB2 8RU, UK

Published in the United States of America by Cambridge University Press, New York

www.cambridge.org
Information on this title: www.cambridge.org/9780521102919

First published 1982
This digitally printed version 2009

A catalogue record for this publication is available from the British Library

Library of Congress Cataloguing in Publication data
Main entry under title:
Public enterprise in less-developed countries.
Selected from papers prepared for the 2nd
BAPEG conference held in April 1980.
1. Underdeveloped areas – Government business
enterprises – Addresses, essays, lectures.
I. Jones, Leroy P. II. Boston Area Public
Enterprise Group.
HD3850.P83   338.7´4´091724   82–1206

ISBN 978-0-521-24821-1 hardback
ISBN 978-0-521-10291-9 paperback

Contents

v

Part III.   How are decisions made in practice?

Part IV.   How do public enterprises behave in international markets?

Contributors

Yair Aharoni
Faculty of Management
Leon Recanti Graduate School of Business
Tel Aviv University

Muzaffer Ahmad
Institute of Business Administration
University of Dacca

V. V. Bhatt
Public and Private Finance Development Economics Department
World Bank

Janet Kelly Escobar
Harvard Center for International Affairs

J. Finsinger
International Institute of Management
Wissenschaftszentrum Berlin

Malcolm Gillis
Harvard Institute for International Development

John B. Howard
International Center for Law in Development

Glenn P. Jenkins
Harvard Institute for International Development

Leroy P. Jones
Department of Economics
Boston University

Donald R. Lessard
Sloan School of Management
Massachusetts Institute of Technology

Brian Levy
Harvard Business School

Richard D. Mallon
Harvard Institute for International Development

Michael Manove
Department of Economics
Boston University

Edward S. Mason
Harvard Institute for International Development

J. M. Mintz
Department of Economics
Queen's University

Dani Rodrik
United Nations Commission on Trade and Development

Paul S. Rosenstein-Rodan
Center for Latin American Development Studies
Boston University

Ravi Sethi
National Academy of Administration
Indian Administrative Service

Pankaj Tandon
Department of Economics
Boston University

Bruce Vermeulen
Department of Economics
Boston University

Raymond Vernon
Harvard Center for International Affairs

I. Vogelsang
Department of Economics
Boston University

Lawrence H. Wortzel
School of Management
Boston University

Figures and tables

Figures

xiii

Tables

Preface

The Boston Area Public Enterprise Group (BAPEG) is a multidisciplinary group of scholars dedicated to understanding the public enterprises operating in the world's mixed economies. The first BAPEG conference focused on public enterprises in industrialized nations and resulted in the publication of *State-Owned Enterprises in the Western Economies,* edited by Yair Aharoni and Raymond Vernon. The second BAPEG Conference in April 1980 concentrated on public enterprises in less-developed countries with mixed economies. Some 70 papers were prepared for the conference, of which 29 were selected for discussion. The selections in this volume were chosen from the larger group to illustrate the range of issues addressed by the assembly.

The conference was attended by 68 scholars, government officials, and public-enterprise executives from 19 countries in South Asia, Africa, Latin America, Eastern and Western Europe, and North America. We would like to thank all the participants, whose lively comments contributed to the revised selections that appear here. We would also like to thank the Rockefeller Foundation, Ford Foundation, U.S. State Department, and Fund for Multinational Management Education, whose financial support made the conference possible. We are similarly indebted to Leita Kaldi of the Harvard Institute for International Development and to Susan Weise of the Boston University Public Enterprise Program, who served as energetic and capable administrative coordinators.

1 Introduction

Leroy P. Jones

1.1 Are public enterprises a useful unit of observation?

Public enterprise is a hybrid organization whose understanding requires a multidisciplinary perspective. As an "enterprise" it sells its output. It therefore performs functions (e.g., production, finance, and marketing) that are the concern of management specialists and is subject to the pressures of various markets, which are studied by economists. On the other hand, as a "public" organization, it is owned and/or controlled by the government or its agent. It is therefore subject to direct and indirect pressures from bureaucrats, politicians, and the public at large – groups that are studied by experts in public administration, political science, law and sociology. The chapters in this volume are accordingly a diversified group in terms of disciplinary approach.

The public enterprises studied are themselves a heterogeneous group, varying both within and across countries. As hybrids, public enterprises share characteristics of traditional government units and private business enterprises, with some being closer to one pole than to the other. Some, such as British Petroleum, are essentially autonomous and behave very much as large private enterprises operating in similar markets and with similar separation of ownership from control. At the other extreme are institutions, such as some development banks, that act largely as vehicles for implementing government policy by transmitting subsidized credit to individuals for purposes determined by bureaucratic and political processes. The public enterprises of the broad middle ground between these two extremes are of primary concern in the discussions presented here.

The overlap between public enterprises and other units of production leads some to deny the efficacy of public enterprise as a separate field of research. Their views were represented in the conference discussions. It was argued that large-scale private enterprises, particularly multinationals, exhibit most of the characteristics of many public enterprises, including monopoly or oligopoly market structures; goal conflicts between owners and managers (and between managers at different levels and between those of different units); complex, hierarchical bureaucratic decision structures; information impactedness; difficulty of measuring and rewarding individual performances in joint-product endeavors and

1

so on. Further, private enterprises – particularly large, highly visible ones – are also subject to governmental and public pressures through taxes and subsidies, legal regulation, informal guidance, and media pressures. Public and private enterprises alike are called upon to pursue noncommercial social objectives and to support the political aspirations of particular individuals and groups. In this view, the study of public enterprise should simply be one segment of the study of large-scale business organizations.

This opinion was rejected by the majority of conference participants. The characteristics of large businesses after all overlap with those of government bureaucracies, on the one hand, and with small businesses, on the other. Is there then only a single legitimate unit of observation – namely, the production unit – with all variants being merely special cases? In theory this is fine, and a completely general model could conceivably be developed, incorporating all the variables determining the behavior of all forms of organization. In practice, of course, this is impossible and it is necessary to focus on those factors of special importance in particular settings. It is thus natural for different scholars to specialize in the study of political parties, governments, public enterprises, large-scale business in general, multinationals in particular, small-scale business, and nonprofit organizations.

A similar dialogue has been repeated within the field of economics where it is sometimes argued that applied fields such as development, agriculture, trade, health, education, regulation, and industrial organization have no special status because the tools of analysis applied in these fields are drawn from the general kits of micro and macro theory plus quantitative methods. Although this is true, it is also true that the problems to which the tools are applied have special characteristics that require the development of special-purpose tools. It is no accident that econometric techniques evolved far more rapidly in agricultural economics (where there are large numbers of similar producers) than in the study of governments or large business organizations (where to get large numbers one has to suppress critical differences). Further, at the applied level the institutional setting exercises an important influence, and non-economic factors need to be taken into account. Applied fields thus belong in the realm of political economy rather than economics. This is certainly true of public enterprises, where economics, management, and the sociopolitical analysis all have roles to play.

Even so, are public enterprises sufficiently different to constitute a separate unit of observation? Most conference participants felt the answer was yes. Public enterprises differ from traditional government units in being subject to the pressures of the markets in which they buy and sell, but they also differ from large private organizations in being subject to *direct*, or internal, government control. Governments, of course, can influence private managers *indirectly*, or externally, by passing laws, imposing taxes, and jawboning, but this is quite different from public enterprises where government has the power to hire and fire the manager. For a private manager, on the other hand, the discipline imposed by the capital market is typically the major determinant of his tenure. The conflict between public and private goals and procedures is thus central in a public enterprise but tangential in private enterprises. These and many other differences between public institutions (those not selling their output), public enterprises, and private enterprises struck most conference participants as being sufficient to justify a distinct specialization within the broader study of the economic consequences of organizational behavior. The chapters that follow illustrate many of these differences and may help the reader to form his or her own judgment.

1.2 What determines the size and structure of the public-enterprise sector?

What determines the partitioning of the enterprise sector of a less-developed country (LDC) with a mixed economy into public and private spheres? Is it largely the result of random factors such as historical accident and ideological predilection? Or, are there systematic underlying forces at work that are susceptible to analysis and that are applicable across a variety of countries with divergent experiences and political proclivities? The two chapters in Part I address these questions from a comparative international perspective. One, however, focuses on microeconomic efficiency and the other on political economy as explanatory variables.

In Chapter 2 Jones and Mason point out that there is surprising and substantial uniformity in the use of public enterprise in LDCs. Countries as ideologically diverse as India and South Korea have public-enterprise sectors that are quite similar in size, structure, and rate of growth. More broadly, in the majority of LDCs public enterprises produce shares of GNP that fall within a fairly narrow range of 7 to 15%. Moreover, many outlying observations are explicable in terms of economic structure alone: Nepal is on the low end because of an exceptionally small role for the sorts of modern industries susceptible to public operation; Saudi Arabia is on the high side because of heavy reliance on petroleum. Much of the variance within the modal size range is similarly explained by differences in economic circumstances rather than historical accident or ideological predilection. Similarities in the structure of the sector (the particular industries chosen for public operation) are even greater.

These facts suggest that public enterprise can at least in part be understood as the response of pragmatic governments to similar problems faced in the process of development. Public enterprise is simply one tool among many at the government's disposal for altering the path of a mixed economy. Other intervention mechanisms include taxes and subsidies, antitrust, various forms of regulation, and informal administrative guidance. Insofar as pragmatic considerations dominate, the public operation of a particular industry will depend on a comparison of the benefits and costs of public enterprise as compared to alternative intervention mechanisms. Benefits are conceived as following from intervention where *market failures* lead a private producer to behavior incompatible with social-welfare maximization. Costs occur as a result of *organizational failures* (e.g., failure of public enterprises to minimize costs of production), and these vary with the intervention mechanism and the characteristics of a particular industry. In which industries are the net benefits of public enterprise likely to be both positive and greater than those of alternative intervention mechanisms? The empirically revealed preferences of LDCs suggest that public enterprise is most appropriate in industries that are large in scale relative to product and factor markets; are capital intensive; have high forward linkages; involve high rent and natural-resource export; produce marketed standardized products; and do not require large numbers of decentralized establishments.

Causation, of course, is multiple, and the economic focus of Chapter 2 is complemented by the sociopolitical emphasis presented by Ahmad in Chapter 3. The latter stresses that decisions affecting public enterprises are made not by neutral social-welfare maximizers concerned only with economic growth but by individuals representing particular class interests and having broader political objectives. In Ahmad's view, public enterprise is thus simply one arena in which contending social forces play out their quest for dominance, in this case competing for control of the actual or potential enterprise surplus. As an example, consider the comparison of India and South Korea, which share the common public-enterprise characteristics identified above. Ahmad notes that these are basic industries where risk is large, payoff is deferred, and expected returns are low. He then argues that the capitalists are pleased to leave such uncertain ventures to the state, so long as producers' goods are sold at a subsidized rate to the private sector, leaving a handsome, but hidden, subsidy in the capitalists' pockets. In this view, what is common to India and Korea is not market failure but the effective configuration of social forces.

Ahmad goes on to illustrate the political economy approach by identifying five different prototypical public-enterprise roles, with brief national examples of each. The regimes vary with both the relative power of different social classes and the fashion in which independence was achieved from the colonial power. He also devotes attention to the dynamics of class conflict and the way in which this affects the stability and operational efficiency of the public-enterprise sector.

1.3   Principal–agent relationships: Who should control public enterprises?

One of the most common topics in the public-enterprise literature is the problem of multiple objectives. Public enterprises are called upon to pursue a mix of commercial and noncommercial objectives, which can include such diverse goals as earning profits, redistributing income, subsidizing particular regions and sectors, earning foreign exchange, generating employment, and increasing the probability that the party in power will be reelected. Having such a plethora of objectives can be equivalent to having no objective, and management is all too often left free to pursue its own interests or a constantly shifting, incoherent mix. To alleviate this problem it is naturally suggested that some explicit mechanism for establishing trade-offs be established. For example, the Nora Committee in France[1] recommended that public enterprise be run on a strictly commercial basis with any noncommercial objectives being compensated at negotiated incremental cost. Logic notwithstanding, such schemes have not been notably successful.

Part of the explanation for this failure may be that the problem is misstated. As Leonid Hurwicz of the University of Minnesota pointed out in conference deliberations, the real difficulty is one not of multiple objectives but of plural principals. The simplest private enterprise faces a conflict between reducing inputs and costs while increasing output and revenues. Various programming techniques are available for handling more complicated cases, and much of the economics profession is concerned with establishing weights (prices) to allocate resources so as to maximize objective functions involving multiple objectives. The real difficulty occurs when different individuals have different preferences. For a private enterprise, this is a comparatively minor problem because the various stockholders are likely to have similar trade-offs that can be captured in the objective of profit (which is still a complex variable incorporating weights on various conflicting objectives). Similar agreement is unlikely on the weights of the various elements of the social-profit function of a public enterprise. The Ministry of Labor may be interested primarily in employment, the Ministry of Finance in profit, the politicians in low prices in an election year, and so forth. The underlying problem is thus one of plural principals with different objective functions.

Aharoni (Chapter 4) faces this problem explicitly in asking whether the public enterprise is "an agent without a principal." He argues that the traditional conceptualization is mistaken in viewing government as the shareholding, goal-setting principal and the enterprise as executing agent. Rather, the public at large is the principal for whom a variety of agents act, including various political parties, government ministries, and public enterprises. Each agent's view of the public interest is naturally influenced by its own self and group interests, thus diminishing its ability to establish trade-offs objectively on behalf of the public. It is then not surprising that public-enterprise managers sometimes view themselves as having at least as much of a claim on the goal-setting function as their erstwhile bureaucratic and political superiors. Aharoni then suggests a partial but pragmatic solution: "Since there is no one principal, but several tiers of agents, these agents can be forced to argue on choices to be made . . . if independent goal audit is introduced." Such an audit, conducted by a third party, provides a forum for periodic public scrutiny of the actions of various agents.

Howard (Chapter 5) shares Aharoni's skepticism of relying on the government as sole arbiter of the public interest but stresses the role of direct community input, thus bypassing the political and bureaucratic intermediaries. He addresses the problem from a legal standpoint and describes the public enterprise as being "entrusted by, or on behalf of, a community as principal, with power and resources to be used by it, as trustee, for the benefit of members of the community.'' The problem is then to establish legal mechanisms to ensure that the "institutional fiduciary'' role is in fact exercised in the public interest. To accomplish this, Howard places great emphasis on direct community input into the decision process, rather than on indirect input through bureaucratic, political, or managerial agents. Drawing on a variety of international experience, he suggests that this input can be accomplished by: worker, community and consumer representation on boards; devices to ensure effective legal recourse by groups who feel they are ill served by an enterprise; and an infrastructure of intermediary organizations. Howard focuses on the control of public enterprises concerned with implementing the "new development strategies," but his suggestions have far wider applicability, as shown by West European experiments with "codetermination" in manufacturing.

1.4   How are decisions made in practice?

The conflict over objectives does not stop at the enterprise gate but is reflected in differences between actors *within* the enterprise. It is widely recognized that in all large-scale business organizations, management will have interests of its own that may or may not coincide with the interests of the stockholders. In large-scale public enterprises the absence of clearly defined goals, and the multiplicity of lines of communication with, and responsibilities owed to, various government departments and agencies, and the difficulties of measuring performance may well exacerbate the problem of managers pursuing their own interests in opposition to those of the shareholder.

That a public enterprise is a hybrid functioning partly as a market-oriented enterprise and partly as an extension of the government bureaucracy is reflected in the composition of management. In Chapter 6 Kelly identifies two types of managers whom she characterizes as "engineers" and "commissars." The "engineers" are primarily concerned with running the enterprise like a private business and are oriented toward profits or growth. The "commissars," on the other hand, regard their jobs as "one link in a political career," and this cautions moderation and the maintenance of good relations with associated government agencies. The engineers are very much like top and middle managers of private enterprises and tend to be defenders of a commercial orientation, whereas the commissars are unique to the public enterprise and are particularly sensitive to noncommercial and more narrowly political objectives. Enterprise behavior, then, is not just the result of interaction between the enterprise and the center but also of the balance achieved between coalitions within the enterprise. This is very much in the spirit of the new literature on the economics of internal organization, which emphasizes that large enterprises (as most public enterprises are) are not monolithic maximizers of anything but rather coalitions of disparate interest groups within the firm.

Kelly uses her framework to explain differences in the behavior of two similar mineral-based conglomerates, one in Brazil, the other in Venezuela. As Kelly is a political scientist, it is noteworthy that she does not see these differences as being explained primarily by variations in the external political or administrative environment or even in different propensities to appoint commissars as opposed to engineers in positions of responsibility. Instead, outcomes depend primarily on the internal interplay between engineers and commissars, and the balance between them is tipped according to whether economic factors bolster the position of one side or the other.

Bhatt (Chapter 7) also bases his discussion on a case study, this time of a single, smaller enterprise in India. It is somewhat unique in the public-enterprise literature, being an unabashed success story: A new tractor was designed, based largely on indigenous technology; a plant was completed on schedule and at the cost envisioned; except for a strike, full-capacity operation would have been reached in three years as planned; consumer acceptance and demand have been high; and innovation continued, with two new models introduced in four years. This is not exactly the popular image of how public projects operate, and, indeed, the idea was initially rejected at the national level before being picked up at the state level. Bhatt then gives us something approaching a controlled experiment with a single project failing in one institutional environment but succeeding in another. He sees the failure as a result of inadequate linkages among the various national organs involved in technology development, production, and project evaluation, compounded by politically derived discontinuities in the objectives pursued by each. The success was due in part to the entrepreneurial drive of a single individual but also in part to the availability of alternative public-enterprise decision centers. In this view, institutional pluralism to some extent substitutes for market competition in producing pressures for efficient outcomes.

In Chapter 8 Vermeulen and Sethi also look at decision making in India, but rather than taking a comprehensive view of a single firm, they look at a particular decision area across all firms. Specifically, they are concerned with the difference between public and private enterprises in labor relations. They begin with the striking empirical observation that in India over a 16-year period, public firms lost less than one-fifth of the time to strikes (relative to their employment) as compared with private firms. How is this to be explained? Vermeulen and Sethi consider three broad sets of explanatory variables. First, the phenomenon may be due not to the way in which the public sector operates but to the industries chosen for public operation. For example, the public-enterprise sector on average consists of industries that employ far more capital per worker than those in which the private sector is located; this implies both a higher average skill level and a lower share of wages in total costs; and this could in turn generate different bargaining conditions and explain some of the observed public–private differential. A second possibility is that public managers are pushovers at the bargaining table, whether because of a lack of cost-consciousness or a concern for the welfare of the masses. The third

possibility is far more subtle. Vermeulen and Sethi argue that the *process* of negotiation is different because of such factors as less mistrust of the motives of
managers by workers and greater likelihood of a dispute being referred to the
supra-enterprise level for arbitration. Despite a valiant effort, the data ultimately
do not allow Vermeulen and Sethi to reach definitive conclusions as to the relative
contributions of the three sets of factors. Nonetheless, the careful and systematic
presentation of the possibilities leaves the reader with a far clearer picture of the
different environments in which public- and private-enterprise labor negotiations
are handled.

1.5   How do public enterprises behave in international markets?

Differences between public and private behavior are also of concern in the international arena. From the less-developed-country perspective, raw-materials
markets are of primary concern as the wave of nationalizations of the last two
decades has led to strong, and sometimes dominant, positions for public enterprises in petroleum, copper, iron ore, and bauxite. The last two markets are the
objects of study by Vernon and Levy (Chapter 9) and by Rodrik (Chapter 10). The
question in both cases is just how different the strategies of the nationalized firms
have been. As these are case studies rather than abstract theories or popular jour-
nalization, no simple answers are to be expected and none are offered. Nonetheless, the impression left by both studies is that in at least some important respects
the nationalized firms are driven by many of the same economic imperatives that
led their private predecessors, with some similar outcomes.

   In both industries, high fixed costs and economies of scale have limited the
number of participants and thus driven private enterprises to vertical integration in
an effort to reduce risk. The typical pattern was a mine in an LDC linked to a
parent mill in an industrialized country. Nationalization broke this ownership link
but in no way removed the desire of both parties for stable markets. Stability could
be achieved in part by building new mills within the LDCs and in part by negotiating long-term contractual arrangements. Many of the domestic mills are joint
ventures with foreign firms, which undertake foreign marketing, and thus
increase stability. There is also increasing use of intergovernmental enterprises
and state-to-state trade agreements, particularly in bauxite and aluminum.

   Just how effective these efforts at stabilizing markets will be is not yet clear, but
both chapters express doubts. Vernon and Levy note that ''market participants
who are motivated by diverse goals find it more difficult to coordinate their efforts
than those with common goals'' and Rodrik stresses that the instability of political
regimes can be transmitted to the market via state participation. In sum, public
ownership in these two industries does not seem to have reduced the search for
mechanisms to stabilize markets, though it may have reduced the potential for
success.

   Turning from raw materials to manufactured exports, a quite different pattern
emerges. As Jones and Wortzel document in Chapter 11, manufactured exports

from the public-enterprise sector in LDCs have historically been negligible both as a share of public-enterprise output and as a share of total exports. This is due to a combination of market (external to the public-enterprise sector's decision-making structure) and institutional factors (internal to that structure). The market explanation is simply that in LDCs "public enterprises have a comparative *institutional* advantage over private enterprises in activities that are capital intensive; whereas LDCs have a comparative *production* advantage in exporting products that are labor intensive." Institutional constraints follow from the fact that markets for manufactured exports are typically more competitive and risky than the monopolistic or oligopolistic domestic markets in which public enterprises usually operate. Manufactured exports therefore require a more innovative entrepreneurial (as opposed to managerial) attitude, which may be precluded by government policies that encourage risk aversion, restrain necessary expenditures on marketing talent and some forms of foreign promotion, and increase reaction time to rapidly changing foreign market conditions. Analysis of the interplay between market and institutional factors then leads to different policy prescriptions for the public-enterprise role in promotion of manufactured exports in three distinct situations: consumer goods under early "importer pull," consumer goods under later "exporter push," and producers' goods.

1.6   How do public-enterprise managers respond to risk?

Whereas Jones and Wortzel are concerned that public enterprise may be *less* appropriate in risky environments, there is a body of received literature suggesting they may be *more* appropriate. This is the Arrow and Lind[2] argument that the real cost of absorbing uncorrelated risk is reduced as it is spread over larger ownership units and that public enterprises are the ultimate vehicle for distributing risk across the entire population. The difference between the two views is between normative and positive statements. In principle, public-enterprise decision makers *ought* to be more risk neutral than their private counterparts; in practice, government control procedures and adverse selection in some countries may make them decidedly more risk adverse.

Tandon (Chapter 12) focuses on the effect of hierarchical structure in compounding risk aversion. As have several other writers in this volume, he stresses that a public enterprise is not a monolithic maximizer of social welfare (or any other objective function) but a collection of individuals operating in their own self-interest. He then asks how individual risk profiles are aggregated into an enterprise risk profile. He reaches three conclusions. First, in a hierarchy the imperfection of information flows can increase the uncertainty faced by decision makers at higher levels. Second, the presence of risk aversion at various levels tends to accumulate through the hierarchy, making the enterprise more risk averse than any individual within it. Third, even if individuals are risk neutral, the enterprise can be risk averse. All of these conclusions are equally valid for public and private hierarchies, but the problem is more severe in public enterprise for three reasons. First, the public enterprise ought to be risk neutral. Second, individual public-enterprise managers may be risk adverse. Third, the compounding effect increases with the depth of the hierarchy and the public-enterprise decision chain is typically longer and more discontinuous, as it typically includes both the enterprise and the supervising government agencies.

Gillis, Jenkins, and Lessard (Chapter 13) also are concerned with the normative theory of the public-enterprise attitude toward risk and emphasize that, contrary to the requirements of the Arrow and Lind argument, the risk faced by many public-enterprise projects is not unsystematic and diversifiable within the economy. This is particularly true in small, open LDCs or where third-party finance is included. This leads them to conclude that a risk premium should often be charged on public-enterprise capital, and, more generally, to a consideration of the role of finance in public-enterprise operations. They are particularly concerned with countering the notion that public-enterprise finance "does not matter" because as custodian of all national resources, the government should be neutral between, say, funds that come directly as government equity and those provided indirectly through government-controlled banks. What this argument ignores is the link between finance, managerial incentives, and performance. Financial structure in part determines the distribution of surplus between the enterprise, the state, and other actors, including managers. Retained earnings may enter the manager's utility function because he is a seeker of autonomy or because he takes pride and satisfaction from expansion. Finance then affects not only the distribution of surplus but also its magnitude, as it alters managers' motivation to produce surplus. Retained earnings are, of course, only a single element in the managerial utility function, and the goal of improving performance by improving reward functions needs to be considered in a broader context.

1.7   How are incentive systems to be designed?

If better performance cannot be distinguished from worse, managers can be neither guided to improve performance nor rewarded for doing so. In the absence of a direct link between the societal and managerial benefits from enterprise performance, it is only to be expected that decisions will be made that increase the latter at the expense of the former. It is clear that at least part of the widely perceived inefficiency of public enterprise is due to the absence of such a link. It is equally clear that the absence or imperfections of performance-linked incentive systems is no accident. Such systems are exceedingly difficult to construct in an environment of multiple objectives, plural principals, incorrect market prices, imperfect information, risk, and an abundance of nonpecuniary links between enterprise and managerial welfare. Previous efforts at developing rigorous incentive systems (e.g., Bergson[3], Domar[4]) have therefore been partial in nature. The chapters in this section are similarly limited in scope but nevertheless extend our knowledge of what needs to be incorporated into a complete incentive system.

Finsinger and Vogelsang (Chapter 14) deal with the common situation in which the public enterprise has a monopoly. The profit-maximizing price is then not welfare maximizing, resulting in too little output at too high a price under private operation. The usual solution is for prices to be set by some superior government ministry or regulatory body, leaving it to the enterprise to meet demand at that price and at minimum cost. This system suffers from one fundamental defect, which is that necessary information on demand and cost functions resides in the enterprise and is only imperfectly transmitted to the center. For example, the enterprise will quite naturally endeavor to convince the center that costs are as high as possible in order to increase their flexibility and thus the scope for reward. One solution is to continually expand the staff at the center until they know all there is to know about the enterprise. This is at best a waste of scarce talent and is probably doomed to failure in any event. Another possibility is to decentralize the price-setting function to where the information is and to set a performance index that leads the enterprise to maximize social welfare rather than enterprise profit. Finsinger and Vogelsang derive such an index in a partial-equilibrium framework. The proofs are complex, but the solution is simple. The bonus in a particular period is a function of a performance index that incorporates changes in both profits *and* in consumer surplus. This is measurable in terms of standard accounting data, assuming that all prices reflect social scarcity. If not, shadow prices would have to be used, and this is an obvious limitation to the solution. Further, as the authors recognize, there is the standard intertemporal problem (a counterpart to the ratchet effect in Soviet incentive systems) in which management may not move directly to the optimum in this period because doing so would reduce or eliminate their potential for bonus in the next period. Another set of problems involves second-best considerations. Finsinger and Vogelsang deal with one of these in suggesting a variant of their index that minimizes the partial-equilibrium welfare loss associated with imposition of a balanced-budget constraint.

Manove (Chapter 15) is similarly concerned with the asymmetrical distribution of information between the government and the enterprise and with the problem of deriving correct signals to ensure that the enterprise will act in the public interest. His general scenario is one in which the center knows the benefits of production but has only partial information on costs, whereas the enterprise is ignorant of benefits but has complete information on costs. This is a quite realistic situation both in terms of cost data being imbedded in the enterprise and, particularly in LDCs, in the imperfections of market prices requiring central calculations of social benefits. To make the problem tractable, he deals with the particular case in which the marginal costs are constant but in which the curve shifts from period to period according to exogenous events, some of which are specific to the enterprise and some of which affect the entire industry. The center knows the long-term mean and variance, but only the enterprise knows the specific short-term situation. He then considers the best possible outcome under three alternative institutional arrangements: a central planning scenario in which the enterprise is given a quantity target; a regulatory environment in which the enterprise is given a price and allowed to maximize profits; and a public-enterprise situation in which the enterprise is given a response function that makes production levels dependent on the cost parameters known only to the enterprise. Not surprisingly, the public-enterprise outcome is superior to the other two because it allows full use of information on both costs and benefits.

1.8   How does public enterprise compare with other intervention mechanisms?

Like Manove, the two authors in this section are concerned with comparing public enterprise with other intervention mechanisms. Mallon (Chapter 16), however, shifts the policy objective from efficiency to equity. Many governments have specified income distribution as a goal, but the Malaysian experience is probably unique in combining: explicit selection of a particular ethnic group as the beneficiary; a focus on creation of new (as opposed to redistribution of existing) entrepreneurial wealth as the means; and heavy reliance on public enterprise as the instrument. Mallon describes how the development of ethnic Malay entrepreneurs was first pursued through the traditional mechanisms of providing credit and technical assistance, encouragement of savings and investment, and development of human capital. When these entrepreneurial support efforts failed to produce results sufficient to satisfy political requirements, a switch was made to entrepreneurial substitution. Public enterprises were established with the avowed objective of progressively increasing Malay managerial and equity participation to the point where divestiture was possible. This necessarily meant investment in largely small-scale firms in direct competition with existing private firms and therefore created a public-enterprise sector of quite atypical structure by LDC standards. Mallon then asks just how cost-efficient use of public enterprise has been in comparison with the entrepreneurial support alternatives. The data does not allow him to reach definitive conclusions, but the analysis does lead to policy prescriptions as to how the costs associated with public enterprise might be reduced.

Mallon thus brings us full circle in returning to the question of "why public enterprise?" In Chapter 17 Mintz writes in the same vein but deals with theory rather than practice. He identifies the welfare loss associated with one particular market failure and compares public·enterprise with alternative intervention mechanisms for achieving the efficiency conditions.

Mintz considers the market failure that occurs when imperfect capital markets limit private risk sharing, thus increasing the real cost of investment and reducing its level below that which is socially desirable. This is obviously the case in LDCs, where stock markets are either nonexistent or extremely limited in scope. Mintz shows that government equity participation can substitute for (though not improve upon) a perfect capital market. Moreover, he argues that except in the limiting case of uncorrelated project returns, the optimal government share will be less than 100%. That is, optimal risk sharing generally requires mixed enterprise. Mintz also considers alternative forms of intervention. Government debt participation – common to LDCs – not only cannot accomplish the objective but retards it, as investor risk is compounded through leveraging. Tax and subsidy schemes can sometimes achieve the desired results but only over a narrower range of circumstances. In sum, although risk sharing is only one argument for mixed enterprise, the Mintz analysis suggests that government minority ownership deserves a closer look as part of the bag of tools used by LDCs to foster industrial development.

One of the mandatory self-depreciating stories told in introductory economics courses concerns the man who lost his car keys in his front yard at night but was found searching for them under the streetlight because the light was better there. The implied choice between rigor and relevance was the subject of some lively interchange among the heterogeneous conference participants, who ran the gamut from practical men-of-affairs to abstract theoreticians. Given the underdeveloped state of public-enterprise research, this was both healthy and unsurprising. To exaggerate, the choice is between using rigorous methods to generate definitive statements about trivial problems and using soft, "intuitive groping" to make questionable assertions about critical issues. The selections in this volume represent a broad range on the continuum thus defined. The goal is to move the light toward the problem without forgetting that, in the interim, critical practical decisions must be made using informed but imperfect judgment.

Notes

1 Simon Nora, *Rapport sur les enterprises publique* (Paris: La Documentation française, Apr. 1967).
2 Kenneth Arrow and Robert C. Lind, "Uncertainty and the Evaluation of Public Investment Decisions," *American Economic Review* 9, No. 3 (June 1970):367–78.
3 Abraham Bergson, "Managerial Risks and Rewards in Public Enterprises," *Journal of Comparative Economics* 2, No. 3 (Sept. 1978) : 211–25.
4 Evsey D. Domar, "On the Optimal Compensation of a Socialist Manager," *The Quarterly Journal of Economics* 88, No. 1 (Feb. 1974):1–18.

Part I

Why public enterprise?

2 Role of economic factors in determining the size and structure of the public-enterprise sector in less-developed countries with mixed economies

Leroy P. Jones and Edward S. Mason

2.1 Introduction

The issues

What is to be explained is the size and structure of the public-enterprise sector[1] in mixed economies, in particular those in less-developed countries (LDCs). The numerous reasons for establishing or retaining public enterprises can be consolidated into four groups:

1. Ideological predilection
2. Acquisition or consolidation of political or economic power
3. Historical heritage and inertia
4. Pragmatic response to economic problems

Although we will be concerned primarily with the fourth (economic) group of factors, we begin by briefly considering the competing–complementary explanations. Causation is multiple, and it is necessary to be explicit about what is being left out as we focus on economic determinants.

Ideological predilection

What does it mean to say that ideology has influenced the choice of public enterprise? We take it to mean that the decision rests not upon an unbiased examination of means in relation to ends in a particular case but upon a prior belief that certain forms of organization are generally preferable to others.

Work on this chapter was partially supported by a Ford Foundation grant to the Boston University Public Enterprise Program. We are indebted to Peter Evans, Richard D. Mallon, Jan Tinbergen, and John Sheahan for their comments on an earlier draft.

This does not imply that all choices influenced by ideology are irrational. In some cases the decision would be the same if based on an unbiased examination of the relation of means to ends. More important, ideology can influence ends as well as means. A belief in the merits of a "socialist pattern of society" can lend extra value to expansion of employment or redistribution of income, favoring investment decisions promoting those ends. But whatever the ends, there remains the choice of appropriate means. For example, income can be redistributed by taxation as well as by public ownership. The Scandinavian countries have chosen the former means, with relatively small public-enterprise sectors but very high levels of income redistribution via taxes to finance transfers and public services. Eastern Europe, on the other hand, chooses public production as the means of satisfying consumption requirements. Given the aim of income redistribution, which mix of means is preferable in a particular setting? Ideology biases this difficult decision in a particular direction and may lead to choices in which inferior means are chosen to attain particular ends. It is only if public or private enterprise is regarded as an end in itself (e.g., a capitalist concern for freedom of opportunity or the preference among some socialists for nonhierarchical production relationships) that the pragmatic choice among alternative forms of organization becomes moot.

There is no economy in which a dominant ideology does not exercise some influence. Ideologies favorable to public enterprise in LDCs may be described simply as socialism but are more commonly associated with a modifier – Arab, African, or Burmese socialism or the pursuit of a socialist pattern of society. The modifiers are intended to convey a nondoctrinaire recognition of specific local conditions, but there can be little doubt that such ideologies provide facilitating environments for public enterprises. Conversely, the establishment of public enterprise is much more difficult in a country such as the Republic of the Philippines, which has inherited the United States' antipublic bias.

Acquisition or consolidation of political or economic power

This is obviously related to ideology but is conceptually distinct as decisions are made not according to some preconceived position but according to the consequences of particular actions. Decisions to establish, retain, or divest a public enterprise are not made in a political vacuum. In the struggle for power among various interest groups, ownership and control of economic units are instruments for advancing certain interests and frustrating others.

The nationalization of foreign-owned enterprises in Egypt following the Suez War in 1956 eliminated potential centers of opposition to Nasser's revolutionary government. Although ideology certainly had some influence in 1960 and 1961, it is significant that Nasser's promulgation of the Charter of Arab Socialism came after nationalization rather than before. The dominant motivation can be interpreted to have been a consolidation of political power through the elimination of the economic base of political components.[2]

The quest for economic power may also play a role. Ahmad (Chapter 3) sees various classes struggling over the surplus generated by the public enterprises. Evans argues that there is a symbiotic relationship between multinationals and public enterprises that supports capitalist interests.[3] He also emphasizes the role of public enterprise in furthering the interests of the "state bourgeoisie," which controls and manages the enterprises.[4] Sobhan and Ahmad describe a situation in Bangladesh where the interests of the capitalist class were served by public enterprises whose pricing policies allowed capitalist middlemen to usurp surplus in a system that was ostensibly operated to benefit the masses.[5]

Financial and political interests of course interact. It has been argued that in India the existence of a strong business class (which must be relied on for political funding) has exerted its influence in retarding progress toward the "socialist pattern of society" advocated by the dominant political party. In Korea under the Rhee regime, the public banking system was used to channel campaign funds to the ruling political party.[6]

Historical heritage and inertia

In the wake of colonial exodus (Korea in 1945) or a liberation war (Bangladesh in 1972), new governments often have little short-term alternative but to take over substantial responsibilities in the industrial sphere. Once an enterprise is in public hands for any significant period of time, there then develops a strong inertia (defended by various interest groups) that tends to keep it in the public sector regardless of ideology or performance. The influence of inertia is particularly visible in situations in which the locus of political power changes drastically. Post–Allende Chile is one of the few cases of broad-based divestiture of public enterprises. Elsewhere, public enterprises established under one regime or philosophy exhibit remarkable staying power even in the face of later antagonistic governments. Employees, as well as civil servants (and sometimes consumers), have clear vested interests whose defense can impede denationalization. Less dramatic evidence of the operation of inertia occurs with economic development. A country might establish its first fertilizer plant in the public sector on the legitimate grounds of inadequate private entrepreneurship. It may well remain public 15 years later when the private sector has proven itself capable of running far larger and more complicated projects.

Pragmatic response to economic problems

In their pursuit of economic goals, governments have a variety of centralized and decentralized institutional arrangements to choose from. These range from purely competitive market organizations through private enterprises guided by taxes, subsidies, and various kinds of direct controls and joint and cooperative ventures of various sorts to publicly owned and controlled enterprises. A pragmatic, non-ideological government would view public enterprise neutrally as simply one tool among many. It would then select a tool on the basis of institutional comparative advantage derived from evaluation of the benefits and costs of each form for dealing with a particular problem in a particular industry.

Now, no country operates in such pristine isolation from political and historical conditions, but conversely, no country can totally ignore economic factors. Even the USSR places truck gardening in the private sector and even the United States uses public enterprise for the postal system. Less ideologically biased mixed economies – particularly in the LDCs – might be expected to be much more heavily influenced by pragmatic considerations. That, at least, is the first major theme of this chapter. In the words of Talcott Parsons: "The balance between governmentally controlled and free-enterprise industry is to a far larger degree than is generally held a pragmatic question and not one of fundamental principles."[7]

The second major theme of this chapter is that economic factors must be understood to include both costs and benefits of public operation and that these must be evaluated in comparison with those of institutional alternatives. Public enterprises are sometimes inefficient, but the alternatives create their own problems. Large family groups in LDCs, regulated monopolies in the United States, and credit-subsidized or tariff-protected private firms also create distortions.

Our third major theme is that the net benefits of public operation – and the resulting institutional comparative advantage – are sufficiently uniform across countries to have both predictive and prescriptive value in determining the structure and, to a lesser extent, the size of the public-enterprise sector.

None of this should be misconstrued as an argument for economic determinism in which political, sociological, and historical factors are impotent. Far from it; as already stated, causation is multiple. The limited role of this chapter, however, is to analyze only the contribution of economic factors.

2.2   Evidence on size and structure

a. The question

To the extent that the choice of public enterprise is pragmatic, and to the extent that the determinants of institutional comparative advantage apply across countries, then similar countries facing similar problems will choose public enterprise to a similar extent. The result would be identifiable regularities in the size and structure of the public-enterprise sector across countries. To what extent do such regularities exist?

b. India versus Korea

A comparison of India and the Republic of Korea provides a useful starting point, as the public-enterprise sectors of both are well developed and well documented but spring from quite different ideological predilections.[8] In India the prevailing view has been that

the adoption of the socialist pattern of society as the national objective, as well as the need for planned and rapid development require that all industries of basic and strategic importance, or in the nature of public utility services should be in the public sector.[9]

In Korea, on the other hand:

private ownership of production should unconditionally be encouraged except in instances where it is necessary to control it to stimulate national development and protect the interests of the people.[10]

In short, public enterprise is typically viewed as a "necessary evil" in Korea, an appellation reserved for private enterprise in India. What difference does this make in practice?

In the early 1970s the share of GDP originating in the public-enterprise sector was virtually identical in India and Korea at about 9%. If this result is surprising, part of the explanation may be due to differences in sectoral structure: India is much more agrarian and public ownership is universally less prevalent in agriculture than in industry. This is reflected in the fact that as a share of nonagricultural GDP, India's public-enterprise sector becomes somewhat larger than Korea's (15% vs. 13%). If this remains surprising, it might be because a simple static comparison of levels disguises quite different trends. True, from 1960-1 to 1972-3 the Indian public-enterprise sector increased its share of the economy by 80%, whereas from 1963 to 1972 the Korean sector share expanded by only 50%. However, because the Korean economy was growing more than twice as fast as India's during this period, the Korean public-enterprise sector actually grew much faster than India's (14% real annual growth rate vs. 8%).

Perhaps ideology reveals itself in structure rather than in size. Table 2.1 gives a single-digit comparison of the industrial composition of public-enterprise output in the two countries. There is only one really striking difference – in transport and communication. This is due primarily to the share of railways: In both countries railways are public, but Korean railways are a much smaller share of total transportation than in India, as Korea is geographically a very small country and India a very large one.[11] The difference is thus not due to a different public–private choice but to different industrial structures. In sum, and even allowing for errors in measurement, the impact of ideology seems undetectable: The dominant feature of a comparison of the size, trend, and structure of the public-enterprise sectors in India and Korea is one of similarities rather than differences.

c. Other countries: size

The reader who suspects that India and Korea are atypical in their similarities and that the set of LDCs as a whole exhibits substantially more diversity is correct. In the absence of careful statistical work using common definitions it is difficult to be

Table 2.1. *Percentage of public-enterprise sector in value added of various industries: Korea and India, 1971-2*

Industry	Korea[a]	India[b]
Agriculture, forestry, fishing	0.2	1.8
Mining	32.6	36.3
Manufacturing	16.4	13.3
Electricity, water, etc.	71.7	83.8
Construction	4.9	4.8
Trade	1.2	3.2
Transport, communication	30.8	61.4
Finance	83.5	84.0[c]
Other	0.5	1.6
Total	9.1	9.4

[a] Leroy Jones, *Public Enterprise and Economic Development: The Korean Case* (Seoul: Korean Development Institute, 1975), p. 78.

[b] N. S. Ramaswamy, V. J. Kesary, P. V. George, G. K. Nayar, V. G. Kamath, and P. D. Deenadayalu, *Performance of Indian Public Enterprise* (New Delhi: Standing Conference on Public Enterprises, 1978), p. 96. These shares are reported in constant prices, but current price shares are identical because deflation of public enterprise current price data was done at the single-digit level using national accounts deflators (Ramaswamy et.al., pp. 98–104).

[c] The source gives 25.4%, but there is an incompatibility as "ownership of dwellings" is grouped with "finance." As a rough adjustment we use a figure of 84%, which is the 1973 share of loans plus deposits in the public banks. Vadilal Dagli, ed., *Commerce Yearbook of Public Sector: 1974-1975* (Bombay: Mahatme, 1974), pp. 90-1.

precise, but in terms of size, the sector's contribution to GNP would seem to range from lows in the vicinity of from 2 to 3% (Philippines, Nepal) to highs that may approach or exceed 50% (Saudi Arabia). Further, diversity within the manufacturing sector is probably even greater. As already noted, agriculture has a low publicization[12] propensity, so that even wholesale public ownership of industry may leave only a modest share of GNP in the public-enterprise sector in a largely agrarian economy. For example, in Bangladesh public enterprises are estimated to account for 56% of value added in mining and manufacturing (and for 80% of large-scale manufacturing) but for only 8% of GDP.[13]

A substantial part of this diversity, however, is explained by differences in resource endowments. Most important in this regard is mining, which has a relatively high publicization propensity (one-third in India and Korea and three-fourths or more where oil is a prominent resource). The largest public-enterprise sectors therefore occur where large-scale mining generates a large share of GNP.

The size difference between such countries as Iran, Bolivia, and Saudi Arabia, on the one hand, and those such as India and Korea, on the other, are thus due not to ideology or history but to differences in resource endowments.

Available data suggest that the bulk of mixed-economy LDCs fall in a much narrower range. In an International Development Research Centre sponsored study of seven Asian nations, the size of the public-enterprise sector ranged from a low of 2% of GDP in Nepal to a high of 12% in Sri Lanka, with Thailand intermediate at 4% and India, Bangladesh, Pakistan, and Korea in the 8% to 9% range.[14] On the basis of this evidence plus scattered impressions elsewhere we suggest that the bulk of public-enterprise sectors in LDCs fall in the fairly narrow range of 7% to 15% of GDP.[15] This modal range appears to include such diverse countries as Korea, India, Taiwan, Brazil, Pakistan, Bangladesh, Singapore, Sri Lanka, and Mexico. Outlying observations are explained by differences in both resource endowment and ideology and history, as is variance within the modal range. The Philippines is at the low end for ideological reasons, whereas Nepal is there because of a particularly primitive economic structure. The bulk of the high observations occur for economic reasons (high national-resource extraction) with a few for ideological (Tanzania) or historical (Egypt, Turkey) reasons.

Other countries: structure

The similarities in structure in India and Korea have even wider applicability than do the similarities in size. Pryor has compared Eastern and Western Europe where the *level* of public-sector activity ranged from 9% to 71%[16]. There was nonetheless great similarity in the *pattern* of nationalization as measured by a high and statistically significant rank correlation coefficient of ownership shares in a one-digit industry classification and a significant correlation within a two-digit mining and manufacturing ranking. That is, although countries differed markedly in the *level* of public-enterprise use, there were marked similarities in *structure* with the same industries having the highest publicization propensities across ideological boundaries. Sakong I1 has produced similar results at the one-digit level for a seven-nation sample of Asian countries.[17]

In sum, the exceptional similarity of the public-enterprise sectors in India and Korea is due to a constellation of factors – history, ideology, interest-group struggle, and pragmatic responses to different economic conditions – which act in offsetting directions and just happen to balance out in these two countries. Elsewhere, national differences often act in reinforcing, rather than offsetting, directions and create much greater variance of outcome. Nonetheless, our survey of the available empirical evidence suggests that this variance is much less than might be expected and that much of it is due to differences in economic conditions. This supports the notion that underlying economic factors play a significant causal role. We now explain why this might be so.

2.3 Benefits and costs of public enterprise in an optimal economic order

a. Market failure versus organization failure

To focus on pragmatic economic considerations we assume away the influence of ideological, historical, and political factors and imagine a rational decision-making entity exclusively concerned with maximizing social welfare through a choice among a wide variety of centralized and decentralized institutions.[18] Public enterprise is then simply one among many tools available for achieving the government's goals, and the choice of this tool is a function of the costs and benefits associated with its use as compared to those of other institutional forms.

Discussion of the behavior of such a mythical beast by no means implies its existence. It is nonetheless of interest for at least three reasons. First, some governments sometimes try to make some decisions on pragmatic grounds and in these cases the availability of a cost–benefit framework has both predictive and prescriptive value. Second, at the opposite extreme where pragmatic considerations are likely to be totally ignored, there is some interest in being able to distinguish situations where the net cost of the public-enterprise choice is low from those where it is high. Finally, in the most common case where all factors enter into the decision, the pragmatic cost–benefit calculus may play a substantial role at the margin. In most mixed-economy LDCs there will be pressures both for and against further extensions or contractions of the public-enterprise sectors. The pro public-enterprise forces are more likely to win those battles where they also have pragmatic arguments on their side and vice versa. Occasionally, the imbalance between the forces will provoke a wholesale shift in one direction or the other, but subsequent adjustments at the margin may still follow predictable patterns. In Pakistan ideological nationalizations in 1972–4 were followed in 1977 by *selective* denationalization along lines predictable on pragmatic grounds.[19]

We are engaged in what Tinbergen terms a quest for the "optimum organization of the economy."[20] The first step is the specification of an interdependent set of desirable *outcomes*, one subset of which is the marginal conditions of pareto efficiency. The second step is the choice of a set of *institutions* to achieve the desired outcome. Two polar institutional possibilities are a perfectly centralized planning system and a perfectly decentralized market system. Our particular concern is with an intermediate mixed institution (public enterprise) that combines the potential for centralized direction of some decisions with response to market signals in others.

Under what conditions will public enterprise be part of the optimal economic order? We structure our answer to this question in terms of the costs and benefits associated with this choice. These could be classified in many ways, but we utilize two broad categories:

1.   Benefits can be had from government intervention where market failures lead a profit-maximizing private producer to behavior incompatible

with social-welfare maximization;

2. Costs occur as a result of *organizational failures* associated with a specific intervention mechanism. A particular institutional tool (say public enterprise) may achieve an *intended* deviation from private behavior (say, willingness to price at marginal cost rather than marginal revenue in a natural monopoly) but may at the same time produce *unintended* deviations (say, cost inefficiency) that must be compared with the costs associated with other intervention mechanisms (say, price and profit regulation under private ownership).

This classification reflects the notion that enterprise outcomes can deviate from the welfare norm for two reasons:

1. Incorrect *external* signals of economic opportunity
2. Incorrect *internal* responses because organizational and/or behavioral characteristics create nonmaximizing behavior by the firm (individuals or coalitions *within* the firm may of course still be maximizing)

Economists have traditionally been most concerned with the former problem, leaving the latter to management and public-administration scientists. There are, however, several rapidly evolving bodies of economic literature that address the organizational-failure problem under such headings as "*X*-efficiency theory," "behavioral theories of the firm," "property rights," and the "economics of internal organization."[21] It is our contention that the insights from these materials must be brought to bear in assessing the costs of the choice of public enterprise relative to other organization forms.

We approach the problem of an optimum organization from the point of view of a laissez-faire economy, examining the areas in which market failures may call for some type of intervention. It could be approached equally well from the point of view of a fully centralized economy, asking in what areas a decentralization of decision making or a limitation of controls on economic units may be desirable. The only difference is that the costs of centralization (organizational failures) become the benefits of decentralization and vice versa.

b. Benefits: market failures

The concept of market failures in the context of welfare economics is well known and here we provide only an overview. Pareto efficiency is a condition whereby no one can be made better off without making someone else worse off. As such, it is a necessary, but not a sufficient, condition for a "good" economic system. It is necessary because, regardless of our value judgments,[22] it is desirable to undertake a reallocation if it makes someone better off without harming anyone else. It is not sufficient because we may reject a *particular* pareto efficient allocation if we:

1. Do not accept the initial wealth (and subsequent income) distribution with which it is associated

2. Reject consumer preferences (e.g., for drugs over nutritious food or for child labor over education or for current consumption over savings for old age)
3. Consider the social relations of production to have value independent of the value of inputs and outputs

Such a specification of *outcomes* thus constitutes part of Stage 1 of Tinbergen's scheme for selection of the "optimum organization of the economy."

Stage 2 consists of specifying a set of instruments for achieving the marginal conditions. Under certain highly restrictive conditions (discussed later) perfectly decentralized decision making (either via private ownership or market socialism as per Lange–Lerner) can achieve the marginal conditions and thus serve public welfare without intervention by centralized authority. Any deviation from these conditions can be broadly defined as a market failure (to achieve the marginal conditions via decentralized decisions) and creates the *potential* for improvement via government intervention. We utilize a somewhat narrower definition of market failure by decomposing the broad definition into organizational failures (internal to the firm) and (narrow) market failures (external to the firm).

Pareto efficiency is attained when marginal social costs equal marginal social benefits for all activities. The two most commonly cited circumstances in which markets fail to produce these results are decreasing cost technology and external effects. In the first case, the larger the firm, the greater the cost advantage, so that profit-seeking activity leads to exit of all but the single largest firm, creating a natural monopoly. In less extreme cases the result is oligopoly, with resulting opportunities for concerted action to constrain production, raise prices, and enjoy excess profits. In the second case, activities generate costs (e.g., pollution) and benefits (e.g., some forms of worker training) to society that do not enter the firm's calculus, which means that even where marginal costs equal marginal benefits from the narrow enterprise perspective, they will not do so from the broader social perspective. There is then an argument for replacing the invisible hand of the market with the visible hand of government to increase social welfare by restoring the social marginal conditions.

These considerations lead Tinbergen to conclude (in part) that "a mixed order seems to be optimal showing the following structure: (a) a public sector of considerable extent takes care of all activities showing external effects or indivisibilities of some importance, while activities that show neither of these characteristics can be carried out by a private sector."[23]

This statement is of course only a first approximation and needs to be both modified and extended. The modification is that the specified conditions create only a *motive* for intervention and not a case for a particular *means* of intervention. Public enterprise is only one way of restoring the marginal conditions and alternatives (regulation, taxes, and subsidies, etc) must be considered. Further, the benefits must be set against the costs (see the following subsection). The extension is that additional sources of market failure need to be appended to the Tinbergen pair. Although there is no widely accepted morphology of market failures, other commonly cited categories include public goods, merit goods, information imperfections, and lumpy capital. Two additional reasons that deserve mention in the context of LDCs are dynamic considerations and artificial monopoly, topics to which we now briefly turn.

The pareto-efficiency conditions are generally stated in static (single-period) terms, but there is in principle no difficulty in extending it to a dynamic multiperiod formulation. Now costs and benefits occur in different time periods and what must be equated is the net present vparticular decision. The practical difficulty is that as these costs and benefits recede into the future they need to be discounted not only for forgone opportunities and preferences but also for increasing uncertainty in an unknowable future. In LDCs the future is particularly uncertain because of information imperfections, political instability, and the absence of vehicles for risk spreading. An investment may then be socially desirable but perceived as privately undersirable because of a low expected rate of private return.

These problems become greater as we move from small-scale traditional activities to large-scale modern activities with long gestation and payback periods and unknown production technology and marketing conditions. It is the function of entrepreneurs to solve these problems, but entrepreneurial failure will be greater in LDCs. Economies advance in large part through innovations in technology, marketing, management, and so on, and optimal levels of innovation cannot be achieved if left solely to private initiative in LDCs. Further, innovation often requires abandonment of traditional ways so that Schumpeter's "creative destruction" is an essential part of the development process. If private entrepreneurs prefer a low, but certain, return in traditional activities to a larger expected return with higher variance in modern activities, there is again room for positive government intervention.

Monopoly can be artificial as well as natural, that is, created by the efforts of man rather than dictated by the necessities of technology. There can be conspiracies among firms, individuals, and governments, producing unfair practices designed to force the exit of, and preclude the entrance of, competitors; efforts that are sometimes accompanied by bribery and strong-arm tactics. These practices are certainly significant in many LDCs. It is commonly held that the wholesale rice trade in some southeast nations in some periods has been controlled by ethnic Chinese using force and political payoffs. Perhaps more important, monopoly enforced by political influence can occur in factor markets, most noticeably in those for credit and foreign exchange. If large family groups control existing industry and exert political power as a result, they can influence factor allocations, reduce entry, and distort marginal conditions across many product markets.

This last observation leads to a critical compounding factor in the theory of government intervention. Markets are interdependent so that distortions in one market are transmitted to others, creating divergences between private and social

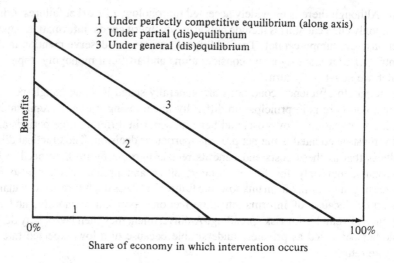

Figure 2.1. Potential benefits from government intervention.

marginal costs and benefits even in markets that are themselves otherwise undistorted. Recognition of such constrained general equilibrium considerations, where there exist unremedied distortions in some uncontrollable markets, can justify intervention in other controllable (but themselves undistorted) markets as a second-best solution. For example, the existence of public goods plus the impossibility of a poll tax means that other markets must be distorted by taxes to generate the revenue to finance the public good.[24]

The argument of this subsection can be summarized in terms of Figure 2.1 and the following propositions:

1. Under certain highly restrictive assumptions, decentralized markets yield pareto efficiency and there are no benefits to be had from intervention (curve 1, along axis)
2. Violation of any of these conditions creates market failures whose removal by government intervention could yield benefits in those markets. The potential-benefit curve slopes downward, as some markets are more distorted than others. It intersects the abscissa, as not all markets are distorted in the partial-equilibrium sense (curve 2)
3. In constrained general (dis)equilibrium, the interdependence of markets can justify intervention in virtually all markets (curve 3).

Costs of intervention

Although a rational case can thus be made for intervention in virtually any market, our pragmatic government will set the benefits of such intervention against its costs. These costs may be of two sorts. First, there are the resource costs – largely manpower and intertemporal delays – involved in central planning boards, regulatory agencies, tax bureaus, and like institutions at the center, plus those incurred at the enterprise level in providing information, bargaining, and designing a means of circumventing the intervention mechanism. The second set of costs, probably much more important, is the tendency of intervention institutions to generate new problems in attempting to solve old ones. A tool is selected to achieve *intended* deviations from idealized private behavior and ends up creating *unintended* deviations as well: A public enterprise is created to avoid the problems of private monopoly but ends up producing with excessive costs as well; a system of price and profit regulation of private enterprise is set up for the same reason but also results in excessively capital-intensive investment decisions; a credit subsidy is designed to encourage exports but also results in interest arbitrage and land speculation; jawboning may temporarily reduce price increases but incur implicit government commitments that create new problems when due. Examples of such costly unintended deviations associated with various intervention institutions could be expanded indefinitely. Our purpose, here, however, is merely to stress that such costs are by no means confined to the public-enterprise problems discussed here but are associated to one degree or another with *all* intervention mechanisms.

Around the world public enterprises are often accused of inefficiency. This is not surprising. Public enterprises are a hybrid, sharing characteristics of government bureaucracies, on the one hand, and private enterprises, on the other. As an "enterprise," they must face a market test of the acceptability of their product, and this imposes one set of pressures on management. As a "public" organization, they must be responsive to the needs of dominant political forces and are subject to the constraints and opportunities afforded by being part of the civil-service chain of command. Given the necessity of trade-offs between these two sets of pressures, it is not only unsurprising but positively predictable that the outcome will often be suboptimal by the standards of one side or the other or both. This is not to excuse the result or suggest that its most deleterious consequences cannot be mitigated but only to suggest that certain efficiency costs are likely to be incurred in choosing the public-enterprise tool.

The inefficiency to which we refer is not so much that associated with traditional allocative efficiency (choice of the wrong price–quantity bundle) as with failure to minimize costs of production for the quantity actually chosen. Both the popular and academic literature on public enterprise are replete with instances of this form of behavior; here we only outline the more important causal antecedents.

Public enterprises often operate under bureaucratic systems that control processes rather than outcomes. Procurement patterns, for example, typically mandate formal bidding procedures and multiple official ministerial approvals regardless of economic cost. An Asian fertilizer plant was shut down for more than a month by bureaucratic impediments in obtaining replacement parts from

Europe, which could otherwise have been gotten in a few days. The cost? Roughly $200,000 *per day* of downtime. The benefits? Avoidance of corruption and over-charging on equipment worth $100,000 at most. Assume 30 days excess downtime and 100% corruption via kickback. It then cost $6 million to save $100,000[25]. The time-consuming traditional rules of government are difficult to reconcile with the needs of an organization that must operate in a dynamic market.

A second kind of problem involves the use of political influence to transfer income from the public to various special-interest groups, be it unemployed brothers-in-law, retired generals, politically potent unions, constituents back home, or industrialists who want the public output at a low price. There is a narrow line here between the legitimate and the illegitimate. A major function of government is to transfer income from one group to another. The difficulty with public enterprises is that the transfers can be so readily hidden from those who pay the freight in terms of increased taxes, higher inflation, or lower government expenditures on health, education, or welfare.

A third difficulty is that public-enterprise decision makers often have little incentive to control costs. In part this can result from recruitment practices (short-term political appointees as chief executives) and in part from civil-service pay structures that preclude merit bonuses. More fundamentally, however, it is seldom possible to distinguish "good" from "bad" performance. If there are both legitimate and illegitimate reasons for losing money and no techniques for distinguishing between the two, managerial performance cannot be judged. A public manager under pressure to hire unproductive workers has little reason to resist, as any effect on profit can be hidden by attribution to government pricing policies on inputs or outputs.

A list of this sort could be extended indefinitely; our purpose is merely suggestive. There are no necessary reasons for public enterprises to fail to minimize costs but a host of sufficient ones. Although such costs of public enterprise are real, they must be compared with the costs of alternatives.

Private firms also experience managerial failures, and the resulting costs must be taken into account in determining the net advantage (or disadvantage) of public enterprises in particular industries. As Comanor and Leibenstein argue, the major disadvantages of monopoly may not be the social cost of misallocation – "too little production and too high a price" – but that the absence of competitive pressure yields excess costs for what *is* produced.[26] In the less-developed countries the prevalence of family firms with· accompanying nepotism may produce similar results. Further, Sheahan argues that the unwillingness of some LDC entrepreneurs to dilute family control can lead to suboptimal investment in large-scale projects unless the government intervenes.[27] This list could again be both extended and debated, but the general point is clear. Private enterprise, like public enterprise, may not behave as profit maximizers, and these internal organizational failures must also be considered in assessing the costs and benefits of intervention.

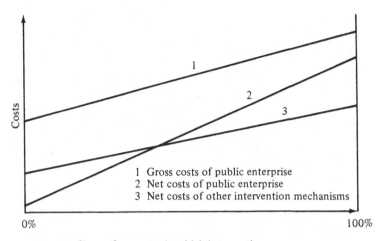

Figure 2.2. Costs of public intervention.

The argument of this subsection may be summarized in terms of Figure 2.2,[28] which incorporates the following propositions:

1. Gross costs of public enterprise: If the problems of public enterprise are greater in some sectors than others, the slope of the curve will be positive, reflecting increasing marginal costs as increasingly inappropriate activities are brought into the public domain. The level of the curve is a function of the efficacy of the public-enterprise control system.

2. Net costs of public enterprise: Private organizations also suffer organizational failures and these must be netted out in evaluating public enterprises. This curve necessarily lies below the gross cost curve by an amount varying with the efficacy of private enterprises in particular countries and particular industries.

3. Net costs of alternative forms of intervention: This is defined as with number 2 but for the best alternative form of intervention. It is sometimes above and sometimes below the public-enterprise curve on the assumption that one institutional form will have a comparative advantage in some activities and another form in others.

Equilibrium

Equilibrium occurs at the intersection of the various cost and benefit curves, partitioning the economy into public-enterprise and controlled and uncontrolled private sectors as shown in Figure 2.3.[29] For some activities, the costs of any form

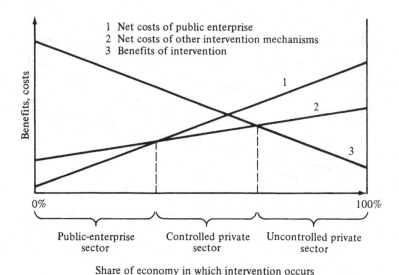

Figure 2.3. Partitioning of economy according to costs and benefits of intervention.

of intervention exceed the benefits and these can best be left in the uncontrolled private sector. For other activities, the costs of public enterprise are less than both the benefits and the costs of alternatives, thus determining a public enterprise sector. In the remainder of the economy, the costs of alternative intervention mechanisms are below both public-enterprise costs and the benefits of intervention, thus suggesting a controlled private sector.

Insofar as (1) countries face identical economic conditions (i.e., have identically positioned curves), (2) ideological, historical, and political influences are neutral, so that decisions are made on the basis of social-welfare maximization, (3) information on relative costs and benefits are widely available, and (4) distributional considerations are neutral, the equilibrium will be uniform across countries and national institutional partitionings will be identical. As these conditions are nowhere fulfilled, uniformity is not to be expected, but insofar as pragmatic considerations have influence, there will be at least pressures in this direction. This is the notion behind "convergence theory," which predicts and finds increasing similarities between economic institutions in the United States and the USSR.[30] Even if economic conditions are identical and distributional considerations are ignored, however, complete convergence is still not to be expected because in the middle range net benefits minus costs will be not only small but indeterminate because of information imperfections. There is thus likely to be a substantial range over which ideological and political predilection can and will operate at no great economic cost, and the United States and the USSR could be expected to settle at opposite ends of this band of indeterminancy.

Our contention is that this argument applies to the public-enterprise sector in LDCs. In similar countries there would be a common realm of institutional comparative advantage for public enterprise. There would also be a band of indeterminacy in which ideological and political factors would alter the outcome at no great expense, but economic pressures would over time force countries within this band. Countries differ, however, so that even purely pragmatic governments might still differ in their use of public enterprise. How might these differences affect the appropriate realm for public enterprise in LDCs as opposed to more-developed countries (MDCs)?

Costs and benefits in LDCs

How do the relative positions of the curves vary between MDCs and LDCs and within the LDC set? We make no pretense to being able to answer this question, as so little systematic comparative work has been done on the cost side. For example, consider the fact that the United States uses regulation and formal antitrust to deal with monopoly and oligopoly, whereas most of the rest of the world's mixed economies handle the same problems through a mixture of public enterprise and informal "administrative guidance" (the latter exemplified by countries as diverse as France and Japan). Why is this so? Is it because ideological bias blinds one set of countries to the institutional advantages of alternatives? Is it because the cost differences are really negligible as between forms of intervention? Or is it because the costs vary in different historical, political, and cultural nexuses and each country has chosen an optimal solution for its own environment? The comparative systems literature, in focusing on the polar extremes of planning and markets, has tended to ignore such issues of institutional choice, which are most relevant at the margin in mixed economies. We do not propose to redress this sort of imbalance here but merely to suggest a few factors that may be germane in determining the outcome.

A pragmatic choice as to the optimal organization of production is likely to differ substantially between LDCs and MDCs. Differences on the benefit side are clear-cut in favoring more intervention in LDCs, whereas those on the cost side probably argue in the opposite direction, making the net results indeterminant on a priori grounds without detailed study of relative magnitudes.

It is virtually tautological to argue that potential gross benefits from intervention are greater in LDCs, as extensive and pervasive market failures are part of the definition of underdevelopment. Information is absent, impacted, or costly. There is a shortage of capable entrepreneurs and managers. Externalities abound. Markets are small, so natural monopolies and oligopolies (which are a function of scale relative to market size) are much more common. Factors such as these affect the ability of markets to allocate resources and achieve the marginal conditions.

In MDCs both supply and demand curves are likely to be smoother, facilitating marginal adjustments as consumer tastes and better information, together with higher incomes and a greater variety of products, encourage substitution and easier adaption to price and quantity changes. On the supply side the greater mobility of factors geographically, and among various types of activity, tends to equalize factor prices and accommodate factor use to changing profit opportunities. In LDCs, on the other hand, the relative absence of these conditions tends to produce more and greater market failures and lack of opportunity for exploiting potential innovations. Demand and supply curves are not smooth and differences are discrete rather than marginal. On the demand side, handicaps of communication, transportation, and information yield different prices for similar products and the absence of variety discourages substitution. On the supply side, lack of factor mobility and the relative absence of market intermediaries tend to produce large differences in factor prices and factor availability both geographically and among different activities. In sum, market failures are more widespread and significant in LDCs.

Taken alone, the foregoing would argue for greater government intervention in LDCs. Consideration of cost factors, however, argues in the opposite direction. Shortages of entrepreneurial and managerial talent and of information constrain the public sector as well as the private. As a consequence, LDCs typically lack the competent and relatively uncorrupt civil services required to effectively administer controls and do not command the pool of experienced administrators and managers required to run public enterprises efficiently. As a consequence, our imagined body of pragmatic decision makers at the top do not have the same set of choices among various forms of organization that their counterparts might be expected to have in developed countries. Administrative cost considerations of this sort have led some experts to be much more skeptical of the wisdom of giving as large a role to public enterprise in LDCs as in MDCs. Administrative weakness is as much a characteristic of underdevelopment as market failure.

If gross costs of intervention are thus higher in LDCs, net costs are certainly less so because the organizational failures of private enterprise are also greater. Public enterprises may be far from exhibiting cost-minimizing behavior, but what of the family-run conglomerates that are often the institutional alternative?

The relative positions of the two net cost curves also might be expected to vary between LDCs and MDCs. If intervention in small-scale decentralized activities is more costly via public ownership as compared to tax–subsidy combinations, and if such activities – notably agriculture – constitute a larger fraction of output in LDCs, the public-enterprise tool will dominate alternative intervention mechanisms over a smaller fraction of national output. On the industry side, relative factor endowment may argue for more small-scale, labor-intensive activities where public-enterprise intervention is similarly more costly.

The various curves will also differ substantially across the highly heterogeneous set of LDCs. In part this will be due to differences in economic conditions. Large deposits of extractable natural resources will lift gross benefits in some sectors in countries so endowed and raise the left-hand side of the gross benefit curve. Small countries will have a greater fraction of the economy susceptible to natural monopoly and oligopoly than will larger countries at similar stages of development. Finally, the level of development varies greatly across the LDCs with some much closer to the MDC pole than to other LDCs.

Cost curves may also vary as a result of differences in political and cultural heritage, though this is far more hypothetical. "Hard" political structures may enable more effective control of public enterprises and reduce their costs relative to alternative means of intervention. The hierarchical orientation of East Asian Sinitic cultures may shift curves in the same direction if these cultures are more capable of handling the centralized forms of large-scale organizations as compared to more individualistic cultures. Differences in bureaucratic tradition – say British, French, American, and Sinitic – may have profound effects on the relative efficacy of different intervention mechanisms. Also, the degree of political, economic, religious, and ethnic homogeneity may alter the degree to which it is possible for a government to concern itself with such mundane matters as relative economic costs and benefits.

Finally, the relative positions of the cost curves are not immutable even within a particular country. Indeed, much of the public-enterprise literature is concerned with investigation of institutional structures that will reduce the gross costs of public enterprise. Although the historical record suggests skepticism as to the potential for rapid change, the possibility remains that better documented research can convince top decision makers to make the changes necessary to lower the gross cost curve.

If the net effect of this bewildering set of offsetting considerations is a priori agnosticism, sobeit. This merely points to the need for careful research leading to country- and industry-specific decisions rather than guidance by ideological predilection or historical inertia.

Ranking of activities

It is obviously of considerable practical interest to be able to rank activities according to their appropriateness for public operation. Three sorts of classification scheme might be used:

1. Industrial classification (e.g., cement on the left, truck gardening on the right)
2. Popular classification (e.g., basic or heavy industry on the left; light industry on the right)
3. Technical classification (e.g., those industries that are large relative to the product and factor markets on the left)

It is our contention that the technical form has far more normative and predictive power, and that the other two forms are useful only insofar as they serve as proxies in particular countries at particular times.

Consider the cement industry, which is certainly "basic" in the sense that its output is critical to the growth of most modern sectors. Yet the net benefits from its nationalization are likely to be high (or even positive) only in those countries where its scale is large relative to product and factor markets. By modern standards, cement establishments are relatively small in absolute size and require only a relatively simple mechanical mixing technology. A medium-size economy is therefore capable of sustaining a fairly large number of such plants and it should be one of the earlier industries that private entrepreneurs are capable of financing and operating. A small economy, on the other hand, may be capable of sustaining only a single plant; and a very primitive economy may find finance and operation beyond the capacity of indigenous entrepreneurs and managers. Korea has 20 cement establishments, and these are all private. Sri Lanka has only 3 units and these are all public. Although ideological, historical, and political factors have played a role in determining these different outcomes, they are both quite consistent with a pragmatic solution. Popular and industrial descriptions are thus useful primarily as proxies for underlying technical characteristics. As the latter vary with national economic circumstance, the former are likely to be misleading in particular cases.

Consider the steel industry. Here scale with modern technology is large relative to product and factor markets in all but the largest and most developed economies. Here the "basic" and "industrial" proxies would seem to serve well. Although this is true if we confine ourselves to LDCs, the analysis does not extend to MDCs. To be sure, steel has been increasingly subject to nationalization (or other major forms of government intervention) in MDCs, but this has little to do with its "basic" nature or even its scale. Rather, it is because a combination of technological obsolescence and shifting relative prices makes its production increasingly noncompetitive in countries that were previously dominant. If there is a divergence between the social and private costs of exit (costs of reallocating labor and the presence of interest obligations, which represent private costs but social benefits), there is an economic argument for government intervention to defer bankruptcy until social marginal costs fall below social marginal benefits. Steel may be heavily public in both MDCs and LDCs, but the reasons are quite different, as are the policy implications. In one the goal is to manage decline systematically and in the other to manage growth. Hiring, training, and investment decisions are accordingly quite different.

"Nationalism" is another popular category that needs to be looked at in terms of its underlying technical motivations. As a political or ideological description it has explanatory value, but as an economic category, it is a rather broad proxy. Although expropriation of foreign firms is occasionally undertaken on a wholesale basis for ideological reasons, selective nationalization is far more common. What explains this is the differential industrial propensities to publicization. It is no accident that natural-resources extraction has the highest propensity. First, there is often a large pure economic rent to be extracted, and if institutional constraints (bookkeeping practices, transfer prices) make problematic the domestic expropriation of these rents via taxation, there is an economic argument for nationalization on the benefit side. Second, as pointed out by Vernon and Levy (Chapter 9), the costs of nationalization are a function of the existence and availability of alternative managerial and engineering skills (either through the training of nationals or the existence of an international factor market where such skills can be hired). The timing as well as the pattern of nationalization is thus explicable in part in terms of the underlying technical characteristics of the industry.

As another example of the importance of going beyond industrial classifications, consider export-oriented mineral extraction. For reasons just given, such activities are particularly likely to be in public enterprises. Sri Lanka, however, has left gemstone mining largely in private hands, despite its economic importance, economic rents, and countervailing ideological predilection. Why? Because these gems are typically found in alluvial deposits, requiring mining by a few men working in small widely separated pits. The technology of production is similar to truck gardening and its very small scale makes for high net costs of centralization. The rent is accordingly extracted by a monopsonistic public-marketing organization, but production is quite naturally left in private hands.

In sum, traditional and industrial descriptors can be useful proxies, especially in particular national settings. They are nonetheless only proxies, and serious attempts at ranking activities requires attention to underlying technical characteristics. We now consider some partial evidence on just what these characteristics are.

2.4   Evidence on revealed institutional advantage of public enterprise

The issues

In Section 2.2 we presented evidence suggesting that public enterprises are not randomly distributed but concentrated in particular industrial sectors. We now go a step deeper to ascertain the underlying technical characteristics of those industries chosen for public operation. The question is whether or not those characteristics define areas where the net benefits minus costs of public enterprise are liable to be particularly high. To the extent that they are, we have further confirmation of the role of pragmatic economic considerations in determining the size and structure of the public-enterprise sector. These revealed preferences also provide some preliminary guidance on the ranking of activities in terms of their appropriateness for public operation. The Korean case is first examined in some detail.

Korea: size relative to product market

The single most striking characteristic of the Korean public-enterprise sector is output-market concentration.[31] In 1972, 76% of public-enterprise value added was in markets that were egregiously imperfect (i.e., monopoly, monpsony, bilateral monopoly, or regulated oligopoly). Three-quarters of the remaining public-enterprise output was in manufacturing sectors with an output-weighted, International Standard Industrial Classification four-digit, four-company concentration ratio of 0.73, compared with 0.51 for the manufacturing sector as a whole. Public enterprises thus operated overwhelmingly in imperfect output markets, with at most 10% of value added sold in reasonably competitive markets.

The converse also held, with public enterprises dominating highly concentrated industries. For the mining and manufacturing sector, this is readily documented. Among all four-digit industries with four-firm concentration ratios of 0.70 or greater, there was at least one public enterprise in each of seven sectors, which together accounted for 73% of sales in the concentrated industries. Outside manufacturing no comparable statistics are available, but it is difficult to think of any major concentrated activity in Korea that does not have substantial public-enterprise participation.

Given this high correlation between public enterprise and imperfect competition, what was the direction of causation? One possibility is that the government used its power to protect its enterprises from competitive pressures. This is clearly the case with the Office of Monopoly (cigarettes and ginseng) where the goal was straightforward revenue maximization. In virtually all the other cases, however, enterprises have been in the public sector because they operate in imperfect markets rather than vice versa.

In sum, the single characteristic of size relative to product markets thus provides striking support for the hypothesis of economic pragmatism.[32] Virtually the entire sector in Korea consists of activities where gross benefits are likely to be particularly large for this reason alone.

Korea: size relative to factor market

Size relative to factor markets is a second technical characteristic defining activities where gross benefits are likely to be large. Using absolute enterprise size as a proxy, the correlation is notable but less impressive than for output-market concentration. Twenty of Korea's 50 largest enterprises were in the public sector in 1972, including 12 of the 16 largest. How might this result be explained in terms of cost and benefits? Gross benefits of intervention are liable to be high in such activities for two reasons:

1.   Private entrepreneurial market failures will be greater the larger the scale of the activity relative to the accumulated stock of entrepreneurial capital and experience.
2.   The dangers to the public of extensions of private market power increase with size.

Both these factors are only imperfectly reflected in our proxy measure, the first because our unit of observation is too large, the second because it is too small. The relevant measure for many entrepreneurial market failures is the establishment (rather than the enterprise), as it determines the technologically minimal scale. Some large Korean private enterprises consist of many establishments that have accrued sequentially in activities that are essentially small scale (trade, plywood, sugar, textiles, miscellaneous foodstuffs, highway transport, etc). Large enterprises need not exceed entrepreneurial capacities even when large establishments do. In addition, the rapidly expanding entrepreneurial capacity has meant that by the 1970s even relatively large establishments were within the capacity of private entrepreneurs (e.g., the first oil refinery was built in the early 1960s with public participation, the next two with private participation).

The relevant measure of economic power is the conglomerate family group, so that the enterprise measure used above substantially understates their influence. In fact, the size of such groups in Korea is growing rapidly and the government has made only the most modest efforts to restrict that growth. However, there has been a major effort to constrain the *influence* of this size by keeping the banks in the public-enterprise sector. By controlling credit allocation to the highly leveraged conglomerates, the government is able to constrain their influence.[33]

The foregoing gives a partial explanation of why enterprise size is a significant but imperfect predictor of inclusion in the public-enterprise sector. However, it covers only gross benefits, and net costs must also be considered. Many of the large private enterprises are in activities that are decentralized (e.g., trade) or produce export-oriented products requiring innovative foreign marketing (e.g., clothing), and in these sectors the costs of centralized, risk-averse decision making may be high.

Korea: capital intensity

Entrepreneurial market failures, and thus gross benefits of intervention, are likely to be higher in the most modern, capital-intensive, high-technology industries. Capital intensity (as measured by the ratio of the capital stock to employee compensation at the 117-sector level in 1972) for the public-enterprise sector is more than three times that of the Korean economy, almost triple that of the nonagricultural economy, and almost double that of Korean manufacturing. Public-enterprise manufacturing enterprises are themselves roughly twice as capital intensive as manufacturing as a whole. Public enterprises are thus overwhelmingly capital intensive in Korea.

The converse also holds, though to a somewhat lesser extent, with the capital-intensive sectors generally influenced by public operation. Of the 11 most capital-intensive sectors in the Korean economy, public enterprises produce virtually all output in 4 and are significant (10 to 50% of the market share) in 6. The single capital-intensive sector without public participation – cement – is instructive. Here high capital–labor ratios are combined with relatively small scale and relatively simple technology, so that entrepreneurial failures are likely to be absent.

Korea: high forward linkages

If the costs of administering intervention are significant, and rise with the size of the sector being centrally directed, it makes sense to concentrate intervention in those "basic" sectors where removal of distortions is particularly beneficial so that transmission to downstream users can be avoided. This can be measured using the Hirschmanian concept of linkages. Forward linkages represent sales to intermediate (rather than final) users, and backward linkages reflect purchases from intermediate producers. Industries with high linkages may thus have greater impact on other productive sectors and might be taken as representing "the commanding heights" of the economy.[34] In Korea, the public-enterprise sector as a whole has high forward linkages but modest backward linkages relative to the entire nonagricultural economy. Further, the public-enterprise manufacturing sector (excluding the consumer-oriented Office of Monopoly) has very high forward linkages relative to Korean manufacturing as a whole and virtually identical backward linkages.

Korea: export orientation

The Korean economy is heavily export oriented, yet the public-enterprise sector plays a negligible direct role. Only about 4.9% of public-enterprise output is exported, accounting for only 5.3% of total exports. In part this reflects the fact that Korean exports on the average are labor intensive, whereas public-enterprise production is capital intensive. It may also, however, reflect high organizational costs of public operation in an area where quick decisions, rapid adjustments, and innovative marketing are prerequisites to success (Jones and Wortzel, Chapter 11).

Korea: multicollinearity

The technical factors just described correlate with one another, of course, as well as with the dependent variable of publicness. When all the cross-correlations are positive, the characteristics just discussed, taken as a group, come very close to being both necessary and sufficient for publicness. Virtually all industries that are large relative to product and factor markets, are capital intensive, have high forward linkages, and are not export oriented have public participation. Where the cross-correlations are negative, trade-offs emerge. For example, consider those manufacturing sectors that are both highly concentrated (concentration ratios greater than 0.70) and large (1977 sales greater than $15 billion Korean dollars). Of 15 such sectors there is no public participation in 9, all of which have very low forward linkages (sugar, beer, candies, soft drinks, dairy products, paint, watches and clocks, meat processing).

In sum, the revealed determinants of the costs and benefits of publicness are multiple. Product-market concentration has a very large single-factor explanatory power, but the other elements also play an identifiable role.

Other countries: similarities

Because Korea has a particularly pragmatic, growth-oriented government, the explanatory power of the foregoing variables might be expected to be particularly large. Although we know of no other country where sufficiently detailed work has been done to permit similar quantification, casual empiricism suggests that technical factors play a major role in most countries. A few scattered pieces of evidence supporting this notion are:

1. Trebat, writing on Brazil and Mexico, observes that "in both countries (we can identify) a core group of 30–50 enterprises which, because of their size or influence on resource allocation, are the backbone of the respective public enterprise sectors. With some exceptions (e.g., CONASUPO in Mexico), these tend to be public enterprise monopolies or oligopolies."[35] He further reports that in 1978 the 10 largest enterprises in Brazil were all public enterprises, as were 7 of the next 15 largest firms.

2. Of the 52 largest LDC firms listed in *Fortune's* 1979 list of the 500 largest non-U.S. industrials, 34 were public enterprises. Further, these public enterprises accounted for three-quarters of total sales by listed LDC firms, as opposed to less than 10% for public enterprises among listed MDC firms.[36]

3. In Indian manufacturing in 1977–8, the 7 largest enterprises were public as were 12 of the top 16.[37] A list of the public-enterprise share of output in 135 mining and manufacturing product lines gives no less than 78 in which public enterprises produced from 90 to 100%, with 37 more in the 50 to 90% range.[38] The 100% category includes an impressive array of commodities ranging from petroleum to turbines to vitamin B_2.

Although these data are hardly definitive, they are certainly suggestive. The alternative to public enterprise is not the perfectly competitive private enterprise of economic theory but private monopoly or oligopoly. Writ large, the pattern of public enterprises in LDCs does not on the average seem inconsistent with pragmatic choices based on a cost–benefit calculus.

Based on theory, careful examination of the Korean data, and casual perusal of limited data elsewhere, we would propose the following hypothesis: The sectors where the benefits minus costs of public ownership are likely to be highest in mixed-economy LDCs are those with the following characteristics:

1. Large in scale relative to product market
2. Large relative to factor markets
3. Capital intensive
4. High forward linkages
5. High rent, natural-resource export

6. Standardized products, easily marketed
7. Not requiring decentralized establishments

Other countries: exceptions

Although all countries are liable to have many individual exceptions to the fore-going hypothesis (e.g., small, sick companies taken over through conversion of debt to equity by public banks), their aggregate output would seem to generally be small relative to the public-enterprise sector as a whole. There are nonetheless a number of countries where, in addition to the sectors defined above, there is substantial aggregate output from small, differentiated producers of consumer goods.

In Malaysia, the government has a conscious policy of improving the lot of the ethnic Malay population, in part by integrating them into the entrepreneurial class (Mallon, Chapter 16). One major vehicle has been the establishment of large numbers of small public enterprises with a view to turning them over eventually to emergent Malay entrepreneurs. There is thus an ethnic distributional dimension to entrepreneurial failure. Available stocks of ethnic Chinese and Indian entrepreneurs could readily have undertaken such activities without public-enterprise intervention. The simple distribution-neutral efficiency conditions that we have focused on have thus been subordinated to what is perceived as a higher social goal.

In Bangladesh, wholesale nationalization at liberation resulted in large numbers of small, consumer-oriented enterprises moving into government hands, where they remain.[39] Two factors seem to have been at work. First, there was an ideological predisposition toward public enterprise on the part of some decision makers. Second, on the pragmatic side, the exodus of West Pakistanis and Biharis may have left inadequate numbers of domestic entrepreneurs and managers. To the extent the latter factor was operative, one would expect eventual divestiture of the smaller-scale activities as a domestic entrepreneurial class develops, as per the Malaysian plan.

Indonesia, like Malaysia and Bangladesh, has large numbers of small-scale public enterprises; unlike them, it is difficult to discern any pattern of explanation.[40] They are scattered across the literal and figurative landscape in a plethora of industries that combine public and private activity in a most eclectic pattern. If our analytic benefit–cost framework has any value, this is likely to entail rather substantial social costs.

These three examples serve to reemphasize two features of our approach. First, although economic factors explain a great deal, they do not come close to explaining everything. Second, where cost–benefit factors are ignored, or over-ridden, economic loss is likely to accrue. In Malaysia, these extra costs may be offset by distributional benefits, but in Indonesia, there would seem to be largely deadweight loss.

2.5 Conclusion

Our analytic framework may be summarized in the following propositions:[41]

1. The share of the public-enterprise sector in GNP is (by definition) the product of the industrial structure (the share of GNP generated in each sector) and the publicization propensity (the share of public enterprise in each sector).
2. The overall publicization propensity is a function of underlying economic, historical, political, and ideological propensities.
3. The economic publicization propensity in turn depends upon a purely pragmatic comparison of benefits and costs of public enterprise.
4. Benefits are conceived as flowing from the removal of imperfections resulting from market failures external to the enterprise.
5. Costs are conceived as following from organizational failures internal to the enterprise; and costs associated with public enterprise must be compared with those of alternative institutional intervention mechanisms.
6. Benefits and costs are a function of technical characteristics that have *both* an industry-specific and a country-specific environmental component – such as minimal efficient scale (an industry character-istic) relative to market size (a country characteristic).

Our low-order empirical survey suggests the following hypotheses for mixed-economy LDCs:

7. The share of the public-enterprise sector falls in a narrow range, with the majority of countries in the 7 to 15% region.
8. Much of the variance in GNP shares is explained by differential indus-trial structure (especially the share of large-scale mining) and this makes the publicization propensities even more uniform across coun-tries than the GNP shares.
9. The historical, political, and ideological factors operate largely as country-specific shift parameters, meaning still greater uniformity across countries in the economic publicization propensities.
10. The economic propensities still vary across the countries for the same industry, primarily because the environmental characteristics differ[42] (e.g., the minimum efficient scale of cement is large relative to Sri Lanka's market but small relative to Korea's).
11. More controversially, in most countries, the economic propensities seem to dominate the historical, political, and ideological factors in deter-mining the overall publicization propensity.

As an illustration, India and Korea generate virtually identical shares of GDP in the public-enterprise sector. This is due not to identical levels of the entire first layer of explanatory variables (industrial structure and the publicization propensity) but to rough correspondence, with differences that happen to offset one another. In the same vein, the similarity of the overall publicization propensity subsumes offsetting differences at lower levels of explanation. However, major differences between the two countries in ideology, history, and political factors seem to us to play only a minor role in explaining the overall publicization propensities, leaving the major role to be played by economic propensities.

Thus the major theme of this paper has been that economic factors – reflected in the costs and benefits of institutional choice – explain a great deal of the observed size and structure of public-enterprise sectors. There are, of course, countries in which other factors are quite important. Malaysia has established many small public enterprises to help ethnic Malays. Bangladesh took over many small-scale enterprises after its liberation struggle. Although economic considerations explain much, they do not explain everything.

We have made statements that are at once descriptive, predictive, and normative. This linkage can be justified only through some form of economic Darwinism: Governments do best that are rational and in the long run make choices consistent with pragmatic welfare maximization. A strong version would amount to single-causal economic determinism. This is absurd. The evidence clearly shows substantial divergence in the size, and to a lesser extent the structure, of public-enterprise sectors. Whereas a very important share of these differences is attributable to international variations in economic conditions, much is also clearly due to non-economic factors. There is nonetheless sufficient similarity across countries to support a weak version of economic Darwinism in which causation is multiple but in which there is a clear contribution from governments that respond *as if* they were rational welfare maximizers. Although this may be because decisions, in fact, are made on the basis of careful cost–benefit calculations, it more often results because economic conditions serve to constrain alternative decisions at the margin. For some activities the net costs of a wrong decision are so great that ideological predilection is eventually overcome. For other activities the net costs are smaller but still sufficient to tip the balance one way or the other when decisions are the result of political compromise between competing interest groups. In such circumstances a normative theory of the costs and benefits of public ownership and control also has descriptive–predictive value.

One major implication of our analysis is that institutional choices do matter a great deal in determining economic outcomes. Organizational failures are as important as market failures in explaining suboptimal economic performance. The failure of mainstream economists to direct much attention toward this source of economic inefficiency suggests a supoptimal allocation of professional resources.[43]

Our analysis implies a need for interdisciplinary studies of the effect of institutional choices on economic outcomes. Economists' empirical work generally explains outcomes only in terms of market variables. Other social scientists examine the behavior of various institutional structures without examining the economic costs and benefits of that behavior. Research strategies that recognize outcomes as a function of both markets and institutions are needed. This is particularly true of those institutional forms intermediate between market and plan, which constitute the marginal opportunity set of mixed economies. Public enterprise, a particularly important subset, ultimately can be fully understood only in terms of its institutional opportunity costs.

Notes

1 A short definition of public enterprise encompasses organizations owned and/or controlled by governments (central, provincial, and local) and financed largely by selling in a market. For a more elaborate definition and a discussion of alternatives see Leroy P. Jones, *Public Enterprise and Economic Development: The Korean Case* (Seoul: Korean Development Institute, 1975), pp. 22–42.

2 See Patrick O'Brien, *The Revolution in Egypt's Economic System* (New York: Oxford University Press, 1961), p. 214.

3 Peter Evans, "Multinationals, State-Owned Corporations, and the Transformation of Imperialism: A Brazilian Case Study," *Economic Development and Cultural Change* 26, No. 1 (Oct. 1977):43–64.

4 Peter Evans, *Dependent Development: The Alliance of Multinationals, State and Local Capital in Brazil* (Princeton: Princeton University Press, 1979).

5 Rehman Sobhan and Muzaffer Ahmad, *Public Enterprise in an Intermediate Regime: A Study in the Political Economy of Bangladesh* (Dacca: Bangladesh Institute of Development Studies, 1980).

6 Leroy Jones and Il Sakong, *Government, Business and Entrepreneurship: The Korean Case* (Cambridge: Harvard University Press, 1980), pp. 105–6.

7 Talcott Parsons, "Some Reflections on the Institutional Framework of Economic Development," in *The Challenge of Development,* ed. Alfred Bonne (Jerusalem: 1958), p. 123.

8 Except as noted, all data in this subsection come from two sources: N. S. Ramaswamy, V. J. Kesary, P. V. George, G. K. Nayar, V. G. Kamath and P. D. Deenadayalu, *Performance of Indian Public Enterprises* (New Delhi: Standing Conference of Public Enterprises, 1978); and Jones, *Public Enterprise and Economic Development.*

9 "Industrial Policy Resolution of 1956," in Government of India, *Second Five Year Plan* (New Delhi: Central Statistical Organization, 1956), p. 47.

10 Park Chung Hee, *Our Nation's Path* (Seoul: Hollym, 1970), p. 218.

11 Railways were 32% of transport and communications in India in 1972–3 but only 10% in Korea in 1973. Thus, if the Korean rail system had been as important as India's, the public-enterprise share of transport and communications would have risen to 53% in Korea vs. the 61% figure reported for India. Calculated from Jones, *Public Enterprise and Economic Development,* pp. 76 and 236, and Government of India, *Statistical Abstract 1975* (New Delhi: Central Statistical Organization, 1976), p. 409.

12 This cumbersome term is used to refer to both the take-over of existing firms (i.e., nationalization) and the establishment of new ones.

13 Sobhan and Ahmad, *Public Enterprise in an Intermediate Regime,* pp. 7–17.

14 Il Sakong, "Macroeconomic Aspects of Public Enterprise in Asia: A Comparative Study," working paper, (Seoul: Korea Development Institute, 1979), pp. 47–50.

15 Many reports of higher shares are simply incorrect. A common fallacy is to take public-enterprise *sales* as a share of GDP or GNP. Definitional problems generally

create only small errors, except where there is a failure to distinguish between the public-enterprise sector and the public sector as a whole. Another common source of difficulty is using the much higher asset or investment shares as a proxy for value-added shares.

16 Frederick L. Pryor, "Public Ownership: Some Quantitative Dimensions," in *Public Enterprise: Economic Analysis of Theory and Practice*, ed. William G. Shepherd (Lexington, Mass.: Lexington Books, 1976), pp. 3–22. Measured as a share of employment. Note that the "public sector" includes "public institutions" – which do not market their output (e.g., the military) – as well as public "enterprise."

17 Sakong, "Macroeconomic Aspects of Public Enterprise in Asia," p. 55.

18 The use of a market-failure approach to explaining the size and structure of the public-enterprise sector in LDCs is hardly novel. Predecessors include John B. Sheahan, "Public Enterprise in Developing Countries," in *Public Enterprise: Economic Analysis of Theory and Practice*, ed. William G. Shepherd (Lexington, Mass.: Lexington Books, 1976), pp. 205–33; Deepak Lal, "Public Enterprises," mimeographed (London, 1977), and Jones, *Public Enterprise and Economic Development*, pp. 13–18.

19 Some 2,000 small-scale decentralized units in rice and flour milling and cotton ginning were divested. See Investment Advisory Centre of Pakistan, *Role of Performance of Public Enterprises in the Economic Growth of Pakistan* (Karachi: IACP, 1979).

20 Jan Tinbergen, "Optimal Organization of the Economy," in *Public Expenditure Analysis*, ed. Balbir S. Sahni (Rotterdam: Rotterdam University Press, 1972), pp. 21–35.

21 For introductions to these bodies of literature, see Harvey Leibenstein, *Beyond Economic Man* (Cambridge: Harvard University Press, 1976); Henry Simon, *Administrative Behavior* (New York: Macmillan, 1976); Oliver Williamson, *Markets and Hierarchies* (New York: Free Press, 1975); Eric Furubotn and Scetozar Pejovich, *The Economics of Property Rights* (Cambridge, Mass.: Lippincott, Ballinger, 1974); and A. M. Spence, "The Economics of International Organization: An Introduction," *Bell Journal of Economics*, 6, No. 1 (Spring 1975):163–72.

22 This does not pertain, of course, if a negative value is placed on an increase in the welfare of some individual or group.

23 H. Linnemann, J. P. Pronk, and Jan Tinbergen, "Convergence of Economic Systems in East and West," in *Comparative Economic Systems*, ed. Morris Bornstein (Homewood, Ill.: Irwin, 1974), pp. 493–510. Also see Jan Tinbergen, "The Significance of Welfare Economics for Socialism," in *On Political Economy and Econometrics: Essays in Honor of Oscar Lange*, ed., the Anniversary Committee of the Polish Scientific Publishers (Oxford: Pergamon Press, 1965), pp. 591–9.

24 Examples of second-best interventions in terms of public-enterprise pricing are found in Abram Bergson, "Optimal Pricing for a Public Enterprise," *Quarterly Journal of Economics* 36, (Nov. 1972):519–44, and W. J. Baumol and W. J. Bradford, "Optimal Departures from Marginal Cost Pricing," *American Economic Review* 60, No. 3 (June 1970):265–83.

25 Leroy P. Jones, "Performance Evaluation of Public Enterprises: A Methodology with an Application to Asian Fertilizer Plants," mimeographed (Boston University).

26 William S. Comanor and Harvey Leibenstein, "Allocative Efficiency, X-Efficiency and the Measurement of Welfare Losses," *Economica* 36, No. 3 (Aug. 1969):304–9.

27 Sheahan, "Public Enterprise," pp. 206–10.
28 A case can certainly be made that the curves are not linear but "*U*-shaped," reflecting initial scale economies in supervision. We omit this complication as it does not alter the main points of our argument.
29 Figure 2.2, like the one that precedes it, has only heuristic value, because a particular activity need not, and generally will not, be horizontally coincident on the different curves. That is, it may be on the left of the benefits curve but on the right of one of the cost curves. Only benerve that, when positive, depicts a public-enterprise sector.
30 E.g., see Linnemann, Pronk, and Tinbergen, "Convergence of Economic Systems."
31 All data in this subsection are from Jones, *Public Enterprise and Economic Development.*
32 That public enterprises overwhelmingly sell in imperfect output markets also has a major implication on the cost side. To the extent that public operation entails cost inefficiencies, these must be financed somehow. In noncompetitive internal markets these may be passed on in part to the consumer, whereas in competitive internal or export markets they cannot. This fact by no means reduces the real costs of public enterprise but does serve to mask them and reduce pressures for reform.
33 For elaboration on the role of family conglomerates in Korea and the role of public banks in controlling their behavior, see Jones and Sakong, *Government, Business and Entrepreneurship*, pp. 101–10.
34 Direct plus indirect domestic linkages are theoretically superior measures but at this level of generality yield similar results and for present purposes do not warrant the greater expository detail. See Jones, *Public Enterprise and Economic Development,* pp. 98–105.
35 Thomas Trebat, "Public Enterprises in Brazil and Mexico: Comparative Structure, Control and Performance," mimeographed (New York: Bankers Trust, 1980), pp. 15, 18.
36 Leroy Jones, "Public Enterprise in Less-Developed Countries," *Wall Street Journal,* Dec. 7, 1979, p. 15.
37 Documentation Centre for Corporate and Business Policy Research, *The Future of Public Sector in India* (New Delhi: DCCBPR, 1979), pp. S-63–4.
38 Ibid., pp. S-6 to S-13. Figures are largely in quantities, so it is not possible to calculate how large a fraction of public-enterprise output is in highly concentrated industries; however, there can be no question that the figure is very high.
39 See Sobhan and Ahmad, "Public Enterprise in an Intermediate Regime."
40 See Malcolm Gillis and Ralph E. Beals, *Tax and Investment Policy for Hard Minerals: Public and Multinational Enterprise in Indonesia* (Cambridge, Mass.: Ballinger, 1980).
41 The propositions also could be formalized, of course, in a set of equations involving vector and matrix algebra, but for present nonquantitative purposes, the verbal equivalent will suffice.
42 And to a limited extent because optimal technical characteristics vary with factor endowment to the extent that factor substitution is possible.
43 For elaboration on this argument in a wider context, see Charles Wolf, Jr., "Economic Efficiency and Inefficient Economics," *Journal of Post-Keynesian Economics,* No. 3 (Fall 1979):71–82.

3 Political economy of public enterprise

Muzaffer Ahmad

This chapter represents a *political-economy* approach to understanding the existence and behavior of public enterprises. It begins with a critique of the pure economic approach not because such an approach is irrelevant but because it is incomplete. The missing element, supplied here, is the interplay of political, economic, and social forces that affect the policy making of the state toward public enterprise. Although I bring together many disparate ideas from the literature, in no sense is this a complete survey. The purpose is only to illustrate the political-economy type of analysis. My aim is to seek broader answers than the usual narrow technical economic ones.

3.1 Traditional economics versus political economy

Neo classical economics has endogenous limitations because it assumes away the interwoven linkages between polity, society, and economy. The interplay of social forces has little impact on the analysis, except as it indirectly affects the market through such measurable variables as income distribution. This branch of economics typically assumes "economic men" who are free and rational, who pursue their individual self-interests by maximizing perceived utility, and who operate in perfect markets. Further, it uses concepts of equilibrium and optimality that, though defined with mathematical precision, are at best only an approximation of reality.[1] Political economists find this high degree of abstraction difficult to accept amid the reality they perceive. They find the quest for "harmony" unrealistic as they see conflicts of interest unfold every day. They see group interests as having a reality independent of individual interest. They prefer to study the interplay of socio-political forces in a historical context. They hope to observe the devolution of dialectics in an imperfect situation where concepts of equilibrium and optimality are only distorted visions. In this scheme, polity and economy are not divorced from each other but instead interact through the interplay of social forces. Indeed, this is the subject matter of political economy.[2]

In writing this chapter the author has benefited from his work with Professor Rehman Sobhan and comments by Professors Edward S. Mason, Gustav Papanek, Peter Evans, John Sheahan, and Leroy P. Jones. However, the author alone is responsible for all errors that may remain.

The concern of economists with public enterprise has largely been confined to traditional microeconomic concerns with pricing and investment decisions. The possibility of public production of goods for private consumption is usually either ignored or considered to be an aberration. Even those who take a more realistic view of public enterprise focus narrowly on market-failure explanations, thus committing an error of omission in ignoring social forces (Jones and Mason, Chapter 2). This is in the tradition of economics that is purported to have been developed as impersonal, value free, and politically and socially neutral. In a free-enterprise economy this neutrality ensures the continued dominance of capitalists.[3]

In spite of economists' reservations there has been a growth in public enterprises across the ideological spectrum.[4] Because of this and because nonsocialist countries use this tool, it has been suggested that the phenomenon of public ownership is not necessarily central to socialist objectives. This is true in the sense that public enterprise can be used to achieve nonsocialist objectives (e.g. under state capitalism). Although social ownership is thus not a sufficient condition for the achievement of socialist goals, it remains a necessary condition.

A claim that ideology is unimportant has been prompted by the perception that the scope of public-enterprise activity is heavily conditioned by pragmatic economic factors. In pure neoclassical economics, public enterprise is unnatural, as in a perfect economy with pure competition such a phenomenon would be unnecessary. Because neither a perfect economy nor pure competition exists, the government reaches a deviant situation through various forms of intervention, including consultation, regulation, taxes and subsidies, and direct ownership. Public enterprise is then a policy of last resort. Adherents of this approach believe in a minimal public sector (including government) and it is allocative and operational efficiency – perceived in terms of equilibrium and optimality – which assume primordial importance.

3.2 Political economy: an alternative approach

What do the many variants of political economy offer as an alternative? The basic concern is the close inter-dependence of economy and polity. In contrast to the traditional grudging acceptance on narrow economic grounds, the political economist considers the public enterprise as a positive politico-economic institution in a given socio-political situation.[5] The essential point is that public enterprises are capable of generating *surplus*. The ownership of the public enterprise in theory lies with the state, but in practice this is a nonoperational entity. Real control normally lies with one or more groups working through a political party, a bureaucracy, a technocracy in the enterprise, and/or workers. This provides control of productive resources and the level and distribution of surplus. The competing social forces not only manifest themselves in the ownership-control-operation nexus but also extend into strategy, management, and result.[6]

Contrary to the economists' assumptions, public enterprises come into being not only because of market failure but also because of sociopolitical exigency and interest-group activity. It makes more sense to think of interactive systems in which social forces, political power, and economic policy are related. Society does not necessarily display consensus, symmetry, or consistency through such mechanisms as voice, preference, vote, or choice. Rather, the manifestation of deviance, coercion, and tension through dominance, dependence, and violence are common. Thus the harmony of market equilibrium sought through the participation of rational but "atomistic" individuals who sustain democratic equity through vote is merely an idealized picture that has never existed (nor is it likely to exist).

It is therefore necessary to think of a *total* social system consisting of economic, political, and societal subsystems. The societal subsystem shows the configuration of interest groups that interact with each other in the political arena to gain or retain control of productive resources in the economic sphere. These resources are critical because they are the key to social dominance. The political subsystem is the reflection of this societal subsystem as the groups attempt to arrive at, or impose, a set of collective goals. The economic subsystem then has the function of actualization of goals through the production of goods and services. In sum, the societal subsystem defines the players in the game, the political subsystem defines the rules of the game, and the economic subsystem sees the game played.

The thesis is that there are at least two groups in the societal subsystem: One group has the privilege of making decisions because of its control over productive resources, the other offers active or passive compliance. Compliance can be formalized, say, by a vote. Political, military, or bureaucratic groups – or a combination thereof – are dominant when they command resources through control of the political subsystem and, by extension, the economic subsystem. Dominance changes only if command over productive resources changes.

The pattern is not static. The dominated group may change its character, and compliance may become shaky, thus requiring changes in social, political, and economic policy. Economic policy is the reflection of the interest-achievement effort of the dominant group in quest of survival and supremacy embodied in the state apparatus itself.

Political power is an extension of societal domination based on production relations. In capitalistic society, productive resources are controlled either directly or indirectly by owners of capital. The polity then works to maintain the dominance of capitalists. This requires a production relation where private financial profit is the primary measure of efficiency. Once the social subsystem is disturbed, the polity must adjust to protect the interest of the owners of capital. This requires intervention in the "free" economic system through such concepts as social benefit–cost analysis and through attempts at income redistribution. Such efforts function only as an accommodation process, however, so long as the basic mode of capitalistic society remains intact.

Surplus in a socialist society has a parallel, of course, to profit in a capitalist society. The qualitative difference comes in who controls the surplus. The quantitative calculation also differs as prices and costs have different meanings in a market-controlled economy as opposed to a controlled-market economy.

Focusing on the distribution of surplus as the critical variable suggests a new dimension for classifying public enterprises. Although traditional categories (e.g., based on legal status, industry, or market failure) are useful, it is even more important to identify the impact on the private sector. At one extreme, the public-enterprise sector may totally *supplant* the private-enterprise sector and have no meaningful interaction with the private sector in the mobilization, utilization, production and distribution of goods, savings, and surplus. This is the case where there is no leakage of surplus to the private sector, for example, in a tobacco monopoly covering procurement, production, and distribution. At the other end of the spectrum is a public enterprise that is totally *supportive* of private enterprise in the sense that surpluses are wholly or partially transferred to the private sector, for example, the production of an intermediate input that is sold at an advantageous price to the private sector. Such a situation occurs when the private-enterprise sector is politically supportive of the controlling group. Between these two extremes is a continuum that manifests different and changing degrees of supplantation and support.

To summarize, in a political-economy framework, public enterprises represent control over the use of productive resources and especially over the generation and distribution of surplus, be it actual or potential. Although such control has its origin in the societal and political subsystems, there is also an iterative feedback.

3.3   The nature of the contending social forces

The relationships between social forces do not easily lend themselves to such time-honored collective notions as a community utility function. One might conceivably agree to welfare functions of particular interest groups that are then weighted by a dominance factor. This would result in an aggregate welfare function very similar to that of the dominant group but slightly adjusted to attain the compliance of the dominated group.

State policies reflect the efforts of contending social forces to promote use of resources in a manner that benefits the controlling social class. History is replete with examples of this. Monarchy and dictatorships are extreme cases that need no elaboration. Even in democracies, political parties with different class bases exist and coalitions of these groups affect the policy making of the state. Thus studies aimed at understanding policies involving the allocation of resources must be viewed more in the fashion of game theory. This is not necessarily a zero-sum game, where the gain of one is the loss of the other; but, at times, where the sum to be divided may grow, inherent in the game is the condition that the share becomes less for the subordinated group.[7]

In developing countries, authority is represented very strongly in the state and the government because other institutions of modernization and mobilization are weak. Hence, the dominant social force is also dominant in government, and this allows the utilization of public enterprise for consolidation of its power.

3.4   Evolution of social forces in the colonial period

Although the focus of this discussion is on post colonial, mixed-economy LDCs, their societal systems were formed under the influence of colonial powers. It is thus necessary to understand the formation of social relations in that period in order to understand its manifestation in the post colonial period.

The contending forces shaping the policy in a developing country are both internal and international. Because of past imperial domination, there is likely to be a governmental and service bureaucracy that outnumbers groups engaged in production activities in modern non traditional sectors. Bureaucracy in a colonized society is likely to wield considerable influence because of its proximity to power, and this provides the bureaucracy with opportunities to control productive resources. This is done in a pattern to maximize the safety of the interest of the colonizer.

In LDCs there may be a small number of landed bourgeoisie and perhaps a small group of large bourgeoisie who grew under the benign influence of the imperial dominators. Even though these groups cannot generally be classed as bourgeoisie in the generally accepted sense, they are influential as a concentrated and organized interest group. For historical and class-interest reasons they prefer to interlock with foreign corporate or state interests. There also exists a military class whose interest is comparable to this dependent national bourgeoisie and generally aligns itself with them. This is not to deny the possibility that during a nationalist struggle there could have been limited growth of a national bourgeoisie who ventured into industry. With independence, and even before, this bourgeoisie could play the role of a comprador group, aligning with external interests.

Thus, a post colonial society may have a group, which may be termed bourgeois, composed of high bureaucrats in government and military and commercial establishments as well as financiers, traders, and industrialists. There also exists a class of petty bourgeoisie who are small property owners, in small businesses, or in low-level professional jobs. In addition, the proletariat (i.e., those who sell labor) exist in large numbers. This categorization is often complicated by a low level of class awareness resulting from extended kinship and other socio-cultural values and relationships.[8]

I have already referred to the link between the national social class and the colonial metropolitan group. Their presence is manifest in private metropolitan capital, government capital (reflecting the interests of the group that controls the government), or foreign institutions, which have a residual of dominant capital in their organization and operation.

A special case is described by the Latin American "dependencia" theory. It generally deals with the interaction between the multi-nationals and a post colonial power elite who have common interests. The state then plays a supportive role for promotion of multinational and national bourgeois capital.[9]

This paradigm of external and internal forces needs to be supplemented by a classification based on the nature of the decolonialization process. The colonial power may or may not have created a gentry consisting of bureaucrats and the military and also may or may not have promoted the commercial bourgeoisie from which the national capitalist group normally emerges.[10] Further, the decolonialization process may or may not have been peaceful, and an armed conflict is likely to create a polity antagonistic to metropolitan power. Finally, because of constraints of resources and institutions, the state could be influenced by international institutions committed to metropolitan interests.[11]

3.5 Categories of public enterprise in dominant–subordinate countries

Because many elements determine the social configuration in the postcolonial period, there is wide divergence among the LDCs. However, consideration of five basic patterns will suggest how the colonial experience affects the postcolonial interplay of social forces and how this in turn affects the role of public enterprise.

First, the colonial power may have allowed the emergence of a national bourgeoisie that was dominant at the time of a *peaceful* transfer of power. This group is often a comprador bourgeoisie having a mutually supportive relationship with international capital. One would not expect expansion of public enterprise in such a situation, and no nationalization would be anticipated. One would, however, expect expansion of the public sector to support and subsidize the growth of the private capital. For example, the state may operate risky high-technology projects in basic industries, absorb any loss, and sell at a low price to private producers who then enjoy comfortable profits with little effort. The scope and depth of private industrialization thus remains limited to low-risk and high-return areas, with the high-risk and low-return areas covered by the public sector.

An example is India, which emerged as an independent state through peaceful negotiation and with an influential indigenous bourgeoisie. Independence further entrenched the bourgeoisie and created an opportunity for it to expand its dominance at the expense of imperial interest.[12] Initially, existing foreign capital entered into partnership with national bourgeois enterprises, but with time and experience the national groups became the dominant partner.

Under these circumstances public enterprise has generally played only a supportive role. Public enterprise indeed grew but without prejudice to the private sector. It undertook investment in high-risk and low-return sectors, in high-technology sectors, and in sectors where externalities for the private sector were large.

Public enterprise coexisted with the private sector in part to salvage the weak private units. The only case where the private sector was supplanted was that of banking and insurance and this was prompted by political necessity.[13] Public-enterprise investment grew nearly twofold in the 1960s, but the share of the private sector in fixed capital formation increased compared to that of the public sector. The private sector was free to expand within designated sectors, and the growth of the private sector in India was accompanied by a growing concentration and polarization of the ownership of assets.[14] Industrial capitalists in India have done reasonably well under the regime of verbal socialism.[15] In this sense, Jones and Mason's static comparison in Chapter 2 of South Korea and India fails to recognize the impact of the interplay of social forces. The real cause of the similar use of public enterprise in the two countries is not economic similarity but the equivalent dominance of national bourgeoisie in both polities.[16]

A second case occurs where the transfer of power takes place under conditions of conflict. This is likely to mean that the bourgeoisie cultivated the support of the petty bourgeoisie and the proletariat during the struggle for liberation. It then becomes politically inappropriate to hand over control of foreign enterprises directly to the national bourgeoisie on achieving independence. Instead, they utilize indirect control through state ownership, with management in the hands of an agent of their class. This may mean a nominal expansion of public enterprises, a process that may be reversed if the national bourgeoisie continues to consolidate power and if the proletariat or petty bourgeoisie fail to organize. A growing private sector is further encouraged by foreign or international development organizations that, in the name of economic efficiency, merely look at profit and loss and suggest policies that restrict the role of public enterprise.

Bangladesh is a good example. At the time of the partition of India there existed no high bourgeoisie in East Pakistan, despite some landed aristocracy. In the early days of Pakistan, bureaucratic control and political leadership remained in the hands of non-Bengalis, and the benefits of state policies encouraging the development of a national bourgeoisie were monopolized by immigrants and Punjabi groups. In the 1960s the unpopularity of free enterprise and a market-control philosophy of development led to a policy of sponsored capitalism in East Pakistan. Thus a nascent bourgeoisie was created by the political power of Pakistan. This process was disrupted when liberation was attained with the leadership of a party whose base was a petty bourgeoisie group of small traders, industrialists, officials, and surplus farmers. Given their modest political and economic power base, they needed the cooperation of students, peasants, and workers. Thus the abandoned assets of Pakistani bourgeoisie could not be taken over by a national bourgeoisie. Meanwhile, radicals pushed through a policy of nationalization that led to an expansion of public enterprise. However, the petty bourgeoisie saw to it that the nationalized sector remained an island. The absence of commitment and cadre allowed for dissipation of assets and surplus mainly to traders with political linkages. As the bureaucracy hampered the efficient operation of the public enterprises, the aid givers found it expedient to push carefully and candidly a policy of reversal.[17]

A third situation occurs when the proletariat and/or petty bourgeoisie gain supremacy via a prolonged armed conflict. This results in a sharp change in the composition of political power. If this power is not strangled by a combination of metropolitan and imperialist power, a meaningful expansion of public enterprises could occur. This can only be sustained through the cooperation of supportive states, petty bourgeoisie, and the proletariat. Examples of such a case are found in North Korea, Vietnam, and Algeria.[18]

With the increase of Japanese influence and ultimate domination the Korean peninsula went from a feudal land to a subordinate economy tied to the Japanese metropolis. This opened up avenues of Japanese capitalist penetration but crippled nationalist capitalistic development. However, Japanese finance did develop hydropower and chemical industries after World War I. They had also developed heavier industries in preparation for World War II. Japan created a landlord class by decree in 1906 and this alienated the exploited peasantry. A small class of comprador bourgeoisie arose in administration, commerce, and industry and worked in collaboration with Japanese capital. Japanese extraction of raw material for their own industries made domestic cottage industries difficult to maintain, and the encroachment of Japanese goods in the Korean market made other industries unprofitable. Under these circumstances the nationalist movement grew and in the 1920s and 1930s it was increasingly militant. Defeat of the Japanese in World War II left an independent but divided Korea. North Korea proceeded to build a popular base through land reform. This entailed the confiscation of all the land owned by the Japanese, the Korean collaborators, and land owned in excess of five *cho* per family. Rented land and lands of religious units were distributed to tenants. The movement also promulgated sweeping regulations to make working conditions in industry humane. This strengthened the worker-peasant alliance for a mass-based government, which proceeded to take over most economic activity, allowing the national capitalists to survive at only the most subordinate level.

The lesson of this approach is that once the appropriate social reforms are carried out to create a mass-based party with real power, the nationalization of the main branches of the economy yields the economic surplus previously expropriated by colonialists or capitalists. The process was simplified in North Korea by the exodus of the weak and disorganized national bourgeoisie to the more congenial South and aided by supportive states such as the Soviet Union and China.[19]

A fourth case occurs when there is no small national bourgeoisie, the transfer of power is peaceful, and foreign capital remains dominant until the national bourgeoisie emerges. A variant occurs where the transfer has taken place through violence and public enterprise becomes dominant with support from sympathetic states and the middle class as in Angola. An example of the more common peaceful variant is found in Nigeria.

Historically, Nigeria evolved from an artificial aggregation of tribes. Ruling families constituted the indigenous elite. Urbanization, Westernization, and political development helped this "old" elite, through access to overseas education, to acquire a Western way of life and professional and governmental jobs. They became the "new" national bourgeoisie and held positions of influence in independent Nigeria, which had gained freedom peacefully through negotiation. This traditionally privileged, but small, group would have retained control of the upper stratum of society but for an exploding demand by educated youth.[20]

Because of the absence of a national bourgeoisie with education, skills, and ability, Nigeria initially followed a policy of welcoming any expatriate industrial development activity. As the new elite grew, policies changed. In 1962 the government declared its intention of enabling "Nigerian *businessmen* to control increasing portions of the Nigerian economy."[21] Private enterprise was encouraged through the classical means of developing infrastructure and incentives. Public enterprise came not to satisfy socialist ideology but to channel public funds to private capitalists, to meet certain social needs, to run public utilities, and in general to provide support to private entrepreneurs. Thus a study of ownership and control structures of business enterprise in Nigeria in 1970 shows the unimportance of Nigerian shareholding vis-à-vis expatriate shareholding, the dominant role of expatriate institutions in large business enterprises, and the relatively stronger hold of expatriates on the boards of Nigerian companies. Only in 1972 did the Nigerian bourgeoisie begin to reserve certain areas for Nigerians.[22]

A fifth situation occurs when the transition is peaceful but the petty bourgeoisie, with a coalition of rich farmers, coalesce to promote state intervention and to keep the bourgeoisie at bay and the proletariat enthused about approaching socialism.[23] This requires a deliberate restraint of the growth of the national bourgeoisie and the encouragement of the aspirations of the proletariat. Once the petty bourgeoisie themselves grow and become the national bourgeoisie, the nature of the coalition changes and public enterprise may again assume a supportive role. Such a state is often marked by changes in foreign relations and an increase of foreign assistance from the free world. This is illustrated by the case of Sri Lanka.

Sri Lanka attained independence through peaceful negotiations without allowing discontinuities to create a vacuum. As the indigenous bourgeoisie was in embryo, in the immediate postindependence period a coalition of the national bourgeoisie and the colonial bourgeoisie perpetrated their dominance. In this phase, public enterprise played a role in support of private enterprise. However, the effort to create a capitalist entrepreneurial class out of feudal plantation owners was not a success. In 1956 the first political alliance of workers and petty bourgeoisie encouraged the moderate expansion of public enterprises without prejudice to the private sector (as in India). Public enterprise played a complementary role economically and also helped in the evolution of the petty bourgeoisie into a national bourgeoisie. This strengthened class then used the instruments of public enterprise to promote themselves into a capitalist group. After 1965 they began taking advantage of state-sponsored financial assistance programs and incentives. In 1970, however, the worker–petty bourgeois alliance reversed the policy, and the government proceeded to use public enterprise to attack the power of foreign capital, feudal interest, and the national capitalist group. Nationalization policies pursued by a coalition of workers and petty bourgeoisie helped in the rapid growth of public enterprise in Sri Lanka. The alliances of social forces were again reversed and the national bourgeoisie came into power. The new government wasted no time in changing the role of public enterprise. This example illustrates Michael Kalecki's point that an intermediate regime with a dominant public-enterprise sector can survive only if a coalition of petty bourgeois, middle class, and wealthy farmers works with the support of sympathetic states.[24]

This discussion shows that it is essential to distinguish the conditions in which public enterprise plays a dominant role from those in which it is only supportive. The supportive role occurs when a national bourgeoisie exists and is in control of the polity and is facilitated by support of foreign capital and international agencies. In this case public enterprises provide support and incentives for private enterprises.[25] However, the national bourgeoisie may fail to achieve progress in spite of this support. The bourgeois class then realizes that the state is the only channel by which to stabilize the situation and accommodate capital, and they, in their own interest, broaden state production but under their own control. Management is arranged in such a way that the surplus eventually finds its way into the promotion of their class. In some Latin American economies notable examples are found.

Though the foregoing fivefold typology is not exhaustive, this descriptive analysis has illustrated that the historical evolution of class interest is a major cause of the expansion or contraction of the public sector. This is not fully recognized in the conventional discussion of "entrepreneurial failure." The political-economy approach goes beyond economic factors. It sees entrepreneurial support as a manifestation of a policy of dominant social forces and entrepreneurial substitution as the result of an interplay of contending forces.

3.6 Stability of public-enterprise regimes

As already shown – notably in the case of Sri Lanka – public-enterprise regimes are dynamic rather than static. They change with shifts in the underlying balance of social forces. The process starts with the political displacement of foreign interests. So long as the polity is controlled by them, further changes are deferred and the public sector plays a supportive role. Once a large petty bourgeoisie develops and aligns itself with rich peasants to control the polity, further change comes through the political dominance of this alliance, which leads, in turn, to the assumption of the dominant role by the public sector. The further evolution of this "intermediate class" (consisting of petty bougeoisie and rich farmers) may ultimately reverse the process because of a sharpening of conflict with the proletariat. Only if the latter assumes control of the polity will public enterprise achieve a dominant role.

Situations that are stable with respect to public enterprises are also common, so long as stability is understood as having only medium-term implications. All such cases require a stable polity, which would, in turn, assume stable social relations among the contending forces. Two stable situations exist at the two ends of the scale.

At one extreme there is a dominant capitalist group, which uses public enterprises in a supportive role. This group's power increases with economic growth, keeping the petty bourgeoisie and the proletariat disinclined to organize for a conflict. The failure of the national bourgeoisie (through ineptitude or metropolitan linkage) can eventually destabilize such a situation, as can a sharpening of conflict resulting from increasing inequity. A case in point is Pakistan, particularly West Pakistan.

Power in Pakistan has been concentrated in the hands of a bureaucratic-military elite, who coalesced with the new industrial class that was formed from immigrants and the Punjabi trading class. The bureaucracy provided cheap capital through low interest rates, cheap labor through the control of trade unionism, cheap raw material by allowing terms of trade to move against agriculture, and cheap machinery through an overvalued currency and protection. Public enterprise was to play the role of promoter of private enterprise and this it did splendidly, and the system was stable for a long period. Destabilization was due to the eagerness of the ruling alliance to protect economic gains by denying the political process demanded by regional configurations of social forces.[26]

The other stable situation occurs at the other extreme with the near absence of a national bourgeoisie and the dominance of the proletariat in a mass-based state. Thus, the most stable case of public-enterprise dominance occurs where the national bourgeoisie is effectively eliminated as a source of power (as in North Korea). There, public enterprise has legitimized itself with the proletariat, who lack the capacity to control productive resources directly and who thus prefer social control in their own interest. With an efficient technocracy and a cadre committed to using the public sector in the interest of the masses, stability is possible. A case in point is North Vietnam.

Even such a pure situation is not entirely conflict free, however. With the progress of public enterprises, the dominance of technocracy increases and the technocrats can begin to play a role comparable to that of the petty bourgeoisie. In the absence of a strong, ideologically committed polity, the new class can eventually undermine the collective nature of the society.[27]

An example is Yugoslavia after World War II. Property was transferred from the private sector to the state to facilitate a change in production relationships, reorganize the national economy, and transform the capitalist system into a socialist one. The state sector grew considerably, and it was asserted that the state sector was the highest form of social ownership. This centralized approach required the merger of government administration and business management under direct political party leadership. This burgeoning postwar bureaucracy did indeed constitute a new class, and there was a recognizable alienation of peasants and workers from the party and the trade union. As Yugoslav local loyalties and individualism reaffirmed themselves, the polity had to respond with decentralization, social (as opposed to state) ownership of the means of production, associated labor organizations, market orientation, and self-management. Even with expanded participation at the enterprise level the system renders sufficient power to the political and management elites.[28]

A third stable regime is the intermediate regime where numerically dominant petty bourgeoisie and the rich peasants coalesce to form the polity and utilize public enterprise to promote an amalgam of their interests supported by international socialist capital and state capitalism. They also pursue a policy to uproot the feudal class and to appease the peasants. Such a regime can be stable when it benefits the numerical majority of small traders, investors, farmers, and workers through seepage of potential surplus. An example is Algeria.[29]

Stability, however, does not mean the disappearance of conflict, particularly in such an intermediate regime where the petty bourgeoisie is dominant. The genesis of conflict lies in the controversy over control. The contenders are the state bureaucracy, the party machinery, the enterprise technocracy, the aspiring private sector, and the workers. Even without the national bourgeoisie in the wings and without international capital supporting either block, the germs of social instability exist, and this invariably affects the role and performance of public enterprise.

Hence, stated strongly, stability requires the continued dominance of a particular class. The nature, outlook, and interests of this class define the role and relevance of public enterprise.

3.7 Conflict within the public-enterprise sector

Even where the structure of the public-enterprise sector is apparently stable, there is conflict over policies within the sector. The public-enterprise sector becomes one arena in which opposing forces contend. Conflict is manifested in the processes of control that are directly linked to the generation and distribution of surplus. The actual surplus of the firm is merely the residual, so that control over processes allows dissipation of potential surplus either through leakage to intermediaries (suppliers, wholesalers, and retailers) or through higher wages, salaries, benefits, and so on. Similarly, actual surplus may be inflated by low transfer prices on inputs or deflated by high transfer prices. Free-market practices cannot resolve the conflict, as they do not represent relative push and pull in the critical political decision-making mechanism.[30]

One manifestation of such conflict is in the issue of autonomy versus accountability. Under one stable condition (i.e., where the bourgeoisie is dominant), discretion will be left with the public enterprises that are directed by technocracies sympathetic to the bourgeoisie class. Because of class identification, the bureaucracy and polity have no fear of challenge from this group. Potential challenge could come only from the petty bourgeoisie and, more importantly, from labor, if and when workers become organized.

In the other stable condition (where the regime is mass based), the technocracy is under the control of the polity, and enterprise autonomy is limited within the perimeters set by political control. Here, the potential for conflict lies with the technocracy turning into a new class or with the workers coming into conflict with the party over the use of surplus. Only a strong polity ensures the continuity of stability with a defined set of work assignments.

The third case of stability (intermediate regimes) is the most vulnerable and is immediately threatened when the coalition of urban petty bourgeoisie and surplus farmer is threatened by changing terms of trade (between agriculture and industry) or by the evolution of petty bourgeoisie to national bourgeoisie. In this case the small business group wants to maintain maximum control to ensure against unfavorable developments.

In unstable situations the conflict is sharpened and authority factually devolves to the temporarily dominant group. It opts for maximum control, generally through the state bureaucracy, which typically becomes the servant of the dominant group (either by actually aligning with this group or by assuming a subservient profile). Though the intent to control is strong, the extent and depth of control may actually be weak.[31]

3.8 Generation and distribution of surplus

It is my contention that the use of resources under the control of public enterprise is dependent on the character of the polity. Where controlled by the national bourgeoisie, public enterprises are used to foster private enterprise by supplying public-sector goods and services to the private sector below cost. They also express interest in minimizing costs, if that can be done without disturbing their gain as suppliers of inputs. On the one hand, their interest lies in selling to public enterprise at higher than market prices and, on the other, in buying from public enterprise at below cost. Such a situation naturally limits the capacity of the public sector to generate surplus.

A polity that is controlled by the working class, on the other hand, would like to see nominal employment grow and wages and benefits increase beyond that which the enterprise should normatively yield. There may be complaints about top-heavy management and their privileges. If production is of mass-consumption goods, workers would prefer to see prices raised but to be paid themselves in-kind. If the industrial working class is linked to the rural low-income group, as is the case in many LDCs, the working class would advocate high prices for industrial raw materials and subsidies for necessities. In an intermediate regime, the urban middle class would advocate price control at the mill gate and higher prices for agricultural produce, which is used either as a wage good or as industrial raw material. In an unstable situation, when the polity has not been able to resolve its contradictions, policies are also unstable. In all these cases, the generation of surplus in public enterprises is adversely affected and resource utilization may not be optimized.

The distribution of surplus, like its generation, is intricately related to a set of public policies toward capital structure, amortization, and taxation. At one extreme the government may treat all expenses as grants, and the funds as sunk, and may also take away any operational surplus so long as no opposition is mounted by the technocracy and the workers. At the other end of the scale, all investments are treated as loans, and funds are to be recovered through a depreciation account, with the enterprise subject to business taxes. In this case, given the same level of performance, the surplus generated is smaller as parts of it have gone to the government under different accounts. Licensing procedures, exchange rates, interest rates, credit allocations, and other policies also affect the size of the surplus.

Both mass-based regimes and a petty bourgeoisie–dominant polity would desire to maximize surplus and would adjust these policies accordingly. In a petty bourgeois polity in transition to a national bourgeoisie, surplus would be maximized, but with a generous wage-salary-benefit structure. This group might come in conflict with the private sector, which would opt for fixing prices at the factory level. The party functionaries might encourage this in order to take a part of the surplus for their own class. This may engender a conflict not only with the enterprise technocracy but also with the workers. In the bourgeois-dominant polity, the trading bourgeoisie is more organized and able to establish a set of policies that generate surplus for them through input-pricing and output-marketing mechanisms.

These considerations raise problems for economic-efficiency studies of public enterprises, particularly in unstable conflict situations. Only by studying the polity's impact on resource use and on generation and distribution of surplus would we be able to obtain a clearer picture of the role of contending social forces. With that as datum, the efficiency criterion needs to be recast by explicitly accommodating sociopolitical factors if such analysis is to be meaningful.

Policy making is as much a political act as it is economic. This is not to say that economic analysis is irrelevant but to underscore its limited focus on factors affecting performance and profit of public enterprise, and thus the use of such may indeed further the class interest of a particular social class.

Let me now summarize the differences between an economic approach and a political approach. Economists seem to view public enterprises as a necessary corrective institution in a second-best situation and they look for ways of making it work in a free-market environment even though that may be a highly controversial objective. The political economist sees public enterprise as a natural phenomenon in the sociopolitical process and in some cases as a necessary institution. He studies how it works and why it works the way it does, keeping the interplay of social forces paramount in his consideration. Thus for an economist, public enterprise appears in cases of market failure, whereas for the political economist, it may exist as a shield from the market phenomenon itself. In the case of a national bourgeoisie or foreign-capital–dominant situation, where public enterprise plays a subservient role, economic analysis predominates and the political-economy approach yields similar conclusions. Elsewhere, quite different results are obtained.

Notes

1 John G. Gurley, "The State of Political Economics," in *Modern Political Economy,* ed: James H. Weaver (Boston: Allyn & Bacon, 1973), pp. 55–69; and Herbert Gintis, "Alienation and Power: Towards a Radical Welfare Economics" (Ph.D diss., Harvard University, 1969).
2 Michael Zweig, "Bourgeois and Radical Paradigms in Economics," *Review of Radical Political Economics* 3, No. 2 (1971):43–58.
3 Nico Poulantzas, *State, Power, Socialism* (London: National Labour Board, 1978).
4 Frederick L. Pryor, "Public Ownership: Some Quantitative Dimensions," in *Public Enterprise: Economic Analysis of Theory and Practice,* ed. William G. Shepherd (Lexington, Mass.: Lexington Books, 1976), pp. 3–21.
5 Muzaffer Ahmad, "Whither Public Enterprise," *Political Economy* 2 (1974):297–312; Rehman Sobhan and Muzaffer Ahmad, *Public Enterprise in an Intermediate Regime: A Study in the Political Economy of Bangladesh* (Dacca: Bangladesh Institute of Development Studies, 1980).
6 Rehman Sobhan, "The Political Economy of Public Enterprise in Asia," mimeographed (Oxford University, 1978); Muzaffer Ahmad, "Issues in the Political Economy of Public Enterprise," mimeographed (Dacca: Bangladesh Institute of Development Studies, 1978).
7 James Petras (with Kent Trachte), "Liberal, Structural and Radical Approaches to Political Economy: An Assessment and Alternative," in *Critical Perspectives on Imperialism and Social Class in the Third World,* ed. James Petras (New York: Monthly Review Press, 1978).
8 Sobhan, "Political Economy," p. 9.
9 Peter Evans, *Dependent Development: The Alliance of Multinationals, State and Local Capital in Brazil* (Princeton: Princeton University Press, 1979).
10 A. Mukerjee, "Indian Capitalist Class and Congress on National Planning and the Public Sector," *Economic and Political Weekly* 13, No. 35 (Sept. 2, (1978):1516–28.
11 Prabhat Patnaik, "Imperialism and Growth of Indian Capitalism," in *Studies in Theory of Imperialism,* ed. Roger Owen and Robert B. Sutcliffe, (London: Longman, 1972), pp. 210–25.
12 Asim Choudhry, *Private Economic Power in India* (Delhi: People's Publishing House, 1975).
13 R. K. Hazari, *The Structure of the Corporate Private Sector* (Delhi: Asia Publishing House, 1966).
14 Agnus Maddison, *Class Structure and Economic Growth* (New York: Norton, 1971).
15 Muzaffer Ahmad, "Public Enterprise in South Asia – A Study in Comparison," Monograph, Yugoslavia (Ljubljana: International Center for Public Enterprises in Developing Countries, 1980).

64   Why public enterprise?

16 Ibid.
17 Marnia Lazreg, *The Emergence of Class in Algeria* (Boulder, Colo.: Westview Press, 1976).
18 William B. Quandt, *Revolution and Political Leadership: Algeria* (New York: Harper and Row, 1970).
19 Ellen Brun and Jacques Hersh, *Socialist Korea* (New York: Monthly Review Press, 1976).
20 Hugh H. Smythe and Mabel M. Smythe, *The New Nigerian Elite* (Stanford: Stanford University Press, 1960).
21 Federation of Nigeria, *National Development Plans* (Lagos, 1962-8).
22 Sayre P. Schatz, "Economic Environment and Private Entrepreneurship in West Africa," *Economic Bulletin of Ghana* 35 No. 4 (1973):42-56; E. O. Akeredolu-Ale, "The Evolution of Private Indigenous Entrepreneurship in Nigeria," in *Industrial Development in Nigeria*, ed. O. Oteriba and M. O. Kayode, (Ibadan, Nigeria: Ibadan University Press, 1977), pp. 47-63; Eno J. Usoero, "Government Policies, Politics and Industrial Development Strategy in Nigeria, 1947-1974," in ibid., pp. 64-73; M. E. Blunt, "The Place of Ideology in the Origins and Development of Public Enterprises in Nigeria," *Nigerian Journal of Economic and Social Studies* 6, No. 3 (1964):333-49; and Tesea Turner, "Nigeria: The State and MNCs," *Review of African Political Economy* 5 (1976):63-79.
23 M. Kalecki, "Observations on Social and Economic Aspects of Intermediate Regimes," in *Essays in Developing Economies* (Humanities Press, 1976), pp. 30-7.
24 A-Jayeratswami Wilson, *Politics in Sri Lanka* (New York: St. Martin's, 1974).
25 James Petras, "State Capitalism and Third World," in *Critical Perspectives on Imperialism and Social Class in the Third World*, ed. James Petras (New York: Monthly Review Press, 1978), pp. 84-102, and Evans, *Dependent Development*.
26 Gustav Papenek, *Pakistan's Development, Social Goals and Private Incentives* (Cambridge: Harvard University Press, 1967); and Akhlakur M. Rahman, "The Role of the Public Sector in the Economic Development of Pakistan," in *Economic Development of South Asia*, ed. Gossage Robinson and Michael Kidron (New York: Macmillan, 1970), pp. 69-89. and Stephen P. Lewis, *Pakistan: Industrialization and Trade Policies* (New York: Oxford University Press, 1970); and Lawrence J. White, *Industrial Concentration and Economic Power in Pakistan* (Princeton: Princeton University Press, 1974): and Sobhan and Ahmad, *Public Enterprise in an Intermediate Regime*, p. 8.
27 Richard P. Farkas, *Yugoslav Development and Political Change* (New York: Praeger, 1975); Branko Horvat, *The Yugoslav Economic System* (White Plains, N.Y.: International Arts and Sciences Press, 1976); Rudolf Bicanic, "Economic Policy in Socialist Yugoslavia" (Cambridge: Harvard University Press, 1973); and Peter Jamberek, *Development and Social Change in Yugoslavia* (Lexington, Mass.: Lexington Books, 1975).
28 Sobhan and Ahmad, *Public Enterprise in an Intermediate Regime*, p. 8.
29 Quandt, *Revolution and Political Leadership: Algeria*.
30 Sobhan and Ahmad, *Public Enterprise in an Intermediate Regime*, pp. 469-88.
31 Ibid., p. 8.

Part II

Principal–agent relationships: Who should control public enterprises?

4   State-owned enterprise: an agent without a principal

Yair Aharoni

State-owned enterprises (SOEs) comprise a large and rapidly growing sector of the economy in the majority of countries in the world today. They have been established to achieve a broad array of public policy purposes in very diverse political and economic systems. Typically, they account for half or more of total government investment, and in 1978 the international borrowings alone of public-sector enterprises amounted to more than $30 billion, equal to the total foreign borrowings by central governments in the past year.[1] As international exporters, importers, and investors, SOEs are helping to shape the emerging structure of trade and payments relations in the 1980s. Their presence outside their traditional domain of public utilities is being felt especially in natural-resource–based and modern high-technology industries with high barriers to entry, in which private multinational firms have heretofore taken the lead. They are moving into a dominating position also in senescent industries such as textiles, shipbuilding, and steel, where the government moved in to save present firms from going under.

Yet despite the proliferation of SOEs since World War II, we actually know very little about the way they are managed. One reason for this lack of knowledge may be the tendency of economic theory to assume a perfect-market economy, in which firms passively transfer inputs procured in a perfect market into output sold in similar markets. Until recently, little attention has been paid to the problems and cost involved in managing an enterprise. By the same token, early socialist theoreticians saw the nationalization of production facilities as a way to achieve some equity and reduce "exploitation." They, too, however, did not pay much attention to the problem of managing the enterprises once nationalized. Rather they assumed – naïvely as it turned out – that "society will be transformed into a huge organization for cooperative production" in which everyone will work in accordance with the national plan.[2]

In the real world, firms do not operate in a neoclassical competitive environment. Rather, they have certain size and are managed hierarchically; the managers operate under uncertainty, and the information collected is costly.

The help of Ravi Ramamurti, my research assistant at the Harvard Graduate School of Business Administration, and that of anonymous reviewers is gratefully acknowledged.

Uncertainty cannot be fully eliminated by the use of contingency contracts. Under these conditions, the management of the firm has discretion in the choice of strategies, product lines, organizational forms, and policies. They are guided not by an internalized need to achieve a prescribed plan but by other motivations. Thus, managers may use their discretion to expand their staff or to achieve slack or on-the-job leisure.[3] One cannot assume that all decision makers in the economy are working together to achieve identical goals. Therefore, the relationships between managers and the state officials controlling them, as well as the negative and positive incentives to managers, are of crucial importance.

One way to look at the relationships between managers and owners of firms is in the terms of the principal–agent theory. An agency relationship exists when one party (the agent) acts on behalf of another (the principal). The two parties have unequal interests but may have an incentive to cooperate. Contractual arrangements are sought that will induce an agent to behave as if he was maximizing the welfare of the principal. Most analyses of agency relationships assume that the agent can choose a line of action that, together with exogenous events, determines the payoff. The principal is assumed to be unable to change the payoff.

The relationships between owners and managers of business firms are examples of agency relationships. Managers are contracted to act on behalf of (private or public) shareholders. However, as in all agency relationships, the manager is assumed to act to maximize his own interests. Therefore, a "perfect" contract would structure the manager's incentives to correspond exactly to those of the shareholders. In real life situations, no contract is expected to meet this standard, and agency costs are more than the costs specified in the contract.

What are these additional costs? First, there are certain costs of detecting decisions incongruent with the shareholders' interests. The higher the costs of monitoring managers' behavior, the larger their discretion. In real life, monitoring costs are high because the principal (shareholder) does not have an independent source of information. In addition, under uncertainty, optimal decision making depends on the risk preferences of managers and shareholders, which may not be identical. Moreover, to avoid replacement costs, shareholders may allow managers a certain amount of discretion.[4]

All these types of agency costs – distinct managers' interests, monitoring and detection costs, replacement costs – as well as such environmental variables as uncertainty about strategy, are likely to apply to SOEs. However, the agency costs cannot be conceptually defined in SOEs because the principal is not identifiable. The notion that the government or the minister is the principal and that the enterprise is the agent is misleading. Rather, the populace as a whole is the principal, with a variety of agents acting on its behalf. These agents include various government ministers, members of parliament, managers of firms, and so on. All these agents are in fact a coalition – a group working together who share *some*, but not all, goals. SOE shares are not traded in the market, and the populace does not have an effective voice in their direction and control. As state ownership does not necessarily imply social ownership, the mechanism of goal formulation is an important one. A case can be made that SOE management has as legitimate a claim to the participation in the goal formulation on behalf of the principal as do the other agents. The multiple and often ill-defined objectives make performance measurement almost impossible. As a result, the market may police SOE managers much less than in the case of private enterprise.

These problems of social ownership are developed in Sections 4.1 and 4.2. In Section 4.3, an independent of multiple legitimate claimants to the goal-specification function.

4.1 Shareholders without shares

Private firms are owned by individuals who may buy or sell ownership rights at some price. SOEs are ultimately owned by all citizens of a country and are financed from the general pool of funds mobilized by the government through taxes or other means. However, the SOE "shareholders" do not hold any shares that can be traded in the market, and no market mechanism allows them to signal their views on the performance of the enterprise, nor can they take part in a proxy fight for a take-over bid. Therefore, the citizens of the country do not have even the minimal influence enjoyed by shareholders of a modern corporation.

The state is not a person, not even a single organization. It acts through a variety of ministers, legislators, and civil servants, who are themselves agents of the general public. These different agents invariably see their mission as different from one another. Thus, different objectives are sought by different government ministries, and interorganizational conflicts are normal phenomena. These conflicts affect the process of SOE goal specifications. A government official concerned with foreign affairs may see the reduction of the state's dependence on imported technology as a prime goal and therefore seek an increase in the SOE research and development budget. The minister of labor may see the state's role as maximizing employment and thus favor more labor-intensive procedures for the SOE. The finance minister, viewing himself as "the shareholder," may want the firm to pay higher dividends. Yet another minister, whose agency buys the firm's output, may seek to reduce its prices. These competing representatives cannot be considered *the* principal of the firm whose interests are well defined. Consequently, no "perfect" contract can structure managers' incentives so that their interests will match the principal's goals. These goals are rarely, if ever, stated explicitly and trade-offs among them are not agreed. Thus, different agents give the enterprise conflicting, parallel commands, which turn SOEs into hybrids, expected to achieve both traditional economic goals in the marketplace and all sorts of social goals: help for the poor, increased employment, a redistribution of income, development of laggard regions, and so on. They are also expected to achieve political goals such as the avoidance of perceived domination by foreign multinationals, developing of new technologies, and enhancement of the glory of the state. Several agents seek to resolve the ambiguity of goals in ways that suit them best. Goal conflicts among state agents are sometimes "solved" by formally assigning two or more of these objectives to an SOE. At other times, conflicting commands are faced by SOEs because several external agents of society, rightly or wrongly, view SOEs as legitimate tools for achieving overall national goals. Thus, the principal (the populace) is represented by a loose coalition of agents: sponsoring minister, the treasury, the civil servants, other ministers, and the parliament. Their decisions are influenced by all sorts of interest groups – consumers, labor unions, and others – all of which claim at least some right to participate in the process of goal formulation. Even in countries with a decentralized framework of control, there is a continuous flow of ex ante intervention in various decisions.

Can the principal be assumed to be a collective term for a coalition of ministers, interest groups, civil servants, trade unions, and parliament members? Even such an assumption does not seem to hold, as SOE managers often try to influence the process of goal specification, resist the imposition of certain goals in many different ways, and claim the right to participate in the formulation of goals.

4.2   Legitimacy of goals and strategies

There are three major explanations for the ability of SOE managers to resist certain goals imposed on them by various government agencies. The first is the difference between managers' self-interest and that of other state agents. This is by now a well-theorized phenomenon in both large diffused ownership corporations and SOEs. The notion that professional managers single-mindedly operate the firm to maximize profits has long been rejected. It was replaced by "behavioral" or "managerial" theories.[5] This difference in self-interests is also at the root of the agent – principal problem and the view of the firm as a set of contracts.[6]

Second, SOE managers can afford to resist certain goals because it is difficult to measure their performance. In a private firm, managerial performance is scrutinized by the board of directors, which in turn is viewed as a market-induced institution. In an SOE, managerial performance cannot be gauged, because of the many conflicting and ill-defined objectives. Moreover, in many countries, the control structure is not clearly defined, and the board cannot discipline or replace a manager, at least not without a lengthy negotiation with a sponsoring minister and other agents. Therefore, although a market for the services of managers does exist,[7] and although managers might be dismissed, the policing of managers is much more difficult. In such a situation, ambitious managers may be able to achieve more discretion than private-sector managers. Less ambitious managers, faced with conflicting goals and restrictions, may simply choose to defer to governmental constraints. In extreme cases, managers may develop what Phatak called the "don't rock the boat syndrome."[8] With this approach, managers avoid changes that may alienate any powerful groups: Redundant workers are not dismissed, erring staff are not disciplined, no obsolete plant is closed, and no organizational changes are made. In short, managers simply develop apathy.

Third and most important, managers consider themselves to be the trustees of the "real" interest of the state at least as much as the government employees. Managers sometimes bring to their job the same set of values and ideologies that belong to the rest of the business world. As they see it, the intervention of various government ministries to achieve non-economic goals is an encroachment on their prerogatives as the trustees of the economic interests of the firm. SOE managers would probably argue that if the government, for social reasons, wants an enterprise to deviate from its economic mission, it should compensate it for the economic losses incurred. Such a point of view has been presented independently by public committees on SOEs in different countries.[9]

Managers of large corporations accept the legitimacy of the shareholders' interests, although they may not always actually pursue those interests. SOE managers may question the legitimacy of demands from government, not only because they try to maximize their own utility but because they perceive the "real" goals of the amorphous principal – the state – to be different. Further, many of them maintain that operational efficiency requires that decisions on objectives and strategy be made within the enterprise itself. In here lies the major difference between SOEs and large private corporations with diffused ownership. SOE management feels it has as legitimate a claim to goal specification as other agents. The government may require the SOE to avoid price increases to combat inflation, to procure locally made and more expensive goods or to maintain the size of its labor force to secure employment, or to pursue certain objectives perceived as important in achieving a short-term political gain. In all these cases, managers may have different perceptions of the legitimate role of the enterprise. They see it as their legitimate right – even their duty to the "real" interest of the state – to try to evade the issue or even fight openly against such a request. They would thus attempt to avoid the order, get around it, or procrastinate. In certain cases, managers may even bring "their" cases before the public by leaking information to the press or by applying to the president or prime minister to appeal a sponsoring minister's decision.

In summary, the behavior of an SOE cannot be explained within the principal-agent theory. Rather, an SOE should be viewed not only as a set of contracts among factors of production but as a coalition of the managers, the board of directors, government ministers, civil servants, parliament members, and others. The principal of the property-rights theory and the classical theory of the firm does not exist. Instead, there are different members of a coalition who share the belief that its survival should be maintained by the continuation of the enterprise.

The actual outcome and degree of discretion managers enjoy in their operations seem to be the result of a fight for power among the various agents of the state. Managers of SOEs seem to spend more time than their private-sector counterparts in managing the environment and aiming at co-opting the controlling agencies or assuring their allegiance. The outcome of this fight for power, that is, the actual strategic choices made, can be predicted only in terms of contingency theory. Although it is beyond the scope of this chapter to propose such a contingency theory, a few examples may be helpful.

The ability of an SOE manager to choose the strategy he prefers and the objectives he sees as most relevant is a joint function of his personality, the legal and institutional environment in which he operates, and the time and expertise of those monitoring him. In general, experience shows that the bigger the firm is, the more independent it is of the government (by generating its own funds), the more technical the information needed to operate the enterprise, and the more expertise concentrated in management at the firm level, the more management can dictate goals. In addition, management enjoys more discretion in its strategic choices when it operates internationally (by being at least partially outside the domain of government control), has a large number of customers and product lines, has a greater freedom to choose its customers, product lines, and suppliers. Finally, the degree of goal congruency is a crucial variable. The more legitimate are the demands of government agencies in the eyes of the manager, the more he will abide by them. I have discussed these points extensively in another publication.[10] Here it is enough to note that the real problem is to define the legitimate role of different state organs and the dimensions of social controls. In practice, these dimensions are ill defined, and conflicts on goals constantly occur.

Even in the rare case in which goals are explicitly stated, they eventually are modified in the daily operations of the enterprise through numerous managerial decisions once the enterprise is established. The lack of performance measurement makes it difficult to monitor these changes. In addition, actual monitoring systems used by different government controllers often lead to distortion.

The complex relationships between the SOE and its environment cannot be solved by an "optimal contract," because the optimality characteristics are ill defined. Different agents of the state, including the managers of the enterprise and their controllers as well as other constituents, look for ways to reach some quasi resolution of conflicts, often by ill-defining the objectives of the enterprise or by official requirements to achieve multiple and conflicting goals.

Lack of agreement on goals seems to be at the root of many difficulties pointed out by studies of SOEs. In the public-administration literature, the problem is referred to as "the accountability vs. autonomy" issue: SOEs are said to need "enough" autonomy to run their business operations without having to face the rigid difficulties inherent in the bureaucratic structure of government. At the same time, it is felt that an SOE should be accountable to government and parliament, and the latter should dictate its goals. Yet, the balance between "autonomy" and "accountability" has never been satisfactorily struck. The preceding analysis shows that this is no accident. The way the coalition of forces is structured bars the definition of precise goals. Even in less complex situations, as pointed out by Cyert and March, a quasi resolution of conflicts is a way of life.[11] However, even though conflicts cannot always be solved, they can be brought into the open to force decision makers to be confronted with several concrete choices. As there is no one principal but several tiers of agents, these agents can be forced to argue on choices to be made – and therefore implicitly on the goals – if independent "goal audit" is introduced, embodied in a broader comprehensive audit, as an integral part of the institutional design. Note that because goals are formulated as a result of interaction in a coalition, different institutional designs may change membership in the coalition and the relative power of different coalition members.

4.3 Comprehensive audit

The term *comprehensive audit* is used here in the sense suggested by Churchill and Cooper.[12] In compreshensive audit, the process of objective appraisal is extended to all aspects of management. The auditor is not necessarily a CPA, nor does he stop at the accounting attest function. Comprehensive audits are not restricted to financial transaction: They are extended to an examination and appraisal of the propriety of the objectives pursued and the methods used, effectiveness in stating objectives and in attaining them, and finally, the efficiency of performance as measured by the benefits received and the resources utilized.

Comprehensive auditing is done by a third party – someone whose interests are not identical with those who are audited or with the government ministry sponsoring the enterprise. The auditors are also agents who may have their own views about the "proper" objectives to be pursued. Also, the development of a comprehensive, audit scheme requires a considerable amount of skill. However, comprehensive audit is a major step in assuring that SOEs are accountable along socially relevant dimensions. In doing so, questions of goals pursued and the "right" objectives are put on the agenda of a public debate once the results of the audit are published.

Comprehensive audits have been tried by different state auditing organs – the General Accounting Office in the United States, the Cour des Comptes in France, the Auditor General in Canada, and the State Controller in Israel are some examples. In all these cases, it seems that such an audit helps to alleviate the lack of a principal. The audits by themselves, of course, cannot create agreed objectives. Different individuals continue to hold different points of view about the propriety of the objectives pursued, but the publication of comprehensive reports brings the conflict to the surface. It also helps in discussing the propriety of objectives actually pursued. This is an important development in an area where agreement on objectives is difficult to obtain and their achievement difficult to control. Needless to say, the impact of the report is largely a result of its general availability to the public. A report presented to management, and to it alone, will not have such an impact.

It might be noted that the existence of the audit creates an audit-anticipation effect.[13] Objectives that management, or the government, feels are improper in the eyes of the public will not be pursued in the first place. The very anticipation of an audit changes the behavior of those that expect to be audited.

To be sure, the institutional mechanism of comprehensive audit is not free of side effects: It costs money and requires managers to divert their energies from managing the enterprise to answering requests for audit. In addition, SOEs may be reluctant to reveal commercial information, as full disclosure puts them in a position of comparative disadvantage by allowing them less commercial secrecy than their private counterparts. Finally, in a parliamentary regime, as the government controls the parliament, state comprehensive audits may be less effective than one might wish. For that matter, state comprehensive auditing may be even less effective in regimes where democratic institutions are less powerful and less diffused, and where checks and balances in the political systems are not adhered to. In fact, in some such regimes, the government may not allow such audit to be carried out in the first place.

A variation of a "goal audit" may be one in which the government decides on the objectives of each enterprise at the time of creation and on an internal governmental body that reports directly to the board of directors and the government as a whole rather than to a specific sponsoring ministry without publishing the results. This may result in a redefinition or clarification of goals as the avoidance of publicity may reduce the resistance of the ruling coalition to such an audit. However, it may also reduce its effectiveness, as publicity is important in deciding on SOE objectives and priorities while keeping some modicum of freedom.

4.4 Conclusions

The agency-costs theory cannot be applied directly to the measurement of the costs of managing SOEs. By the same token, Williamson's definition of discretion does not apply.[14] Both the agent-principal theory and the Williamson hypothesis about discretion assume a clear objective and an identifiable principal. Therefore, Williamson can measure the size of discretion, at least conceptually, as the difference between the maximizing of the welfare of the principal and the actual behavior of the agent plus the cost of the contract. The major problem faced by organizational designers in planning the institutional relationships between SOE management and its constituents is that they somehow have to face the issue of a precise definition of the goals of the state in the establishment and operation of the firm.

The problem of setting goals for SOEs is to a large extent insoluble. As long as we do not have a theory of the state, as long as we do not know what the legitimate objectives of such enterprises are, how they are decided, and who decides on both objectives and trade-offs, there is no way to give a normative answer to whether or not the performance of a certain enterprise is "socially desirable." Yet individuals have a feeling of what is legitimate and what seems to be in the public interest. Therefore, an independent audit of goals and objectives, at least under some conditions, may make the problem recognizable and thus partially solvable. At the very least, the decisions of management and other state agents may be subjected periodically to public scrutiny and subsequent adjustment. Without an open system of goals statement and auditing, state ownership may degenerate into a shift of power to a new managerial or bureaucratic class instead of achieving socially desirable objectives.

Notes

1 "Public Sector Enterprise: A State in the Market," *The Economist*, Dec. 30, 1978, p. 41.
2 N. L. Burkharin and E. Preobrazhensky, *The ABC of Communism* (London: Penguin, 1969), p. 114. English translation of 1920 Russan original.
3 O. E. Williamson, *The Economics of Discretionary Behavior: Management Objectives in a Theory of the Firm* (Englewood Cliffs, N.J.: Prentice-Hall, 1964), pp. 49–52.
4 For examples of optimal literature, see M. Harris and A. Raviv, "Some Results on Incentive Contracts," *American Economic Review* 68 (Mar. 1978):20–30; M. Harris and A. Raviv, "Optimal Incentive Contracts with Imperfect Information," *Journal of Economic Theory* 20 (Apr. 1979):231–59; B. Holmström, "Moral Hazard and Observability," *Bell Journal of Economics* 10 (Spring 1979):74–91; and S. Shavell, "Risk Sharing and Incentives in the Principal and Agent Relationship," *Bell Journal of Economics* 10 (Spring 1979):55–73.
5 For a discussion of these theories, see W. Baumol, *Business Behavior: Value and Growth* (New York: Macmillan, 1959); H. Simon, "Theories of Decision Making in Economics and Behavioral Science," *American Economic Review* 49 (June 1959):253–88; R. Cyert and J. March, *A Behavioral Theory of the Firm* (Englewood Cliffs, N.J.: Prentice-Hall, 1963); R. Marris, *The Economic Theory of Managerial Capitalism* (New York: Free Press, 1964); and Williamson, *Economics of Discretionary Behavior.*
6 Two well-known examples are A. Alchian and H. Demsetz, "Production, Information Costs, and Economic Organization," *American Economic Review* 62 (Dec. 1971):777–95; and M. Jensen and W. Meckling, "Theory of the Firm: Managerial Behavior, Agency Costs and Ownership Structure," *Journal of Financial Economics* 3 (Oct. 1976):305–60.
7 E. Fama, "Agency Problems and the Theory of the Firm," *Journal of Political Economics* 88 (Apr. 1980):288–307.
8 A. Phatak, "Governmental Interference and Management Problems of Public Sector Firms," *Annals of Public and Cooperative Economy* 40 (July-Sept. 1969).
9 Some well-known examples are the Nora Committee report in France (*Rapport sur les entreprises publique* [Paris: La Documentation française, Apr. 1967]); the white paper on nationalized industries in the United Kingdom (*Nationalized Industries: A Review of Economic and Financial Objectives* [London: HMSO, 1967], Commnd. 3437); the Israeli Government Companies Law 5737-1978 (*Sefer Ho Chukkim* 770 [1978]:163); the Statsföretag law in Sweden; and Canada's privy council report on crown corporations (*Crown Corporations: Direction, Control, Accountability: Government of Canada's Proposals* [Ottawa: Privy Council Office, 1977]).
10 See Y. Aharoni, "Managerial Discretion," in *State-Owned Enterprise in the Western Economies*, ed. Y. Aharoni and R. Vernon (London: Croom Helm, 1981), pp. 184–93.
11 Cyert and March, *Behavioral Theory of the Firm.*

12 N. Churchill and W. Cooper, "Comprehensive Auditing" (paper presented at meeting of Institute of Chartered Accountants of Ontario, Ottawa, June 12, 1978).
13 See N. Churchill, "The Effects of an Audit" (Ph.D diss., University of Michigan, 1962). A summary of the relevant material is available in N. C. Churchill and W. W. Cooper, "Effects of Auditing Records," in *New Perspectives in Organizational Research*, ed. W. W. Cooper, H. J. Leavitt, and M. W. Shelley (New York: Wiley, 1964), pp. 250–75.
14 Williamson, *Economics of Discretionary Behavior*.

5 Social accountability of public enterprises: law and community controls in the new development strategies

John B. Howard

5.1 The thesis

The ultimate goal of development should be a strong state, a strong economy, and a strong community. The new development strategies stress the need for a strong community, which conventional development strategies have tended to ignore. The new strategies compel attention to a basic dilemma of development: the potential conflict between the concentration of power in government and market organizations to promote development and the capacity of people, particularly the disadvantaged, to share responsibility for developmental changes in their own lives.

This chapter regards conventional roles of public enterprises and positivist notions of law as an instrument of the state as illustrative of this dilemma and as contributing to the weakening of the community. What is required to implement the new strategies is, first, the recognition that public enterprises *are* socially accountable and have as one of their roles the strengthening of the community, as well as the state and the economy.

To perform such a role, a public enterprise has to combine the advantages of a state agency and a community organization. This purpose is served by viewing the powers and resources vested in the public enterprise and bearing on the community's well-being as a developmental trust and the public enterprise as an *institutional fiduciary* subject to community, as well as state, controls. The fiducial form of public enterprise linking its state and community roles is the counterpart of the corporate form of public enterprise that links its state and market roles.

Accordingly, control systems, including legal systems, for holding public enterprises socially accountable should include community, as well as state and

The author is especially grateful to Clarence Dias, president of the International Center for Law in Development, for unfailing support and wise insights during the preparation of this chapter. He is also indebted to other law-in-development colleagues – Reginald Green, Yash Ghai, and William Robson – for their criticisms of earlier versions.

market, controls in order to assure that enterprise activities serve the well-being of the community at both national and local levels. Local community self-help organizations, which share responsibility for development, also act as important control entities. They serve as vehicles for the collective exercise of the rights of individual beneficiaries to demand performance by public enterprises and provide a basis upon which to build nationwide community organizations that can hold public enterprises socially accountable at the national level.

5.2 The issues

The existing public-enterprise literature deals almost exclusively with market control and government control (via the legislature, executive, and judiciary) but largely ignores control by the community itself. The standard approach was reflected in an international workshop in Yugoslavia where it was suggested that "control systems should not be looked upon as being of a restrictive nature but as a shorthand expression of all government and public relations with public enterprises which [have] a near imperative impact on public enterprise management."[1] The main concern of the workshop was with public enterprises as instruments of state policy and as business organizations, and with the interface between government and enterprise management, including the latter's involvement in making policy. It was noted that effective management of public enterprises depends upon the system of controls, both for internal managerial purposes and for external accountability to public authorities, and that excessive state controls endanger the "autonomy" of the enterprises (i.e., in their role as business organizations).

Although the workshop acknowledged the importance of the "social accountability" of public enterprises, it devoted only limited attention to it and to community controls. It noted that control systems for public enterprises differ from control systems for private enterprises in part because of the variety of social goals that public enterprises are obliged to pursue as a matter of national policy. There is a need for public opinion to make itself felt and for opportunities to ventilate public grievances. An important element in a control system is a "culture" of professional management that would include, in addition to business management skills, a mature understanding of all sectors of the public interacting with public enterprises, such as consumers, local communities, and workers, as well as private enterprises in the case of mixed economies. But the workshop did not explore the subject of social controls any further.[2]

This chapter, in effect, takes up where the Yugoslavia workshop and existing literature leave off. It focuses on the interface between public enterprise and community and addresses three basic questions. First, what are the roles of public enterprises in achieving the goals of the new development strategies? Second, what is the contribution of law to these roles? Third, what configuration of state, market, and community controls will support these roles and help make public enterprises both effective and socially accountable?

5.3 Public-enterprise roles in new development strategies

Public enterprises,[3] as development institutions, are viewed here as having three roles: as state agencies, as business organizations, and as community fiduciaries. Corresponding to these roles are three control systems[4] (comprised of controls and control entities) relating to the interfaces between public enterprise and state, market, and community, respectively.

Under conventional development strategies, oriented primarily to economic growth, public enterprises were created to obtain the advantages of both state agencies and business organizations: the former assuring state control over the implementation of policy and the latter assuring "autonomy" for exercising commercial discretion subject to market controls.

Yet state and market controls have proved inadequate to hold public enterprises accountable for their impact on society. This inadequacy has assumed new proportions as the roles of public enterprises have changed in the process of development.

The state has vastly expanded its general role as trustee, on behalf of the people, of the nation's resources and welfare through a variety of public-enterprise roles: as landlord to rural cultivators or urban householders, creditor to small farmers and slum dwellers, and the provider of social security to the poor, in addition to their relations as employer to workers and producer to consumers.

State and market controls over public enterprises in these new roles have failed to resolve a basic dilemma of development: the potential conflict between the concentration of power in government and business organizations to promote development and the capacity of the people for self-reliant development. Instead, the result of development has been overdependence of people on government and market, with expanded opportunities for arbitrariness, discrimination, exploitation, and intimidation by organizations in their dealings with individuals, especially the disadvantaged.

Resolution of this dilemma became a central concern of development strategy in the 1970s. Frustration with the widespread failures of the conventional, growth-oriented development strategies, in both capitalist and socialist countries, has led to the formulation of new development strategies.[5] These are oriented to economic growth but also to the meeting of basic human needs and the promotion of self-reliance, together with the reconstitution of societal relationships conducive to these goals. The new strategies seek to resolve the dilemma of development in favor of the people, with particular attention to the disadvantaged.

But public enterprises have no monopoly of responsibility for implementing such strategies. Indeed, there is mounting evidence that the effectiveness of national development programs depends to a large extent on the types of local and intermediate institutions that bear on development. Examples of these are local self-help organizations based on membership, such as farmer and worker production cooperatives, slum dwellers and other neighborhood associations, community-based credit institutions, and intermediate institutions that provide legal, organizational, and other professional services to the disadvantaged.[6] On the one hand, such organizations depend in varying degrees on resources under the control of state and market institutions, including public enterprises. On the other hand, such organizations serve as control entities in enabling their members collectively to exercise controls over public enterprises so as to hold them socially accountable.

These organizations may be viewed as constituting a community sector,[7] distinct from the state sector and the market sector, which constantly threaten to swallow it up. Certain countries, recognizing the potential contribution of community organizations to development, particularly as they bear on the disadvantaged, have embarked on national development programs that aim to create new community organizations and to strengthen existing ones.[8]

To implement these new development strategies, public enterprises must share responsibility for development with these community-sector organizations. The corollary of this proposition is that the effectiveness of many public-enterprise programs depends (1) on the type of local and intermediate organizations that bear on such development and (2) on the social accountability of public enterprise in its relationship with the intended beneficiaries and their organizations. The current spate of interest within development circles in local, participatory, productive enterprises of the disadvantaged thus needs to be matched with a similar interest in socially accountable public enterprises.

5.4   Examples of shared responsibility for development

Following are several programs that illustrate shared responsibility between public enterprises and local community-based organizations for development of the community sector.

Nepal's small farmers' group credit program

In this example,[9] a national agricultural bank (the public enterprise), in a pilot project, has successfully capacitated disadvantaged small farmers to share in responsibility for development projects and wider community activities. It accomplished this by making loans to only homogeneous groups of 15 to 20 farmers who were held jointly liable for repayment and by providing community organizers to help each farmer group establish and run an organization for joint planning of their production (e.g., in crop or livestock production) and related activities. The key to motivation is that credit is extended to only the small groups, with no collateral other than credible plans for income-raising action. The bank supports the groups with an integrated program of credit and organizational and technical assistance.

By learning to work together as groups, the small farmers have achieved a number of results: a substantial increase in income, a widening range of productive activities, election to *panchayats* and membership in cooperatives, the capacity to present their cases in large meetings and before government officials, and an end to exploitation by middlemen. The pilot projects demonstrated the possibility and value of economic and social cooperation among the poorest of the peasantry.

From the standpoint of the present chapter, a number of points are interesting. A working partnership was established between the public enterprise and organizations of the beneficiaries based on:

1. Recognition of the need for organizations of the beneficiaries so that they could share responsibility for the development process
2. Recognition of the social accountability of both public enterprise and the small farmers' groups
3. A clear distinction between, and articulation of, the functions of the public enterprise in charge of the program and the beneficiary groups
4. Facilitation of the organization of beneficiaries through group organizers who acted as catalysts (rather than substitutes) for self-reliant decision making
5. Public-enterprise standards and procedures for securing credit and back-up support that were responsive to the needs of the beneficiaries and conducive to their organization for self-reliance
6. A proposed expansion of the program based on articulation of development strategies at the local, national, and international levels

Although the legal aspects of the program were not explicitly reported, they are clearly present and are likely to become more important as the small farmers' group credit movement expands and more formal linkages are established between the small groups, the federation of groups, the cooperatives, and private and public institutions with the resources needed for continued development within a new structural framework.

Philippine communal irrigation systems

In this example,[10] a national irrigation administration undertook to promote communal irrigation systems (as distinct from a national system). It fielded community organizers among client farmers to assist them in strengthening their associations' roles in planning, expanding or newly constructing, and operating the communal systems by providing initial technical and financial assistance to the associations. The administration evaluated its record of success and failure and concluded that the tasks of the program required it to achieve a new set of skills and adopt a basic reorientation and restructuring suitable to the partnership relations required for the interface between the administration and the farm community. Among the recommended changes were: decentralization in order to respond to the diversity of social and technical needs in different communal systems; integration and coordination at both headquarters and field levels between technical and social experts; and change in the administration's budget and control systems to take into account joint farmer control over communal irrigation projects and to enable the administration to provide accountability in financial matters to the farmer organizations.

Agriculture production cooperatives

Agricultural production cooperatives[11] have been established in many parts of the third world (e.g., Sri Lanka, Tanzania, Peru), usually with government initiative or support, as an alternative to state collective farms and private individual farming. The cooperatives illustrate a tripartite sharing of responsibility between small farmers, state agencies, and the cooperative managers. The cooperatives' internal problems are characterized by the divergence of interests among the three. The small farmers are interested in:

rewarding income and services, autonomy of personal life, scope for individual and local initiative, meaningful opportunities to influence decisions affecting individuals and local groups, and, for the most ambitious, opportunities to advance within the institutionalized structure of the group farm and ancillary organizations as well as possibilities for engaging in at least some private family farming.

State agencies are interested in

increased production, greater investment which may require restraining consumption, widespread access to income-earning and other opportunities for the rural population, discouragement of the emergence of economically successful individual peasants as a superior social class, increasing the base of political support in the rural society for those holding national power.

The cooperatives' managers are caught between a duality of interests "in dealing effectively with outside agencies while at the same time identifying with the concerns and objectives of members within their sphere of responsibility."[12] These diverse interests need to be reconciled in a tripartite sharing and differentiation of responsibilities for development programs. Even more difficult than internal problems has been the problem of external relations with large producers, government, and labor unions.

Experience with production cooperatives in their efforts to achieve self-reliance points up the need for public enterprises that (1) provide a variety of supporting services to strengthen the cooperatives; (2) adopt an incentive-based participatory approach instead of a top-down bureaucratic approach; and (3) facilitate expansion of successful local cooperatives over a wider geographic area.

5.5 Practical obstacles to social accountability

The foregoing examples of specific instances in which public enterprises and community organizations have collaborated reveal varying degrees of success. What are the obstacles to such success? There are three main practical arguments against a development strategy that would make public enterprises directly accountable to the community. One is that the persons who wield power inside or outside government will strongly resist any diminution of the advantages that accrue to them from their lack of accountability for that power.[13] Such resistance is, of course, basic to the dilemma of development referred to earlier, but to advance such an argument while professing the goals of the new development strategies is hypocritical and makes the goals a matter of rhetoric without reality.

A second argument is that the disadvantaged lack the capacity to share responsibility for development, that the effort to capacitate them to do so is both time consuming and tiresome, and that it is not a realistic alternative to the conventional top-down approach of most public enterprises. There is increasing evidence, however, that the disadvantaged do have such capacity[14] and that effective programs can be designed and implemented when the government and the enterprise officials concerned are responsive to the needs and cultural patterns of the intended beneficiaries[15] and when self-help organizations are established with built-in mechanisms to hold public enterprise socially accountable.

A third argument is that embattled public-enterprise managers, already barely coping with state controls, will view the introduction of community controls as an additional, and unjustified, threat to the discretion and autonomy of the enterprise as an efficient, well-managed business organization. Yet this need not be the case. To resolve the problem of shared responsibility between enterprise and government, one proposal made from the manager's standpoint is that the annual development program be designed by the manager and government officials together, thus defining the limits of the manager's discretion and providing the basis upon which the manager is held accountable for his performance.[16] In other words, the program would limit the manager's liability. However, an annual program may include certain social targets (e.g., credit for small farmers or low-cost housing) for the accomplishment of which a conventional approach may be inadequate. Therefore, the enterprise manager, faced with a situation of uncertain control over the social participants in the program, is confronted with three choices. He may opt for a minimum of discretion, which the government will resist if it is serious about accomplishing the social targets. He may opt for a maximum of discretion because the unknowns make it impossible to structure his mission in advance, in which case he runs the double risk of having government make a scapegoat of him for failure and of creating a decision-making process within the enterprise in which lower-level staff eschew action of any sort in their dealings with the public for fear of sticking their necks out, so that all decision making is concentrated at the top echelon. Or he may opt for designing an annual program for the enterprise that includes the inputs of self-help organizations and the tasks for which they are responsible. By accepting the realities of working at the interface between enterprise and community, specifying the tasks of the community organizations and helping to capacitate them for the tasks, the manager delineates the enterprise's social accountability but also limits and structures the discretion and therefore the liability of the enterprise. The program provides the basis upon which the enterprise is evaluated and judged, by both the government and the public.

The underlying point is that state and market controls are inadequate to limit and structure the discretion that a public-enterprise manager needs for official dealing with community organizations. They must be supplemented with community controls to make the enterprise program effective and to make the accountability of the enterprise manager commensurate with the scope and content of his discretion.

5.6   Legal foundations of social accountability

In their new development roles, public enterprises exercise important functions in the process of law – in lawmaking, law implementation, and law compliance. The enterprises require discretion to perform a quasi-legislative function (e.g., rule making) and a quasi-judicial function (e.g., settlement of disputes), as well as administrative and managerial functions. For example, they may need to have discretion:

1. To determine the localities within a country that will benefit from a rural or urban development program
2. To establish criteria by which individuals and groups qualify for services under a development program and to make rules for the refusal, reduction, or termination of services
3. To determine compensation to be paid for rental or purchase of land
4. To hear and dispose of cases of disputes between themselves and beneficiaries and to establish the standards and procedures to be adhered to by complainants
5. To provide extension services, including organizational and legal services
6. To capacitate disadvantaged groups and establish new relations between them and more powerful groups in society

These are formidable powers, which go beyond the traditional roles of state administrative agencies and business organizations. They represent functions of governance by which public enterprises link the process of law with the process of development and make the process of law an important concern of development strategy as it bears on public enterprise. If community organizations are to share responsibility for development with public enterprises, they need also to share in control over the process of law.

The positivist notion of law, on which conventional development strategies rely, is inadequate to provide this linkage between the process of law and governance and the process of development. For governments adopting the views of legal positivism,[17] law is an instrument of the state and a public enterprise is a state agency, obliged to follow the rules of law laid down by the state, with a minimum of discretion of its own.

A different notion of law is needed for the new development strategies: one that (1) enables people, through self-help organizations, to share responsibility for developmental changes in their own lives and to share control over the process of law and governance that bears on such changes and (2) enables public enterprises that have an impact on society to perform a vital and socially accountable role in strengthening the community.

5.7 Legal obstacles to socially accountable public enterprises

The tradition of legal positivism will not easily be dislodged. Nevertheless, there are currents in many countries in a direction favorable to such a community role and to the presumptions that public enterprises are socially accountable and that individuals and community organizations, which share responsibility for development, are entitled to exercise controls over enterprises that have a vital impact on their lives and communities. Following are several areas in which there is movement to eliminate the legal obstacles to socially accountable public enterprises:

Sovereign immunity

Under positivist notions, law is, in effect, what the government says it is, and without its consent, there is no legal redress for private citizens for violations of their legal or constitutional rights by government officials, whether through honest mistakes or deliberately wrongful acts. In an extreme form, the doctrine of sovereign immunity prevents individuals and groups from pursuing their claims against government for the tortious acts of its officials and institutions, for violations of civil and political rights, and for other wrongful activity in carrying out its development programs. Although the notion of sovereign immunity persists in varying forms from country to country, the scope has been eroded over time.[18]

Public enterprise as an instrument of the state

Legal positivism includes the notion that a public enterprise is an instrument of the state and is not itself accountable for the propriety of its actions when it follows state laws. A contrary view, embraced by many, if not all, countries is the ideal of "constitutionalism," according to which public officials are accountable for their exercise of discretionary power. According to this ideal, which goes beyond the written constitution as a framework of law, all organized power, whether of public or private institutions, is derived from the people and must serve socially acceptable ends; powerholders are accountable to others than themselves and by criteria other than those they alone define, both for the ends they choose and the means they adopt to pursue those ends.[19] This notion of "institutional accountability" extends to positive obligations to *take* certain actions essential to people's well-being as well as to negative obligations *not* to take certain actions that violate people's rights.[20] It also embraces institutional actions affecting *group* rights as well as *individual* rights.[21]

Social control by the state through law

The phrase *law as social engineering* has in recent years and in certain quarters acquired a derogatory connotation because authoritarian governments have accomplished their developmental aims by the manipulative use of laws and legal institutions to justify and impose developmental changes and by the abandonment of law whenever it ceases to serve their purposes.[22] Roscoe Pound, the originator of the term, viewed law as one means of social control, the merits of which are to be judged by its social consequences.[23] With this perspective, he saw in legal history

the record of a continually wider recognizing and satisfying of human wants or claims or desires through social control; a more embracing and more effective securing of social interests; a continually more complete and effective elimination of waste and precluding of friction in human employment of the goods of existence – in short, a continually more efficacious social enginerering.[24]

Pound acknowledged that an engineering interpretation of law might be abused by an authoritarian government.[25] To avoid the trap of authoritarianism, he stressed the importance of the context of social control. "Today social control is primarily the function of the state and is exercised through law" yet this is not self-sufficient.[26] Law must function on a background of other less direct, but not less important, agencies, such as family, religion, and education. Justice must transcend the ruler, that he may be judged. Pound thus explicitly recognized the need for community controls over government, yet he failed to address fully how they can be exercised through law. The notion of law as social engineering, in the spirit in which Pound conceived it but without the priority he gave to social control by the state, can be a useful concept in designing and constituting a system of community controls that enables the people to share in control over developmental change and to democratize the process of law (see Section 5.8).

Legal controls over discretion

Discretion lies at the heart of the law governing public enterprises and the monitoring of their performance by other bodies. Legal controls of discretion have been an important means, for example, in striking a balance between state control and market autonomy of public enterprises under conventional development strategies.

Gunnar Myrdal, in his extensive study of the countries of South Asia, was troubled by the failure to control the exercise of discretion of public officials in what he termed "soft states," that is states deficient in law observance and enforcement.[27] His proposed remedy for converting such states into "hard states" was greater reliance on non-discretionary controls and compulsion, which some persons characterized as the remedy of authoritarian government. Yet it seems clear that what Myrdal was seeking is *authoritative* rather than *authoritarian* government. In an earlier work,[28] he writes of the need for a strengthened system of community controls, which he subsequently found lacking in his Asian studies and the prospects for which he perhaps concluded were unpromising. Nevertheless, his proposed remedy is illustrative of a development strategy that views law primarily in positivist terms as the rules laid down to implement state policy.

Myrdal found American law to have similarities to the law of soft states.[29] Yet in the United States, following a period also characterized by the excessive use of discretionary power by public officials, the current emphasis is not to minimize discretion or to maximize its control but to eliminate unnecessary discretion beyond that commensurate with the tasks to be undertaken and to find the optimum control for confining, structuring, and checking discretion accordingly. Where, for example, legislation does not provide the necessary standards, state agencies have been encouraged to develop, in the process of policy and decision making, their own standards that can serve as a public basis both for administrative handling of issues and cases and for judicial review of administrative actions.[30] Such a course, however, may also be of doubtful effectiveness in the absence of strong community controls that can ensure that the exercise of official discretion is indeed in the public interest or not unduly influenced by more powerful groups to the detriment of intended disadvantaged beneficiaries.

Controls by disadvantaged persons

A central problem in holding public officials and public enterprises socially accountable is the difficulty that the common person, especially the disadvantaged person, has, individually or collectively, in enforcing legitimate claims against powerful organizations.

In what has been termed a worldwide ''access to justice'' movement,[31] many countries have devised a variety of new legal institutions and broadened legal representation so as to enable common persons to prevail against powerful organizations for the latter's wrongful acts. The difficulty of the common person is compounded in the case of persons disadvantaged by reasons of powerlessness arising from poverty, minority status, sex, age, or geographical diffuseness. In such cases, the opportunities for exploitation, discrimination, and intimidation by more powerful groups, inside and outside government, are enhanced by the superior control such groups have over the conduct of public officials, whether through state and market controls or through social controls. This superior control results in the sustained enjoyment of a disproportionate share of the resources entrusted to public enterprises for purposes of development.

To remedy this situation it is not sufficient to provide access to powerful organizations by disadvantaged persons. What is required is that the system of state, market, and community enterprises be revamped with the aim of strengthening the role of disadvantaged individuals and groups in the process of development. This requires a threefold approach: the creation of new forms of public enterprises and public-enterprise programs based on shared responsibility for development; the organization of the disadvantaged for purposes of self-help; and the designing of new arrangements to enable the disadvantaged to exercise controls over public enterprises to hold them socially accountable.

Examples of the first two were given earlier in Section 5.4. Examples of the third, given below, are drawn from movements to create new legal arrangements and resources to enable disadvantaged groups and communities to hold public enterprises socially accountable:

1. Creating legal institutions to meet the needs of individuals in disadvantaged groups, such as ombudsmen and public or private attorney generals with power to take initiative in cases of infringements of the law or damage to the public interest by public enterprises.[32]

2. Giving broadened legal representation and legal assistance to a wide range of relatively powerless disadvantaged groups (e.g., the poor, ethnic minorities, children, women, workers, consumers, local communities) before government agencies, public enterprises, legislatures, and courts.[33]

3. In many countries efforts are being made to go beyond the "delivery of legal services" by members of a professional bar (often indifferent or antagonistic to the needs of the disadvantaged) and to provide disadvantaged persons with the collective capacity to use and shape the process of law for meeting their own needs. Examples are: the inclusion of specially motivated community organizers and lawyers in the extension services of public enterprises and other state agencies; the use by disadvantaged communities of their own community organizers and lawyers for purposes of self-help and for exercising controls over public enterprises;[34] and the systematic effort of certain private bodies to educate disadvantaged local groups and communities about their rights and the process of law and to study the characteristics of disadvantaged groups and what types of participatory legal services will best meet their needs.[35]

5.8 Public enterprises as fiduciaries

When a nation commits itself to the new development strategies, it must have as one of its goals the strengthening of the community, as well as the state and the economy. To achieve these goals, public enterprises must perform three roles as development institutions: as state organizations, as business organizations, and as community organizations. To hold public enterprises accountable for these roles requires three interlocking control systems (comprised of controls and control entities), corresponding to the interfaces between public enterprises and state, market, and community, respectively. The laws governing the conduct of public enterprises (which the enterprises themselves help to shape) are an important part of the control systems. The laws work through authoritative controls in the form of standards and procedures, sanctions and remedies, rights and duties, and so on. These controls differ according to the role of the public enterprise.

As an instrument of the *state*, public enterprise operates within a set of *hierarchical* relationships and is subject to external *mandatory* controls of the state, bearing on matters such as direction, supervision, and coordination of enterprise activities, internal structure, appointment and dismissal of personnel, budgeting and procurement. Performance is judged primarily in terms of *obedience* in carrying out government policy. As a *business* organization producing and marketing goods and services, public enterprise operates within a set of *bargaining* relationships and subject to external *price* controls of the market, bearing on matters such as supply and demand, costs and wages, capital and credit, competition and monopoly, and so on. Peformance is judged primarily in terms of *efficiency* and *foresight* in making use of available resources and market opportunities. As a community agency, public enterprise operates within a set of *fiducial* relationships and is subject to external *participatory* controls, bearing on matters such as impact on local communities, quality of working conditions, quality of products and services, quality of environment, economic security, job opportunities and training, and so on. Performance is judged primarily in terms of *social accountability* in meeting the needs of the community.[36]

A particular public enterprise may be subject, in practice, to a combination of external controls. These may reinforce or conflict with one another, and some may be exercised by an alliance of particular groups, for example, certain ministers, enterprise officials, and social elites.

The notion of law in legal positivism, on which conventional development strategies tend to rely, stresses the state and business roles of public enterprises but is weak on their role in dealing with the community. The "autonomy" of a public enterprise as a business organization provides a measure of commercial discretion to follow the rules of the market as recognized or regulated by the state. This autonomous role is epitomized in the corporate enterprise form,[37] by which a public enterprise as a state agency adopts the role of a market-sector organization with appropriate state controls (such as ministerial representation on the enterprise board of directors and external financial and policy controls).

The social accountability of a public enterprise for its exercise of discretion in dealing with the community sector, however, has not been similarly addressed, with the result that it has not been adequately controlled. Public enterprises have sometimes been given too little discretion to be effective in performing their social roles or too much discretion, so that in neither case are they socially accountable. The remedy lies in providing them with a degree of "autonomy" as a community organization. This autonomous role is epitomized in the form of an institutional fiduciary, subject to appropriate state controls, so that it can combine the advantages of a community organization and a state agency.

The characteristics of a fiduciary organization, as the term is used here, are that it is entrusted by, or on behalf of, a community as principal with power and resources to be used by it, as trustee, for the benefit of the members of the community.[38] The relationship between fiduciary and beneficiaries is characterized by the obligation of the fiduciary to act in the beneficiaries' interest and the right of the beneficiaries to demand performance by the fiduciary of its trust. The relationship between fiduciary and principal may be defined by charter or statute, but the obligations of the fiduciary arise from the trust undertaking itself, and the terms of the charter or statute cannot derogate from the fiducial obligations or the beneficiaries' rights. The fiduciary is also under a general duty, because of the dependence of the beneficiaries on the relationship, to act with special care and candor in the performance of its trust.

A community enterprise is a particular form of fiduciary organization that is engaged in the production and/or distribution of goods or services based on initiatives and leadership from within a community and oriented to community goals. They may have relations with organizations in the state and market sectors, but the community remains the primary control entity.

To institutionalize the interface between public enterprise and community promises to be no less difficult than past efforts to institutionalize the interface between public enterprise and market. In both cases, public enterprises as state agencies are required to take on a role characteristic of organizations in another sector: in the case of the market sector, the form of a corporate enterprise; in the case of the community sector, the form of an institutional fiduciary. Neither role can be adopted in *toto*, however, but must be adapted to the role of public enterprise as state agencies and be subjected to appropriate state controls.

There are four ways for a nation that is committed to strengthening the community to differentiate the roles of state and community organizations in a relationship of shared responsibility for development:

1. The government may provide certain benefits (e.g., credit via a public enterprise) to *individuals* within a given local community as part of a general nationwide program.
2. The government may *operate* its own enterprises to handle certain programs in particular local communities (e.g., provide low-cost housing to slum dwellers).
3. The government may *support* (e.g., organize, assist, and regulate) community enterprises (e.g., production cooperatives for small farmers through a public agricultural bank).
4. The government may *authorize* its public enterprises to undertake joint ventures with local community enterprises.

Whatever approach or combination of approaches is taken, the government must deal with the problem of the social accountability of enterprises at both the national and local level. Several principles (which are not narrowly legal in the sense of depending mainly on enforcement by the courts) can help to solve this problem and thus avoid the all-too-familiar obstacles of a top-down style of management and a bypassing or absence of local controls:

1. Relationships should be established between a public enterprise and the community that resemble, so far as feasible, the fiducial relations between a community enterprise and the community. Arrangements might include, for example: the use of local community organizations to make, or participate in, community impact studies; the creation of a community trust to which both the public enterprise and the local community would contribute for implementing a specific project of local development; and the capacitation of local community organizations to enable intended beneficiaries to exercise their rights, individually or collectively, to demand performance by the public enterprise.
2. Public enterprises should be decentralized and their social/technical teams need to be familiar with local conditions not only because of the diversity of local communities but also because of the need to achieve a sense of confidence in each local community.
3. Local community controls should be utilized or created to guide public-enterprise activities toward the meeting of local needs to assure that the obligations to the local community are not eroded by the self-interest of those within the enterprise and that controls over management performance are shared by local organizations.
4. There should be "transparency" of management[39] at all levels, that is, candor and disclosure, with the burden of proof on the national and local enterprises that their performance is proper.
5. National community controls should be utilized or created to facilitate the expansion to provincial and national levels of successful experiments with socially accountable enterprises at the local level (i.e., there needs to be an infrastructure of self-help organizations and of intermediary organizations supportive of their purposes).

Although the foregoing principles indicate the direction in which changes are needed, including changes in law, to institute community controls of public enterprises, the difficulties in making such changes are not to be minimized.

5.9 Control systems for socially accountable public enterprises

Before considering control systems for public enterprises, it is useful to comment briefly on some relevant lessons to be learned from private enterprises.

Private enterprises

The notion of "institutional accountability" examined in the preceding section is compatible with the notion of a country (e.g., the United States) as a "bargaining society," in which competition in the market serves as an external curb on abuse of economic power.[40] But with the rise of the big business corporation and the transfer of power from shareholders to professional managers who are virtually unaccountable to society, serious questions have arisen concerning "the social legitimacy of both the market and the big business corporations."[41] Today, market controls over business corporations are increasingly being supplemented not only with state (legislative, judicial, and executive) controls but also with a range of community controls and internal (self) controls concerned with making the business corporation socially accountable. As a consequence, the point has been made that it may be easier to achieve social accountablity for private enterprises than for public enterprises.[42]

Especially noteworthy in the foregoing experience is the convergence of views concerning the roles of a private enterprise as a business organization and as a socially accountable instrument of society. For example, many big corporations in the United States have established, at the top level of policy making, "public responsibility committees of the board."[43] These committees assist the boards in determining policy with respect to a range of complex and sensitive social issues: for example, the philosophy of the enterprise concerning its public responsibility, affirmative action to discriminate in favor of disadvantaged groups in society, relations with local communities, environmental quality, product quality and safety, consumerism, occupational safety and health, employee issues, charitable organizations, and government relations. On the one hand, such an approach can be viewed as an expression of concern for the "social role" of a private enterprise: its public purpose and fiducial obligations, the social purpose of, and limitations upon, private property. Or it can be viewed, at least in part, as "good business," that is, as part of the "marketing concept" in accordance with which an alert enterprise foresees shifting social priorities (e.g., an emerging demand for environmental protection) and sets out to produce the goods and services to meet the envisaged needs.[44]

Public enterprises

What then are the appropriate configurations of state, market, and community control systems (control and control entities) for holding public enterprises socially accountable for their role in strengthening the community sector? The keystone of such control systems is the fiducial relationship between the public enterprise and individuals and organizations in the community sector. From the standpoint of the public enterprise, the important aspects of this relationship are: the nature of its trust and program; discretionary powers commensurate with its social accountability; and a set of internal (self) controls established by board and management in conformity with the right of beneficiaries and their organizations to demand performance by the enterprise.

The functions of these control systems are to clarify, publicize, fulfill, and monitor the role of a public enterprise as an institutional fiduciary in strengthening the community. The systems cut across conventional fields of law such as administrative law, constitutional law, company law, the law of social organizations, and human-rights law.

The following checklist of elements relevant to the more adequate design and implementation of laws governing public enterprises is based on past experience. It is not intended as a set of prescriptions but as a basis for experimentation and studies that will bring innovation and improvement in control systems for public enterprises.

1. *Internal (self) controls and control entities*
   a. An "enterprise program" that contains the targets, resources, and roles for which the enterprise is responsible and on the basis of which enterprise performance is to be evaluated and judged by external state, market, and community control entities
   b. A governing board that is accountable to the community,[45] assisted by a "social accountability" committee to advise the board on all aspects of the enterprise's relationships with the community and/or representatives on the board from major segments of the public (e.g., workers, consumers) affected by the enterprise
   c. At the level of the managerial staff, a "management culture" that includes not only management skills but also an understanding of the segments of the public with which the enterprise interacts (an understanding produced, e.g., through specially designed workshops and inclusion on the enterprise staff of members of disadvantaged groups)
   d. Institutional rules and regulations, standards and procedures for exercising and monitoring the exercise of discretion that are responsive to needs and rights in the community sector
   e. An institutional tradition of integrity, predictability, disclosure, and fairness at all levels of employees having contacts with the public
2. *Community controls and control entities*
   a. Community-based organizations, constituted under laws supportive of their role in sharing responsibility in development, that can exercise collective controls over public enterprises on behalf of their members and can undertake joint ventures with public enterprises
   b. Arrangements enabling intended beneficiaries of a public-enterprise program to demand (individually or collectively, by direct action of confrontation or negotiation or through legal channels in pursuit

of administrative or judicial remedies) performance by the public enterprise of its trust

c. Legal resources that enable the disadvantaged to exercise their right to demand performance by public enterprises, and the linkage of such right with rights relating to association, standing, access, participation, disclosure, burden of proof, fair hearing, and so on

d. An infrastructure of intermediary organizations (e.g., the professions, the media, political parties) that are responsive to the needs of the disadvantaged

3. *State controls and control entities*

a. Constitutional controls in the form of directives of state policy or fundamental rights or provision of special treatment for disadvantaged sectors of the population

b. Agencies of the legislature or political associations charged with general responsibilities to monitor the activities of public as well as private enterprises that impinge on community concerns, such as the welfare of disadvantaged groups and the quality of the environment

c. Employment and procurement regulations and requirements and services of a bureau of public enterprises or a social accountancy service

d. Controls by special tribunals or the regular courts

4. *Market controls and control entities*

a. The changing demand of consumers for goods and services with beneficial features (e.g., safe, energy efficient, nonpolluting) and their anticipation and supply by competitive public and private enterprises

b. The public image and goodwill of a competitive enterprise that has a favorable impact on local communities and segments of the public

c. Market controls exercised through the countervailing power of labor groups in collective bargaining, through holding companies and other forms of layered organization, and through tripartite councils of government, management, and labor in industrial sectors[46]

5. *International controls and control entities*

a. Policies and practices of international aid organizations that affect the creation, programs, and conduct of public enterprises and their social accountability[47]

The roles of public enterprises in strengthening the community and the control systems for holding them socially accountable have yet to be fully designed and made operative. Among the basic obstacles are:

1. The lack of reliable information about the impact of public enterprises on local communities, particularly on disadvantaged groups, and about

the operation of existing control systems for public enterprises

2. The need to change attitudes and capacities on the part of political leaders, public-enterprise managers and staff, professional personnel and community leaders and members

3. The inadequacy of existing organizations and notions of law and administration

The creation of socially accountable public enterprises requires a systematic effort and a variety of legal innovations, organizational experiments, and action-oriented research projects addressed to these obstacles and involving participation by and dialogue among, the different groups whose sharing of responsibility is vital to the success of the enterprises.

Notes

1 International Center for Public Enterprises in Developing Countries, *Control Systems for Public Enterprises in Developing Countries* (Ljubljana, Yugoslavia: ICPE; 1979), p. 5.

2 A partial exception was the paper on control systems for Yugoslav enterprises, which described the country's Basic Organizations of Associated Labor and Social Accountancy Service (1979).

3 The term *public enterprise* as used in the BAPEG conference encompasses organizations owned and/or controlled by governments (central, provincial, and local) and financed largely by selling a product or service in the market. See Chapter 2, note 1. Although the thesis of this chapter applies to such organizations, it is also applicable to a broader class of organizations such as those providing social services in urban development, including services to the disadvantaged. See William A. Robson, "Public Enterprises as a Function of Economic and Social Development," *Annals of Public and Cooperative Economy*, Vol. 44 (Oct.–Dec. 1973), which is concerned with public enterprises in countries with a mixed economy rather than those in countries where the state has a monopoly of economic enterprise.

4 The term *control* is used, as it was in the Yugoslavian workshop, to include support as well as constraint, incentives as well as disincentives.

5 See, e.g. The Dag Hammarskjöld Foundation Report proposing "another development" *What Now* (Uppsala: Dag Hammarskjöld Foundation, 1975); *Another Development: Approaches and Strategies,* ed. Marc Nerfin (Uppsala: Dag Hammarskjöld Foundation, 1977) and *Development Dialogue* Vol. 2, Towards a Theory of Rural Development (Uppsala: Dag Hammarskjöld Foundation, 1977); International Labour Office, *Meeting Basic Needs: Strategies for Eradicating Mass Poverty and Unemployment* (Geneva: ILO, 1977) and *The Basic Needs Approach to Development: Some Issues Regarding Concepts and Methodology* (Geneva, 1977); Address by Robert S. McNamara, president, to the Board of Governors of the International Bank for Reconstruction and Development, (Sept. 26, 1977); Organization for Economic Co-operation and Development, *1977 Review, 1978 Review; Liaison Bulletin of the Development Centre* (1977) and *OECD Observer* (November 1977). The international dimension of the problem is discussed in Johann Galtung, "Grand Designs on a Collision Course," *International Development Review,* No. 3-4 (1978): 43–7 and Johann Galtung, "What Is a Strategy," in International Foundation for Development Alternatives (IFDA), *Dossier 6* (Nyon, Switzerland: IFDA (1979); Roger D. Hansen, *Beyond the North-South Stalemate* (New York: McGraw-Hill, 1979). For a critique of the new development strategies

from a conceptual standpoint, see Reginald H. Green, "Basic Human Needs: A Strategic Conceptualization Towards Another Development," IFDA *Dossier 22* (Nyon, Switzerland: IFDA, 1978); for an Asian perspective, see Godfrey Gunatilleke, "Asian Perspectives: A Background Note" (Paper presented at a meeting of the Marga Institute, Colombo, Mar. 10-12, 1978); in terms of the rhetoric–reality gap, see Joseph Collins and Frances Moore Lappe, "The World Bank," IFDA *Dossier 5* (Nyon, Switzerland: IFDA, 1979).

6 See, e.g., Joel D. Barken, Frank Holmquist, David Gachuki, Shem Migot-Adholla, "Is Small Beautiful? The Organizational Conditions for Effective Small-Scale, Self-Help Development Projects in Rural Kenya," (University of Iowa, Department of Political Science occasional paper, Dec. 1979); International Center for Law in Development, "Law and Legal Resources in the Mobilization of the Rural Poor for Self-Reliant Development," IFDA *Dossier 12* (Nyon, Switzerland: IFDA, 1979) p. 69; Anupam Mishra and Satyendra Tripathi, "Chipko Movement," in *People's Action for Development with Justice*, ed. Radhakrishna, (New Delhi: Gandhi Peace Foundation, 1978); Upendra Baxi, "Notes on the Relevance of Legal Resources for Participatory Organizations of the Rural Poor: The Case of the Chipko Movement" (paper, 1979); Ana Gutierrez Johnson and William Foote Whyte, "The Mondragon System of Worker Production Cooperatives," in *Industrial and Labor Relations Review* 31, no. 1 (Oct. 1977); 18–30; "*Community Development Corporations: A Strategy for Depressed Urban and Rural Areas,"* Ford Foundation Policy Paper, 1973; and John A. Echeveste, "TELACU: Pioneers in Economic Development," *Opportunity* 2 (Fall 1978): 16–19.

7 The term *community* as used in this chapter designates a number of people usually associated in the same locality, having common organization, and subject to the same laws, which need not be uniform throughout the community but provide a common framework within which organization and laws may differ for different subcommunities. At the local level, with which this chapter is primarily concerned, a village or neighborhood group or disadvantaged group may be a community (or subcommunity); at a higher level the nation may be a community; at the highest level the organized world society may be a global community. A community does not always exist and may need to be created. The term *community organization* is used to designate an organization that is based on and/or oriented toward strengthening a particular community.

8 Examples from very different countries are the creation within the constitution of Ecuador of a new "communitarian sector," distinct from the public sector and the private-property sector and the creation in the United States, with foundation and business financing, of a nationwide program to provide support for "self-help community and neighborhood groups."

9 Dharam Ghai and Md. Anisur Rahman, "Rural Poverty and the Small Farmers' Development Programme in Nepal" (International Labour Organization report, Oct. 1979); Prakash Lohani, "Small Farmer Development Programme in Nepal" (Paper presented to Workshop on Small Farmers' Development and Credit Policy, Kathmandu, Apr. 1980).

10 Felipe B. Alfonso, "Farmer Participation in the Development of Communal Systems: Skills and Structural Implications," *Philippine Agricultural Engineering Journal* (1980), pp. 28–31.

11 See Peter Dorner, ed., *Cooperation and Commune: Group Farming in the Economic Development of Agriculture* (Madison: University of Wisconsin Press, 1977).

12 Quotations taken from ibid., p. 10.

13 The community processes in this phenomenon, called "mobilization of bias," are examined by Peter Bachrach and Morton S. Baratz, *Power and Poverty* (New York:

Oxford University Press, 1970).

14 See, e.g., Mary Racelis Hollnsteiner, "People as Policy Makers: the Participative Dimension in Low-Income Housing" (Paper presented at International Conference on Low-Income Housing, Technology and Policy at the Asian Institute of Technology, Bangkok, June 7-10, 1977); and "Development from the Bottom-up: Mobilizing the Rural Poor for Self-Development," (Report prepared by Mary Racelis Hollnsteiner for the Food and Agriculture Organization, Manila, 1978; published in abridged form in Hollnsteiner, "Mobilizing the Rural Poor Through Community Organizations," *Philippine Studies* 28 (1979); 387-416.

15 Examples of the techniques used for this purpose are seminars on the peasantry for judges in Peru's Agrarian Reform Tribunal and working sessions held for the Philippine National Housing Administration within a targeted disadvantaged area and attended by persons from that area.

16 P. K. Basu, "Linkage Between Policy and Performance: Empirical and Theoretical Considerations on Public Enterprises in Mixed Economy Less Developed Countries" (Paper presented at second BAPEG conference on Public Enterprise in Mixed Economy LDCs, Boston Apr. 1980).

17 See, e.g., "Legal Positivism," in *Encyclopedia of Philosophy* (1967), 4:418, and "Positivism," in *International Encyclopedia of the Social Sciences* (1968), p. 389.

18 It is only in recent years that the U.S. Supreme Court has made it easier for individuals to sue their government by stripping local governments of absolute immunity from damage suits for civil-rights violations and by rejecting federal government claims of absolute personal immunity for most federal officials from damage suits for constitutional violations. See *New York Times*, June 8, 1980, p. 20E.

19 James Williard Hurst, "Legal Elements in United States History," in *Law in American History*, ed., Donald Fleming and Bernard Bailyn, (Boston: Little, Brown, 1971), pp 3-4. See also Hurst, *Law and Social Order in the United States* (Ithaca, N.Y.: Cornell University Press, 1977).

20 Although most U.S. constitutional history has emphasized what the government cannot do, in the past half century, the notions have emerged that the due-process clause of the Constitution *permits* social-welfare legislation and in certain instances *requires* it. The emergence of "a judicial concept of constitutional duty" is described by Arthur Selwyn Miller, "Towards a Concept of Constitutional Duty," in *The Supreme Court and the Judicial Function*, ed. Philip B. Kurland (Chicago: University of Chicago Press, 1975), p. 187. Under the U.N. Covenant of Social and Economic Rights, the government of a signatory state has positive duties to achieve certain minimum social and economic goals. But these duties are abstract and can be evaded on the grounds of lack of resources or organization. The notion of public enterprises as fiduciaries concretizes the positive obligations and lays the basis for the rights of beneficiaries to demand performance.

21 In the United States, in spite of the prevailing view that human rights are individual in nature, there is growing recognition of group rights in instances of weakness that require affirmative or compensatory action to promise equality (e.g., blacks, women, children) or survival of a community based on fundamental and enduring interests (e.g., ethnic groups such as Indians and Hispanics). See Vernon Van Dyke, "Human Rights and the Rights of Groups," *American Journal of Political Science* 18 (Nov. 1974): 725, and Vernon Van Dyke, "Justice as Fairness for Groups?" *American Political Science Review* 69 (June 1975); 607. In India and Malaysia there are constitutional provisions for the protection of the rights of untouchables and Malays.

22 See, e.g., the description of Nkrumah's use of law in Ghana by S. K. B. Asante, "Law and Society in Ghana," in *Africa and Law: Developing Legal Systems in the*

African Commonwealth Nations (1968).

23 See, e.g., "Roscoe Pound," in *International Encyclopedia of the Social Sciences*, p. 395.

24 Roscoe Pound, *An Introduction to the Philosophy of Law*, rev. ed.,(New Haven: Yale University Press, 1954), p. 47.

25 Roscoe Pound, *Interpretation of Legal History* (Cambridge University Press, 1930), p. 164.

26 Roscoe Pound, *Social Control Through Law* (New Haven: Yale University Press, 1942), pp. 25–26.

27 Gunnar Myrdal, *Asian Drama: An Inquiry into the Poverty of Nations* New York: Pantheon, 1968).

28 Gunnar Myrdal, *Beyond the Welfare State* (New Haven: Yale University Press, 1960), p. 70.

29 Gunnar Myrdal, "The 'Soft State' in Underdeveloped Countries," *UCLA Law Review* 15 (June 1968): 1118–1134.

30 See Kenneth Culp Davis, *Discretionary Justice: A Preliminary Inquiry* (Baton Rouge: Louisiana State University Press, 1973).

31 Mauro Cappelletti and Bryant Garth, "Access to Justice: The Newest Wave in the Worldwide Movement to Make Rights Effective," *Buffalo Law Review* 27 (1977–78):181.

32 See ibid., for a variety of such institutions.

33 For this purpose, "public interest" law activities have been undertaken in a number of countries. Concerning the United States, see Ford Foundation, *The Public Interest Law Firm: New Voices for New Constituencies* (New York: Ford Foundation 1973). Indonesia, Colombia, Sri Lanka, India, and other developing countries have undertaken similar activities.

34 The International Center for Law in Development is encouraging studies of the "legal resources" needed by disadvantaged groups and communities in third-world countries to provide them with the skills and capacity for self-reliant development. See James C. N. Paul and Clarence J. Dias, *Law and Legal Resources in the Mobilization of the Rural Poor for Self-Reliant Development* (New York: ICLD, 1980).

35 Pioneering efforts of this type are a project to strengthen the legal resources of landless sugar workers in the Philippines, a nongovernmental Chilean Institute for the Study and Development of Legal Aid, a Legal Services Institute established in the United States by the Harvard Law School in cooperation with the Greater Houston area, and a National Street Law Institute located in Washington, D.C.

36 Robert A. Dahl and Charles E. Lindblow, *Politics, Economics and Welfare,* 2nd ed. (Chicago: University of Chicago Press, 1976), use a fourfold classification system of controls as between "leaders" and "followers": price, hierarchy, polyarchy, and bargaining. I distinguish between the source of controls (state, market, and community), the control systems or the relationships within which controls are exercised (hierarchical, bargaining, and fiducial), and the controls (mandatory, price, and participatory).

37 See, e.g., Wolfgang Friedmann, "Governmental (Public) Enterprises," *International Encyclopedia of Comparative Law*, Vol. 13 (International Encyclopedia of Comparative Law) *Business and Private Organizations*, p. 3.

38 The notions of trust and fiduciary have historic roots in most legal systems, including Roman, Hindu, Islamic, European, civil law, and common law. As might be expected, the application of the common principles involved has varied in different systems. This chapter is an initial attempt to explore the application of the principles to community organizations and public enterprises as institutional fiduciaries or trustees. Among possible references, see the introduction in Sir Ernest

Barker, *Social Contract* (New York: Oxford University Press, 1962); G. W. Paton, ed., *A Textbook of Jurisprudence*, 4th ed. (Oxford: Clarendon Press, 1972); *Corpus Juris Secundum* (Brooklyn: American Law Book, 1967), Vol. 36A; *Black's Law Dictionary*, 5th ed. (St. Paul, Minn.: West Publishing, 1979); *International Encyclopedia of Comparative Law*, Vol. 6, Chap. 11; S. K. B. Asante, "Fiduciary Principles in Anglo-American Laws and the Customary Law of Ghana – A Comparative Study," *International and Comparative Law Quarterly* (Oct. 1965): 1144–1188; *Encyclopedia of Islam* (Leiden: Brill, 1960); Anwar Ahman Qadir, *Islamic Jurisprudence in the Modern World* (Bombay: Tripathi, 1963).

39 *Transparency* is the term used in the report of the Yugoslavia workshop on public enterprises discussed in Section 5.2. In recent administrative law cases, United States courts have just begun to shift the burden of proof from the complainant (proof of impropriety) to the government agency (proof of propriety).

40 See Hurst, *Law and Social Order in the United States*, pp. 59 and 245.

41 Ibid., p. 273.

42 James Q. Wilson and Patricia Rachad, "Can the Government Regulate Itself?" *The Public Interest*, No. 46 (Winter 1977):3.

43 See Michael L. Loudal, Raymond A. Bauer, and Nancy W. Treventon, "Public Responsibility Committees of the Board," *Harvard Business Review* (May-June 1977): 40. Other steps taken by corporations to meet their social responsibilities include the establishment of departments or foundations for public giving, the loaning of staff members as experts to local communities, and the encouragement of staff members to work in local community organizations.

44 See Charles W. Gross and Harish L. Verma, "Marketing and Social Responsibility," *Business Horizons* (Oct. 1977):75.

45 See, e.g., Neil W. Hamilton and Peter R. Hamilton, *Governance of Public Enterprise* (Lexington, Mass.: Heath, 1981), p. 113.

46 Not surprisingly, some of the best illustrations of market controls over public enterprise are to be found in the United States, where the most common form of public enterprise is the public authority, a government-owned organization (primarily at the state and local level) that raises capital by issuing revenue bonds in the private money market and invests it in public facilities. Examples are the Authority of the Port of New York and the New York Metropolitan Transportation Authority. A recent study of public authorities has found that the planning process is shaped and limited by financial market controls (e.g., the private banks' view of what constitutes financially viable public authority projects) to a degree that the resulting policy biases prevent adequate consideration of the authorities' impact on the national or local economy or the physical, social, and political environment. The study's only recommendations bearing on social accountability are greater public access to information and a management more open to viewpoints from society. Annmarie Hauck Walsh, *The Public Business* (Cambridge, Mass: MIT Press, 1978).

47 See International Legal Center, *The Impact of International Organizations on Legal and Institutional Change in the Developing Countries* (New York: ILC, 1977).

Part III

How are decisions made in practice?

6 Comparing state enterprises across international boundaries: the Corporación Venezolana de Guayana and the Companhía Vale do Rio Doce

Janet Kelly Escobar

Because of the diverse forms of state-owned enterprises (SOEs), scholars still differ considerably over basic issues concerning their behavior. More agreement is possible, however, when a relatively homogeneous subset of state enterprises can be studied. Comparative analysis of Air France and of a state-owned agricultural enterprise in Cuba would probably offer little in the way of useful generalizations; it makes more sense to build up hypotheses from cases that are more likely to have commonalities. This chapter examines, through detailed case studies, two similar state-owned conglomerates in Venezuela and Brazil, the Corporación Venezolana de Guayana (CVG) and the Companhía Vale do Rio Doce (CVRD), and constructs a model for analyzing the kind of behavior found to be typical in both.

6.1 Comparability of CVG and CVRD: a short description

As state-owned enterprises go, CVG and CVRD have significant similarities that provide a rich field for comparison. CVG was founded in 1960 as a regional development corporation whose ambit included the huge southeastern portion of Venezuela, at the time largely empty and backward, although blessed with important mineral and energy resources. CVG's original mandate was three-fold: direct the nascent steel industry, build up the hydroelectric facilities in the area, and provide the human and physical infrastructure not only for these two industries but also for the development of new industries in Guayana.

The research for this chapter was made possible by support from the Corporación Venezolana de Guayana and the Harvard Institute for International Development, as well as by the cooperation of the Companhía Vale do Rio Doce. Much of the information was collected in the course of interviews with managers from the two companies during 1979. Particular thanks are also due Professor Raymond Vernon for his support for the project. Of course, the author alone is responsible for any errors and for all the conclusions drawn in the course of the study.

103

Table 6.1. *Subsidiaries of CVRD and CVG by industry, 1978*

Industry	CVRD	Status[a]	CVG	Status[a]
Iron ore	CVRD division	C-D	Ferrominera Orinoca	C-S
	Amazonia Mineração	C-S		
	Minas del Rey D. Pedro	C-S		
	Caraça Ferro e Aço	C-S		
	Minas da Serra Geral	C-S		
	Itavale Ltda.	A		
	Others	C-S		
Iron-ore pellets	CVRD division	C-D	Sidor division	C-S
	Nipo-Brasileira de Pelotização	"C-S"		
	Italo-Brasileira de Pelotização	"C-S"		
	Hispano-Brasileira de Pelotização	"C-S"		
High-iron briquettes			Minerales Ordaz	C-S
			Fior de Venezuela	A
Steel	Siderbrás	A	Sidor	C-S
Chemicals, fertilizer	Mineração Vale Paranaiba	C-S		
	Fertilizantes Vale do Rio Grande	C-S		
Wood, paper, pulp	Floresta Rio Doce	C-S	CVG	C-D
	Empreen d imentos Florestais	A	C.A. Pulpa y Papel	A
	Celulose Nipo-Brasileira	"C-S"		
Bauxite	Mineracao Rio do Norte	A	Bauxiven	C-S

	CVRD		Partner	
Alumina	Valenorte (holding)	A	Interamericana de Alumino	C-A
Aluminum	Valenorte (holding)	A	Venalum	C-S
	Valesul	C-S	Aluminio del Caroní	A
Shipping related industries	Navegação Rio Doce Ltda.	C-A	Puerto de Hierro	A
	Seamar Shipping Corp.	A		
Railroad	CVRD division	C-D	Ferrominera division	C-S
Ferroalloys			Venbozel	A
Electricity			Electificación del Caroní	C-S
Banking, finance	Itabira International	C-S	Sociedad Financiera Atlántica	C-S
	Rio Doce International Finance Co.	C-S		
Marketing	Rio Doce Europa	C-S	CVG International	C-S
Other	Rio Doce Geologia e Mineração	C-S	Metalmeg	A
			Cementos Guayana	A
	R.D. Engenharía e Planejamento	C-S	Fanatracto	A

[a] C-D, holding company performs function directly; C-S, activity of subsidiary; "C-S", activity of subsidiary controlled in practice by partner; C-A, activity of affiliate controlled by CVRD or CVG; A, activity of affiliate.

Source: CVRD, *Annual Report* (1978); CVG, "Estados Financieros," (December 1978).

Although CVG took direct charge of the infrastructure, subsidiary and affiliated companies were formed for all the productive, or business, activities of the holding company. The range of CVG interests spread to mining, the manufacture of intermediate products, aluminum, banking, and a variety of other fields. Despite earlier expectations, CVG's subsidiaries have not often generated investment funds from their own operations, so that the holding company has not yet come near to being a self-sufficient or self-financing entity – it remains dependent on the government for new funds for investment.

The 1970s brought a multiplication of spending plans in Venezuela, made possible by large increases in revenues from the oil sector. This in turn meant accelerated investments by CVG, especially in steel. The result is that CVG is now trying to recover from a prolonged case of indigestion. In recent years, CVG has found that it could no longer expect ever more official capital with no questions asked. Increasingly, capital for new industrial projects has been routed through a recently created state institution, the Venezuelan Investment Fund (FIV). The FIV thus began to vie with CVG for some control over the firms in which both now held shares. Rival state entities in other regions also began to clamor for a share of funds for industrial development, arguing that the wealth should be shared a bit more. Consequently, CVG is entering its second 20 years of life with great power and influence but also with problems for the future.[1]

CVRD of Brazil is similar in many ways to CVG. At the end of 1978 the consolidated assets of CVRD were listed at $2.5 billion (American billion) and those of the CVG at $1.9 billion.[2] CVRD was founded in 1942 with the instigation, help, and pressure of the United States and Great Britain to ensure their future sources for iron ore. The company's humble beginnings restricted it to iron-ore mining and export, with little in the way of grand social aims.[3] Since 1942, CVRD has come a long way. It became a holding company not unlike CVG, with affiliates in shipping, bauxite, aluminum, pelletizing, wood and pulp, and so on. As Table 6.1 shows, the correspondence in business activities between CVRD and CVG is striking.

Aside from the similarities in lines of business, CVG and CVRD find themselves selling in some of the same markets abroad (e.g., iron ore and aluminum) and operating in domestic markets that show some of the same characteristics – oligopolistic, protected, fast growing. Both have entered into joint ventures with private interests, foreign and domestic. In most cases, domestic partners are other state enterprises.

Naturally, there are also differences. The far more favorable balance-of-payments situation in Venezuela contributes to significant differences in the needs and preferences of the two governments with respect to their SOEs. Another environmental difference is in the kind of government in power: Brazil has currently what has been called a bureaucratic-authoritarian system run by the military, whereas Venezuela enjoys a civilian democracy with two main parties, smooth changes of power, and so on (since 1958). CVRD, given its origins, is still principally an iron-ore company, with the status of being the largest single exporter of iron ore in the world. CVG's iron-ore business was acquired more recently and has a more limited scale.[4] CVRD also can claim to be a *national* company, rather than an organization devoted to a particular region as in the case of CVG. All the same, until recently, CVRD's operations remained mainly in the state of Minas Gerais, the location of the iron-ore deposits. Thus, even in the regional development sense, CVRD and CVG display significant similarities, even if CVG's area of potential action remains more limited.[5]

6.2 A model for comparing SOE behavior

CVG and CVRD often behave differently. Although the literature now existing on SOEs suggests that such differences are not random, it nevertheless leaves the observer groping for some way to make sense out of the variety of behaviors detected in such complex organizations. Too often, hypotheses attempt to characterize the whole organization (e.g., "risk averse," "X-inefficient," etc.) when in fact different parts function differently in response to varying conditions. The model presented here attempts to provide a framework to allow analysis of behaviorial regularities in SOEs and still predict a high degree of variability of types of behavior within a single firm and among firms.

Assumptions

This model makes seven assumptions. First, SOE behavior is defined as the behavior or set of policies of its core decision-making group, or "coalition."[6] The coalition's make-up can vary according to the company and its constitution and practices. It is usually made up of key managers at the top level of the corporation and perhaps some members of the board of directors. The core group may differ, depending on the policy area involved.

Second, the coalition within the company consists of two types: the *engineers* and the *commissars*. Engineers, as their name implies, concern themselves chiefly with directing the firm. They do not view themselves as social workers. They exhibit the good and bad qualities of businessmen in general; like managers in private enterprise, they also concern themselves with their own advancement and their personal security within the firm. But engineers do generally see the firm's betterment as in their own self-interest.[7] In short, the engineer is assumed to choose strategies prompted by the same basic motivations as his colleague in private enterprise, although he does confront a different political environment, which he may have to manipulate for his own good or that of the firm.

(There is one exception to this view of the engineer. To the extent that managerial salaries in an SOE are significantly lower than those in comparable private industries, one would expect the engineer in the SOE to be inferior in capabilities and perhaps different with respect to levels of motivation. This exception does not apply, however, in the cases of CVG and CVRD, because salary gaps between public and private industry do not appear to be so great as to make them into dumping grounds for inferior managers.)

In contrast to the engineer, the commissar's principal interest lies outside the firm. The current government or officially recognized groups (labor, the military, professional groups, etc.) probably appoint *all* state enterprise directors and high-level managers or can veto their appointments, so that it is not political appointment that distinguishes the engineer from the commissar. What does differentiate them is the motive behind the appointment and the attitude of the appointee. For the commissars, days spent in a state-owned company make up a season in a political career. The commissar may well judge that satisfactory performance by the state firm will enhance his career or the position of his party or sponsoring group, in which case he and the engineers will assume common qualities. When he receives no external directives, he will also tend to adopt the perspective of the engineers in the firm. More often, however, the commissar's goal is to fill some function distinct from the purely operational.

In cases of joint ventures between the state and private industry, there will be directors and managers appointed by the private partner as well. These representatives can usually be viewed as engineers, but to the extent they subordinate the welfare of the SOE to the welfare of the mother company, they are also serving interests external to the firm.

Engineers and commissars do not represent the children of light and the children of darkness in this scheme. Nor can an individual claim to be purely one or the other. At any time, however, a given SOE will be directed by some relatively fixed mixture of engineers and commissars. The point is that *the two groups, and the balance between them, provide the dynamics of goal conflict within the firm.*

The third assumption is that within the coalition there are four principal motivating forces: (1) social subsidization, (2) profit maximization, (3) risk minimization, and (4) autonomy maximization.

Fourth, SOEs are always required to support some level of social subsidization. Social subsidization carries a special meaning here: *a company engages in social subsidization when it acts to benefit some groups as a result of external compulsion.* By this definition, it should be clear that social subsidization need not imply welfare maximization. Commissars will urge subsidization for whatever groups their sponsors favor. Subsidization of "some groups" could in fact imply costs to other groups that result in net welfare losses. It is not uncommon to find state enterprises taking from the poor and giving to the rich – often for reasons that on their face appear to be meritorious.

Fifth, as it is assumed that engineers are motivated by the same forces as businessmen in private industry, it follows that they are driven by a profit-maximization motive. It should be understood, however, that *"profit maximization" as used here is an umbrella concept that represents a variety of maximizing goals associated with the long-term health of the firm in conventional terms.* At different times, these could include revenue goals, market-share goals, production goals, and the like. Adjustment among firm goals will be modified in part by what individual engineers see as good for themselves and by their influence in the core decision group. Like managers in private industry, engineers usually press for maximization strategies that favor their own divisions – production managers identify production goals as primary for the firm; finance managers tend to press for profit goals.

Sixth, risk minimization is the complementary side of profit maximization. It also subsumes a variety of possible responses whose *main aim is to blunt the effects of uncertainty for both the company and the individual manager*. Again, this motivation should be the same for engineers in SOEs as it is for businessmen in private enterprise, assuming that conditions of employment do not grossly differ.

Seventh, given the natural drives among engineers toward profit maximization and risk minimization, their incentives to perform acts of social subsidization will be low. Commissars will favor acts of social subsidization, depending on their orders. This conflict gives rise to a special class of behavior in engineers: autonomy maximization, that is, "freedom to make decisions related to operation and strategic management practices without government interference."[8] As this model allows for interference from sources other than the government, the definition might be expanded to include all outside interference.

Now, managers in private enterprise may also pursue autonomy strategies, seeking independence from boards of directors or stockholders, à la Galbraith's technostructure. In those cases, the managers usually think that they can run the company better than the owners or directors.[9] Autonomy-maximization strategies of engineers in SOEs contain this element of wanting freedom to do the job better but also something else. We assume here that *engineers seek autonomy to avoid as much as possible social-subsidization requirements*. Thus, for engineers, autonomy maximization is not an end in itself but rather an instrumental goal in service of profit maximization and risk minimization. Given rational calculations, an engineer will not pursue an autonomy strategy at all costs – if he goes too far, he risks his job, government support for the company's projects and so on.

Commissars representing the government have, of course, much less interest in autonomy maximization. At times, a commissar from a nongoverning party might seek to undermine the authority of the party in power; he may ally himself with the engineers to do so. Commissars representing private partners in the SOE will certainly seek autonomy from government intereference and also try to increase the role of the partner in decision making. A commissar representing the army or labor would also have his distinct goals. Ideal types require extreme foundations, of course, and even the most faithful commissar will have some ideas of his own about how to further the national good. Yet the very real differences between engineers and commissars on questions of social subsidization and autonomy create an inner tension with the SOE. The greater the social-subsidization level required, the greater will be the conflict within the managing coalition over the proper behavior of the firm.

Table 6.2. *A model for comparing SOEs*

Policy Area	Social Subsidization	Profit Maximization	Risk Minimization	Autonomy Maximization
Pricing: competitive policy	Domestic price minimization Foreign revenue maximization Do not compete with domestic Industry	Exploit monopoly power abroad and at home	Cartel agreements with existing competitors Prevent new entrants to market	Operate in competitive markets
Marketing: contracts policy	Sell to politically chosen markets	Market aggressively Use government help for sales, contracts.	Favor long-term contracts	Avoid government help and interference
Supply policy	Favor local suppliers or government-chosen sources	Seek lowest cost	Long-term contracts Multiple sources	Multiple sources
Employment policy	Subsidize employment if necessary "Fair wages"	Minimize labor costs Rewards and punishments to employees	Maximize flexibility Seek job security for oneself	Maximize flexibility Seek job security for oneself
Diversification policy: products and markets	Invest at home only Take over sick firms Avoid competition with healthy firms Attention to social rate of return	Diversify products and markets according to investment potential	Prudent diversification Avoid speculation	Diversify, especially via subsidiaries Invest abroad
Finance and tax policy	Generate internal sources of funds Pay taxes and dividends	Secure cheapest finance Get subsidies Avoid taxes and dividends	Get government loans and guarantees Seek legal tax breaks	Minimize taxes and dividends Reinvest surplus

Partnership policy	Maximize national control Joint ventures where necessary	Take partners when financially sensible	Use partners as credit guarantors, sales outlets, suppliers, etc.	Use partners as counterweight to government and other pressures
Information policy	Share information with authorities Advertise the positive	Disclosure only if necessary; selective information release	Hide negative information	Hide negative information

The model

Table 6.2 illustrates tentatively the structure of the model. It organizes, within the terms of the assumptions, possible ranges of behavior for state-owned enterprises in eight policy areas. It exposes policy conflicts likely to trouble managing coalitions that will be resolved by a political (power) process among their members.

The eight policy areas of the model are not meant to be exhaustive, although they do include actually or potentially most major decision areas confronted by SOE managers. Several areas were omitted, mainly because there is insufficient data at present to extend the case studies into these areas.

The remainder of this chapter will examine CVG and CVRD within the context of the model presented, using the case method to analyze for each policy area the dynamics of policy determination in the holding companies and their subsidiaries. The emphasis will be on coalition politics within the SOE among the current mix of engineers and commissars in charge. In dealing with the overall behavior pattern of an SOE, it can be said that it will range within the limits of two extremes, or ideal types:

> SOE as textbook example   ⟷   SOE as textbook example
> of private enterprise   of government agency

If every policy of the company fell into the second column in the model in Table 6.2 (profit maximization), the SOE would be a pure textbook type of private enterprise; by the same token, if all policies fell into the social-subsidization category, the SOE would approach the status of being a pure government agency. But it is for the hybrid character of the typical SOE in mixed economies that this model is most suitable.

To sum up, it is the goal of this chapter to show that:

1. Overall behavior in SOEs tends to be mixed.
2. The range of managerial strategy tends to be greater in SOEs than in private enterprises because of the complications of outside influences.
3. Specific behavior in different policy areas of an SOE will vary with respect to the four categories of behavior (profit maximization, risk minimization, autonomy maximization, and social subsidization).
4. Different policies within a single SOE are likely to appear to be inconsistent, although taken as a whole they may provide a "baroque solution" to a complex of divergent forces.

Because this model seeks to capture the complexity and the variability of SOE behavior, it makes small claim to finding simple explanations or predictions for why a particular SOE does or will do *X*. But within the limits of its range, the remainder of this chapter will attempt to explore the determination of behavior of CVG and CVRD in the policy areas suggested by the model.

6.3   CVG and CVRD observed

Pricing and competition policy

In international markets with many suppliers, a state-owned company will have no choice but to price competitively if it wishes to sell its good abroad. Engineers will at least get the benefits of autonomy should they have to operate in the rough and tumble of such international markets. Should a government feel pressure to increase exports for balance-of-payments purposes, it will encourage its SOE to be a revenue maximizer in its export activities. Equally, if any monopolistic power can be gained, both engineers and commissars will agree on exploiting that power. If the government does not concern itself with exports in the area of the SOE in question, however, it may well impose restrictions that inhibit sales in international markets. In iron ore, CVG and CVRD illustrate these tendencies.

The Venezuelan government is hardly desperate for balance-of-payments improvements through iron-ore exports, given ever-growing export receipts from the oil sector (1975 oil exports were valued at $8.3 billion vs. $279 million for iron-ore exports).[10] Before Venezuelan mines were nationalized in 1975, U.S. Steel had mined Venezuelan ores and shipped the bulk of them to the United States. To protect tax income, the Venezuelan government set minimum export prices for the ore based on high American domestic prices. After nationalization, Ferrominera, the unified state iron-ore company, found itself forced to continue the prenationalization policy of charging high prices, even at the cost of lower sales. Whereas the government feared a sort of postcolonial giveaway of natural resources, the former owners saw no reason to favor Venezuelan ores as they no longer owned the mines. Export sales, therefore, are half of what they formerly were in the best years. There is evidence that the managers of the company remaining from prenationalization days would much prefer a different strategy, but their influence is limited in part by their past association with the American companies. To the commissars, they are a bit suspect.

The Brazilian government's need for export performance is well known, so that with regard to export goals, the commissars and the engineers agree. The goal is export revenue maximization (as opposed to profit maximization) in iron ore. The world iron-ore market, within limits competitive, results in impersonal forces that leave CVRD engineers with a high degree of autonomy. As there is not much opportunity of exploiting monopoly power, the Brazilian strategy dictates that CVRD avoid joining international cartels, which might restrict output (e.g., the Association of Iron Ore Exporting Countries, or APEF), and that it simply try to find the balance of price and volume that maximizes export earnings. Incidentally, Venzuela *is* a member of APEF. In contrast, CVRD's strategy has meant fast-growing exports in the last 10 years and relatively stable exports even during the last several years of decline in the world steel industry.

The comparison between CVRD and CVG/Ferrominera in their respective domestic markets is also interesting. Both the Brazilian and the Venezuelan governments favor cheap iron-ore inputs as a boost for their domestic steel industries, and both control the internal price. In Venezuela, however, the government's ability to impose a social-subsidization policy in this respect appears to be greater for several reasons:

1. In Brazil, private iron-ore companies operate alongside CVRD, so their pressure prevents an unprofitably low price.
2. CVG/Ferrominera is a smaller company than CVRD and thus has less political influence.
3. Ferrominera's chief customer is another CVG subsidiary, Siderúrgica del Orinoco, or Sidor. In the coalition politics of CVG, Sidor's engineers have far more clout than Ferrominera's, as Sidor is older, larger, and has long been considered a "national champion." Sidor also loses money, whereas Ferrominera made profits, at least through 1979.

Thus, in Ferrominera's case, the possession of domestic monopoly power seriously restricted autonomy and weakened its case against a subsidized price to Sidor. Only when Ferrominera was also in danger of losing money in 1980 was the government disposed to raise the price for domestic iron-ore sales.

The cases of other CVG and CVRD industries illustrate some of the above tendencies further. Steel is really a peripheral part of CVRD's business, as it has only small minority interests in other state steel firms. For CVG, however, steel is central and a dominant focus of its efforts. For the Venezuelan government, steel is likewise central, representing a huge investment in "development." Although the government may talk quite a bit about future exports of steel from Sidor, the absence of balance-of-payments pressures translates into only weak demands for foreign currency inflows from this sector. The government does wish to demonstrate that revenues from oil have been successfully invested in diversification of the economy, however, so that token or subsidized exports are possible and even likely. However, if exposed to a free market in steel, domestically or internationally, Sidor would cease to exist. Thus, both engineers and commissars came to agree that the company should be granted monopoly power at home, through a combination of protective tariffs and the granting of an official monopoly on steel imports (which are then resold, usually at a profit). Although there is a successful private steel company, Sivensa, its success rests heavily on the fact that the two companies have divided the domestic market between them by mutual agreement. Even though Sidor does get this special treatment from the government, it still faces limits on the extent to which it is allowed to exercise monopoly power domestically. Steel, after all, is an input to *other* industries the Venezuelans wish to develop, so the Development Ministry does control prices. Sidor's engineers spend much time and effort trying to get price increases, arguing constantly both in private and in the public news media.

Sidor thus exemplifies the shifting politics implicit in pricing policy: Because competition is out of the question, the company seeks monopoly power domestically and engages in a tug-of-war over the government's desire for social subsidization of private industry via low domestic prices.

The aluminum industry provides more variations on the theme. Valesul, the aluminum company in Rio owned by CVRD, will be entering a domestic market in competition with private local producers, both national and foreign. This gives the company a certain amount of operating autonomy. There are limits on the government's tendency to control domestic prices, as too onerous a price-control would lead to the exit of private industry from the field. This would conflict with the Brazilian strategy of promoting the private sector.

Alcasa, the CVG–Reynolds joint venture (50:50 until 1980), confronts a slightly different situation, as until recently it had a monopoly on primary aluminum production in Venezuela. This would normally mean more social-subsidization requirements and less autonomy for the company, but actually, the 50% ownership of the company by a foreign corporation decreased the power of the commissars in CVG and prevented the appointment of commissars in Alcasa. Alcasa remained free as long as it did not exploit its monopoly power too fully – and, indeed, Alcasa's prices were always set just comfortably above world levels but with less of a margin over the world price (about 10%) than found in other sectors of private Venezuelan industry. This restraint did not prevent Alcasa from charging higher prices in neighboring countries where there was a LAFTA tariff preference.[11] This behavior could be expected, given the likely congruence of commissar and engineer ideas on the subject.

Both CVG and CVRD have second aluminum companies, Venalum and Valenorte, respectively, and both have Japanese partners and an export orientation. Both have long-term sales contracts with the Japanese partners. Both sales contracts give discounts to the Japanese. Neither company has yet reached the point where it has to compete on the free-world market for aluminum, although CVG's Venalum may presently be at that point. Both governments took on partners to get exports not otherwise available and to stimulate an industry in which going it alone is both risky and technically difficult. Engineers have the option neither to exploit international monopoly power nor to enjoy the autonomy of operating in a free market; the only strategy left to them is also the strategy of the commissar: to wring as high a price as possible from the Japanese. Press reports and interviews in both companies provide evidence that the governments have renegotiation in mind, the outcome of which will be subject to Professor Vernon's "obsolescing bargain" and the usual determinants of bargaining power.[12]

Marketing and contracts policy

State-owned enterprises usually enjoy significant protection in domestic markets either because they operate monopolies or because they work out market-sharing arrangements with competitors. In countries that profess to a degree of capitalism, it would be rare for a government to wish to destroy a private competitor through price wars or similar sharklike activities. Engineers might wish to wipe out or weaken the competition, but commissars generally will not. In Brazil, CVRD engineers do worry about the disadvantages they suffer in their domestic iron-ore markets, but the reality is that mine location serves as the determinant of who sells to whom.[13] Only in Valesul, its Rio aluminum company, has CVRD come near to competing with the private aluminum companies serving the rich southeast of the country. Even though their production failed to cover needs, private companies mounted a campaign to move Valesul out of "their" territory. They formed an alliance with the minister of mines, arguing against *estatização*, or state take-over of the economy. Valesul allied itself with Rio de Janeiro interests who wanted more local investment and jobs and who used the press to make the domestic aluminum interests look like lackeys of foreign imperialism.[14] Valesul won in the end, in part because the private sector's argument that it could supply the whole market was weak, in part because Valesul engineers could exploit the lack of a coherent government policy on the question.

In Venezuela there is less domestic competition with the private sector and thus fewer "marketing" problems for state firms like CVG. There can be competition *within* the public sector. When there is competition between state enterprises in a home market, engineers in each company in question use a variety of competitive tactics to assure themselves of a maximum share of the domestic market. Engineers maneuver for position against other SOEs because the domestic market is *usually* more lucrative than the international market, where the cold winds of competition blow hard.[15] Commissars have no political preference as long as there are no special reasons for their sponsors to favor one company over another. Barring such special conditions, commissars are likely to back their own companies.

In CVG, two cases of intra-SOE rivalry stand out. The steel company, Sidor, currently faces the imminent creation of a new steel company in the west of the country. If steel demand had grown as predicted, by 1985 domestic demand would have begun to outstrip Sidor's installed capacity of 4.8 million metric tons. Siderzulia, the potential competitor, was scheduled to have a nominal capacity of 1.3 million tons by 1983.[16] Sidor, fearing overproduction, used market studies and cost studies to alert planners to the fact that Siderzulia should be delayed. In fact, the government appears to have accepted Sidor's view, as it put off all negotiations with potential Siderzulia partners (which still have not been chosen as of this writing) for a couple of years. This was wise, given that total Sidor sales in 1980 reached only 1.9 million tons.[17]

To a lesser degree, some jockeying for domestic position also appears to have occurred between the two CVG aluminum companies, Alcasa and Venalum. As the original monpolist, Alcasa received assurances that Venalum would not sell in the domestic market, except to one company, which would process molten aluminum for export. Despite the original agreement, however, it was not unlikely that Venalum engineers might covet some of Alcasa's customers. Indeed, several Venalum engineers mentioned that they had received "unsolicited" inquiries from Alcasa customers who thought that Venalum quality would prove superior. The natural competition between Venalum and Alcasa engineers may now be resolved by the decision of the government to take a majority interest in Alcasa, perhaps leading to a merger of policy making.

As for international marketing questions, recent observers have noted the tendency of SOEs to behave differently from private enterprises in foreign sales strategies.[18] One theme of such observations is that governments provide aid to SOEs in international markets, enabling them to obtain sales not otherwise available. Engineers, needless to say, would like such aid from the revenue point of view and may appreciate it more if it gives longer-term stability. They may at the same time hesitate to entwine themselves too tightly in a government network, especially if the government deals begin to provide political gains to the state instead of economic gains to the SOE. CVRD in Brazil has welcomed government-supported barter sales of iron ore in Eastern Europe and elsewhere, for instance.[19] In fact, a competing private iron-ore exporter complained that it should be let in on some of these deals too.

A long-term sales contract imposed on Alcasa by the CVG brought a contrary response from engineers in the subsidiary. When Alcasa needed capital infusions from its two owners in 1979, the private partner, Reynolds, began to balk at putting up more money. Reportedly as part of these negotiations, Reynolds received a contract to buy aluminum from Alcasa far below the market price. The interesting part is that local engineers within Alcasa saw the contract as negative for Alcasa itself and prejudicial to future sales in the Andean market. It can easily be seen here that in a joint venture, "engineers" representing a large company like Reynolds and "engineers" representing the local partner will have different criteria for optimal operations. CVG favored the agreement as a second-best solution because Alcasa needed the capital, but the end result was that the state bought out Reynolds shares to shift majority control to the Venezuelan Investment Fund (lessening the control of both CVG and Reynolds).[20]

With regard to preferences for long-term contracts, which Professor Vernon hypothesizes may be greater than in private enterprises,[21] CVRD and CVG do not provide much evidence, with one significant exception. In practically all cases of SOE–private-enterprise joint ventures, a long-term sales contract to the private partner was involved. As such arrangements were struck long before operations began, the engineers have few resources to influence them. Both commissars and local engineers tend to think that the bargain should be renegotiated later, so any resulting conflict will probably take place along national lines (local engineers and commissars against foreign engineers). Changes will depend on shifts in relative bargaining power. Already such a conflict has shaped up between Brazilians and Japanese in Valenorte and perhaps between Brazilians and their partners in pelletization. Similar testiness appeared in remarks about the terms of sales agreed on at the time of the creation of CVG's Venalum.

Supply policy

The model shows potential conflicts within the firm over where the SOE should buy its inputs. As developing countries, both Brazil and Venezuela have reason to impose the social-subsidization rule in favor of domestic suppliers. The impulse to do so would seem to be stronger in Brazil for balance-of-payments reasons. In fact, Brazil's tremendously complicated set of regulations requiring domestic purchasing is imposed on *both* private and state enterprises. CVRD engineers might wish they could buy from the lowest-cost supplier, but in most cases they simply cannot. Their only expedient is to claim that quality differences require foreign purchases, but there are limits to such claims.[22]

As could be expected, Venezuela's pressure for favoring local suppliers is weaker, although present (the government *does* want to stimulate domestic diversification). In Sidor, it was decided that contracts for earth-moving equipment, construction, and the like would necessarily go to Venezuelan companies on the assumption that there was enough domestic competition (more than one bidder) to justify this restriction. In favoring local suppliers, the Venezuelan government gives more favors to state enterprises than to private industry, usually to ensure the solvency of the SOE. Some SOEs benefit from this (if they are the local suppliers being favored) and others lose (if they are forced to buy from the other). One finds fewer such examples in CVRD because it tends to be relatively self-sufficient, owning its own railroad, ships, and so on.

A few examples from Venezuela: CVG companies must use the shipping services of the state company, Compañía Anónima Venezolana de Nevegación (CAVN). Ferrominera, Alcasa, and Venalum all complain about the quality of service, price, and reliability. Commissars from CVG support the subsidiaries in their complaints but do not go so far as to question the propriety of favoring CAVN. In one case, Ferrominera's engineers fought to arrange an alternative shipping contract with the former owner, U.S. Steel, to which CAVN objected. As it involved a battle between state enterprises, the issue was eventually decided by the president.[23] Alternatively, as has been mentioned, Sidor is an SOE that benefits from local supply requirements, as various regulations force private firms to buy Sidor products.

Supply policy also can be affected by more purely political considerations and may involve international relations. In at least one case, the Venezuelan government agreed to an alumina supply contract with Jamaica, at a concessionary price to the hard-pressed Jamaicans. The unwilling buyer, Venalum, risked a confrontation by refusing to go along with the volume specifications. This defiance, which involved a CVG manager who was hostile to the party in power, resulted in an altered agreement. Company–government conflicts, then, are subject to negotiation.

Employment policy

Engineers usually prefer, if the market permits, to work at the fullest capacity and with the fewest possible workers consistent with smooth operations. For both business and autonomy reasons, engineers want flexibility in making this sort of decision. Yet even among engineers (in private and public enterprises) one does expect to find the self-serving tendency to want to expand staff to increase one's personal importance or to maximize autonomy.[24] Although normally the owners can be expected to check such tendencies, students often find that governments use their SOEs to achieve such macroeconomic ends as employment maximization. Another influence in favor of employment creation in SOEs might be the desire of commissars to build up groups of faithful supporters thankful for jobs granted. But such hypotheses are difficult to prove, as there is rarely a good standard of comparison.

The evidence from CVRD and CVG gathered thus far hardly proves a case one way or the other. However, both cases do point to the dangers of uncritically assuming heavy pressures for employment creation or maintenance. In Venezuela hard-core unemployment does occur in marginal sectors, but this condition coexists with labor shortages at all but the most unskilled levels. The government therefore has little reason to push for featherbedding in CVG industries. Engineers in various companies did discuss their desires to streamline employment by efficiency improvements, but as all the companies have been growing, it is again difficult to know if such weeding out has occurred.

Despite the foregoing, CVG does provide one case of real cutbacks: Ferrominera. As noted earlier, iron-ore production has fallen far below its peak of the mid-1970s, implying that at least some workers would have been redundant. Were they laid off? Engineers claimed that they tried *not* to lay off their most skilled workers, for fear of never recovering them in better times. Additionally, both engineers and commissars prefer that declines in the industry should not become objects of public attention, signaling as they would defects in the post-nationalization process. One sign of artificial employment maintenance is the fact that production has risen significantly above sales volume. In 1980, total sales were 13.6 metric tons, but production reached 16.1 million tons.[25]

Given the far more serious employment situation in Brazil, the government might be predicted to fit more closely the pattern of requiring employment sub-sidization in its SOEs.[26] By the late 1970s, however, a number of factors worked in the contrary direction. One is the economic "crisis," which prompted the government to impose belt tightening throughout the entire governmental apparatus. CVRD had to accept an overall hiring freeze, and management therefore set ceilings for each of its divisions. Engineers grumbled at their loss of flexibility but could at least rejoice that they were not being made into employers of last resort. To provide themselves with some flexibility in hiring, they used some contract labor for some unskilled positions. Engineers can also thwart government efforts to use SOEs as sources for political appointments. A Valesul manager proudly recounted how that company managed to reject a list of employees sent over by the ministry by requiring examinations for jobs. (One commissar did get an executive-level job, but that was considered a small concession that the company could easily live with.)

In summary, the sketchy evidence at hand shows that SOEs need not demonstrate classic cases of obesity in employment. Engineers prefer to run a tight organization if possible, and economic problems may produce employment restraints rather than employment creation. SOEs will always employ some commissars, of course. Even that, as will be seen, may not always be such a bad thing.

Diversification policy: products and markets

Normal business instincts impel engineers to favor product and market diversification, at least where risk remains low. Of course, risks for companies abroad tend to be high in general, whereas risks for SOEs at home tend to be lower than the norm. Thus, engineers are likely to have a domestic bias that is reinforced by the more purely domestic perspectives of the commissars. To the extent that SOEs do diversify, their autonomy grows apace. The complexity of a multiple-subsidiary company makes it all the more difficult for the politicians or the public to know what is going on.

In principle, product diversification does not conflict with social-subsidization requirements unless it requires scarce outside capital or unless it interferes with markets already claimed by other companies. As for purchasing existing firms, engineers try to resist as much as possible having to take over failing companies, but governments the world over resort to the SOE bailout for social reasons. In the same spirit, commissars may want to hold on to sick subsidiaries, whereas engineers would normally cut their losses. One can thus imagine internal conflicts over what to do about virtually all diversification questions involving foreign investment, new capital, entering into competition with existing companies, or bailing out losers.

With regard to foreign investment by SOEs, observers have spotted large SOEs from developed countries acting like garden variety multinational corporations.[27] The political constraint against such behavior should be greater in developing countries where the whole purpose of the SOE is, in theory, the development of the *home* country. Neither CVG nor CVRD has yet made an investment abroad except as an ancillary part of its main lines of business. CVRD has considered such investments (coal mining in Canada, iron-ore processing in Egypt and Mexico) but has not yet carried through on any. Both companies have sales subsidiaries abroad, and CVRD has both a finance subsidiary in the Caribbean and a shipping company registered in Liberia. The regional development mission of CVG could account for the fact that CVG's engineers face stricter limits on investment choice.

In terms of domestic diversification, both CVG and CVRD have added new lines of business, within the limits set by government policy on competition. In only two cases has CVG taken over companies known to be failing. The first was Minorca, a subsidiary of U.S. Steel in which USS was pressed to keep a 49% share at the time of the nationalization of its iron-ore interests in 1975. In 1980, CVG also bought out the foreign shares in the troubled Venbozel formerly owned by the French company Nobel. But continued operations were in doubt as losses have continued in both companies.

CVRD maintains investments in some uneconomic mines for purely social reasons, but these are small enough not to create significant drains on resources. CVRD's diversification policy appears to be limited only by government restrictions forbidding entry into industries where private enterprises or other SOEs already operate.[28] Kept out of steel and other downstream industries in the southeast, CVRD looked to the north and to diversification into other minerals – copper, manganese, and so on. There have also been strategic moves by company management to ensure CVRD's future role in controlling those mineral resources.[29] As the presence of private competition is the chief limit on SOE diversification in such mixed economies, CVRD is making the rational preemptive move from the engineer's point of view. Like the best generals, they are striking where the enemy is not.

Financial and tax policy

Engineers try to procure, when unconstrained, the cheapest finance available, like their private-industry equivalents. If this means government financing or subsidies, autonomy usually suffers. SOEs are freest when they finance themselves, particularly with self-generated funds. The government has no particular desire to spend its resources to support SOEs. Thus, arguments for government loans depend on persuading the purseholders that the SOE itself is an object worthy of social subsidization. The second-best solution for the SOE is a government handout of equity capital without strings or a hidden subsidy that no one will remember exists.

For years, CVG managed to keep relative financial autonomy because the government willingly advanced equity infusions on the ground that it would make a high social rate of return in the future. Whatever the social return, the financial rate of return has not yet lived up to expectations. When the 1970s arrived and brought increased oil earnings, one might have expected even greater official indulgence, but not so. The avalanche of petrodollars raised fears of mindless spending and inflation, and in response the government set up the Investment Fund (the Fondo de Inversiones, the FIV), whose job was to invest the new wealth responsibly. The FIV has become powerful by insisting on owning shares rather than giving loans, thus diluting the ownership of some SOEs among state bodies. CVG and FIV are uneasy partners; CVG commissars at the holding-company level view these developments with profound dismay, as their relative power in the government hierarchy has diminished. This inter-commissar rivalry is possible because the government has been willing to let its representatives "fight it out" without directives from above about what would be a desirable outcome.

Faced with similar choices, CVRD has managed more successfully to finance itself, although expansion plans in recent years have begun to strain this ability. In trying to arrange financing for the Carajás iron-ore project, which was originally to be a joint venture with U.S. Steel, CVRD has faced tough bankers' conditions. In an effort to reduce overall capital outlays, CVRD also moved to lessen its equity obligations for the first stage of the Albrás aluminum project.[30] In fact, one of the most important sources of capital for new projects is the partner in joint ventures. As we shall see, this expedient brings its own problems.

As engineers prefer autonomy with regard to investment policy, they try to maximize the retained earnings of the SOE. Both taxes and dividends remove resources for autonomy from the firm. In fact, tax payments from CVRD and CVG appear to be rare, even when compared to the private sector. CVG itself pays no taxes because of its status as a development institute; among its subsidiaries, the situation is almost the same. Thus far, only Ferrominera has paid any significant taxes, apparently because the tax law affecting it was devised before nationalization. CVRD has been almost as successful as CVG, mainly avoiding taxes by investment tax credits and the like.

The reasons an SOE both wants subsidies (profits expansion) and does not want them (autonomy loss) should now be clear. What both engineers and commissars predictably prefer is a subsidy that is hidden from both the public and curious political opponents. Hidden subsidies rarely make a company dependent on political whim, as few people even notice them. Welfare economists may write volumes about how all subsidies must be overt and accounted for – but that is exactly what people in SOEs do *not* want. Governments might in some ways like the idea of an open subsidy system, but even they want to create the impression that the SOE is doing better than it is. Why do governments seem so weak in demanding a financial return from their SOEs? Perhaps because SOE managers have an easy time convincing governments that resources kept in the firm are resources spent on development. Or at least the governments are easily convinced.

Partnership policy

As the model in Table 6.2 shows, all parties involved in running SOEs – governments, commissars, and engineers – at times have reasons to favor joint ventures. There are reasons not to favor them too, depending on domestic capabilities in capital raising and management. Ideally, of course, a government likes control over its SOEs; often, however, it does not have the resources to go it alone. Engineers may like private partners to the extent that the power of the commissars is thereby reduced, but once there is mixed participation, especially foreign participation, *the nature of the managing coalition changes radically.* Engineers placed by the outside partner develop two loyalties: one to the SOE itself and one to the stronger, mother company, which really determines their long-term career chances. In cases of conflict of interest between private shareholder and SOE, they are like the commissars for the private owners. Self-interest in this case produces conflict among engineers on some questions, even though they might ally themselves on all other questions. As we have seen, commissars in one SOE do not seem to appreciate joint ventures with other SOEs – perhaps they even dislike this kind of joint venture the most.[31]

Both CVG and CVRD have extensive joint ventures with private-sector partners. Rarely does either one hold minority ownership (de jure) in any company where a foreign partner is in the majority. CVRD was considering giving up its control over Albrás, but only temporarily and because of a lack of capital. In a few other cases, CVG and CVRD hold minority shares where the majority partner is national. Managers representing different partners are likely to struggle for operating control, whether engineers or commissars. This conflict is especially clear in CVG's Alcasa and Venalum, where local personnel resent the influence of Reynolds personnel. In effect, local engineers suspect their colleagues of being commissars for the partner company instead of being fellow engineers. In Ferrominera, similar patterns were found involving pre- and post-nationalization managers and even involving conflict between local personnel who formerly worked for one or the other of the former concessionaires. Government commissars support the local engineers on nationalistic principles as long as they do not suspect them of allying too closely with foreign or private partners. If trends thus far show anything, it is that these pressures will prompt the government to buy out foreign partners if conditions permit. The Venezuelans bought up controlling Japanese shares in Venalum not long after new oil revenues eased the problem of capital shortage; conflict also led to the recent take-over of majority control in Alcasa.

CVRD's joint ventures follow a pattern similar to those of CVG. Foreign partners are a sort of necessary evil, particularly when export contracts form part of the initial package. In the one case where CVRD took over foreign shares (AMZA-Carajás), the initial move came from the foreign partner, U.S. Steel. CVRD engineers and commissars profess to be happy with the outcome, despite the financing problems it implies.[32] CVRD does not generally share ownership with other government entities, except in steel, and in that case some unhappiness with the situation was expressed. In another case, CVRD danced another variation on the joint-venture theme. Minas Serra Geral, an iron-ore company, is a joint venture with Japanese steel interests, mainly Kawasaki Steel. CVRD owns 51%. Why foreign partners in an area that CVRD could presumably develop itself? Perhaps CVRD simply wanted capital otherwise unavailable. Perhaps CVRD was looking ahead, as this venture forms part of a wider relationship with Kawasaki Steel, which is the chief partner in the building of a new steel company located at CVRD's port at Tubarão.

A word about private local partners: In both Brazil and Venezuela the governments profess a desire to encourage local capitalism. In Brazil, the government goes so far as to claim that it hopes to give up control of many SOEs as soon as private enterprise can take over, presumably on the condition that excessive industrial concentration does not result. But joint ventures with foreigners are far more common because of the greater resources available to multinational corporations compared to local industry, even in countries as developed as Brazil and Venezuela. Whether or not a real denationalization will ever take place is another question – but both engineers and commissars would probably resist. (Engineers may complain about having to put up with the government as owner, but even lame men grow accustomed to their crutches.)

Information policy

It is a private peeve of researchers that state-owned enterprises tend to be secretive. This does not distinguish them from private enterprises, surely, but the idea of public service leads one naively to hope otherwise. Engineers naturally seek to advertise good results and to hide bad ones, from both the public and the government. Commissars and their external counterparts tend to agree on this point, at least with respect to keeping the *public* only partially informed. Thus, the incentives for disclosure are practically nil. At least when private companies keep secrets, governments feel like adversaries and pass disclosure laws requiring reports and the like. Most SOE constitutions similarly define requirements for annual reports, but given the incentives for sugarcoating, these must be approached with care.

The government does not want information that it might judge unsuitable for public ears. Unfortunately for the bureaucrats and politicians, they suffer a distinct disadvantage vis-à-vis the engineers, as the engineers have a day-to-day knowledge of the firm that outsiders lack. Here the role of the commissar becomes important: Commissars can alert the government or outside interests to events worth noting. This may even be positive, depending on the effectiveness of the commissar.

CVG offers many examples of these tendencies. Annual reports are hard to come by, and for many subsidiaries, these are practically internal documents. CVG annual reports have been issued as much as three years late. Press releases are often less than lucid. The press may fall down on the job also, however, especially as journalists often ''report'' but rarely analyze. One institution that does disseminate valuable information in Venezuela is the Contraloría General of the Congress. Naturally, it is considered to be excessively negative, but its investigations have led to actual firings for ineptitude and corruption.

Some of the same attitudes surface in CVRD. There the engineers expressed some disdain toward the ministry in charge, saying that the ministry knows little of what goes on, understands it less, and that therefore they (the engineers) try to have as little to do with it as possible. CVRD *seems* somewhat more open with standard public information, but this apparent difference could have much to do with the fact that CVRD's performance has been less embarrassing. And although one would expect Brazil's press to be reticent about criticism, they have at times been allowed to go quite far in making "constructive" criticism of the public sector.

6.4 Conclusions

One expectation of this chapter was that SOEs would exhibit complex behavior, not subject to simple categorization. This was not only because governments set unclear goals but also because even the traditional profit maximizers, the engineers, face internal conflicts. As a result, the overall behavior of the typical SOE in developing mixed economies like Brazil and Venezuela tends to be a mélange, varying according to policy, power shifts, and the business and economic environment. The examples given here certainly showed a wealth of conflict within the firms, as well as between them and the governments and other bodies controlling them. This conflict approach better allows us to get at the richness and variability of SOE behavior than a more monolithic approach.[33]

Looking at SOE behavior at disaggregated policy levels also permitted a more detailed analysis of the possibilities of SOE actions and showed as well the necessity for a fairly detailed knowledge of the political and economic context in which the SOE operates. I would argue that we are not yet and probably never will be at the point where we can make broad statements like "SOEs are risk takers," or "SOE managers are less profit-conscious than managers in private industry." What we can do is specify under what conditions an SOE is more likely to take risks or pursue profits. Even this kind of analysis demands a view of the interactions among policy choices in the firm.

The assumption that a large class of managers of SOEs are similar to private-enterprise managers in terms of goals (but not in terms of tactics available to them) is strongly supported by the cases of CVG and CVRD. It explains not only strictly textbook maximizing behavior but also subsidy-seeking and self-seeking behavior. Also, the engineers' drive for autonomy opens up extra lines of action, adding further realism and complexity to the picture.

The chapter looked at CVG and CVRD principally from the vantage point of a single period in which the research was carried out. This perhaps created the false impression that the balance between engineers and commissars within the companies was a given. In reality, this too must be a variable. A dynamic view of change in the SOE would have to incorporate some theory of change, in which perhaps the government–SOE bargaining process itself is the motor of evolution. Alternatively, changes in performance[34] or changes in government needs alter the balance, as would environmental events like market reversals.

If it seems that this chapter failed to advance far down the road toward predicting regularities and making general statements, it should be remembered that we did not have much hope of this at the outset. But neither can it be said that CVG or CVRD emerged as either unpredictable or irrational, as in explaining their behavior, the simple framework offered here provided a reasonable method for making sense out of rather complex and apparently contradictory policies.

Notes

1 For information on the CVG, see its Annual Reports and, particularly, República de Venezuela, Corporación Venezolana de Guayana, *Informe Quinquenal: 1974-78.*
2 According to CVRD, *Annual Report* (1978), and CVG, "Estados Financieros" (Dec. 1978). The exchange rates used were those prevailing officially at the end of 1978. Exchange-rate vagaries can be extremely important in the case of Brazil.
3 From the beginning, however, a fund for the development of the Rio Doce area was set up. A short history of the CVRD, "Escola Superior de Guerra," mimeographed (June 25, 1964), was prepared by the company itself.
4 In 1978, CVRD exported 42 million tons of iron ore (excluding iron-ore pellets from subsidiaries of 1.9 million metric tons). In the same year, CVG's iron-ore subsidiary exported only 12.9 million tons, which was far below the high export year of 1974, when CVG exports reached 26 million tons. Data from CVRD, *Annual Report* (1978); República de Venezuela, Ministerio de Minas y Energía, *Hierro y Otros Datos Estadísticos* (1976); CVG, *Annual Report* (1978).
5 One event that could increase the similarities between CVG and CVRD would be the reform of CVG's structure, which is sporadically discussed in Venezuela. One idea calls for splitting CVG into two separate entities: a regional development agency and an industrial holding company.
6 As in Kalman J. Cohen and Richard M. Cyert, *Theory of the Firm: Resource Allocation in a Market Economy* (Englewood Cliffs, N.J.: Prentice-Hall, 1965), p. 331.
7 Richard Schmalensee, *The Control of Natural Monopolies* (Lexington, Mass.: Lexington Books, 1979), p. 97, drawing from J. B. Sheahan, "Public Enterprise: Ideas from West European Experience" (Paper presented at the American Economic Association Annual Meeting, New York, 1977). Also, O. E. Williamson, "A Model of Rational Managerial Behavior," in Cohen and Cyert, *Theory of the Firm*, Chap. 9.
8 Accepting the definition offered in Robert W. Sexty, "Autonomy Strategies of Government-Owned Business Corporations in Canada" (Paper presented at the State-Owned Enterprises Conference, Harvard University, March 27, 1979), p. 9.
9 J. K. Galbraith, *The New Industrial State* (New York: New American Library, 1967), Chap. 7.
10 Banco Central de Venezuela, *Informe Económico* (1975), pp. A-176 and A-184.
11 In at least one sales contract, according to an Alcasa manager, Alcasa sold aluminum to a Peruvian buyer for 24% above a sales price to an international dealer.
12 *Metal Bulletin*, June 3, 1980.
13 E.g., an internal CVRD economic review noted CVRD's disadvantages resulting from poor mine location and relatively limited reserves in the Minas Gerais industrial region. See Superintendencia de Orcamento e Desenvolvimento, "Boletín de Conjunctura Internacional," No. 1 (May 1977).
14 Various newspaper stories on the conflict before the public between February and May 1979. Supporting Valesul were such articles as "A Guerra do alumino," *Tribuna da Imprensa*, March 9, 1979, and "Transferencia para o Norte tornará a Valesul inviável," *Jornal do Brasil*, March 16, 1979.
15 High domestic prices are most probable in developing countries with mixed economies, where production inefficiencies are likely to exist, thus producing higher costs and dependence on protection. The exception to the rule whereby SOEs compete for domestic sales applies to situations where the domestic sale price is controlled at a very low level, usually for political reasons. In Venezuela, for instance, the national oil companies do not compete seriously for domestic sales outlets because the controlled price of gasoline is far below international levels.
16 Fondo de Inversiones, *Memoria Anual* (1978), p. 50.

17 CVG Sidor, *Informe Anual* (1980), p. 19.

18 For instance, Raymond Vernon, "The International Aspects of State-Owned Enterprises," mimeographed (Harvard University, July 1979), and M. M. Kostecki, "International Implications of State Trading by the Advanced Countries" (Paper presented at the State-Owned Enterprises Conference, Harvard University, March 27, 1979); also, Douglas F. Lamont, *Foreign State Enterprises: A Threat to American Business* (New York: Basic Books, 1979).

19 It should be understood that "barter" in this context does not necessarily mean that CVRD itself trades iron ore for something else. The barter could be a wider deal involving other parts of the Brazilian state, in which promises are made to buy or trade some good in return for the iron-ore sale. In a recent deal, for instance, Poland agreed to buy iron ore in return for Brazilian use of Polish equipment and technology in coal production. See *Metal Bulletin*, May 6, 1980.

20 As of Dec. 15, 1980. *El Universal*, Jan. 7, 1981.

21 Vernon, "International Aspects of State-Owned Enterprises," p. 16.

22 An interesting example is the hiring of foreign, often Chinese, sailors for the CVRD shipping subsidiary Docenave. CVRD managers mentioned that the Brazilians do not make the best sailors, and they try to resist government pressures to "hire native." One engineer strategy has been to register some ships under flags of convenience.

23 Here one could perceive an alliance between the foreign company involved (U.S. Steel) and the local engineers in Ferrominera, whose interests coincided. For an official account of the argument, see República de Venezuela, Contraloría General, *Informe* (1978).

24 Cohen and Cyert, *Theory of the Firm*, p. 355.

25 Banco Central de Venezuela, *Informe Económico* (1980), p. 229.

26 "Dependency" theorists would probably *not* predict that Brazil's government would use SOEs for employment creation. In this view, state enterprises and private enterprises are engaged in a mutually supportive venture to develop the country in alliance with foreign capital and without regard to income distribution questions. One author who refers to labor-repressive policies in Brazil is Peter Evans, *Dependent Development: The Alliance of Multinational, State and Local Capital in Brazil* (Princeton: Princeton University Press, 1979).

27 Robert Gilpin, *U.S. Power and the Multinational Corporation* (New York: Basic Books, 1975), pp. 242–4.

28 Although limitation on competition between SOEs and private industry seems to be typical of developing countries with mixed economies, it may not apply to developed countries. This could be explained by the fact that private industry is weaker in developing countries, where the supposed purpose of SOEs is to supplement the private sector, not to make life more difficult for it.

29 See "Superintendency for Carajás?" *Metal Bulletin*, June 6, 1980.

30 *Metal Bulletin*, June 3, 1980.

31 E.g., see "La CVG pierde influencia," *Número* (Caracas), June 8, 1980.

32 "CVRD Looks for Carajás Takers," *Metal Bulletin*, May 2, 1980.

33 The same point is made by Donald P. Warwick in "A Transactional Approach to the Public Enterprise" (Paper presented at the second BAPEG conference on Public Enterprise in Mixed Economy LDCs, Boston, Apr. 1980). Although the language in Warwick's paper is different from that used here, the basic conflict-oriented approach is the same.

34 In this context, Albert Hirschman's *Exit, Voice and Loyalty: Responses to Decline in Firms, Organizations and States* (Cambridge: Harvard University Press, 1970) offers some challenging ideas about individual and mass behavior under conditions of change.

7 Decision structure, technological self-reliance, and public-enterprise performance

V. V. Bhatt

The characteristic feature of the development process – since World War II in both the developed and the developing countries – is the deliberate assumption by the state of the function of regulating the pace and pattern of socioeconomic development. The major declared objectives of state policies in less-developed countries (LDCs) include sustained progressive improvement in the levels of living, reduction of inequality in the distribution of income, wealth, and economic power, and technological self-reliance (which constitutes both an instrument as well as an objective). It has been difficult, however, in a large number of LDCs to translate these multiple and often conflicting objectives into *operative goals*[1] of the various *holons*[2] – subsystems of the government organizational system – with the result that these objectives, in actual fact, have remained largely of *ceremonial* significance.

The economist's solution to this problem is quite simple. When the multiple objectives are appropriately weighted, there is a consistent preference or objective function. Given "right" prices – decision signals – it would not be difficult to choose the best course from *all* the possible alternative courses of action.[3] However, this is not how organizations function in the real world of considerable complexity and uncertainty. The operative goals and the information structure – or to use Arrow's expressive phrase, the agenda[4] – of each subsystem is a function of its location in the multileveled hierarchy of the government system,[5] its past history,[6] the quality of its top management,[7] and the complexity of its task and social environment.[8] It is thus essential to study the decision structure and processes of the organizational system and how they change.

The Swaraj tractor case is interesting from many points of view. It is related to technological self-reliance, which is one of the major declared objectives of a large number of LDCs. It indicates the *different yet rational* response of various parts of the governmental system to a common problem – the problem of responding to a concrete case of indigenously developed design, the Swaraj tractor. It shows how the entrepreneurial ability of a few individuals had fruitful results because of the *existence* of (1) a plurality of decision centers with different agendas and (2) the technological infrastructure necessary for creative adaptation of modern technology. At the same time, it pinpoints the limitations of the existing

129

decision structure and processes from the point of view of the objective of technological self-reliance and suggests the organic functional linkages required for
institutionalizing this objective. Thus, this case study has relevance not only for
India but also for other LDCs that have similar problems and objectives.

This chapter is divided into three sections. The Swaraj story is only briefly
narrated in Section 7.1, as this case has been discussed in considerable detail elsewhere.[9] The decision structure and behavior of the various concerned subsystems
are analyzed in Section 7.2. In the final section, an attempt is made to indicate, in
the light of this case study, an alternative decision structure that could effectively
shape the operative goals of the concerned subsystems so as to reflect the objective
of technological self-reliance.

7.1   The Swaraj story

Before presenting the Swaraj tractor case,[10] it is essential to give some background
with regard to the tractor industry in India. Farm mechanization started only after
World War II. The domestic production of tractors, however, started in 1963–4
with a licensed installed capacity on a two-shift basis of 16,000 units by three firms
– Tractor and Farm Equipment (TAFE), Eicher Tractors India, Ltd. (Eicher), and
Hindustan Tractors, Ltd. (HTL) – the first with a capacity of 7,000 units, the
second with 2,000 units, and the third with 7,000 units. TAFE was permitted
foreign collaboration with Massey-Ferguson of the United Kingdom in 1961,
Eicher with Eicher of the Federal Republic of Germany in 1961, and HTL with
Motokov of Czechoslovakia in 1960. As against this domestic capacity, it was
estimated that the demand for tractors would increase substantially as a result of
the adoption of the new agricultural strategy in Punjab, Haryana, and western
Uttar Pradesh (the parts of India growing wheat on irrigated land). However, in
view of relatively small holdings, the problem faced by the planning commission
was to identify the type of tractor that would suit the budget and the needs of
farmers with small to medium landholdings.

The commission had estimated the demand for tractors to be 40,000 units per
year by 1968–9, of which half was expected to be for tractors in the range of 20 hp
and below. For the small farms in India it was essential to have low horsepower,
multipurpose tractors suited to their needs and resources. The multinational
companies were producing tractors of 30 hp and above, using obsolete technology. Russian assistance was sought in 1965, but this implied a large foreign-
exchange cost and a large number of Russian experts. At any rate, the Russians
suggested the purchase of 20-hp tractors from Czechoslovakia. Mr. M.M. Suri,
the director of the Central Mechanical Engineering Research Institute (CMERI),
one of the national laboratories under the auspices of the Council of Scientific and
Industrial Research (CSIR), convinced the planners that India had the capacity to
design, engineer, and manufacture a 20-hp tractor suited to the specific Indian
conditions. The CMERI team (under the leadership of Mr. Suri and his deputy,

Mr. Chandra Mohan) set to work on this design and by 1970, after repeated experiments and trials, the Swaraj tractor design was completed. It passed the rigorous test of the Tractor Training and Testing Station (TTTS), a test that only two other tractors (Zeteor and Massey-Ferguson) had passed.

Thus, by 1971, the Swaraj tractor was ripe for commercial production. But the question was: Who would adopt this innovation? Earlier, the prototype was constructed with the assistance of a public-sector concern – the Mining and Allied Machinery Corporation (MAMC) – and it was expected that MAMC would be able to undertake the tractor project with the addition of only some balancing equipment. But in the 1967–71 industrial recession, MAMC had incurred financial losses and was not willing to take the additional risk involved in the production of the new tractor. Although another public-sector concern – Hindustan Machine Tools (HMT) – did want to diversify and go into the tractor business, it did not want to take the risk of producing the Swaraj Model; it preferred Zeteor, a 20-hp tractor of Czech design, on the ground that it was a production model, whereas Swaraj was still a prototype. Neither the central government nor the CSIR nor the National Industrial Development Corporation (NIDC) – the central government industrial consultancy organization – actively supported the results of the Swaraj experiment, although it had been initiated as a result of a decision at the highest level. However, they did support several other projects with foreign collaboration, which produced tractors in the range of 30 hp and above.

It was at this stage that a state government unit decided to produce the Swaraj tractor. The Punjab State Industrial Development Corporation (PSIDC), set up in 1966 with the object of promoting medium and large industries in the state, obtained an industrial license to manufacture the Swaraj tractor in 1970.

The PSIDC contacted the CMERI and requested the latter to release the five engineers who had worked on the Swaraj design for its new firm, Punjab Tractors, Ltd. (PTL). Simultaneously, it appointed the consulting firm M/s Suri & Associates, organized by Mr. Suri after he left the CMERI, to prepare a detailed project report and undertake the entire installation and commissioning of the plant along with the company's engineers (the CMERI group). The detailed project report was completed by the middle of 1971. The next question was: How to finance this project?

The central government was not willing to provide the required resources and the state government did not have the necessary surplus. So the PSIDC and the PTL approached the Industrial Development Bank of India (IDBI). The IDBI was set up in 1964 as an apex development bank to promote industrial development, particularly viable projects that could not obtain financing from the other institutions. Its charter is broad and flexible; it can finance any sound project, irrespective of ownership, organization, and size. Its top management had changed by the time the PTL approached it. Under this new management, the IDBI had taken up active promotional work with regard to the identification of project ideas in backward states and had a firm policy of supporting domestic technical consultancy services as a link between technological research and the production system.

But with the new IDBI management, PTL was not completely confident of obtaining financing to the tune of from 85 to 90% of the project cost. The lack of sponsorship by the central government and the skepticism about the project's success expressed by both the CSIR and the NICD made the PTL somewhat diffident about getting IDBI support. They therefore suggested only a modest project (capacity output of only 5,000 tractors) with a capital cost of less than Rs. 40 million.

The IDBI criteria of project selection were two: (1) domestic resource cost of saving one U.S. dollar should be equal to or less than Rs. 9.5 and (2) internal rate of return of the project should be 15% or more per annum. In addition, it required the promoter to contribute at least 15% of the project cost. The Swaraj project met the domestic resource-cost criterion, but the project's internal rate of return came to only 13% per annum and the PTL was unable to contribute more than 10% of the project cost.

But the IDBI top management was so much impressed by the quality of the detailed report, the Swaraj experiment, and the managerial capacity, technical competence, and motivation of the three critical groups – PSIDC, PTL, and the technical consultants – that it was, somewhat to the surprise of the PTL, willing to arrange for almost 90% of the financing of the project. The construction work as well as the installation of plant and equipment started immediately after the IDBI sanction of financial assistance in March 1972.

The performance of the PTL since 1972 has been remarkable both with regard to its cost and time schedules and the manner in which it faced and tackled the problems as they arose:

1. The project was completed in 105 weeks, by the end of March 1974, *as anticipated.*
2. The actual project cost, in spite of inflation, was more or less as expected – in fact it was somewhat lower – with regard not only to the total cost but also to the cost under each head.
3. The PTL started manufacturing the Swaraj tractor (Swaraj-724) on April 1, 1974, and reached its full-capacity output in 1978 (5,000 units) in spite of raw-material shortages, inflationary pressures, and financial stringency. It would have reached full-capacity output by 1977, as was anticipated, but for an unfortunate labor strike.
4. Swaraj has been, *as was expected,* a successful model, judging from the farmers' response. The PTL has been able to sell its entire output. Its distribution and service system has been superior to that of any other manufacturer in India.
5. It developed through its own research and development work two new designs – Swaraj-735 and Swaraj Economy; the first was introduced

by the end of 1975, the second year of its operation, and the other in 1978. The Swaraj Economy is the cheapest tractor in the international free market for equivalent performance and the PTL entered the export market in 1979.

It is worth mentioning that this new experiment in developing a product based on indigenous technology and know-how won recognition from the central government, which was not prepared to sponsor the Swaraj project in 1972. In 1975 the PTL was awarded the National Gold Shield, the country's highest award, for its contribution to the development of indigenous technology, know-how, and consultancy services. It is ironic to learn that the central government is still considering licensing another tractor plant with British Leyland collaboration.

7.2 Decision process: problems and conjectures

Such is the story of the Swaraj tractor. It raises several problems for analytic inquiry, problems relating to the behavior of various agencies. The following questions arise with regard to the Swaraj story:

1. Why did the central government not sponsor this project?
2. Why did the Punjab government take the risk of undertaking this project? What were the nature and characteristics of its decision process that accounted for its success?

Central government behavior

The decision to develop an indigenous tractor design was taken, at the initiative of the CMERI, by the *apex* decision-making body: the planning commission. The task was set to the CMERI under the direction of a Committee of Technical Experts (CTE) comprising representatives of industry, agricultural universities, farmers, and the Tractor Training and Testing Station. That this project and the objective of technological self-reliance that it represented had the support of the power system was indicated early. The CMERI could induce even the prime minister to intervene in the decision process in favor of the Swaraj experiment, when the agriculture minister was about to conclude an agreement with Czechoslovakia for the production of Zeteor tractors. Again, it was because of this high-level support that the CMERI could get the assistance of a public-sector concern, the Mining and Allied Machinery Corporation (MAMC), in developing the prototype.

But this phase of high-level support for the objective of technological self-reliance did not last long. Immediately after the work on Swaraj started, the prime minister was changed as well as the members of the planning commission. The director-general of CMERI's parent organization, CSIR, who had supported the Swaraj and similar experiments, retired and a new one with a different agenda was appointed; the new director-general emphasized research but *without links* with the industry. Mr. Suri consequently resigned to start his own consulting firm, Suri & Associates.

Thus by the time (1971) the Swaraj tractor was ripe for commercial production, the objective it represented had lost the support of the apex of the power system. The decision to implement the Swaraj project was thus to be taken by the concerned subsystems in the light of their own value systems.

The CSIR was lukewarm about the project. In a sense, being the apex body supervising the efforts at scientific and industrial research, the CSIR would be expected to support actively the Swaraj project. The CSIR did not have previous experience of this type and did not build the crucial information channels required for such a purpose; its agenda – operating goals and information structure – was related only to research and not to its application. It had no links with the Ministry of Industry nor with industry in general; it was responsible for its funding to the Department of Science and Technology, which judged it purely on the basis of its research activities. It was again because of the initiative of the CMERI and the CTE that CSIR even agreed to patent the Swaraj process with the National Research and Development Corporation (NRDC).

The NRDC in fact had the function of supporting and even promoting the projects based on the research results of the national laboratories, for which it had the patents. But the NRDC was also under the Department of Science and Technology and did not have the necessary links with industry to perform such a promotional function. It was passively supportive of the Swaraj project – it was in its interest, as it would get the patent fees if some industrial concern adopted its patent – but it did not play an active role.

The Industry Ministry did not want to take the risk of starting a new enterprise. It was in charge of public-sector industrial concerns, which were not that successful financially and were subject to considerable criticism in the Parliament. So it did not want to take the risk of starting a new one. It would have passively supported an existing *successful* public-sector concern that wanted to branch out into tractor business.[11]

In the field of engineering, there were two such enterprises, MAMC and HMT. The CTE had expected earlier that MAMC would be able to undertake the tractor project with the addition of only some balancing equipment. But in the 1967–71 industrial recession MAMC had incurred financial losses and was not willing to take the additional risk involved in the new tractor project.

The HMT was a financially successful enterprise that wanted to diversify its output by going into tractor production to offset the effects of the industrial recession on its performance. However, it wanted to use its unutilized capacity immediately by first going into assembly of Zeteor tractor parts imported from Czechoslovakia. But the CTE pressed the HMT, at the instance of CMERI, to consider Swaraj. So the HMT asked for advice from the National Industrial Development Corporation (NIDC), which was a consultancy organization sponsored by the central government and was under the Ministry of Industry. The NIDC favored Zeteor as it was a proved production model, whereas Swaraj was only a prototype. The HMT thus selected Zeteor.

With the development of Swaraj, the central government had the opportunity to translate its objective of technological self-reliance into an operative goal. But it could not become an operative goal of any subsystem of the central-government hierarchy as it did not fit into the agenda of any one of them. In these circumstances, the project would have been undertaken only if the prime minister and the cabinet had backed it, as they had done at the earlier stage of the experiment;[12] but the objective of technological self-reliance by this time no longer remained a dominant operative goal of the power system, in spite of its being an important development objective.

Decision making at the state level

In view of the skepticism, for whatever reason, about the Swaraj project on the part of the various central-government agencies, how did it come to pass that the Punjab state government decided to undertake this project? The agency responsible for this in the state government hierarchy was PSIDC. It would be expected from the central-government response that the PSIDC would have reservations. What then were the major considerations on the basis of which the PSIDC took the decision?

The Punjab government and the Punjab farmers were familiar with the whole process of evolution of the Swaraj. After all, the field trials were largely undertaken in the Punjab. The farmers had in a sense become part of this venture, and they had approved this new product, which was expected to save on both capital and operating costs. Further, the Punjabis are proud of their mechanical talents; one of the farmers had in fact successfully done "reverse engineering" – Japanese style – with regard to an East European tractor and had made a similar tractor in his own workshop. (Patent-rights violation prevented this farmer from undertaking small-scale production of this tractor.) Thus, the Punjabis were able to judge Swaraj on its merits and had a certain pride in owning a tractor based on technology and know-how developed in India and, more particularly, by the Punjabis.

This was one consideration. The other was the potential employment impact of the tractor project. The Swaraj was to purchase more than 80% of the components from ancillaries, mostly from the Punjab. And the Punjabis are known for their entrepreneurial and mechanical talents, as a result of which the Punjab boasts the most thriving small-scale industrial sector in India.

Thus the PSIDC was confident about the farmers' response, the employment impact, and, as a result, the financial success of the project. The PSIDC is an independent agency of the Punjab government with the function of promoting industrial development of the state. It is aware that it can perform this innovating function effectively only if its projects succeed in financial terms. For the Punjab government would not, could not, provide subsidies on a continuing basis; and even if it did, such subsidies would affect the ability of the PSIDC to function with a degree of independence and thus its ability to take risks and innovate.

Hardheaded, not romantic, pride in indigenous technology, the farmers' response, and the potential impact on employment and its own resources were the governing factors in the PSIDC's decision to take up this innovative project. For the central-government agencies, Swaraj was an abstraction; it did not have such a direct and visible impact on them as it had for the Punjab government and its agencies.

How do we account for the remarkable performance of the PTL? The comprehensive and illuminating detailed project report, the timely completion of the construction phase without any cost overrun, the timely realization of capacity output, the ways in which the top management tackled problems as they arose – the problem of sources of supply and the liquidity and financial problem – the new models developed through continuing research and development work, all these characteristics of project performance were indeed unique in the financing experience of the IDBI.

The factors that seem to account for this performance are:

1. Selection of the project by PSIDC on the basis of its visible and direct potential impact on its financial resources, Punjab farmers, and employment in small industries.
2. Selection of persons associated with the design of the Swaraj as technical consultants and top management personnel.
3. The powerful non-economic motivation of the technical consultants and top management in making a success of the project (the managing director, Mr. Chandra Mohan, who was on deputation from the CMERI, was to be paid only a salary fixed on the basis of central government scales, and Mr. Suri's fees were much below those charged by other consultants, Indian or foreign).
4. The enlightened development orientation of the IDBI top management and their policies; without the IDBI financial assistance and its own motivation to make it a success, it would have been difficult to undertake this project.

The Swaraj case illustrates the significance of (1) technological infrastructure and (2) the plurality of decision centers for creative adaptation of modern technology in a LDC.

The existence of Technological Research Centers (TRCs), like the CMERI under the aegis of the CSIR, and Technical Consultancy Service Centers (TCSCs), like Suri & Associates, provided the relevant information channels. Of course, the information provided by these channels did not prove decisive for the central-government agencies; their operative goals were determined by their respective locations in the decision structure and the way in which they received signals from their task and general environment. The Punjab state government and its agency, the PSIDC, functioned in a different task and general environment; the existing information channels provided information that was relevant for their operative goals and task environment. But the CMERI did not provide merely information: Without the entrepreneurial ability – the willpower to overcome obstacles[13] – of the Swaraj team at the CMERI, the Swaraj tractor probably would not have seen the light of day.

This entrepreneurial ability produced results because of the existence of a plurality of decision centers with different agendas. If the central government ignored this project, there was a state government that could consider it, or even a private enterprise could be approached. As against NIDC, there was a consulting firm, Suri & Associates. There were again alternative sources of finance; if government could not provide the required finance, IDBI was there to fill this function. In a world of uncertainty, the existence of such a plurality of decision centers with different agendas makes the *competitive learning process* possible and thus provides additional information channels for decision making.

The effective use of such additional information channels is a function of the decision structure. How it needs to be altered to translate the objective of techno-logical self-reliance into operative goals of various subsystems is the question discussed in the final section.

7.3   On restructuring the decision process

To realize the objective of technological self-reliance or the capacity for creative adaptation[14] of modern technology to specific resource endowments, many LDCs like India, Brazil, and Korea have set up a network of research institutes. In India these national research laboratories, or Technological Research Centers (TRCs), are designed around a discipline or technological specialty function under the auspices of the CSIR. But the way in which this technological research function is organized is such that the research system has hardly any communication channels with the production system. That each is under a separate ministry would not matter if these multileveled hierarchies were linked with communication channels at each relevant level. But not having such links, the two systems develop on parallel lines and their agendas do not interact. This structural characteristic appears to be the basic reason why the objective of technological self-reliance normally does not get translated into operative goals of either the· production system or the TRCs.[15]

The CMERI, which is one of the TRCs under the CSIR, tried during 1962-7 at the initiative of its director, Mr. Suri, to link its research with the real problems faced by industry.[16] It tried to identify research problems faced by industrial firms and conduct research on these problems with a view to solving real problems. Such contractual research helped CMERI in doing relevant research as well as in obtaining the financial resources required from industry; it helped the industry in obtaining solutions to its real problems. For this purpose, the CMERI strengthened its staff of academic scientists by recruiting trained industrial technologists with practical experience. The research team was specially built around a problem (project) rather than around a discipline or technological specialty (as is the case with the other TRCs under the CSIR) and was dissolved once the problem was solved. The Swaraj team is an example of such a policy.

However, this individual experiment did not last long. The CSIR asserted its own agenda of research; it did not like the CMERI industrial link and felt that this would be an obstacle to *pure* technological research. In addition, the CSIR top management did not like the CMERI's development as a distinct and financially viable identity, very much unlike its other TRCs, and thus an independent corporation with its own strategic management.[17] Mr. Suri, hence, had to resign.

The lack of communication channels between the production system and the TRCs and the resulting ineffectiveness of research in solving problems relating to creative adaptation of modern technology and upgrading of traditional technology have been emphasized in India's *Draft Fifth Five Year Plan.*[18] But the plan has not identified the concrete shape of these communication channels.

In identifying search or research problems, the crucial role of the design-engineering function is ignored. The Technical Consultancy Service Centers (TCSCs) perform this role and thus constitute a crucial link between the production system and the TRCs. Equally critical is the function of financing; unless the selection criteria of the financial system have a technological dimension, neither the project promoters nor the TCSCs would have an incentive for making "right" technological choices. Thus the financial system and the TCSCs provide channels, which in turn provide signals, for redesigning the setup of the TRCs.

The Swaraj case illustrates the significance of such communication channels between the production system and the TRCs. The organic and sequential relationship among the following tasks and functions seems to have been the crucial factor in the success of this experiment relating to the creative adaptation of modern technology.

Identification of a project idea on the basis of development strategy was the critical first stage. This was done by the planning commission. The identification of available technological choices for this was the second; this was the function of a TCSC (in this case the CMERI performed this function). Identification of a research problem by a TCSC (in this case the CMERI) was the third stage. The research on the problem by a TRC (in this case the CMERI) and the transmission of this research result to the TCSC (in this case Suri & Associates) was the fourth stage. The detailed project report by the TCSC (Suri & Associates) to the project promoter (PTL) and the financial system (IDBI) was the fifth stage. The association of the TCSC (Suri & Associates) with the top management for project implementation was the final stage.

In this organic sequential relationship, the critical functions identifying relevant research problems, embodying the research results meaningfully into a concrete project, and facilitating its implementation – were performed by the TCSC and the IDBI. Without the TCSC, neither the relevant research problem nor a concrete project would have been identified; and without the link between the TCSC and the IDBI, the project would not have become an operational project. It appears from a priori reasoning, as well as from this case study, that the critical links in the process of creative adaptation of modern technology are the TCSC and the financial system; these two provide the essential links between the production system and the technological research system. Without these two functional agencies, the production system and the technological research system are likely to evolve on parallel lines.[19]

Notes

1 On the relationship among high-level goals, operative goals, and selective attention, see Herbert A. Simon, *Administrative Behavior* (New York: Collier-Macmillan, 1976), pp. xxxiv–xxxv.
2 For the word *holon,* see Arthur Koestler, *Janus: A Summing Up* (New York: Random House, 1979), pp. 292–3: "But wholes and parts in this absolute sense do not exist anywhere, either in the domain of living organisms or of social organisations. What we find are intermediary structures on a series of levels in ascending order of complexity; each of which has two faces looking in opposite directions: The face turned towards the lower levels is that of an autonomous whole, the one turned upward that of a dependent part. I have elsewhere proposed the word 'holon' for these Janus-faced sub-assemblies."
3 Simon, *Administrative Behavior,* pp. xxvi–xxvii. In economic theory, price signals indicate imperative decisions; in such a world there is no room for decision making. See John Hicks, *Causality in Economics* (New York: Basic Books, 1979), pp. 90–1.
4 Kenneth J. Arrow, *The Limits of Organization* (New York: Norton, 1974), p. 47.
5 Simon, *Administrative Behavior,* p. xxxv.
6 Arrow, *Limits of Organization,* p. 49.
7 Kenneth J. Arrow, "Limited Knowledge and Economic Analysis," *American Economic Review* 64, No. 1 (March, 1974):1–10.
8 Paul R. Lawrence and Jay W. Lorsch, *Organization and Environment: Managing Differentiation and Integration* (Cambridge: Harvard University Press, 1967), and James D. Thompson, *Organizations in Action: Social Science Bases of Administrative Theory* (New York: McGraw-Hill, 1967).
9 V.V. Bhatt, *Decision Making in the Public Sector: A Case Study of Swaraj Tractor,* Domestic Finance Studies No. 48 (Washington, D.C.: World Bank, 1978).
10 For factual information with regard to the Swaraj story and decisions, apart from Bhatt, ibid., see also G.S. Aurora and Ward Morehouse, "The Dilemma of Technological Choice – The Case of the Small Tractor," *Minerva* (Oct. 1974). These are also the sources for sections 7.2 and 7.3.
11 On the role of the Investment Licensing System of the Ministry of Industry with regard to the Swaraj project, see V. V. Bhatt, "Indigenous Technology and Investment Licensing: The Case Study of the Swaraj Tractor,"*Journal of Development Studies* 15, No. 4 (1979):320–30.
12 On the impact of the power and status system on the operative goals of an organization, see Eric Rhenman, *Organization Theory for Long-Range Planning* (New York: Wiley, 1973), Chap. 4.

13 On the significance of willpower, see Joseph A. Schumpeter, *Business Cycles* (New York: McGraw-Hill, 1939), 1:98–9, and J. M. Keynes, *The General Theory of Employment, Interest and Money* (New York: Harcourt, Brace & World, 1964), p. 161. Personal influence is not merely a result of "perceived high reliability" of information with regard to innovation, the factor emphasized by Arrow, "Limited Knowledge and Economic Analysis," p. 10; rather, it is primarily due to what Schumpeter calls "ability to 'walk alone' and to act on ground untried by experience" or what Keynes calls "animal spirits."

14 On the concept of creative response or adaptation, see Joseph A. Schumpeter, *Essays of J. A. Schumpeter,* ed. Richard V. Clemence (Cambridge, Mass.: Addison-Wesley Press, 1951), pp. 216–27. Adaptive response relates to what Simon calls programmed decisions, whereas creative response relates to what he calls unprogrammed decisions; see Herbert A. Simon, *The New Science of Management Decision* (Englewood Cliffs, N.J.: Prentice-Hall, 1977), pp. 45–9.

15 V. V. Bhatt, *Financial Institutions and Technology Policy,* Domestic Finance Studies No. 54 (Washington, D.C.: 1979).

16 Aurora and Morehouse, "Dilemma of Technological Choice."

17 On the concept of corporation, see Rhenman, *Organization Theory,* Chap. 4.

18 Planning Commission, *Draft Fifth Five Year Plan: 1974–79* (New Delhi: Government of India Press, 1974), Chap. 9, and V. V. Bhatt, *Development Problems, Strategy and Technology Choice: Sarvodaya and Socialist Approaches in India,* Domestic Finance Studies No. 55 (Washington, D.C.: 1979).

19 V. V. Bhatt, "On Technology Policy and Its Institutional Frame," *World Development* 3, No. 9 (1975):651–63.

8 Labor–management conflict resolution in state-owned enterprises: a comparison of public- and private-sector practices in India

Bruce Vermeulen and Ravi Sethi

The contrasts between state-owned firms and private enterprises are nowhere more apparent than in the conduct of labor-management relations. Because public firms are governed by a mix of market and bureaucratic rules, managers of these firms must attempt to satisfy a more complex set of objectives with regard to labor. This chapter considers the impact of these combined market and political-bureaucratic forces on the resolution of labor–management conflicts. Does "publicness" affect the handling and outcome of industrial disputes? Do the mechanisms for resolving conflicts in public enterprises differ systematically from private-sector mechanisms? If so, which of these contrasts are common to all public firms and which result from unique sets of industry- or firm-specific forces? These questions are addressed here with reference to the Indian economy.

Public-enterprise managers often must meet standards of efficiency or profitability and simultaneously fulfill the broader social objectives of the firm. Cost-minimization pressures may require high levels of productivity and labor costs that compare favorably with those of efficient private firms. Social objectives of equity and worker welfare may require firms to act as "model employers," providing above-average earnings, superior working conditions, and greater job security than most private employers. A public firm is also required to function constructively as an instrument of economic development policy, with objectives that may include the manipulation of wages and prices, either to subsidize particular intermediate or final outputs or to contribute to macroeconomic efforts toward wage and price restraint.

Government rarely assigns clear, stable priorities among these competing objectives. In fact, the "optimal" balance of objectives may be quite fluid, responding, and subject, to ongoing political negotiation as new issues, debates, and crises of equity and efficiency arise. Managerial performance in public firms often is judged partly on the basis of an ability to choose and pursue objectives in a politically adept manner, as well as on economic criteria. Because labor policies of

The authors are grateful for comments on an earlier draft by Peter Doeringer, Leroy Jones, Srinivasan Murthy, Lyle Spencer, Jr., and Raymond Vernon. The views expressed, however, are solely the responsibility of the authors.

individual state-owned firms may have important repercussions elsewhere in the economy, the government may usurp the authority of public-enterprise managers and resolve some issues in labor disputes through centralized bureaucratic decisions.

This chapter begins with some intriguing evidence that labor–management conflicts in state-owned firms in India do differ from those in the private sector. Public firms experience dramatically lower rates of strikes, lockouts, and lost time in the course of these disputes. The purpose of this chapter is to consider why this difference occurs. Four principal explanatory hypotheses are proposed and discussed in the light of some preliminary evidence. The first hypothesis offers an explanation based on differences in industrial composition and in the characteristics of public versus private firms. Two hypotheses focus on the privileged treatment of public-enterprise workers, and the fourth hypothesis concerns government's dual role in settling disputes – as "third-party" mediator and as owner of the firm.

The Indian economy is a particularly interesting context for studying these issues. Among the developing nations, India has an unusually diversified and extensive industrial base. Public firms are located in a number of industries and often coexist with private firms in the same industry. Interregional differences in politics and in the degree of industrialization and development also permit an unusually rich assortment of intranational contrasts.

In Section 8.1 recent aggregate trends in industrial disputes are reported. Alternative explanations of the lower time-loss rates in public-sector firms are summarized in Section 8.2, and the four hypotheses are presented. In Section 8.3 the "structural-statistical" hypothesis is considered. After finding that structural factors apparently do not fully account for the differential strike rates, the remainder of the chapter explores three explanatory hypotheses that are based on public–private differences in the labor market. Section 8.4 describes some prominent structural and operational characteristics of Indian labor markets. The model-employer and soft-management hypotheses are presented in Section 8.5, and the government-intervention hypothesis is the subject of Section 8.6. Conclusions are presented in Section 8.7.

8.1 The increasing severity of industrial conflict: aggregate trends in recent years

Strikes and lockouts are among the most conspicuous and costly manifestations of industrial strife. Like the visible tips of icebergs, trends in work stoppages can serve as crude, though potentially misleading, indices of the dimensions of underlying labor–management conflicts. In India's private sector, the incidence of strikes, lockouts, and even serious episodes of violence and killings, escalated rather steadily between 1961 and 1977. Although state-owned firms also experienced increases, strike and lockout rates in public firms have consistently remained markedly lower.

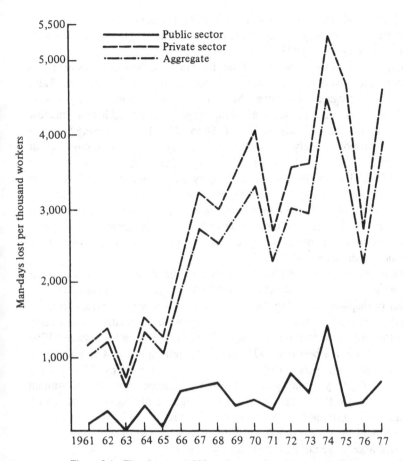

Figure 8.1. Time loss per 1,000 workers employed in manufacturing group of the public and private sector, 1961–77. (Data for 1961–75 from Labour Bureau, *Indian Labour Statistics*, Table 10.4 [New Delhi: Ministry of Labour, Government of India, 1976], p.310; data for 1976–7 computed from tables in "Review of Industrial Disputes in India during 1977," *Indian Labour Journal*, pp. 812–15 and 915–18; and *Economic Survey, 1978–79* [New Delhi: Government of India, 1979] pp. 87–8.

Figure 8.1 illustrates the aggregate, private- , and public-sector trends in man-days lost per 1,000 employees because of lockouts or strikes[1] in manufacturing establishments within the organized sector.[2] These data are at least suggestive of changes in the intensity (and possibly the handling) of labor–management disputes; they also pose an intriguing contrast between public and private firms, which is the focus of this chapter. Where reversals in the prevailing upward trend have occurred, they have tended to be transitory, resulting primarily from national emergency situations (in 1963, 1965, 1971, and from 1975 to early 1977).[3] Total days lost per 1,000 employees in manufacturing rose from an average of 1,047 from 1961 to 1964, to an average of 3,525 for the period 1972–5. After major declines during both 1975 and 1976, resulting from strike prohibitions enforced in the internal emergency, sharp increases in rates of man-days lost were experienced once again in 1977.[4]

The total amount of lost time depends on three factors: the frequency of strikes and lockouts, their average duration, and the number of workers involved. Table 8.1 provides aggregated evidence, for public- and private-sector workers combined, that the overall increase in lost time is partly attributable to an increase in the average duration of disputes. From 1966 to 1975, disputes lasting 5 days or less declined proportionately, as did disputes lasting from 6 to 30 days. Those lasting more than 30 days, however, rose from 9.2% to 23.4% of all disputes between 1966 and 1975. Following the lengthy emergency from 1975 to early 1977, the 1977 data show there was a resurgence of long strikes and lockouts in 1977. The number of workers involved in disputes showed a similar upward trend from 1961 to 1975, whereas the frequency of disputes appeared to decline somewhat. Increases in both scale and duration more than offset any declines in the frequency of disputes.[5]

The issues precipitating work stoppages and the extent to which worker demands were met also changed between 1961 and 1975. There was an increase in the number of disputes involving "indiscipline and violence," whereas issues of wages, allowances, and bonuses declined somewhat in relative importance. Compensation issues were predominant in 48.3% of the disputes between 1966 and 1970 and in 43.1% between 1971 and 1975. Indiscipline and violence were not cited as causes of disputes in 1966-7, but accounted for 9% by 1975.[6] During the 1975-7 emergency, many plants reportedly increased work loads without raising wages. Since then there has been a resurgence of disputes focusing on compensation. Nevertheless, other issues have also remained important and have been pressed with increased militancy. Finally, the number of disputes in which workers' demands were not met at all has increased.

Taken together, these aggregate data document a progression of increasingly long strikes and lockouts, over issues that revolve increasingly around nonwage issues, with worker demands being met less frequently over time. However, these are not the most serious manifestations of what appears to be a steady intensification of strife between management and labor. There has been a growing amount of violence associated with industrial conflict as well, primarily in the private sector. Since 1977 police have used force against workers in a number of work stoppages, and some top management officials and workers have been killed.

When one separates public from private disputes, clear differences emerge. Public manufacturing employees lost an average of only 184 days per 1,000 workers in the period 1961-4, and 786 man-days between 1972 and 1975. Private averages for these two periods, by contrast, were 1,209 and 4,260, respectively.[7] The scale of public-sector disputes has increased, both in terms of average numbers of workers involved per dispute and man-days lost per dispute. However, the number of public disputes has declined, and the incidence of violence has been much lower in state-owned firms.

Table 8.1. *Duration of industrial disputes, 1966–77*

	1966	1967	1968	1969	1970	1971	1972	1973	1974	1975	1976	1977
Total cases for which data are available	2,446	2,655	2,658	2,491	2,730	2,670	3,056	3,116	2,721	1,853	1,373	2,908
Duration (percentage of disputes)												
5 days or less[a]	58.1	55.2	53.3	56.1	53.8	50.5	50.4	49.8	44.7	45.6	59.8	50.0
More than 5 and up to 30 days	32.7	32.5	32.6	33.3	33.0	35.9	37.8	33.5	35.0	31.0	28.2	34.4
More than 30 days	9.2	12.3	14.1	10.6	13.2	13.6	11.8	16.7	20.3	23.4	12.0	15.6

[a] Within this category, there is an approximately equal division between disputes of one day or less and those of between two and five days.
Source: For 1966–75, Bureau of Labour Statistics, *Annual Report* (1976), Table 10.7(c), Table 10.7(c), p. 318, and for 1976–7, "Review of Industrial Disputes in India During 1977," *Indian Labour Journal*, Vol. 20, No. 5 (May 1979), Table 13, p. 893.

The increase of violence makes it especially important to understand the nature and origins of these disputes and differences between violent and orderly conflict resolution. Perhaps the lower rates of dispute-related time loss and violence in public firms hold clues for reducing private-sector tensions.

The remainder of the analysis considers what institutional factors may explain these public–private differences. The broader normative question of whether very low strike and lost-time rates in public enterprises signal successful or problematic industrial settlements is beyond the scope of this chapter. An understanding of what produces the public–private differential is a prerequisite to assessing the relative merits of the public and private mechanisms for resolution.

8.2   Why do public enterprises experience less lost time than private firms as a consequence of labor–management conflicts?

Four explanatory hypotheses

Labor laws often explicitly prohibit the right to strike to public employees, whereas that right is allowed to private-sector workers. Such a difference could explain why public-enterprise lost-time rates are so much lower than those in the private sector. In India, however, strike prohibitions are not a significant factor. During the emergency periods, antistrike restrictions have been imposed and presumably have fallen hardest on government workers and workers in the largest private establishments. These factors have been absent at other times and cannot explain the persistent contrast between the public and private strike and lockout experience since 1961. Four other causal mechanisms are considered that may explain these persistent differences:

1.   The structure–statistical hypothesis: Lower public-enterprise rates of time lost in industrial disputes occur because state-owned firms tend to operate in sectors, industries, environments, or with technologies, that are inherently less conflict prone.

2.   The model-employer hypothesis: Lower public-enterprise rates of time lost in industrial disputes occur because state-owned firms, acting as model employers, provide higher compensation and better working conditions.

3.   The soft-management hypothesis: Lower public-enterprise rates of time lost in industrial disputes occur because public managers tend to grant worker demands without resort to strikes.

4.   The intervention hypothesis: Lower public-enterprise rates of time lost in industrial disputes occur because government intervenes in public- and private-sector collective bargaining and dispute settlements in fundamentally different ways.

The structural–statistical hypothesis suggests that the lower public-enterprise strike rates may simply be a statistical artifact that results from public involvement in the types of activities that experience low rates of industrial unrest whether in the private or the public sector. If the textile industry, for example, has a history of intense labor–management conflicts and frequent strikes – whether because of hard bargaining by management, outmoded technologies, poor working conditions, or some other factor – this industry might have a relatively high rate of lost time under either public or private ownership. If private firms were concentrated in such industries, private-sector lost-time rates would be higher, assuming otherwise comparable dispute-settlement practices.

A test of the structural–statistical hypothesis requires "controlling" for factors that include industry, firm size (in terms of value added, capital stock, and employment), market concentration, technology (as measured by capital–labor ratios and the portion of the work force that is skilled), productivity (value-added per worker), degree of unionization, geographic location, political environment, and demographic composition of the work force. The structural–statistical hypothesis would be supported if these controls eliminated significant public–private differences in rates of lost time; otherwise, "publicness" affects the extent of work stoppages, and it is important to understand the causal role of differences in ownership. How are lower public-sector levels of strikes and lockouts achieved? Do they signal healthier industrial relations or a more coercive public approach? Do public firms in effect buy industrial peace through better compensation and working conditions or through softer, more acquiescent bargaining? If so, are these appropriate policies of a "model employer" or simply a politically expedient indulgence public firms enjoy because they do not face the same market pressures and constraints as their profit-seeking private counterparts? Answers to these questions require a closer look at the operation of labor markets and the processes of conflict resolution in the Indian context.

Most industrial disputes are resolved through some form of negotiation without work stoppages. However, a strike and lockout may occur for a number of reasons. The most common function of either a strike or a lockout is to cause the other party to shift its perception of what constitutes an acceptable settlement.[8] Each party operates with uncertainty about what the other is willing to concede through bargaining. A work stoppage is a means of identifying and changing these respective positions. Where the expected gains exceed the anticipated costs for either party, a work stoppage is likely. There may be no common ground for a mutually acceptable settlement (i.e., a null "contract zone," in the terms of bargaining theorists), or the uncertainties or misinformation associated with bargaining strategies may keep the parties from identifying a basis for settlement.[9] Work stoppages may also occur when the immediate economic gains are nonpositive, that is, to defend a principle rather than to obtain an economic objective.

Union leaders may call a strike as a tactic for unifying their membership or getting them to accept a compromise settlement. The strike may serve as a signal that the leadership could not gain a better settlement through bargaining. Similarly, lockouts may be used as an internal signal between frontline management and stockholders. In the analysis that follows, we abstract from these

intramanagement or intraunion dynamics and focus instead on the external relations between labor and management groups. The remaining hypotheses concern
these interactions.

The model-employer hypothesis focuses on actual and perceived differences in
the quality of jobs as measured by wages and working conditions, which result
from intentional governmental policy. The soft-management hypothesis, also
concerned with relative job quality, concerns differences that result from individual managerial incentives to avoid open conflict rather than from explicit
public policy. The intervention hypothesis emphasizes the nature of government
involvement in the internal affairs of public and private firms and explains strike
activity in terms of differences in expectations, attitudes, and degree of uncertainty and misinformation in negotiations. Each hypothesis is now considered on
the basis of preliminary quantitative and qualitative evidence, which permits only
tentative rather than firm conclusions.

8.3   The structural–statistical hypothesis: Are public firms engaged in less conflict-prone activities?

The aggregate data concerning strikes and lockouts conceal important differences
in the nature of public and private firms and in the economic sectors and industries
in which they are involved. If we consider these differences systematically and
compare public enterprises with only those private firms that are similar, will
firms in the two sectors have closely matched rates of industrial disputes and lost
work time? Do firm and industry characteristics, rather than "publicness" versus
"privateness," account for differences in the level of industrial conflict? Are
factors such as firm size, technology, location, and the extent of unionization
strongly correlated with levels of strike and lockout activity, and do they account
for most or all the differences in lost time experienced by public and private firms?
Is strike and lockout activity primarily historically determined by a unique and
extremely complex combination of events, personalities, and social and technical
relationships of ownership and production in each industry? Or is the nature and
intensity of labor–management conflict determined by uniform characteristics of
individual firms, jobs, and bargaining relationships regardless of the industry in
which they occur? Even if distinct patterns of work stoppages are correlated with
industry or firm traits, these relationships cannot adequately explain why public-
sector loss rates are so much below private-industry rates. They can serve only as
preliminary clues about the underlying causal factors. We return to this point later.

Because adequate firm-specific data were unavailable, relationships between
firm characteristics and industrial disputes could not be directly measured.
Instead, we suggest a set of theoretical links between firm characteristics and
strike behavior and present some data that are only suggestive, because of
multicollinearity and aggregation problems. Firm-level data should be obtained
for a properly controlled test of the structural–statistical hypothesis.

Are public-private differences in firm characteristics key determinants of the levels of industrial conflict?

We consider seven characteristics of the firm that may partially explain differences in public- and private-enterprise strike and lockout experience: firm size, market concentration, technology, location, age, unionization, and political environment.

Firm size. Does firm size account for differences in industrial strife? Economic theory does not suggest an a priori conclusion. Jobs in larger firms may be inherently more impersonal, more specialized, and subject to more worker alienation. However, enforcement of productive labor laws increases with firm size and may reduce the scope of collective bargaining and disputes. Firm size may also be correlated with a number of other factors that affect the incidence of industrial conflict.

Ideally, tests should focus on those underlying correlates for which size is merely a proxy. The published strike data are not disaggregated by firm size. However, large firms certainly have not been immune to industrial disputes recently in India. In fact, "over 30% of all strikes in 1978 are estimated to have taken place in relatively large and modern factories."[10]

Public enterprises are among the largest firms in the economy, measured by employment, fixed capital, or value added. In the organized manufacturing sector about 5% of all firms are publicly owned, yet these state-owned enterprises account for nearly one-fourth of all employment, 26% of value added, and 58% of fixed capital.[11] Average employment in these firms is 403 workers per factory, compared with only 94 among private firms in the organized portion of the economy as a whole.[12] The 10 largest firms in terms of total assets all are in the public sector.[13] If scale does affect the incidence of strikes and lockouts, therefore, it is important to compare public-sector firms with private firms that are comparably large.

Market concentration. Oligopolists may have greater incentives to maintain industrial peace than competitive firms, because a sustained interruption of production may cause a permanent loss of market share. Their oligopolistic rents create a profit pool with which to bargain for industrial peace and stable production through wage premiums and other benefits that are above market-clearing levels. Thus, unions can often gain these concessions. However, unions that overestimate this "ability to pay" may actually strike more frequently. These influences, which are documented in a number of industrial economies, are likely to be important in India as well. If public-sector firms operate in relatively more concentrated markets, this may account for some differences in strike rates.

Technology. Two aspects of technology, the capital intensity of the firm's production process and the occupational composition (specifically the skill intensity) of the firm's work force, may also influence labor–management conflicts. High capital intensity reduces the proportion of labor costs in total costs of production and makes wage concessions proportionately less costly. Like market concentration, high capital intensity is presumed to affect industrial conflict through compensation and working conditions. The wage aspect of these effects is discussed in Section 8.5. However, capital intensity may affect industrial relations more directly. Greater capital intensity usually is associated with a greater differentiation and specialization of labor, which may increase worker alienation.

The skill composition of the work force is also important. Skilled workers tend to have greater market power than unskilled workers, provided that the elasticity of supply among workers is inversely related to the degree of skill. Their added bargaining power may reduce the need to strike to gain wage demands; it also increases the likelihood that a strike action, if taken, will be successful.

Only careful empirical analysis can identify the relationship between technology and the incidence of industrial unrest. Neither firm-specific data nor recent data at the two-digit industry level are published on the skill distribution of workers.[14] Some data are available concerning the relationship between wage rates and factors including capital intensity, skill mix, and firm size, but these are for 1960 and 1964. They do not include strike and lockout information. Dholakia, using these data, reports that larger, more modern facilities with more capital-intensive technologies paid significantly higher wages on average. Both size and technology were found to be important determinants of wage rates.[15] During the same period, non-wage benefits were a higher portion of total earnings in several capital-intensive industries as well.[16]

Data on total emoluments per employee, which are available for 1974–5, confirm that the relationship between size and earnings per worker has continued. Firms with 500 employees or more pay one-fifth to one-third higher total compensation than all firms taken together.[17]

Age of firm. The newness of a firm, or of a particular plant, might influence employee morale through working conditions and possibly through prestige as well. Newness is correlated with size, technology, and market concentration. Newer facilities generally employ more capital-intensive technologies and provide cleaner, safer work environments. Newer plants may on average provide better jobs, an issue that is considered in Section 8.5.

Unionization. Three characteristics of unions seem particularly likely to influence the conduct of industrial relations: the extent of unionization of the work force in a particular plant, firm, or industry; the number of unions representing workers within a given plant and the extent of union rivalry;[18] and the degree of militancy of the dominant union or unions. However, unions in public- and private-sector firms do not appear markedly different in these respects. In most industries where public and private firms coexist, workers in both sectors tend to be represented by the same group of unions. Public-sector firms may be somewhat more unionized on average than private firms, but union membership strength, militancy, and political ties are similar in the two sectors. Union differences among public and private firms therefore are unlikely to account for a substantial part of the difference in man-days lost.

Location. Location can influence the incidence of industrial conflict for two reasons. First, in less industrialized areas, industrial jobs may be much better than alternative local employment opportunities. Cost-of-living and wage rates differ substantially among states as to industrial composition and the proportion of public-sector firms and output in various industries. Political, social, and other local labor market conditions also differ widely. Thus, industrial location may account for some of the public–private differences in labor disputes and conflict resolution.

Political environment. Finally, the composition of local and state government, and the range of ideologies that prevail locally, may influence the incidence and resolution of union–management conflict. Prevailing political ideologies may strongly favor either labor or management. Although these political relationships are not characteristics of the firm, they are particularly important in Indian industrial relations and undoubtedly affect the level of strikes and lockouts. Political ties between parties and unions are utilized to forge compromises that can prevent or shorten lockouts or strikes. How important are the ideological biases of state and local goverments in the outcomes of labor–management conflicts? Does an "anti-union" government stimulate or dampen strike activity? There has been sufficient political diversity in recent state governments in India to permit fruitful empirical analysis of these issues.

Do differences in sectoral and industrial involvement, or differences in the nature and environment of public- and private-sector firms, account for the lower incidence of man-days lost as a result of industrial disputes in public firms?

Several studies of Indian industrial relations have examined strike and lockout data at the one- and two-digit industry level. The usefulness of these studies for our purpose is somewhat dubious, as they involve aggregations across firms that are markedly different. However, the data do demonstrate that controlling for compositional differences at this level would not significantly reduce the differential between public and private lost-time rates.

A meaningful test of the structural–statistical hypothesis requires firm-specific data.[19] The underlying question here is whether the differential in lost time would disappear if state-owned enterprises were compared properly with similar private firms, controlling for all these factors. Several conclusions emerge. Although differences in the sectoral and industrial mix of public and private firms may account for some difference in lost time, these factors cannot account for all the difference. Second, even if they did, we still would not know why or how public and private firms resolve industrial conflicts in different ways, with differing amounts of lost time. Controlling for firm traits rather than merely industrial composition would probably reduce the unexplained public–private differential significantly but would not explain why firm characteristics and strike or lockout rates are correlated.

If we determined, for example, that work stoppages were inversely related to firms' capital–labor ratios, part of the public–private differential would disappear by excluding labor-intensive private firms from a comparison. The causal relationship between capital intensity and disputes would not be illuminated, however. Instead, it would merely point in the direction of subsequent analysis.

The hypotheses discussed in Sections 8.5 and 8.6 focus on causal mechanisms more directly. Each identifies fundamental differences between public and private firms that may account for differences in the amount and severity of industrial disputes. All three are based on comparisons between labor-market operations in the public and private sectors. Before considering these hypotheses, a review of several fundamental characteristics of these markets in India will be useful.

8.4   Some structural characteristics of Indian labor markets

Labor markets vary greatly across the Indian subcontinent. Sharp interregional contrasts exist, for example, in the industrial and occupational mix, the demographic composition of the employed work force, wage rates and costs of living, the degree of unionization, and the political climate. Despite these differences, some broad generalizations about the national labor market may provide a useful backdrop against which to consider labor–management relationships within the organized sector.

Surplus labor and job insecurity

Throughout India, most jobs are outside the organized sector,[20] even in the towns and cities. Such jobs provide extremely low wages, little employment security, and virtually no coverage or enforcement of government protective legislation concerning minimum compensation and working conditions. Employment in the organized sector, public or private, generally is better than in smaller establishments or in the casual labor market. Protective labor legislation is more often enforced, and these jobs provide higher compensation, better working conditions, and greater security. High levels of unemployment and underemployment, however, create powerful market forces that erode these advantages, even for "permanent" workers in the best jobs. As the disparity between market realities and legislated worker protections is expanded, incentives increase for cost-saving violations of these provisions. Protected jobs in the organized sector are in high demand, and employers often are able to defeat trade-union initiatives and to ignore protective labor laws.[21]

Wage levels, determination, and policies

A typical industrial pay package consists of a basic wage plus five special allowances.[22] For many workers the wage package is determined through bilateral collective bargaining at the plant level. Bargaining may occur instead on an industry-wide basis, between national unions and employer associations. Third-party involvement by the government is also common and has been formalized through the establishment of wage boards in a number of industries.[23] Wage boards establish industry-wide basic wage rates, thus reducing the scope of plant-level bargaining.[24] Government intervention also occurs when bilateral bargaining breaks down. Formal machinery exists for conciliation and arbitration. More often the government intervenes informally to negotiate and press for a peaceful settlement.

Government intervention in private-sector wage determination serves two principal objectives. It aids workers in securing wages and working conditions that are "fair" but consistent with price stability, and it secures sufficient industrial peace to ensure an orderly process of economic development. Private-sector real wages for most manufacturing workers stagnated from 1955 until recently.[25] However, government concern for promoting increases to "fair" wage levels, that is, above the existing low market-clearing levels that prevail in the country's unsheltered labor markets, has been expressed in the various national five-year plans.[26] Higher wages and benefits in state-owned firms presumably reflect this goal of "fairness."

Union structure, strength, and politics

About half the non-agricultural work force is estimated to be unionized, with especially strong representation in larger industrial cities and in older industries such as jute, cotton textiles, and the railways.[27] Generally, a number of unions compete politically in each plant.[28] Workers are permitted to join more than one union and few states have established procedures for identifying a single bargaining agent among the unions.

More than 60% of all Indian trade unions are affiliated with five national trade-union coalitions,[29] which are in turn linked closely with rival political parties. The intensity of union rivalries parallels the sharp ideological contrasts and political competition of their party affiliates. Many plants have employer-promoted unions as well. Some industrial conflicts result from interunion rivalries, as union leaders vie for membership by demonstrating their willingness and ability to advocate forcefully worker rights and demands. Conflicts among rival unions may also weaken any attempts to mount a successful strike effort.

Prominent union leaders often become involved directly in state or national elective politics, in ministerial positions in government, or as leaders in the national parties. At the local level, union organizers and leaders often engage actively in local politics and become political brokers, delivering blocks of worker votes to political parties that agree to support worker demands.

To maintain "fair" wages and gain enforcement of existing labor laws amid widespread underemployment, unions rely heavily on political pressure and moral suasion.[30] This has been a pervasive aspect of the Indian labor movement from its origins.[31]

Strikes and lockouts

Even with political backing, a trade union's power to gain concessions from management depends ultimately on the ability to mount a successful strike. The union must be able to deny the employer access to a substitute work force. With so many unemployed and underemployed workers available, Indian unions often must utilize a coercive threat of violence (whether explicit or implied) to dissuade prospective replacements from assuming their jobs.

If a strike stops or seriously curtails production, and if the employer cannot hire alternative workers, the relative strength of labor and management in a strike depends on the financial "staying power" of each side. Unions do not have the means to provide significant strike benefits. When a long strike occurs, therefore, workers either must take temporary jobs in the unprotected sector, or they must rely on the support of other family members during the strike. For management, the impact of curtailed production on profits depends on the availability of inventories and on the potential long-run loss of markets. For society as a whole, the fragile balance and pressing needs of economic development may outweigh these private considerations of costs and staying power.

The cost per day of a strike generally increases as the duration of the strike increases. For workers and employers alike, the consequences of short-term disruptions may be minor, whereas longer strikes may impose severe hardships on workers and seriously damage the employer's long-range market position. Strikes and lockouts usually occur only when expected net gains are positive for employers or workers.[32] For either party, the costs and the benefits depend on uncertainties such as success in securing sustained worker support and curtailing production, effectiveness of retaliatory measures by the employer, balance and influence of public opinion, and impact on the employer's long-range market position. These factors gel or become evident only during the actual course of a strike. Decisions to undertake or accept work stoppages must therefore be based on speculative rather than hard evidence.

Dispute settlement through bilateral collective bargaining

Most worker grievances and demands are resolved at the plant level through direct negotiations between employers and workers. A study of 80 employers and 86 unions in 1972–3 found that nearly 70% of all disputes were resolved through "bilateral collective bargaining" between employers and workers without government involvement.[33] Large private firms, and unions that are plant specific and independent of the national trade-union centers, rely more heavily on collective bargaining than on the "tripartite" methods (with government) described in the following section. Smaller firms more frequently utilize government conciliation services.

"Bilateral" negotiations often involve more than one firm and, in India, usually include multiple unions. The need to compromise and resolve differences among employers, unions, and groups within the unions aggravates the inherent uncertainties of the bargaining process and perhaps leads to more strikes than in bargaining between a single employer and union. Alliances among rival unions, which are necessary for a successful strike, often can be undermined by employers during negotiations.

Third-party involvement by the government

When an impasse is reached in bilateral negotiations, government officials may intervene with or without an invitation from the parties. As in other bargaining contexts, there is formal fact finding, mediation, and arbitration. The parties can also register agreements once achieved to enhance their contractual status. For particularly difficult issues beyond the normal scope of voluntary or compulsory arbitration and wage boards, the government may appoint a commission of inquiry to recommend a basis for settlement.

However, government officials frequently intervene informally instead. A district magistrate or local labor official on learning about a dispute may offer the "good offices" of government to promote bargaining and perhaps mediate a settlement. When industrial disputes are large in scale, state or central government officials may become involved.

Generally, the weaker party in a dispute is more likely to seek expanded, tripartite negotiations and is more willing to empower the third party to arbitrate a settlement. Smaller firms, and trade unions that have weak market positions but strong political allies, have clear incentives to rely on political solutions to industrial conflict. If the union can barter its electoral support effectively, workers often can achieve far better settlements than would be possible through bilateral bargaining.

The government may initiate tripartite bargaining either formally or informally for a variety of reasons. Economic development objectives may require price and wage restraint and continuity of production in key industries. The economic welfare of workers, including target levels of wages, benefits, and working conditions, may require government intervention. According to Meyers and Kannapan:

> The difficulty in developing a committed labour force, the rivalries and weakness of the Indian trade union movement, the failure of many Indian and foreign employers to deal fairly with workers or constructively with trade unions, and the resultant labour discontent and strife have encouraged government intervention in order to control, channel and redirect incipient and actual labour protest.[34]

In addition, political leaders may attempt to build their constituencies by publicly intervening in a management–labor crisis and forging a settlement. The decisive role of fragile alliances and compromises among political parties, unions, employers, and individual leaders greatly amplifies the volatility and uncertainty of the bargaining process.[35]

With these features of Indian labor markets and labor–management relations as a backdrop, we now consider the importance of job quality and of differences in collective-bargaining practices in determining the extent of industrial peace in private and public enterprises.

8.5   The model-employer and soft-management hypotheses: Do public-enterprise workers have less to gain from strikes?

The model-employer and soft-management hypotheses focus on different explanations of the same phenomenon: better wages, benefits, and working conditions in state-owned firms than in their private-sector counterparts. Underlying both hypotheses is the premise that better jobs lessen the probability of strikes by reducing the incremental gains workers can expect from a work stoppage.

Table 8.2 presents some fragmentary evidence that public-private average earnings ratios in 1972–3 were greater than 1.0 in most industries. For industries with strong representation of both public and private firms (including cotton textiles, chemicals and chemical products other than from petroleum and coal, metal products, electrical and other machinery, and transportation equipment), public-sector earnings are substantially higher in almost every case.[36] In industries with wage boards, which establish common, industry-wide basic wage rates, public–private earning differences presumably result from differences in bonuses, hours of work, and local cost-of-living adjustments.[37]

The model-employer hypothesis

As model employers, state-owned firms are expected to provide wages, working conditions, and other benefits that are above the norm for workers in the economy as a whole. According to this hypothesis, public-sector jobs are more attractive and lucrative as a result of deliberate public policy. More detailed comparisons are required to determine the importance of these model-employer effects, which government policy pronouncements emphasize but which managers must balance against other competing objectives.

The soft-management hypothesis

An alternative explanation of the upward bias in public-sector wages and benefits is that workers achieve their demands easily through bargaining. According to this hypothesis, public managers have a bureaucratic disposition to avoid open conflict, and they often accept labor demands rapidly to prevent strikes. Public-sector managers are vulnerable to a multitude of political forces and pressures and may prefer to keep a low profile whenever possible. The consequent reluctance to

Table 8.2. *Per capita annual money earnings of workers earning less than Rs. 400 per month, by industry, 1972–3*

		Average annual earnings, 1972–3		Public–private
Code	Manufacturing industry	Public sector	Private sector	ratio, 1972–3
23	Cotton textiles	3,184	3,109	1.024
24	Wool, silk, and synthetic fiber textiles	2,751	3,218	0.855
25	Jute, hemp, and mesta textiles	1,670	3,495	0.478
26	Textile products including apparel other than footwear	4,262	2,396	1.779
27	Wood and wood products, furniture, and fixtures	3,733	1,906	1.959
28	Paper, paper products, and printing, publishing and allied industries	3,702	2,909	1.273
29	Leather and leather and fur products, except repair	2,196	2,933	0.749
23–29		3,071	2,852	1.077
30	Rubber, plastic, petroleum and coal products	3,387	2,686	1.261
31	Chemicals and chemical products, except products of petroleum and coal	3,594	2,774	1.296
32	Non-metallic mineral products	2,666	2,108	1.265
33	Basic metal and alloys	4,282	2,836	1.510
34	Metal products and parts, except machinery and transport equipment	3,107	2,578	1.205
35	Machinery, machine tools and parts, except electrical machinery	3,217	2,985	1.078
36	Electrical machinery, apparatus, appliances, and supplies and parts	3,586	3,128	1.146
37	Transport equipment and parts	4,138	3,408	1.214
38	Others	3,390	2,564	1.322
30–38		3,486*	2,952	1.131

Note: The averages for industries 23–29 and 30–38 are unweighted.
Source: Computed from Table 4.1 (c), *Indian Labour Statistics*; Labour Bureau, Ministry of Labour (Delhi: Government of India Press, 1976), pp. 74–5. Data compiled from Annual Returns under the Payment of Wages Act, 1936.

provoke labor unrest may lead to systematically better wages, benefits, and working conditions.

We have no evidence yet with which to weight the relative importance of the model-employer and soft-bargaining hypotheses. Just how state-owned enterprises balance stated model-employer objectives against price-stability targets is unclear. Various authors assert that public managers are weak bargainers,[38] but this phenomenon has not been systematically documented. Ideally, we should have information on the determinants of management wage decisions, as well as firm-level data on bargaining outcomes. Data concerning firm location are also important. Whereas the majority of new public-enterprise projects were located in "industrially backward" states between 1961 and 1974, a number of these

Table 8.3. *Annual emoluments per worker by firm size, 1974–5*

Size class (No. of employees)	No. of factories	Average no. of employees per factory	Emoluments (Rs. 100,000s)	Emoluments per worker (Rs.)
0–49	48,559	16.9	20,308	2,466
50–99	7,276	68.6	14,073	2,821
100–199	3,806	137.9	17,043	3,247
200–499	2,587	304.8	35,477	4,500
500–999	984	688.8	41,055	6,057
1,000–1,999	591	1,410.4	53,428	6,410
2,000–4,999	332	2,984.9	66,627	6,723
5,000 and above	82	11,157.8	57,155	6,247
Total	64,217	94.3	305,167	5,042

Source: Indian Institute of Public Opinion, *Quarterly Economic Report*, 88 (Jan.–Mar. 1977):47.

less-developed, low-wage states experienced absolute declines in employment within private firms in the organized sector.[39] The prominence of public enterprises in backward states, which tend to have lower average wage rates than more urbanized and industrialized areas, suggests that public–private earnings differentials may actually be understated by data that do not control for regional location.

A bias in the opposite direction presumably results from being unable to control for firm size. Public enterprises tend to be large firms, and aggregate data on wages by firm size indicate that larger firms pay higher wages. Table 8.3 presents figures for 1974–5. Clearly, public–private earnings and benefit comparisons should be made for firms of comparable size, as firm size is strongly correlated with per worker labor costs.

Better jobs and the level of industrial disputes

To make these hypotheses useful for our analysis, the association between better compensation and lower rates of industrial disputes must be documented. How are better jobs and strike activity related, and how strong is this relationship in comparison with other factors that affect labor–management conflicts? Whether better compensation and working conditions result from model-employer policies or from weak bargaining by management, workers may have little to gain from striking for several reasons. Public opinion may limit additional gains from a strike. If workers are sufficiently privileged in comparison with their private-sector counterparts, public goodwill and political support for "fair" compensation may be jeopardized by demands that are viewed as excessive. Public-sector managers may also acquiesce to union demands to such an extent that workers have few unresolved issues worthy of a strike.

In India public-sector workers seem not to fear reprisals by management. Unlike employees of private firms, they are well protected against job losses, blocked promotions, and other penalties for participating in strikes. Often, rules for promotion prevent supervisory discretion. Government-owned firms have even taken the initiative, informally, in promoting unions.[40] Additional research is needed to determine whether public pressure and managerial acquiescence are key deterrents to strikes.

We turn now to the third type of explanatory hypothesis, which focuses on public–private differences in collective bargaining and conciliation practices.

8.6 The intervention hypothesis: Does government involvement in bargaining reduce public-enterprise work stoppages?

Public–private differences in the collective bargaining process itself may affect the incidence of strikes and lockouts. Even if a public and a private firm were identical in other respects, their differing procedures for resolving disputes might cause strike rates to differ.

The alternative settlement procedures described in Section 8.4 can be grouped in three categories or levels: direct bilateral bargaining between employers (whether individually or in association) and workers (unions or coalitions of unions); informal and formal involvements of local labor officers, magistrates, and other local political leaders; and direct participation of state and central government officials.

Public- and private-sector practices for resolving labor–management conflicts through these three levels of negotiation differ. The premise of the intervention hypothesis is that these differences are crucial in explaining lost-time differentials. The government intervenes more extensively in public-enterprise negotiations. Settlements are thus achieved more frequently without resort to strikes and lockouts.

Public-enterprise labor–management disputes are resolved differently from private-sector conflicts. The bargaining authority of public-enterprise managers is circumscribed and only a limited number of issues can be resolved without government involvement. Third-party involvement (government as political bureaucracy rather than as owner of the firm) occurs earlier in bargaining, and negotiations often move immediately to the state or central government level. Each of these differences contributes to a reduction in strikes.

Issues beyond the authority of public-enterprise managers

The response of any public enterprise to workers' demands may influence trade-union demands at private firms within the same industry (and in related industries) as well as in other state-owned firms. Concessions governing wages and working conditions may serve as models for private-sector settlements even in unrelated industries. Therefore, collective-bargaining agreements in public firms are monitored closely by the Bureau of Public Enterprises (BPE). With rare exceptions, agreements must adhere to PBE guidelines for maximum wages, benefits, and total financial outlays. Managers have no authority to negotiate some issues and usually are unable to exceed PBE limits on others. These restrictions have several important consequences for conflict resolution. The scope of conflict and antagonisms between managers and workers are diminished. Plant managers cannot be blamed for unpopular higher-level decisions and policies. Even when managers have the authority they may choose to submit issues to the BPE to avoid being held accountable by workers for a particular decision. This shared authority for sensitive decisions permits public managers to maintain more congenial labor relations and an atmosphere more conducive to peaceful settlements of other issues over which enterprise discretion is exercised.

Because managerial authority is circumscribed, trade unions often must confront the central or state government rather than a single firm to gain their demands. This requires much greater organizational capability and solidarity on the part of the unions and reduces the potential effectiveness of smaller-scale strikes. The existence of clearly delineated and strictly enforced BPE guidelines also reduces the scope of uncertainty in public-enterprise disputes. Because unions know the government's (and management's) bargaining position on most issues in any dispute, strikes are less necessary than in many private disputes where these parameters must be identified.

Early intervention by the government

The timing of government involvement also differs in public-sector conflict. In the majority of private disputes, government intervention is not invited, and the government takes no initiative to promote a settlement unless failed bilateral negotiations make a work stoppage imminent. In state-owned firms, by contrast, the BPE or other government officials often are involved long before an impasse in negotiations is reached. This may explain both the lower incidence of public-enterprise strikes and the shorter duration of strikes. When an impasse is reached and a strike results, the extent of prior negotiations makes the positions of the parties clearer and discharges some of the intensity and potential for violence.

More frequent involvement of state and central government in negotiations

In addition to earlier government involvement, covering a broader range of issues, public-sector negotiations often move directly to the highest levels of government. Many agreements require budgetary or other policy approval by the state or central government. Local government assistance may be bypassed entirely, or negotiations may occur at both the local and the state or central levels simultaneously. High-level political negotiations tend to produce a settlement that carefully balances political interests and competing government objectives regarding wage and price stability and national economic growth at the same time enhances the welfare of workers. Such a "package" usually embodies the best outcome the trade unions can expect to achieve. If the government renders a judgment informally, unions have relatively little additional recourse. Although formal decisions may be appealed through the courts, informal determinations may only be challenged and overturned through successful large-scale strikes. Unless a government-sponsored settlement violates the underlying balance of interests, unions face a difficult task in mobilizing sufficiently widespread support to force any revisions. When strikes do occur despite mediation efforts by state or national government officials, they are usually shorter than private strikes. Either party may strike to test the power of the other, but the range of uncertainty about political strength on either side usually is small and can be clarified relatively quickly. There have been some important exceptions, such as the nationwide strike of railway workers in 1974, which lasted for many months. In general, however, the more frequent use of high-level government negotiations to resolve public-sector disputes tends to produce fewer, and less-prolonged, work stoppages in state-owned firms than in private firms.

There appears also to be a subtle yet important difference in the labor and management perceptions of each other between the public and private sectors. In private disputes, vehement denunciations by employers and union leaders are common. Typical attitudes are apparently more positive in public-sector bargaining. Public enterprises have a mandate to serve the public interest and are less vulnerable to political attacks in this respect than their private capitalist counterparts. They produce goods and services at prices that are often subsidized and improve worker welfare relative to private-sector workers. The enterprise work force is a key part of the public that the state-owned firm is intended to serve. The workers also represent an important part of the government's political constituency. Although class differences do exist between public-enterprise managers, workers, and the top-level politicians who oversee the enterprises, these differences are mitigated and offset far more than in the private sector by the mutuality of interests suggested here.

Our evidence in support of the intervention hypothesis is anecdotal rather than statistical. It suggests, however, that contrasts in the extent, timing, and nature of government involvement in the process of conflict resolution do play a vital role in the maintenance of greater industrial peace within public-sector firms. The importance and normative implications of the government role in private- and public-sector industrial disputes need to be gauged more closely.

8.7 Conclusion

Substantially lower rates of strikes and lockouts in the public-enterprise sector as compared with private firms in India have been considered through four explanatory hypotheses. The structural–statistical hypothesis states that public enterprises have fewer work stoppages because they engage in activities and have other specific characteristics that are less conflict prone for both public and private firms.

According to this hypothesis, a careful comparison of individual public and private firms with similar characteristics and in similar activities would eliminate this differential. Although individual firm data are not available for such comparisons, this hypothesis seems unlikely to provide a complete explanation.

The model-employer and soft-management hypotheses assert that because of government concerns for worker welfare or because of a desire to avoid politically awkward labor–management confrontations, public enterprises provide better jobs. The marginal gains from strikes are therefore lower for one of several reasons. Although available data suggest that public firms do pay higher wages, the evidence to support these hypotheses is thin. Public firms tend to be larger and more capital intensive, and comparable firms in the private sector pay above average wages as well. The relationship between high wages and low rates of strikes is even less certain. Theory, as is often the case, provides a logic for both greater and lesser rates of disputes and lost time and leaves the issue to be resolved through empirical case studies.

The fourth hypothesis focuses on differences in the nature of bargaining. The more active role of government in public-enterprise disputes is viewed as an important deterrent to strikes. Bargaining and disputes are restricted to a narrower range of issues, and the range of uncertainty is reduced by a widely known and enforced set of public-enterprise guidelines. Limits on the range of labor-related decisions made by managers insulates them from responsibility for many of the more unpopular policy decisions. Early involvement of government in the negotiation of public-sector disputes also may reduce uncertainty and defuse intense conflicts that might otherwise produce strikes. Finally, the participation of state and central government authorities in firm-specific disputes changes the balance of power between labor and management. If unions strike to challenge policies dictated to the enterprise from above, they must match their power aginst the state or national government.

Without more detailed evidence concerning individual firms, it is impossible to offer sound conclusions about the relative importance of these alternative hypotheses. As explanations of the greater degree of industrial peace among state-owned firms, each may provide a partial explanation. Industrial strife in India has been increasing in recent years and has even involved the deaths of some managers and workers. Although strikes served important functions in an industrial-relations system, they are also costly. A better understanding of public–private differences in the handling of labor–management conflicts can provide valuable insights for national labor policies as well as for public policy toward state-owned firms.

Notes

1 The data include strikes and lockouts "connected with [a] specific grievance or demand which lies within the competence of the employers concerned for redressal" and exclude politically motivated work stoppages. See *Indian Labour Journal* 20, No. 5 (May 1979):777 for discussion of the data.

2 The "organized sector" is defined as all public-sector establishments, all private
   nonagricultural establishments with 20 or more workers, and all establishments using
   electric power and employing at least 10 workers.
3 The national emergencies were the Chinese aggression (beginning in Oct. 1962), the
   Indo-Pakistan War (1965), the Bangladesh War (1971), and the more recent internal
   emergency (June 1975 – Mar. 1977).
4 The 1976–7 data separate strikes and lockouts. Lockouts are much more significant
   among work stoppages than in many other countries, accounting for 78% of man-
   days lost in 1976 and 47% in 1977. The internal emergency dramatically reduced
   strike activities (2.8 million man-days lost in 1976 compared with 13.4 million in
   1977) but had almost no impact on lockouts.
5 Bureau of Labour Statistics (BLS), *Annual Report* (New Delhi: Government of India
   Press, 1979), Table 10.8, pp. 812–15 and 915–18.
6 BLS, *Annual Report*, Table 10.7(a), p. 317, and *Indian Labour Journal* 20, No. 5
   (May 1979), Table XI, p. 891.
7 Analyzing data for 1961–9, S.K. Khurana predicted that public-sector strike activity
   would increase to private levels. To date this has not happened. See "Industrial Relations in Private and Public Sector Industry in India: A Comparative Analysis,"
   Indian Journal of Industrial Relations 7 No. 3 (Jan. 1972):411–31.
8 J.T. Dunlop, "The Function of the Strike," in *Frontiers of Collective Bargaining*,
   ed. J.T. Dunlop and N.W. Chamberlain (New York: Harper and Row, 1967),
   pp. 103–21.
9 C.M. Stevens, *Strategy and Collective Bargaining Negotiation* (Westport, Conn.:
   Greenwood Press, 1963).
10 Business India, Ltd., Mar. 19–Apr. 1, 1979. These firms include TELCO, Phillips
   India, Ltd., Wanson India, Ltd., Larsen and Toubro, Guest-Keen Williams, Poysha
   Containers, The Times of India Group, Bajaj Auto, Ltd., and the J.K. Group of
   Companies, and Godrej Nerolac.
11 *Public Sector in the Indian Economy* (Bombay: Economic Intelligence Service,
   Center for Monitoring the Indian Economy, 1978), p. 40.
12 Indian Institute of Public Opinion (IIPO), *Quarterly Economic Report*, No. 88 (New
   Delhi, 1977), p. 47.
13 Food Corporation of India, Bokaro Steel, Hindustan Steel, and the Fertilizer
   Corporation of India, all public enterprises, are the four largest firms in terms of
   assets.The largest private firm is Tata Steel.
14 Data on occupational wage differentials are available from the Labour Bureau's
   Occupational Wage Surveys for 1958–9 and 1964–5. A new survey has been compiled recently but was not available at this writing. Data on skill composition are
   available from a 1956 study by P. Pant and N. Vasudevan, *Occupational Pattern in
   Manfacturing Industries* (New Delhi: Governmental India Press, 1959). Value-added
   data are available more currently, as are data on capital, through the five-year
   plans and supporting documents. However, these data do not include capital–labor
   relationships or industry-specific measures of capital per firm.
15 B.H. Dholakia, "Determinants of Inter-Industry Wage Structure in India," *Indian
   Journal of Industrial Relations* 11, No. 4 (April 1976):445–58. Simple correlation
   coefficients of size with wage rates for 1960 and 1964 are 0.5769 and 0.5623,
   respectively. Coefficients for capital intensity with wages are 0.8263 and 0.7335,
   respectively. All coefficients are significant at the 0.01 level. Size is measured as
   average number of employees per firm; capital intensity is the ratio of gross value of
   fixed assets (current prices) to total man-hours of work in each industry.
17 IIPO, *Quarterly Economic Report*, calculated from table, p. 47.
18 The impact of multiple unions on bargaining outcomes is discussed in Section 8.5.

19 For a more detailed discussion of available data at the one- and two-digit industry levels, see an earlier draft of this paper, available in the working paper series of the Center for Asian Development Studies, Boston University. See also S.M. Pandey and V.K. Pathak, "Inter-Industry Conflict-Proneness in India," *Indian Journal of Industrial Relations* 7, No. 4 (April 1974):521–34.

20 J. Breman, "Labour Relations in the 'Formal' and 'Informal' Sectors: Report of a Case Study in South Gujarat, India," Parts I and II, *Journal of Peasant Studies* 4, Nos. 2 and 3 (Apr. and July 1977):171–205 and 337–59, respectively.

21 Numerous newspaper and journal accounts report cases of employers falsifying records, influencing government inspectors and union leaders, establishing and promoting company unions, precipitating rifts between rival unions, and firing workers who engage actively in union organizing and protests. There have also been instances of fundamental violations of signed industry-wide contracts resulting from tripartite negotiations. See, e.g., R.N. Sharma, "Commitment by Whom: Workers or Owners?" *Indian Journal of Industrial Relations* 14, No. 4 (April 1979) Planning Commission,: 518–34. *Draft Five Year Plan, 1978–1983* (New Delhi: Government of India Press, 1978) p. 15; and numerous issues of *Political and Economic Weekly* (New Delhi). Industries upon which much of the discussion focuses include jute, engineering, and cotton textiles.

22 The supplemental allowances are: a dearness allowance, intended as a cost-of-living adjustment; an annual statutory bonus; a housing rent allowance; a city compensatory allowance to reflect differential living costs among cities; and an incentive bonus. The basic wage typically is the largest component, although dearness allowances are greater in cotton textiles, pharmaceuticals, manufacturing machinery, machine tools, and electrical equipment. The annual bonus, which was originally conceived as a productivity bonus, now generally is a fixed percentage of base pay, usually equaling one month's pay. See G.K. Suri, *Wage System: Its Effective Management* (New Delhi: All India Management Association, 1976).

23 Wage boards have been established in working journalism (May 1956), cotton textiles (Mar. 1957), sugar (Dec. 1957), cement (Apr. 1958), jute (Aug. 1960), tea plantations (Dec. 1960), rubber and coffee (July 1961), iron and steel (Jan. 1962), and coal several years later.

24 See R.P. Verma, "Centralization of Bargaining Structure in India and Its Problems," *Indian Journal of Industrial Relations* 11, No. 3 (Jan. 1976):370–1; and G.P. Sinha, *Industrial Relations and Labour Legislation* (New Delhi, 1977).

25 See S. Palekar, "Wages Under Planning: A Case Study of India," *Indian Economic Journal* 24, No. 1 (July-Sept. 1976):26–49, and *Report of the National Commission on Labour* (New Delhi: Government of India Press, 1969), p. 224.

26 The second five-year plan, e.g., states: "Workers' right to a fair wage has been recognized."

27 Data concerning union membership strength are apparently unreliable because workers often belong to more than one union and because unions have incentives to exaggerate their membership. See C.P. Thakur, "Trade Unions and Social Science Research in India," *Indian Journal of Industrial Relations* 12, No. 1 (July 1976):1–76.

28 Frequently as many as eight or nine unions compete in a single plant.

29 The principal trade-union centers are the National Trade Union Congress (INTUC), the All India Trade Union Congress (AITUC), the Center for Indian Trade Unions (CITU), Hind Mazdoor Sabha (HMS), and the Bhartiya Mazdoor Sangh (BMS).

30 See, e.g., F.C. Munson's study of the printing industry, *Indian Trade Unions: Structure and Functions* (Ann Arbor: University of Michigan Press, 1970).

31 For an excellent account of early appeals to public opinion and political pursuit of

labor objectives, see P. Ghosh and S. Nath, *Labour Relations in India* (New Delhi: Sudha Publications, 1973).

32 For an account of a strike for principle rather than any possible immediate economic gains, see Breman, "Labour Relations." The strike, which clearly could not be won, was called following the unjust firing of a worker.

33 B.R. Patil, "Collective Bargaining and Conciliation in India," *Indian Journal of Industrial Relations* 12, No. 1 (July 1976):41–60.

34 C. Meyers and S. Kannappan, *Industrial Relations in India*, 2nd ed. (London: Asia Publishing, 1970), p. 303. The authors also provide a useful discussion of the history and debate concerning government intervention.

35 One has only to examine a small number of strikes and settlements to know the difficulties inherent in formulating detailed, reliable models to explain and predict bargaining outcomes. Regularities coexist with influences that are unique to each bargaining relationship and settlement.

36 The cotton-textile industry is a notable but peculiar exception. Average earnings over the two years are almost identical in private and public firms. However, public ownership results principally from take-overs of "sick" (bankrupt) firms to avoid large-scale job losses.

37 Wage boards make "no distinction. . . between units in public and private sectors" in setting minimum pay rates, *Report of the National Commission on Labour*, p. 361. Firms do have considerable discretion, however, in total compensation. Overtime pay, e.g., is a large component of earnings and constitutes an important bargaining issue. Public firms reportedly provide greater opportunities for overtime work.

38 For discussions of soft bargaining postures of public managers, see Ghosh and Nath, *Labour Relations* , p. 79, and Patil, "Collective Bargaining."

39 J.C. Jhuraney, "Spatial Changes in the Distribution of Employment in the Organized Sector," *Indian Journal of Industrial Relations* 12, No.1 (July 1976):61–72. States classified as industrially backward include Assam, Jammu and Kashmir, Nagaland, Andhra Pradesh, Bihar, Madhya Pradesh, Orissa, Rajasthan, Uttar Pradesh, Manipur, Tripura, and Goa. Criteria for backwardness were defined in Planning Commission, "Identification of Backward Areas," *Report of the Working Group* (New Delhi: Government of India Press, 1969), as follows: "(1) poverty of people as indicated by low per capita income and low per capita consumption; (2) high density of population in relationship to development of productive resources and employment opportunities; (3) poverty of communications as indicated by small lengths of railways and metalled roads per square mile; (4) high incidence of unemployment or gross underemployment; (5) consumption of electric power."

40 It would be useful to explore ways in which public-employer and government endorsement of union organizing efforts affects public-sector bargaining and industrial disputes.

Part IV

How do public enterprises behave in international markets?

9 State-owned enterprises in the world economy: the case of iron ore

Raymond Vernon and Brian Levy

Only two or three decades ago, international trade was overwhelmingly in the hands of private firms. Today, however, state-owned enterprises hold a strong position in most raw materials, as well as some manufactured products; and the prospects are that this position may grow.

This chapter examines an industry in which state-owned enterprises have greatly enlarged their role in recent years, the world iron-ore industry. The chapter points to a number of conclusions about the effects of state-owned enterprises in international markets. Some conclusions may prove unique for the iron-ore industry, but others promise to apply more widely.

In industries such as iron-ore mining, where the fixed costs are high and where participants are limited in number, individual firms characteristically place considerable emphasis upon strategies that are designed to reduce their market risks. Until the 1970s, large private enterprises in these industries commonly tried to reduce such risks by creating vertically integrated linkages between mine and mill – that is to say, by internalizing the market for iron ore.

When state-owned enterprises became a major factor in the industry in the 1970s, the strategy of linking mines to mills continued to be prevalent wherever both could be located within the same national territory, but vertical integration across national borders became less common. Instead, state-owned enterprises sought other ways to achieve stability in international markets. How successful have they been in reducing the risks and uncertainties of these markets? What has been their effect on the structure of the international market itself? To answer these questions it is necessary first to review some key aspects of the changing structure of the industry.

The research on which this chapter is based was financed in part by the Tinker Foundation, the Ford Foundation, and the Corporación Venezolana de Guayana, and was greatly assisted by the support of the Companhía Vale do Rio Doce. The field work of Janet Kelly Escobar in Venezuela and Brazil was of considerable importance to the authors, as was that of Ravi Ramamurti in India. Sam Citron and Richard Strasser also made substantial research contributions.

9.1   A profile of sources and markets

Changing trade patterns

The location of the world iron-ore industry has depended upon nature's accidents and man's discoveries, producing a fairly concentrated geographical pattern.[1] Nevertheless, the world production patterns for iron ore, shown in Table 9.1, exhibit some startling shifts over the past quarter century. Most notable has been the decline in the relative positions of the United States and France and the rise of those of the USSR, Australia, and Brazil.

Behind these trends lie several important forces. First, the world's steel industry, the principal users of iron ore, has been shifting rapidly. Second, the traditional steel-producing economies have been exhausting their domestic supplies of usable iron ore. In 1977 the United States imported 32.3% of its iron-ore requirements as compared with 7.2% in 1950. Even more drastic changes in source were recorded in the principal European countries. Finally, the new producers of steel – notably including Japan – have been obliged to place far greater reliance on imported ore than the older producers.

Along with the depletion of domestic sources, a decline in the cost of long-haul shipments of ore and other products added to the use of foreign ore sources. Back in 1953, there were no ore transport vessels with a capacity above 20,000 tons. By 1978, 35 ships had a capacity of more than 100,000 tons of ore.[2] The increase in the average size of the ore carrier fleet has led to a marked decline in costs. For instance, the overall costs per ton when shipping ore in a 120,000-ton carrier amount to about one-third of the costs of transporting ore in a 15,000-ton vessel.[3]

In the new patterns of iron-ore trade that emerged, a few country-to-country movements were of particular importance: Australia to Japan, a movement that accounted for more than 20% of the world's international trade in the product; Canada to the United States, accounting for about 9%; Brazil and India to Japan, each representing 6 or 7%; and Brazil to Germany, accounting for 3% or 4%.

Changing patterns of participation

The extraordinary shifts in the world's iron-ore markets have been accompanied by an equally dramatic shift in the participants in those markets.

Thirty years ago, most of the iron ore used by the steel companies of the world came from mines situated within their respective national territories. And most of these mines were linked to the steel mills by ownership or other close ties.

The intimate links between the mills and the mines were a consequence of the oligopolistic structure of both industries; in markets of this sort, transactions conducted on an arm's length basis between unrelated buyers and sellers tend to be fairly costly.[4] In the case of iron ore, these costs are increased by the fact that metal ores are not a totally standardized product, either chemically or physically.

Table 9.1. *World iron-ore production, 1950 and 1977*

Producing country	1950		1977	
	Tons (thousands)	Percent of total	Tons (thousands)	Percent of total
USSR	39,651	16.1	233,947	28.7
Australia	2,453	1.0	95,960	11.8
United States	98,932	40.5	80,718	9.9
Brazil	1,987	0.8	65,942	8.1
China	3,000	1.2	49,211	6.0
France	29,990	13.3	36,400	4.5
Canada	3,281	1.3	52,774	6.5
India	3,125	1.3	40,564	5.0
Liberia			26,082	3.2
Sweden	13,611	5.6	25,015	3.1
Venezuela			21,653	2.7
South Africa	1,189	0.4	15,255	1.9
Chile	2,950	1.2	10,039	1.2
Others	42,293	17.3	60,236	7.4
Total	244,469	100.0	813,996	100.0

Source: American Iron and Steel Institute, *Annual Statistical Report, 1977* (Washington, D.C., 1978), p. 90.

Finding the right ores – or, alternatively, adjusting to the wrong ores – can be costly. The receiver of ore has a high stake in the reliability of the shipper and vice versa.

A second reason for the tendency toward vertical integration has to do with the cost structure of both steel firms and iron-ore mines. Both bear high costs if demand falls off in the periods of downturn,[5] a fact that conduces each to try to capture its downstream customers. In fact, in periods of surplus, the unintegrated iron-ore producer is exposed to the risk that the steel mills will turn to their captive mines for their supplies, using the unintegrated mines as sellers of last resort.[6] On similar lines, the unintegrated steel mills are found worrying about periods of ore shortage, fearful lest the existing supplies will be diverted to their integrated rivals.

Even before World War I, the American steel industry was operating on a vertically integrated basis. And ever since then, the steel firms have directly controlled nearly 80% of their domestic ore sources.[7]

In Europe, meanwhile, with the exception of the iron-ore mines of Sweden, practically all mines have been captives of European steel companies.[8] The Swedish mines were nominally independent; but Sweden's pre–World War II dependence on the German market and the long history of cartelization in the steel industry of Europe suggest that the movements of Swedish ore were controlled by agreements in the downstream steel markets.[9]

Nevertheless, despite the apparent advantages of vertical integration in the iron and steel industry, nonintegrated mines captured considerable shares of the world market in the 1960s and 1970s. Behind that shift lay two principal factors: the emergence of Japan as a steel producer and the emergence of state-owned enterprises as producers of iron ore.

The swift rise in Japan's demands for iron ore began to be evident in the early 1960s at a time when the Japanese government was still loath to authorize direct investments abroad.[10] Nor were the Japanese steel companies themselves exposed at the time to all the stimuli that normally encourage vertical integration. For one thing, as long as they were competing inside the Japanese market they had nothing to fear from one another in terms of iron-ore supplies or iron-ore prices; all of them were joined together, under the leadership of the Ministry of International Trade and Industry, in joint purchase contracts with foreign iron-ore suppliers. In addition, Japan's restrictive import policies protected local steel producers from foreign competition.

In the absence of ownership, Japanese ore buyers during the 1950s and 1960s sought other ways of achieving stability in ore supplies. The Japanese offered long-term procurement contracts and loans to independent mining entrepreneurs, who used these contracts to raise additional capital.[11]

Despite the Japanese example, European and U.S. steel companies were consistent in displaying a preference for direct ownership of the mines. By 1970, Bethlehem, Republic, and U.S. Steel had taken direct ownership of mines in Chile, Liberia, and Venezuela; and by 1976, three-quarters of Canada's ore output was under the control of American steel firms or ore houses closely linked to these firms. By 1970, too, British, Italian, Belgian, and German steel producers had developed substantial ownership positions in the iron-ore mines of Mauritania, India, Liberia, Canada, and Brazil[12]

But as Table 9.2 indicates, between 1964 and 1975 state-owned suppliers began to supplant captive mines as the major source of imported ore. Except for a few locations, the international vertically integrated structure set up by American and European steel companies did not endure. The new situation, as we shall shortly see, was acutely disturbing to some of the world's principal users of iron ore and generated various countermoves on their part.

9.2   The emergence of state-owned enterprises

Their enhanced position

Table 9.3 lists the principal state-owned enterprises that are active in the world iron-ore industry. Two tendencies are clear from the table: that state-owned enterprises have been appearing in the industry with increasing frequency, and that the nationalization of foreign holding companies has become increasingly common.

Table 9.2. *Percentage of imports by Japan, United States, and European Coal and Steel Community countries, by sources, 1950–77*

	1950	1964	1975	1977
Japan				
From independents				
Private	100.0	90.1	66.0	63.7
State owned		9.9	34.0	36.3
Total	100.0	100.0	100.0	100.0
United States				
From sources captive to				
U.S. steel firms	53.9	95.9	44.6	73.1
From independents	46.1	4.1	55.4	26.9
Private	37.7	1.4	2.4	1.5
State owned	8.4	2.7	53.0	25.4
Total	100.0	100.0	100.0	100.0
ECSC Countries				
From sources captive to				
ECSC steel firms	12.3	14.9	21.4	22.7
From sources captive to				
U.S. steel firms	0.9	14.9	9.9	11.1
From Swedish independents	57.8	38.0	15.1	13.2
From other independents	29.0	32.2	53.6	52.9
Private	28.4	22.4	21.2	17.5
State owned	0.6	9.8	32.4	35.4
Total	100.0	100.0	100.0	100.0

Source: United Nations, *Yearbook of International Trade Statistics, 1977* (New York, 1978), pp. 962–3; "1977 Iron Ore Shipments of Companies," *Skillings Mining Review* 67, No. 27 (July 8, 1978):8–9; Walter C. Labys, *"The Role of State Trading in Mineral Commodity Markets: Copper, Tin, Bauxite and Iron Ore,"* paper presented at Conference on State Trading, April 1979, (Montreal: Ecole des Hautes Etudes Commerciales), p. 31a.

The expansion of the operations of state enterprises helped transform the international markets. State enterprises reduced the extent of vertical integration in the industry by preempting positions that private steel firms might eventually have controlled and by cutting back the scope of the private firms' existing positions; by the late 1970s, the state-owned suppliers accounted for almost 40% of internationally traded ore.

What can be said about the business behavior of these enterprises?[13] Our studies suggest that strong generalizations can be made about the factors that bring state-owned enterprises into existence. But once they are in existence, generalizations about their operating policies are considerably more difficult to make.

Table 9.3. *Principal state-owned ventures exporting iron ore, 1978*

Country	Name of establishment	Date established as state enterprise	Iron ore production, 1978 (in thousands of tons)
Brazil	Companhía Vale do Rio Doce (CVRD)	1942	50,574
Sweden	Luossavaara-Kiirunavaara AB (LKAB)	1907–57[a]	23,967
South Africa	South African Iron & Steel Industrial Corporation (ISCOR)	1928	19,796
Liberia	Lamco Joint Venture	1960[b]	10,572
	Bong Mining Company	1963[b]	7,387
India[c]	National Mineral Development Corporation (NMDC)	1958	6,909
	Mines and Metals Trading Corporation (MMTC)	1964	Export trading only
Venezuela	CVG Ferrominera Orinoco S.A.	1974	12,956
Chile	Compañía de Acero del Pacifico S.A. (CAP)	1971	6,935
Mauritania	Société Nationale Industrielle et Minière (SNIM)	1974	6,336
Peru	Empresa Minera del Peru	1975	4,854

[a] The Swedish government held 50% of the company's shares in 1907; in 1957 the government took over the company entirely.
[b] The Liberian government has not attempted to exercise any control over these projects, which are effectively controlled by foreign partners.
[c] Along with the export operations listed here, iron-ore mines captive to state-owned steel companies mine about 12 million tons of ore annually.
Source: Walter C. Labys, *The Role of State Trading in Mineral Commodity Markets: Copper, Tin, Bauxite and Iron Ore* (Montreal: Ecole des Hautes Etudes Commerciales, Conference on State Trading, April 1979), p. 31a; "1978 Iron Ore Shipments of Companies," *Skillings Mining Review* 68, No. 27 (July 7, 1979):12–13.

Origins of the state-owned enterprises

The iron-ore mining industry is one of those sectors that governments usually prefer to have under national control. That desire, however, has not always led governments to set up state-owned enterprises. The decision seems to have turned on three factors: on the nature of the ideology prevailing in the country; on the financial and managerial strength of the country's private sector; and on the country's perception of its capacity to run the operations.

The ideological factor, for instance, seems to have been responsible for the fact that Australia and Canada continue to tolerate the existence of private foreign mining operations on a large scale; largely as a result, foreign mines still account for somewhat more than one-third of internationally traded iron ore. All the nationalizations since 1958, listed in Table 9.3, have taken place in developing countries.[14]

To be sure, even among developing countries, the decision to establish a state-owned enterprise is a highly selective one. Some industries in these countries have been targets for nationalization, whereas others have not. And where nationalizations have been widespread in a given industry, the timing of the decision has varied considerably in different countries.[15]

In the case of Brazil, the opportunity to recapture the national iron-ore industry from foreigners came with the special circumstances that accompanied World War II. An offer by the United States and the United Kingdom to provide capital and markets overcame some of the critical difficulties that often stand in the way of nationalization.

The military-backed Brazilian government that supported the creation of Companhía Vale do Rio Doce (CVRD) in 1942 had previously annulled the long-standing concession of an American entrepreneur to export iron ore, expressing its determination that the Brazilian mining and metallurgical industries were to be developed by Brazilians.[16] The decision to create a state-owned enterprise in steel was taken only after efforts had failed to establish a steel industry owned by private national interests. And once created, the state-owned steel industry continued to seek private local participation.[17]

Consistent with that spirit, local private mining firms have been allowed to carve out a niche for themselves alongside CVRD. And once Brazil overcame the fear of foreign domination, even foreign mining firms were allowed to develop a substantial position in the Brazilian ore industry.[18]

The South African case offers an interesting variant on Brazil. In this instance, the struggle for control was between the Dutch-speaking Afrikaners of the country and the dominant Anglophile businessmen who, though themselves South Africans, had strong ties to the foreign business community. From the 1920s, South African state-owned enterprises, as instruments of domestic industrialization, were used as a countervailing force to the power of the traditional private sector.[19]

The South African Iron and Steel Industrial Corporation (ISCOR), which has dominated South Africa's steel industry since its establishment in 1928, has been active in the iron-ore export business for less than a decade. In the early 1970s the government chose ISCOR over a private rival to develop vast, newly discovered ore resources, a project that entailed the building of a 500-mile railway line through deserted country. Although the railway line was eventually transferred to

South African Railways, ISCOR's early control of the line set the seal on its advantage. In 1979 ISCOR sold 15 million tons of iron ore abroad. Meanwhile, one private firm, a pioneer in the export of iron ore, had already faded away; another private survivor was operating at a small portion of ISCOR's level.

In the cases of both Brazil and South Africa, nationalization was seen mainly as a step in the process of curbing foreign-owned enterprises and their allies in the local economy, not as a step on the road to socialism. Similar motivations were evident in the spate of nationalizations that occurred in the early 1970s in Chile, Mauritania, Peru, and Venezuela.[20] In India, by contrast, the official ideology that accompanied the emergence of state enterprises contained explicit socialist overtones.[21] How deep those convictions ran is a matter for debate. Private business generally continued to play a substantial role in the leading political parties;[22] high government officials at times continued to be drawn from the ranks of private business; and government officials sometimes transferred to the private sector.[23] And some major sectors of the economy were earmarked for continued participation by private enterprise.[24] Finally, the largest private Indian businesses have managed to grow rapidly since independence.[25]

However one may label Indian ideology, it nevertheless called for the close control of enterprise by a government bureaucracy. As subsequent events would demonstrate, that control could be achieved both by ownership and by regulation. The regime that came to control India's iron-ore mines reflected how narrow the gap between the two approaches could sometimes be.

The ideological nuances underlying the decision to establish a state-owned iron-ore enterprise have varied somewhat from country to country. But in all these countries, the propensity to nationalize seems to have been increased by the government's perception that the problems on managing the facilities and marketing the ore were shrinking.

The proposition that national capabilities help to determine the timing of nationalizations is an idea implicit in the concept of the obsolescing bargain.[26] Initially, according to the concept, governments may offer attractive terms to induce foreign firms to make an investment, aware of their own inability to take the project on. But as domestic capabilities to perform complex tasks improve, host governments use their muscle to extract a growing share of the investment's profits. Eventually host countries no longer feel any need to share profits with foreign investors and consider the strategy of owning the mining operations themselves.

The propensity to nationalize is growing over the course of time not only because governments see themselves as becoming more capable but also because they have increasing access to international markets that offer technology without equity strings.[27] In addition, governments are finding it easier to mobilize the financial resources needed for the take-over and operation of state-owned enterprises. In the late 1950s the World Bank refused to help India in the financing of its industrial sector on grounds that the funds were being used by nationalized industry.[28] Today, intergovernmental credit agencies lend readily to state-owned enterprises, although many are barred from lending to private firms.

Finally, one other special factor seems to have speeded the trend to nationalization. Encouraged by the extraordinary events in oil in the first half of the 1970s, many developing countries briefly entertained the expectation that all raw materials were moving into a period of scarcity. Such a period would liberate them from the final restraint that bound them to international companies, namely, the need for a reliable market. That expectation did not last very long – but long enough to stimulate the nationalization of foreign-owned ore mines in several developing countries.

In sum, then, the growth of the state-owned enterprise can be seen as one of the consequences of improved domestic capabilities in the developing countries, coupled with increased access to international capital and technical skills.

9.3 The new international environment

Despite the increased importance of state-owned enterprises in the world's iron-ore markets, certain key characteristics of those markets have remained unchanged. One of these is the high concentration of sellers and buyers. Table 9.4 demonstrates that although the identities of the principal exporters and importers have changed over the years, the degree of geographical concentration has remained very high on both sides of the market, and the actual buyers and sellers have remained very few in number. In 1975 the four largest importing entities accounted for 69% of the international iron-ore trade,[29] and the four largest ore-exporting firms accounted for at least 53% of the trade.[30]

The persistence of this concentration has meant that any given seller of iron ore, unless strongly linked to some specific buyers, was exposed to a high degree of market risk. In their search for such linkages, state-owned enterprises have made considerable use of long-term contracts with foreign ore buyers. Some of these contracts have included firm commitments covering long periods of time that specify both the prices and the volume of the ore to be transferred.[31] Some have linked such commitments to other undertakings, such as a loan to the ore mine from a third party.[32] But others, though dubbed long term, are less firm in nature: They may specify a range instead of a fixed figure for the volume of ore to be sold; they may specify a formula by which the price is periodically to be fixed; or they may simply provide that the price is to be renegotiated periodically.[33] Finally, some trading agreements are only tacit or implicit, representing a continuing relationship between traditional trading partners.

To be sure, firms with long-term contracts are less exposed to market fluctuation than those without such contracts. By 1978, both Germany and Britain had cut back entirely on purchases from the short-term market, which had accounted for

Table 9.4. *Geographical concentration of world trade in iron ore, 1950, 1964, and 1975, in percent*

	1950	1964	1975
World exports: percentage accounted for by:			
Four largest exporting countries	62.6	50.3	65.3
Eight largest exporting countries	82.7	73.9	85.9
World imports: percentage accounted for by:			
Four largest importing countries	65.8	64.3	74.4
Eight largest importing countries	88.3	85.6	91.6

Source: Data for 1950 and 1964 are from Gerald Manners, *The Changing World Market for Iron Ore 1950–1980* (Baltimore: Johns Hopkins University Press, 1971), pp. 344, 348; and for 1975, from United Nations, *Yearbook of International Trade Statistics, 1977* (New York, 1978), pp. 502-3.

about 20% of each country's ore needs in 1974; partly for that reason, both Venezuela and Peru, having canceled their earlier contractual ties upon nationalization, lost ground in Europe. By contrast, volumes traded under various contracts between British Steel and Canada's Carol Lake and various contracts of Brazil's CVRD and Mineracôes Brasileiras Reunidas (MBR) mines resisted the declining trend of ore imports.

Despite these examples, however, experience over the past two decades points to the conclusion that the family of contracts described earlier provides nothing like the stability and predictability in sourcing that is ordinarily associated with ownership. Buyers commonly back away from their commitments when ore is in very easy supply, and the sellers do likewise when ore is in tight supply.[34]

For instance, U.S. Steel did not fulfill the purchase commitments, which it made to Venezuela's Ferrominera Orinoco, associated with the nationalization of its ore holdings in that country.[35] The Japanese now and then have taken delivery of less than the volumes for which they had contracted from Australia; moreover, prices have been adjusted more often and more drastically than was agreed in the supply contracts.[36] The Germans have found a way around a long-term deal with CVRD, under which they were to match their exports from a captive mine in Brazil ton for ton with exports through CVRD.[37]

Notwithstanding the equivocal nature of these so-called long-term contracts, they do of course have a certain utility for buyers and sellers. By reducing the needs of each continuously to search for new partners, they hold down transaction costs and limit the costs of technical adjustments that are associated with changes in the sources of ore. But they do very little to achieve another objective of the ore-exporting and ore-importing enterprises, that is, the reduction of uncertainties associated with changes in supply, demand, and price.

9.4 National politics and international integration

With long-term contracts proving to be no panacea to the problem of international integration, state-owned enterprises have had to search for other ways to deal with instability in international markets. Their responses to this instability have been very different from enterprise to enterprise. And these differences, in turn, stem in part from the distinctive history, the distinctive set of institutions, and the distinctive problems of the country in which each enterprise operates.

Brazil

Brazil's iron-ore industry, as we have already noted, was dominated by a state-owned enterprise for pragmatic, rather than ideological, reasons. Nevertheless, CVRD's operations have been distinctly different in some respects from the operations of a private enterprise. To begin with, the state-owned status of the firm has helped it to gain access to capital on a very large scale. With the help of such capital, CVRD has been the government's agent in the development of a vast infrastructure of railroads, roads, and ports, an infrastructure that has been placed at the service of other enterprises, foreign as well as national. Moreover, CVRD has placed extraordinary emphasis on the import substitution process, throwing as much business as possible to firms based in Brazil. In 1969 only 25% of CVRD's purchases were made in Brazil; but by 1975, more than 80% of CVRD's suppliers were Brazilian-based.[38]

CVRD's state-owned status also has had other effects on its operations. It has, for instance, been involved in various complex deals – government-to-government deals in some cases – involving large-scale two-way swaps of goods and services.[39]

CVRD's close ties to the Brazilian official establishment, however, have not prevented it from taking on many of the characteristics of an ebullient, autonomous private enterprise. In its early years, such tendencies were not much in evidence, inasmuch as CVRD had no substantial cash flows of its own. Once established, however, CVRD developed a considerable quantity of internally generated funds and independent borrowing capacity. Operating on the basis of a rich supply of ores and an efficient infrastructure, CVRD pushed aggressively into world markets, cutting prices as necessary to increase its market share.

More recently, CVRD has begun to develop arrangements that suggest it would like to stabilize the market conditions in which it operates. Thus far, its status as a state-owned enterprise has not prevented it from developing various strong linkages to foreign customers. It has recently constructed three ore processing plants in joint ventures with Italian, Japanese, and Spanish steel companies; it has concurred in the almost fourfold expansion of Ferteco Mineracao, the captive mine of a group of German steel companies, on the condition that the Germans increase their purchases from CVRD as well; and it has agreed to develop a new ore mine jointly with five Japanese steel firms.[40] For the 1980s, CVRD harbors huge expansion plans, which will almost surely require added links with foreign users.[41]

South Africa

In South Africa, as we observed earlier, the gulf between private and state-owned firms has been somewhat wider than in Brazil. The Iron and Steel Industrial Corporation (ISCOR), like CVRD, has received subsidized capital and special infrastructural support. In addition, though, ISCOR has had to contend with government-controlled prices for its steel products, as well as a government-prescribed product range. So far, ISCOR has not developed any strong links to foreign firms, although at one time the firm did seek without success to develop a downstream joint venture with some foreign steel firms.[42]

Venezuela

Unlike Brazil and South Africa, Venezuela has adopted the strategy of achieving stability by domestic integration. Venezuela's state-owned iron-ore undertaking, Ferrominera, has operated under strikingly different conditions from those of Brazil's CVRD or South Africa's ISCOR, reflecting the importance of differences in the domestic setting. For one thing, Venezuela's petroleum exports have relieved the country of the chronic balance-of-payment problems that other developing countries commonly confront. Accordingly, Venezuela has not placed the expansion of its exports very high on its agenda of national objectives. Oil exports have also given Venezuela an exchange rate that has prevented it from emulating Brazil by expanding its exports of manufactured goods.

Perhaps in part for these reasons, Venezuela has been in the lead in trying to persuade other developing countries of the undesirability of price cutting in raw-material exports; indeed, more than any other country, Venezuela was responsible for the creation of OPEC in 1960. In this same vein, Venezuela has looked on the further processing of its raw materials as desirable irrespective of the cost; and it has seen its iron-ore supplies as a resource to be husbanded for an indigenous steel industry that seems destined to be a high-cost producer.

When Ferrominera came into existence in 1975, therefore, it had no burning mandate to expand its output and exports. On the contrary, the company was regarded by government officials as the custodian of properties that would eventually be used to supply raw materials to Sidor, the state-owned steel company. At the same time, however, both Ferrominera and its erstwhile foreign owners saw advantages in maintaining some of their prenationalization ties and in exhibiting the appearance of continuing some of the earlier relationships.[43] Venezuela had no desire to frighten away foreign investors in other industries not ripe for nationalization; besides, the managers of Ferrominera itself wished to continue to sell some of their ore to the former owners, as well as to use the technical services, the marketing services, and the shipping facilities of U.S. Steel. For their part, U.S. Steel and Bethlehem Steel needed time to reconstitute their sources of supply and reduce their dependence on Ferrominera.

Fundamentally, however, Ferrominera has only been marking time until the day when Sidor's needs may be sufficient to absorb its output. Having lost some of its position in U.S. markets as a result of cutbacks in the purchases of its former U.S. owners, Ferrominera has made no apparent effort to fill the gap. Moreover, the company appears to have been•yielding ground to Brazilian competition in European markets. But in light of its underlying mandate, none of these developments has appeared critical to the Venezuelan government.

India

India, like Venezuela, has tried to avoid the uncertainties of foreign markets by turning to domestic integration. Indian policy has long recognized that public and private enterprises might operate side by side in the national market.[44] Accordingly, the interagency Iron Ore Board, in which half a dozen ministries are represented, has applied its policies to all firms in the industry, private and public. Major investments and major trade practices, therefore, have been the subject of high government policy, beyond the control of the management of any single public or private enterprise.

To be sure, the power of the governmental policy board has been augmented by the fact that so much of India's iron-ore industry lies in the government's hands. Part of such ownership takes the form of captive mines attached to the state-owned steel plants of India;[45] the output of these captive mines accounts for about 40% of the nation's annual ore output and is used entirely for internal consumption. A separate state-owned entity, the National Mineral Development Corporation (NMDC), produces another 15%, most of which is exported by the Metals and Minerals Trading Corporation (MMTC), another state-owned enterprise. Small private firms, which mine about one-quarter of India's iron-ore output, have also been obliged to export their ore through MMTC, which arranges for access to an international market that might otherwise be unavailable. Only the large private miners of Goa are allowed to export their ore directly, in order not to disturb their long-standing links to buyers. But even in this case, their export arrangements are held on a short leash.

Despite its general policy, India has allowed a few long-term links to operate. It has tolerated, for instance, the continued exercise of Italian Finsider's right to 2 million tons annually of Goan ore production. And it forged a cooperative venture with an Iranian state-owned steel firm under which the Iranians would finance a new iron-ore project in return for a long-term claim on its ore.[46] But by and large, export goals have been set by government planners, and these have sought to restrict exports of ore in favor of anticipated demands by the domestic steel industry.[47] Furthermore, though the privately owned Goan mining firms are allowed to ship their ore to Japan without the intervention of the MMTC, their contracts with Japanese buyers have been concluded under close state supervision; among other things, contracts in excess of a year or two in duration are prohibited.[48]

In sum, although the state-owned enterprises of different nations have operated under different degrees of supervision and have developed in different directions, they appear to have shared an interest in limiting their risks in foreign markets. Responding to that objective, some have diverted their iron-ore production in increasing proportions to their domestic markets. Those that continue to rely on international markets typically have sought security in various types of long-term arrangements with their customers – but so far with uncertain results.

9.5 Future contours of the international ore market

The public character of state-owned enterprises will no doubt have some influence on the contours of the world ore market. For instance, their public character may influence the structures that replace the ownership ties that once linked the mines and mills of different countries. Here our case studies offer tantalizing hints. In the case of India, for instance, the effect may be trivial; public and private enterprises alike may operate under the same tight governmental strictures. In the case of Brazil, however, the public character of CVRD may well create special inhibitions. We assume – though with little supporting evidence so far – that CVRD will not have the same freedom as a private enterprise to create vertical linkages across Brazil's borders. This assumption rests on the observation that when the managers of state-owned enterprises forge strong foreign linkages, it helps them to slip loose from governmental control. To maintain or restore this control, we expect government officials from time to time to restrict or even to dissolve such linkages. Because so many of the iron-ore producers are state owned, we expect to see an international market develop in which vertical integration across borders is considerably restrained.

Another generalization worth considering is that state-owned iron-ore producers will be less responsive than captive mines to both short-term and long-term changes in international ore demand. That possibility follows in part from our assumption that state-owned enterprises will be compelled to maintain less intimate ties to their foreign buyers. As a result, they may be in a poorer position to foresee a decline in foreign short-term or long-term demand; and even if such a change is foreseen, they may feel less certainty about the relationship of the projected change to their own future sales levels. Finally, in the event that demand actually declines, state-owned enterprises may be slower to adjust production levels than their private counterparts. In periods of declining demand, state-owned enterprises may see their labor costs as fixed and invariant and hence may see no reason to cut their production.

If demand should grow rapidly, rather than decline, there is also a possibility that state-owned enterprises may be less prepared than private enterprises for that development. Again, the state-owned enterprise may lack information or, possessing the information, may be uncertain as to whether it would share in the increase. That handicap, however, could be offset by the fact that some state-owned enterprises by reason of their public character have relatively easy access to the capital needed for expanding their facilities, a factor that could be important in a period of scarce capital and high interest rates.

The increased importance of state-owned enterprises in iron-ore production is also likely to encourage the trend toward vertical integration within national borders, thereby reducing the overall importance of international markets. That view is based on two expectations. First, state-owned mines such as those in Venezuela are more likely to serve their home steel industry as a matter of absolute priority than would be the case if they were privately owned. Second, in recognition of their increasing vulnerability, steel mills in foreign countries that have relied on foreign ores are likely to look for safer sources of ore. Steel mills in the United States are already following that strategy. In response to the erosion of international vertical integration, these firms have turned back to their higher-cost captive-ore sources in North America.[49] The willingness of U.S. mills to rely on relatively costly ores is increased by two factors: by the generous provisions of U.S. tax law, which permit the steel firms to charge a 15% depletion allowance in figuring the taxes on their mining operations, and by the prospect that the U.S. government may restrict the importation of steel from lower-cost sources, including those with access to cheaper ores.

To be sure, neither Japan nor Europe has the option of reverting to a policy of self-sufficiency for its iron ore; nor do many of the iron-ore exporting countries have the option of absorbing their ore production internally. Accordingly, an international market will continue to exist in which the state-owned enterprises will play a major role. One final set of questions to be considered, therefore, is whether the emergence of independent ore producers is likely to presage some OPEC-like agreement in the iron-ore industry. In particular, does the prevalence of state-owned enterprises among these independents make the emergence of a cartel more or less likely?

Here again, one is forced to speculate. Our view is that the existence of state-owned enterprises is more likely to constitute an impediment to such agreements than otherwise. As this review indicates, the various state-owned enterprises involved in the world ore market operate from strikingly different perspectives, pursuing a much more diverse set of goals than would be the case for a group of profit-seeking privately owned mines in an oligopolistic industry. In general, market participants who are motivated by diverse goals find it more difficult to coordinate their efforts than those with common goals.[50] As a result, the fact that so many iron-ore mining operations are state-owned may present an added obstacle to the formation of an effective cartel.[51]

As the role of state-owned enterprises increases, their governments may feel in somewhat better control of their respective national economies and somewhat better equipped to pursue national goals. But the growth of state-owned enterprises could also increase the uncertainties in the world iron-ore market, adding to the difficulties of the importers and exporters that continue to rely on that market. In global welfare terms, it is difficult to say whether the net contribution of the state-owned enterprises will be positive.

Notes

1 See Gerald Manners, *The Changing World Market for Iron Ore, 1950–1980* (Baltimore: Johns Hopkins University Press, 1971).
2 See Lloyd's Register of Shipping, *Statistical Tables* (London: Lloyd's Register of Shipping, 1978), p. 60.
3 Between 1951 and 1965 the costs per ton of ship construction were cut in half, although they increased again thereafter. See Manners, *Changing World Market*, p. 175; and United Nations Conference on Trade and Development, *Review of Maritime Transport, 1976* (New York: United Nations, 1978), p. 26. By the 1970s, the capital cost per ton of building a 120,000-ton vessel was less than 60% that of a 15,000-ton ship; and the operating costs per ton for the larger vessel were one-fourth those of the smaller ship. See R. O. Goss and C. D. Jones, "The Economics of Size in Dry Bulk Carriers," in *Advances in Maritime Economics*, ed. R. O. Goss (Cambridge University Press, 1977), pp. 90–123.
4 See, e.g., Oliver Williamson, "The Vertical Integration of Production: Market Failure Considerations," *American Economic Review* (May 1971), pp. 112–21; see also Peter Buckley and Mark Casson, *The Future of the Multinational Enterprise* (New York: Holmes & Meier, 1976).
5 See F. M. Scherer, *Industrial Market Structure and Economic Performance* (Chicago: Rand McNally, 1970), pp. 192–5.
6 See Raymon Vernon, "The Location of Economic Activity," in ed. John Dunning *Economic Analysis and the Multinational Enterprise,* (London: Allen & Unwin, 1974); see also F. T. Knickerbocker, *Oligopolistic Reaction and the Multinational Enterprise* (Boston: Graduate School of Business Administration, Harvard University, 1973).
7 For details of U.S. controls, see R. B. Mancke, "Iron Ore and Steel: A Case Study of the Causes and Consequences of Vertical Integration," *Journal of Industrial Economics* 20, No. 3 (July 1972):220–9; also Nancy Wardell, "United States Iron Ore Imports: Sourcing Strategies for U.S. Steel Companies" (D.B.A. thesis, Harvard University, 1977), Chap. 2. Much of the remaining 20% has been in the hands of four firms, apparently under the effective control of the U.S. steel producers. See House of Representatives, Committee on the Judiciary, *Report of the Federal Trade Commission on the Control of Iron Ore* (Washington, D.C.: U.S. Government Printing Office, 1952), p. 53.
8 See G. D. Feldman, *Iron and Steel in the German Inflation, 1916–1923* (Princeton: Princeton University Press, 1977), esp. Chap. 4; International Metalworkers Federation, Iron and Steel Department, *The Largest Steel Companies in the Free World* (Steelworkers Conference, Vienna, 1959), pp. 36, 68; Acieries Reunies de Burbach-Eich-Dudelange, *Annual Report, 1975* (Luxembourg, 1976), p. 20; European Group for Financial Research, "The European Steel Industry: A Comparative Study of Twelve Companies," mimeographed (1960), p. 159.

9 See A. F. Rickman, *Swedish Iron Ore* (London: Faber & Faber, 1939), pp. 156–64; see also Ervin Hexner, *International Cartels* (Chapel Hill: University of North Carolina Press, 1946), pp. 203–15.

10 See R. B. McKern, *Multinational Enterprises and Natural Resources* (Sydney, Australia: McGraw-Hill 1976), p. 57.

11 For illustrations of such arrangements in India, see Committee on Public Undertakings (1972–3), *Thirty-Seventh Report: National Mineral Development Corporation Limited, Hyderabad* (New Delhi: Lok Sabha Secretariat, 1973), pp. 1–2, 63. For Australia, see McKern, *Multinational Enterprises*, pp. 206–15; and for South Africa, "Sishen-Saldanha Survey," *Supplement to Financial Mail*, Oct. 1, 1976, p. 11.

12 In two cases, even at this early phase of the internationalization of the iron-ore industry, independent, unintegrated mining firms from the U.S. and Europe set up foreign ventures. These were the Marcona Mining Company – jointly owned by the U.S. mining firms Cyprus Mines and Utah International – in 1952, and Sweden's independent mining company Grangesborg, which began the LAMCO Joint Venture in Liberia in 1960.

13 For the observations of others, see, e.g., M. M. Kostecki, "State Trading in Industrialized and Developing Countries," *Journal of World Trade Law* 12, No. 3; K. D. Walters and R. J. Monsen, "The Nationalized Firm: the Politicians Free Lunch?" *Columbia Journal of World Business* 12, No. 1 (Spring 1977):95; and D. F. Lamont, *Foreign State Enterprises: A Threat to American Business* (New York: Basic Books, 1979).

14 For an example of the developing countries' position, see United Nations, "Permanent Sovereignty over Natural Resources of Developing Countries," Economic and Social Council Resolution 1737, adopted May 4, 1973.

15 See Stephen J. Kobrin, "Foreign Enterprise and Forced Divestment in LDCs," *International Organization* 34, No. 1 (Winter 1980): 65–88. For evidence in the oil industry, see Fariborz Ghadar, *The Evolution of OPEC Strategy* (Lexington, Mass.: Lexington Books, 1977), esp. pp. 20–33.

16 See Peter Evans, *Dependent Development: The Alliance of Multinational, State and Local Capital in Brazil* (Princeton: Princeton University Press, 1979), pp. 89–90. See also John D. Wirth, *The Politics of Brazilian Development, 1930–1954* (Stanford: Stanford University Press, 1970), pp. 111, 112. For details of aborted international efforts to establish a Brazilian iron and steel industry, see Werner Baer, *The Development of the Brazilian Steel Industry* (Nashville, Tenn.: Vanderbilt University Press, 1969), pp. 64–75.

17 Baer, *Development of the Brazilian Steel Industry*, pp. 75, 76.

18 Next to CVRD, which shipped 48.7 million tons in 1978, the largest ore-mining operation is Mineracões Brasileiras Reunidas (MBR) with 1978 shipments of 13.5 million tons; Brazilian interests control 51% of MBR, and the U.S.-based Hanna Mining Company accounts for the other 49%. S.A. Mineracao da Trinidade (SAMITRI) is jointly owned by the European-based ARBED group, with the remaining 40% in the hands of private Brazilian interests. SAMITRI is also a partner in SAMARCO, a joint venture with the U.S. Marcona Corporation. Another private operation, Ferteco Mineracao, is wholly owned by a group of German steel firms.

19 See Heribert Adam and Herman Giliomee, *Ethnic Power Mobilized: Can South Africa Change?* (New Haven: Yale University Press, 1979), esp. Chap. 6. See also David Kaplan, "The Politics of Industrial Protection in South Africa, 1910–1939," *Journal of Southern African Studies* 3, No. 1 (Oct. 1976):70–91.

20 For the Chilean experience, see Theodore H. Moran, *Multinational Corporations and the Politics of Dependence: Copper in Chile* (Princeton: Princeton University

Press, 1974); for Mauritania, see "Senegal, Mauritania, Mali, Guinea," *Quarterly Economic Review*, No. 4, *Economist Intelligence Unit* (London, Mauritania, 1972); for Peru, see John Sheahan, "Peru: Economic Policies and Structural Change, 1968–1978," Center for Development Economics, Research Memorandum No. 72 (Williamstown, Mass: Williams College, 1979), p. 10; and for Venezuela, see Argenis Gamboa, ed., *Nacionalizacion del hierro en Venezuela* (Caracas: Ediciones Centauro, 1974), pp. vi–xv.

21 In 1947, the economic program of the All-India Congress Committee recommended that "in respect of existing undertakings, the process of transfer from private to public ownership should commence after a period of four years," and in 1955 the ruling Congress Party adopted a resolution calling for a "socialist pattern of society." See, e.g., G.C. Agrawal, *Public Sector Steel Industry in India* (Allahabad: Chaitanya Publishing House, 1976), p. 5.

22 See Michael Kidron, *Foreign Investments in India* (London: Oxford University Press, 1965), p. 143.

23 See Helen Lamb, "Business Organization and Leadership in India," in *Leadership and Political Institutions in India*, ed. Richard Park and Irene Tinker (Princeton: Princeton University Press, 1959), pp. 251–67.

24 Ministry of Industry and Supply, Government of India, "Statement of April 6, 1948," in U.S. Department of Commerce, *Investment in India* (Washington, D.C.: U.S. Government Printing Office, 1961), pp. 193–5.

25 See Asim Chaudhuri, *Private Economic Power in India* (New Delhi: People's Publishing House, 1975), pp. 36–7 and 161–5, and Laurence Veit, *India's Second Revolution: The Dimensions of Development* (New York: McGraw-Hill, 1976), esp. Chap. 9.

26 For details of the obsolescing bargain, see Raymond Vernon, *Sovereignty at Bay* (New York: Basic Books, 1971), pp. 46–53.

27 For details of foreign participation in the South African ore-export venture, see South African Iron and Steel Corporation, *Sishen-Saldanha Ore Export Project* (Pretoria, 1974), pp. 32–4. For Brazil, see "World's Largest Ore Port at Tubarão, Brazil," *Skillings Mining Review* 63, No. 39 (Sept. 28, 1974): 6–9.

28 See Edward S. Mason and Robert E. Asher, *The World Bank Since Bretton Woods* (Washington, D.C.: Brookings Institution, 1973), pp. 150–1 and 371–4. According to Mason and Asher, World Bank restrictions on lending to nationalized industries were lifted in 1968. In general, the World Bank has sought government guarantees of loans to nongovernmental borrowers; see ibid., p. 190.

29 Pooling their purchases in each country, Japanese mills in 1975 purchased 47.7% of noncaptive internationally traded iron ore. German mills bought a further 10.7% of the noncaptive internationally traded iron ore through two procurement companies, which coordinated their activities, Rohstoffhandel Gmbh. and Erzkontor Ruhr Gmbh. State-owned monopsonies handle all iron-ore imports for the British and Italians; their trade accounted for an additional 5.8% and 5.1%, respectively.

30 CVRD accounted for 18.1% of noncaptive international supply in 1975. Two Australian mines, Hamersley Holdings and Mount Newman, produced 13.1% and 12%, respectively, of that supply; the Australian government sought to coordinate their sales strategy, but it is not clear how successfully. Malmexport A.B. accounted for a further 10% of the market; and Venezuela's Ferrominera Orinoco for a further 7%.

31 Contracts that India signed with the Japanese in the early 1960s were of this kind; see Deepak Nayyar, *India's Exports and Export Policies in the 1960s* (Cambridge University Press, 1976), p. 364. In the early 1970s British Steel signed contracts

specifying fixed prices for five years with the Canadian Carol Lake project and for three years with the privately owned MBR mine and state-owned CVRD, both in Brazil.

32 An agreement between CVRD and the German steel-firm owners of the Ferteco Mineracao mine was of this type. The Germans agreed to tie their purchases from CVRD to the output of their captive Brazilian mine on a one-to-one basis if CVRD extended a railway to the captive source. Loans proffered to the Liberian LAMCO project were linked to long-term procurement contracts signed by German steel mills.

33 Australian-Japanese long-term contracts permit price and volume flexibility; for instance, in typical contracts volume can vary 10% and price 7.5% around contracted levels; see Ben Smith, "Long-Term Contracts in the Resource Goods Trade," in *Australia, Japan and the Western Pacific Economic Relations*, ed. John Crawford and Saburo Okita (Canberra: Australian Government Publishing Service, 1976), pp. 299–325. Volume flexibility was also built into the long-term contracts between Venezuela's Ferrominera Orinoco and U.S. Steel, with prices pegged to the U.S. Mesabi base price.

34 For a general review, see W. C. Labys, *Market Structure Bargaining Power and Resource Price Formation* (Lexington, Mass: Lexington Books, 1980), pp. 163–195.

35 By 1978, U.S. imports from Venezuela were less than 40% of 1974 levels, a level consistent with such commitments; American Iron and Steel Institute, *Annual Statistical Report, 1978* (Washington, D.C., 1979), p. 77.

36 Smith, "Long-Term Contracts," p. 311.

37 Information provided during interviews.

38 CVRD *Annual Report, 1975.*

39 CVRD has been engaged in arrangements with Mexico and China to swap iron ore for oil; *The Economist*, "Ore for Oil," Dec. 2, 1978, p. 86. For bilateral deals with Poland and Bulgaria, see "$2.5 bn Coal and Ore Pact Between Brazil, Poland," *Financial Times*, July 17, 1978, p. 3; "Rio Ore Deal Seen as Promising," *Financial Times*, July 24, 1978, p. 2.

40 Details have been gathered from various sources, including interviews in Europe and Brazil and CVRD annual reports. See also "The Story of CVRD: Earth's the Limit," *Brazil*, (June 1978), pp. 14–18.

41 The Carajas iron-ore project, which is targeted to come on-stream in the mid-1980s, has a planned capacity of at least 25 million tons.

42 ISCOR, *Annual Report, 1974*, p. 19.

43 See "U.S. Steel, Bethlehem Agree with Venezuela on Plan for Take-over," *Wall Street Journal*, Dec. 18, 1974, p. 33; "Venezuela to Pay U.S. Steel Corp. and Bethlehem," *Wall Street Journal*, Nov. 29, 1974, p. 4; "Venezuela Sets Take-over on Ore," *New York Times*, Nov. 28, 1974, p. 53.

44 Though the Industrial Policy Resolution of 1956 included the iron and steel industry in the state-dominated sector, it noted that "this does not preclude the expansion of the existing privately-owned units, or the possibility of the State securing the co-operation of private enterprises in the establishing of new units when the national interests so require." For a discussion of this resolution, see Francine Frankel, *India's Political Economy 1947–1977* (Princeton: Princeton University Press, 1978), pp. 129–130.

45 With only one significant exception, all the large steel plants of India are state owned.

46 Kudremukh Iron Ore Company, Ltd., *First Annual Report, 1976–77*, p. 6.

Following the Iranian Revolution, Iran cut back its long-term commitment to buy Indian ore by 40%. See "Pitfalls of Selling Iron Ore," *Far Eastern Economic Review* 106, No. 47 (Nov. 23, 1979):58.

47 For a recent example, see "Ministries Differ on Ore Exports," *Economic Times*, Nov. 8, 1979, p. 1.

48 Based on interviews with Goan exporters.

49 Whereas in 1974 28.2% of ore consumed in U.S. steel mills emanated from outside North America, by 1978 the share of ores from outside North America had declined to only 14.4%. American Iron and Steel Institute, *Annual Statistical Report, 1978* (Washington, D.C., 1979), p. 77.

50 See H. H. Newman, "Strategic Groups and the Structure-Performance Relationships," *Review of Economics and Statistics* 9 (Aug. 1978): 417–427.

51 For a presentation of this argument in the context of the oil industry, see Raymond Vernon, "The State-Owned Enterprise in Latin-American Exports," *Quarterly Review of Economics and Business* 21, No. 2 (Summer 1981): 98–114; for a general discussion of the difficulties of establishing an effective cartel, see Richard E. Caves, "International Cartels and Monopolies in International Trade" in *International Economic Policy: Theory and Evidence*, ed. Rudiger Dornbush and Jacob A. Frenkel (Baltimore: Johns Hopkins University Press, 1978), pp. 39–69.

10 Changing patterns of ownership and integration in the international bauxite–aluminum industry

Dani Rodrik

Since World War II aluminum production and consumption have risen at a phenomenal rate thanks largely to rapid increases in demand and widespread discoveries of bauxite sources. The growth of the bauxite–aluminum industry has been accompanied by geographical diversification and an increasingly centrifugal pattern of location. As with other minerals, like copper and iron ore, the role of state-owned enterprises (SOEs) in the industry has been increasingly visible in recent years.

The growth and spread of SOEs within the bauxite–aluminum industry is likely to have a sizable impact on an industry that traditionally has been dominated by a small number of vertically integrated private multinational firms. It is not at all easy, however, to determine a priori what the nature of this impact will be. Will the growing share of mining and production undertaken by SOEs undermine the vertically integrated nature of the industry, thus allowing the emergence of a free market in bauxite? Will SOEs imply the demise of multinational-corporation (MNC) control in the industry? What kind of new integrative mechanisms will arise as SOEs begin their search for stability in an imperfect market? Will the increasing role of third-world governments in bauxite mining put Western imports of ore in jeopardy? Last but not least, what do SOEs imply for the existing patterns of trade in bauxite, alumina, and aluminum?

There has been little systematic research on the implications of SOEs for the world economy, a factor that may account for the rampant speculation that one usually encounters as a response to the preceding questions. Depending on the conditions of different industries, of course, the role SOEs will play in affecting global politics and trade will vary. What follows is an examination of the tensions and adaptations engendered within the international bauxite–aluminum industry by the rising levels of state ownership. As we shall see, the spread of third-world

The author has benefited substantially from conversations with Raymond Vernon and Brian Levy, whose ideas he has borrowed freely. The research for this chapter was supported by the Harvard Business School. The valuable comments received from John Cavanagh, Mieko Nishimizu, and Stuart Holland are also gratefully acknowledged.

189

Table 10.1. *Annual average growth rates in primary aluminum and bauxite production, 1955-76*

Country	Annual growth rate (%)	
	Bauxite	Aluminum
United States	0.4	4.9
Western Europe	2.1	8.3
Japan		14.1
Australia	46.7	28.0
Developing countries	6.3	19.7
Socialist countries	5.6	8.1
World	7.3	7.1

Source: Calculated from United Nations Conference on Trade and Development (UNCTAD), *The World Market for Bauxite: Characteristics and Trends*, TD/B/IPC/Bauxite/2, Feb. 10, 1978, pp. 12-14.

bauxite and aluminum SOEs is giving rise to a network of state-to-state linkages among these SOEs, although the vertically integrated nature of the industry remains the same in essence but changed in form. Thus it is quite possible that we will observe in the early 1980s the emergence of two subsystems of ownership and trade operating side by side within the same industry, linked at various points by joint ventures between state-owned enterprises and private multinational corporations.

10.1 Internationalization of the industry

Aluminum is produced by a two-stage process. Bauxite ore is first converted into alumina by a process of refining. Alumina is then converted into aluminum by a process of smelting.

From its meager beginnings around the turn of the century, the aluminum industry has grown to be one of the most important sectors in the economies of industrial nations. In the postwar era, it has experienced the fastest rate of growth among all minerals industries. Average annual production growth rates both in primary aluminum and in bauxite have been close to 10% for the entire postwar period, rates that compare very favorably with those of copper, iron, tin, and other metals.[1] The growth of the industry has been fostered above all by the highly desirable industrial qualities of aluminum, its favorable price relative to other metals, and the wide availability of sources of bauxite. As Table 10.1 shows, Australia has been by far the fastest grower in both bauxite and primary aluminum. Japan and the developing countries as a group also have experienced significantly high growth rates in aluminum.

Alongside the increase in production have come changes in the geographical location of mining and smelting activity. Until about World War I, both bauxite

Table 10.2. *Percentage of global distribution of bauxite, alumina, and aluminum production, 1955 and 1976*

	Bauxite		Alumina		Aluminum	
	1955	1976	1955	1976	1955	1976
Industrial countries	23.6	37.9	79.7	64.4	82.5	68.9
Developing countries	58.5	48.4	4.1	17.5	0.9	9.3
Socialist countries	17.9	13.7	16.2	18.1	16.6	21.8
Total	100.0	100.0	100.0	100.0	100.0	100.0

Source: Calculated from UNCTAD, *The World Market for Bauxite: Characteristics and Trends*, TD/B/IPC/Bauxite/2, Feb. 10, 1978, pp. 12–14.

and aluminum were almost exclusively produced in North America and Western Europe. After 1912 big aluminum firms began to expand into bauxite mining in the Caribbean region, a process that has been repeated in the postwar era as African, Australian, and other Caribbean deposits were discovered and exploited. Similarly, in aluminum, the process of geographical expansion began in the late 1930s when smelting was started in the USSR and Japan. It is only recently, however, that primary aluminum production has started in developing countries. By 1976, as Table 10.2 shows, only 9.3% of global primary production took place in developing countries. More than half of world bauxite production, by contrast, already came from developing countries in 1955, a share that has declined in the last decade as Australia rose to become the world's leading bauxite producer.

The internationalization of the bauxite industry, therefore, took place at a relatively early stage in the history of the industry. In 1935 the share of imported ores to total consumption in the Organization for Economic Co-operation and Development (OECD) countries plus the USSR stood at 15%; by 1955 this share had risen to 65.7%. Because of the location of new mines in developing countries (mainly in the Caribbean), where they were distant from the smelters of the industrialized countries, international trade in ore became a very important facet of the industry immediately after World War II. As Table 10.3 shows, 62.3% of the bauxite ore produced in the nonsocialist world in 1955 crossed national boundaries. Since 1955 the importance of international flows in bauxite has actually decreased in relative terms as many developing countries attempted to increase the processing of their ore at home. Consequently, international trade in alumina, a midway product between bauxite and aluminum, has increased rapidly at the expense of bauxite trade. Another reason behind the preference for trading in alumina rather than bauxite is the reduced shipping costs of alumina, which is half as bulky as bauxite for any given amount of primary metal production.

The early internationalization of the bauxite-aluminum industry is also revealed in the dependence of the major industrial countries on imported ores. Fully 70.5%

Table 10.3. *International trade as a percentage of bauxite and alumina production, nonsocialist world, 1955, 1965, and 1975*

	1955	1965	1975
Bauxite	62.3	56.1	40.5
Alumina	11.0	24.2	47.9

Source: Calculated from UNCTAD, *The World Market for Bauxite: Characteristics and Trends*, TD/B/IPC/Bauxite/2, Feb. 10, 1978, pp. 12–14, 23–25.

Table 10.4. *Import share as percentage of aggregate bauxite consumption, 1955, 1965, and 1975*

	1955	1965	1975
United States	70.5	85.9	85.4
Western Europe	51.3	50.4	75.3
Japan	100.0	100.0	100.0

Source: Calculated from UNCTAD, *The World Market for Bauxite: Characteristics and Trends*, TD/B/IPC/Bauxite/2, Feb. 10, 1978.

of the aggregate bauxite consumption of the United States in 1955 was supplied by overseas mines. This share climbed to 85.9% in 1965. Similarly, Western Europe's import dependence on bauxite rose from 51.3% in 1955 to 75.3% in 1975. Japan, of course, does not have any bauxite deposits and has always been fully dependent on imports (see Table 10.4).

Because of the geographical incongruity in the location of mines and smelters, the great majority of the trade in bauxite is directed toward the industrial countries. As Table 10.5 shows, the largest markets for international ore are, in decreasing order of importance, the United States, Western Europe, socialist countries, and Japan.

10.2 Evolution of integration

The aluminum industry has historically been a highly integrated industry, both domestically and internationally. A handful of vertically integrated multinational firms own a major part of the nonsocialist world's bauxite, alumina, primary aluminum, and fabricating facilities. The rise of independent firms and especially of state-owned enterprises in the developing nations, together with the increasing risks associated with foreign investment, is now forcing the aluminum majors to adapt their strategies to a changing industry.

Table 10.5. *Destination of internationally traded ore,*
1955, 1965, and 1975

Destination	Percent of ore		
	1955	1965	1975
United States	49.4	59.7	37.1
Western Europe	15.5	13.7	23.8
Japan	3.4	8.5	14.0
Socialist countries	4.7	7.1	15.0

Source: Calculated from UNCTAD, *The World Market for Bauxite:*
Characteristics and Trends, TD/B/IPC/Bauxite/2, Feb. 10, 1978, p. 24.

The aluminum industry was established shortly after the discovery of the Hall–Heroult reduction process for aluminum metal in 1886. Until World War II, the industry was distinctly duopolistic, with the Aluminum Corporation of America (Alcoa) controlling the Western Hemisphere and the Pechiney group in France supplying the rest of the world. Each monopoly was secured through the companies' respective patent rights to the technology of the Hall–Heroult process. By 1909 when Alcoa's patent expired, the company not only had acquired a virtual monopoly over bauxite deposits within the United States but had also come to control important hydroelectric power sources that were potentially crucial for the production of cheap aluminum.[2] In addition, Alcoa was able to protect its monopoly by buying out all prospective entrants in the industry prior to World War II.[3] Like Pechiney in France, the company integrated itself vertically from bauxite mining to the fabrication of finished products.

The duopoly of the prewar era was transformed into an oligopoly immediately after World War II as new entrants joined the American market and as new European cartels failed to materialize. The American government initiated the transition to oligopoly by selling alumina and aluminum capacity to Kaiser and Reynolds with the intention of improving competition in the industry. This increased capacity had been accumulated by the government as part of its war effort. Special incentives and tax benefits were also granted to lure new firms into aluminum production. These policies were quite successful: Besides Kaiser and Reynolds, three other firms (Harvey, Anaconda, Ormet) entered the industry in the early postwar period. Meanwhile in Europe, smaller national firms were established alongside the two giant multinationals, Pechiney and Alusuisse.

Because a major share of the world's high-quality ore deposits was located in the Southern Hemisphere, the aluminum majors extended their reach on an international scale almost from the very beginning of the industry. By World War I, Alcoa had embarked on an aggressive program of exploiting bauxite deposits in the Caribbean. Between 1912 and 1925 the company had acquired a virtual monopoly over the available deposits in Guyana and Surinam – then British

Guiana and Dutch Guiana, respectively.[4] Like Alcan Aluminum, Ltd., Alcoa's Canadian offshoot, the company was interested in mining bauxite in these countries merely for the purpose of supplying refineries in North America. Processing the bauxite near the mining facilities was not considered practical.

After World War II the new entrants into the aluminum industry similarly attempted to establish secure sources of supply by investing overseas. Reynolds and Kaiser both made substantial discoveries in Jamaica, which between 1950 and 1955 rose to become a major bauxite-exporting nation. Reynolds also found bauxite in Haiti and acquired a relatively small mine in Guyana. With the exception of Alcan, none of the majors built alumina refineries in the Caribbean during the 1950s. Alcan's substantially longer shipping routes had made cutting transportation costs a paramount consideration, and the company decided to switch to shipping alumina. Alcan's alumina plants were built in Jamaica and Guyana during the 1950s.

The 1960s witnessed increasing alumina activity in the Caribbean region as the multinationals came under considerable pressure from governments to increase local processing. Alcoa built alumina refineries in Surinam and Jamaica, and two subsequent alumina plants were constructed in the latter country by a consortium of Reynolds, Kaiser, and Anaconda, and by Revere. The only aluminum smelter built in the region was a small one in Surinam owned by Alcoa. Prior to the nationalizations of the early 1970s, the bulk of Caribbean bauxite was still being exported without further processing.

The aluminum majors began to expand toward other areas of the world as substantial deposits were discovered in various parts of Africa and Australia during the 1960s. Alcoa and Kaiser invested in different joint ventures with local capital in Australia; Reynolds took part in a mining project in Ghana; and Alcan and Alcoa joined a consortium to exploit the rich deposits of Guinea. The overseas activities of the European giants increased in this period as well, as Pechiney invested in mines in Greece and Guinea, and Alusuisse acquired interests in Guinea and Sierra Leone.

Also in the 1960s new multinational entrants from Europe and the United States began to compete with the established majors, thus enlarging the aluminum oligopoly. The new oligopolists were frequently firms with interests in other metals, attracted by the high growth and profit potential of the bauxite–aluminum industry. Like the majors, these entrants sought security through vertical integration: By 1973 six of the new multinationals – Rio Tinto (Conzinc), Billiton (Royal Dutch/Shell), Anaconda, Revere, Olin, and Martin Marietta – collectively controlled 12.4% of the nonsocialist world's bauxite-mining capacity.[5]

Unlike the European and North American aluminum firms that have a long history of direct foreign investment, Japanese companies, until recently, have preferred to rely on other forms of linkages for assuring secure ore supplies and have remained vertically unintegrated. Throughout the postwar period, Japan's bauxite imports have been obtained on the basis of long-term contracts, initially

Table 10.6. *Concentration in bauxite mining, 1971 and 1977, in percent*

	1971	1977
Alcoa	16.5	18.7
Alcan	6.6	5.7
Kaiser	15.6	10.8
Reynolds	10.4	4.4
Pechiney	4.9	1.1
Alusuisse	3.3	5.4
Largest 6 firms	57.3	46.6

Source: International Bauxite Association, *IBA Quarterly Review* 3, No. 2 (Dec. 1977):18–21.

with Indonesia but increasingly since the 1960s with Australia. But in recent years Japanese aluminum firms and trading houses have been unusually active in investing in projects around the globe. Japanese interests are currently involved in alumina projects and consortia in Australia, Brazil, the Solomon Islands, Ghana, Indonesia, and the Philippines. Given the magnitude of these projects, it is likely that interaffiliate transactions on the European and North American model will soon assume important proportions in the ore imports of Japan, gradually diminishing the role of long-term contracts with independent producers.

The pattern of foreign investment by North American, European, and Japanese firms in bauxite and alumina has also obtained, at least as distinctly, in primary aluminum production. The predominance of direct foreign investment in all phases of the bauxite–aluminum industry has resulted in high levels of concentration and vertical integration. Tables 10.6, 10.7, and 10.8 provide an overview of the ownership shares of the six largest firms in the industry together with the changes in these shares over time. (Joint ventures and consortia have been apportioned in all cases in proportion to equity holdings.) The picture that emerges is one of dominance by six aluminum majors in all phases of the industry. Although the share of the nonsocialist world's bauxite, alumina, and aluminum capacity owned by these firms has been declining over time, the majors continue to exercise control over most of the industry. The reduction in the levels of concentration is closely related to the rise of state-owned enterprises in the industry, a subject to which we shall turn shortly.

The preponderance of the same six multinational firms in mining and refining as well as in smelting reflects the high level of vertical integration that has accompanied the process of concentration in the industry. Among all commodities, bauxite is probably the one that passes least through competitive markets of buyers and sellers. More than 80% of internationally traded bauxite and alumina is transacted on an interaffiliate basis or various forms of intercompany linkages such as swap

Table 10.7. *Concentration in alumina capacity, nonsocialist world, 1964, 1971, and 1975, in percent*

	1964	1971	1975
Alcoa	19.6	21.2	21.2
Alcan	23.3	14.2	12.3
Kaiser	11.6	11.7	10.9
Reynolds	14.9	10.6	9.7
Pechiney	7.9	10.0	5.9
Alusuisse	4.0	3.1	3.8
Largest 6 firms	81.3	70.0	63.8

Source: U.S. Bureau of Mines, Minerals Yearbook (Washington, D.C.: U.S. Government Printing Office, Selected Years); U.N. Committee on Natural Resources.

Table 10.8. *Concentration in primary aluminum capacity, nonsocialist world, 1956, 1963, 1970, and 1975, in percent*

	1956	1963	1970	1975
Alcoa	23.2	17.3	16.1	13.7
Alcan	26.8	17.8	15.8	12.5
Kaiser	13.0	12.2	9.5	8.4
Reynolds	14.3	14.0	12.3	9.9
Pechiney	4.5	5.7	6.5	8.2
Alusuisse	3.3	2.7	5.4	4.9
Largest 6 firms	85.0	69.7	65.6	57.5

Source: U. S. Bureau of Mines, Minerals Yearbook (Washington, D.C.: U.S. Government Printing Office, Selected Years); U.N. Committee on Natural Resources; Charles River Associates, *An Economic Analysis of the Aluminum Industry* (Cambridge, Mass.: Charles River Associates, 1971), pp. 3–49 to 3–54; R. T. S. McKern, *Multinational Enterprise and Natural Resources* (Sydney, Australia: McGraw-Hill, 1976), p. 148.

arrangements and long-term contracts;[6] the rest goes through an extremely thin spot market. Because the bulk of the bauxite and alumina operations in the developing nations were, until recently, captive links in the chain of vertically integrated multinational firms, the internationalization of the bauxite industry has not resulted in the creation of a world market for bauxite. Consequently, no "market price" for bauxite (or alumina) exists as such.

Because of the tight links between fabricators and smelters, the same situation obtains at the primary aluminum end as well. Only about 2% to 10% of the world's primary aluminum production is traded on the spot market. Although an aluminum contract was established in 1978 at the London Metal Exchange (LME), it is as yet uncertain whether the contract will achieve its purpose. The

Table 10.9. *Aluminum prices, 1954–76, in constant 1973 dollars*

Year	$/lb	Year	$/lb	Year	$/lb
1954	0.38	1962	0.35	1970	0.33
1955	0.41	1963	0.33	1971	0.32
1956	0.43	1964	0.34	1972	0.27
1957	0.44	1965	0.35	1973	0.25
1958	0.42	1966	0.34	1974	0.31
1959	0.41	1967	0.33	1975	0.33
1960	0.39	1968	0.33	1976	0.35
1961	0.38	1969	0.32		

Source: U.S. Bureau of Mines, *Mineral Facts and Problems* (Washington, D.C.: U.S. Government Printing Office , 1976), p. 57.

majors have expressed opposition to having aluminum traded on the LME, claiming that this would lead to speculation.

Various forms of cooperation among the established aluminum producers have historically assured an orderly pattern of aluminum trade with minimal price fluctuations (see Table 10.9). Reciprocal trading, long-term supply contracts, and the exchange of know-how, in conjunction with the recent trend toward joint ventures, are common links among these multinationals.[7] The major European and North American firms have banded together on several occasions to counter a perceived threat to price stability. When cheap aluminum coming from the USSR in the 1960s threatened to disrupt the stability of the industry, major West European producers joined together to establish a "gentlemen's agreement" with the COMECON countries under which the latter undertook to restrict exports to West European markets.[8] Among other institutional expressions of the concern over "excess" supplies and price fluctuations have been Alufinance and Trade Limited – a European bauxite consortium[9] – the European Producers' Aluminum Association[10] and the International Primary Aluminum Institute.[11] These organizations link together almost all large international firms on a consultative basis.

The clubby atmosphere of the bauxite–aluminum industry received its first shocks beginning with the mid-1960s when a number of small, independent, and frequently state-owned smelters entered the industry. As an OECD report points out, most of the new entrants were the consequence of increasing market size in many countries (thereby justifying the creation of national producers) and of the discovery of new bauxite and cheap electricity sources.[12] A wave of nationalizations in the early 1970s and the creation of a bauxite producers' association, the International Bauxite Association (IBA), in 1974 further changed the nature of the industry. Finally, the exploitation of new bauxite discoveries in Latin America and Africa under state auspices limited the expansion opportunities of the majors in those areas. The impact of the rising role of the state on the vertically integrated nature of the bauxite–aluminum industry, however, has so far been surprisingly limited. It is to the consequences of state ownership that we now turn.

10.3   The rise of state-owned enterprises

As we have seen, concentration ratios in the aluminum industry have tended to decline as the number of participants increased. Among the most important of the new entrants in the late sixties and seventies were state-owned enterprises from less-developed countries (LDSs): either nationalized firms or entities created under state auspices with the purpose of developing domestic resources.

To be sure, the industry contained a number of state-owned aluminum producers prior to the rise of SOEs in the developing nations. These were small to medium-sized European producers engaged mostly in supplying the home market. The most important among them were Ardal og Sunndal Verk (Norway), Vereinigte Aluminum-Werke (VAW-Germany), Empresa Nacional del Aluminio (Endasa-Spain), Vereinigte Metallwerke Ranshofen-B (VMRB-Austria), and Alluminio Sarda (Alsar-Italy). Despite their state ownership, the largest of these, Ardal of Norway and VAW of Germany, were run like private firms with little direct support and assistance from their respective governments. The German government, in particular, took special care to avoid granting privileges to VAW.[13] The existence of these SOEs within the industry, therefore, rarely created any difficulties for the majors or any significant stress for the prevalent system of trade and integration. The case of Ardal provides an interesting example of how these SOEs were integrated within the established structures.

Ardal possesses no bauxite, alumina, or fabricating subsidiaries; it is strictly a primary metal producer. The company's success for a long time was due to the selling of its metal on the international market at highly favorable prices – "a tactic which [caused] grumbling from private competitors in the world market."[14] Through its pricing policies, Ardal had built a solid clientele of independent fabricators. The firm obtained its alumina through long-term contracts, paying for it by metal. By 1967, however, Ardal had radically altered its procurement and marketing strategy; that year the company entered the integrated aluminum industry in a deal with Alcan by which the two firms merged their Norwegian interests on a 50:50 basis. (Alcan's share was reduced to 25% in 1974.) Thereafter, Ardal acquired a link to Alcan's bauxite–alumina subsidiaries, as well as to its fabricating concerns; the company withdrew from involvement in the spot market. More recently Ardal has undertaken direct foreign investment on its own in its perennial search for secure sources and customers.

Since the late 1960s the European SOEs have been joined by a rapidly increasing number of state-owned bauxite, alumina, and aluminum producers from the third world. The share of state ownership in the industry has already reached sizable proportions. As Table 10.10 shows, 35.1% of the bauxite-mining capacity of the developing nations is presently owned by SOEs; this ratio declines

Table 10.10 *Estimated world capacity for bauxite, alumina, and aluminum in thousands of metric tons*

	Capacity	Amount state owned	
		Number	Percent
Bauxite (1979)			
Developing countries	50,696	17,772	35.1
Developed market economies	31,940	40	0.1
Total market economies	82,636	17,812	21.6
Total world	101,936	37,112	36.4
Alumina (1979)			
Developing countries	6,750	1,746	25.9
Developed market economies	24,257	1,810	7.5
Total market economies	31,007	3,556	11.5
Total world	38,627	11,176	28.9
Alumina (1980+)			
Developing countries	18,153	8,084	44.5
Developed market economies	30,932	2,445	7.9
Total market economies	49,085	10,529	21.5
Total world	57,625	19,069	33.1
Aluminum (1979)			
Developing countries	2,100	1,078	51.4
Developed market economies	11,998	1,372	11.4
Total market economies	14,098	2,450	17.4
Total world	16,735	5,087	30.4
Aluminum (1980+)			
Developing countries	6,048	3,340	55.2
Developed market economies	13,787	1,760	12.8
Total market economies	19,835	5,100	25.7
Total world	23,522	8,787	37.4

Source: Metal Bulletin, *World Aluminum Survey* (London: Metal Bulletin Ltd., 1977); *Engineering and Mining Journal,* various issues; UNCTAD, *The World Market for Bauxite: Characteristics and Trends,* TD/B/IPC/Bauxite/2, Feb. 10, 1978; U.S. Bureau of Mines, *Minerals Yearbook, 1975* (Washington, D.C.: U.S. Government Printing Office, 1977), 1:193–7.

to the still significant amount of 21.6% for the nonsocialist world as a whole. In alumina and aluminum, 25.9% and 51.4%, respectively, of the developing nations' capacity is state owned; for the nonsocialist world in its entirety these figures drop to 11.5% and 17.4%. These statistics support the view that state ownership is primarily a third world phenomenon: SOEs constitute a far higher share of capacity in developing countries that in developed market economies.

As the growth rate of the industry is also higher in developing nations – in alumina and aluminum as well as bauxite – the role of state ownership is bound to keep increasing in the near future. Table 10.10 contains global-capacity estimates for the first half of the 1980s, which show a distinct increase in the share of SOE capacity. In bauxite the major new addition to world capacity will come from Brazil and Guinea, countries where ore deposits are being exploited by state

Table 10.11. *Nationalizations among bauxite producers*

Company	Year of take-over	Percentage of government equity
Guyana Bauxite Co., Ltd.	1971	100
Friguia (Guinea)	1972	49
Ghana Bauxite Co.	1973	55
Berbice Mines (Guyana)	1974	100
Kaiser-Jamaica Bauxite Partnership	1977	51
Reynolds-Jamaica Bauxite Partnership	1977	51

Source: International Bauxite Association, *IBA Quarterly Review* 3, No. 2 (Dec. 1977):18–21.

entities in cooperation with multinational firms and/or foreign governments. Similarly, the bulk of new alumina facilities will be set up in developing countries wishing to increase local processing and therefore value added. By the early 1980s, the share of SOE capacity to total market economies' capacity will have risen to more than 20%. In aluminum, on the other hand, the energy intensiveness of the smelting process will necessitate the location of most new smelters in developing countries where there are large untapped hydroelectric sources.[15] As Table 10.10 shows, the share of SOE ownership in primary metal will rise to around a quarter of the nonsocialist world capacity during the 1980s.

Why are developing nations increasingly resorting to SOEs to mine and process their mineral resources? The principal factor responsible for SOE creation in the bauxite–aluminum industry, as well as for the establishment of a producers' association in 1974 modeled after OPEC and the drastic increases in bauxite levies imposed on the multinational companies, is the well-known, if poorly understood, phenomenon of economic nationalism in the third world. Since the late sixties, developing nations have taken an increasingly negative attitude toward the alleged benevolence of the international economy and have attempted to reduce dependence on multinational corporations. In contrast to private firms and MNCs, the SOE appeared to be a most useful instrument for achieving national control over the development of local resources in a way consonant with the national interest. As the upper-tier developing nations experienced economic growth and as local elites felt themselves strong enough to curtail at least some of their ties to the industrial economics of the West, the SOEs began to play increasingly important roles in economic development.

The initial major impetus for state ownership in bauxite mining came from a series of nationalizations that swept the industry beginning in the early 1970s. As Table 10.11 shows, since 1971 government take-overs have occurred in Guyana, Guinea, Ghana, and Jamaica. The nationalizations in Guyana and Jamaica were especially significant, as these two countries are major bauxite exporters. (Guinea is a major exporter as well, but the nationalization of the Friguia consortium there involved only minority participation by the government.)

It was Guyana more than any other country that generated a demonstration effect in the industry by nationalizing Alcan's bauxite subsidiary in 1971. The government take-over was prompted by a feeling of frustration engendered by the unresponsive way in which Alcan ran its subsidiary. The government may have been encouraged in its radical posture by the country's near-complete world monopoly in calcined bauxite (which, unlike noncalcined bauxite, is used for nonmetallurgical purposes). Through the state-owned Guyana Bauxite Company (Guybau), the government hoped to increase its bauxite revenues and to expand local processing. In 1974 the other bauxite mine in the country (owned by Reynolds) was nationalized as well, and since then the two operations have merged under the Bauxite Industry Development Corporation (BIDCO).

The nationalization process in Jamaica was started in 1974 when the government drastically raised its bauxite levies from $2.50 per ton to $11.50 per ton, a move that was replicated shortly after by most bauxite-producing nations. In 1977 the Jamaican government signed agreements with Kaiser and Reynolds by which it obtained 51% equity in the bauxite-mining operations of the two U.S. multinationals.

As foreign-owned mining operations were nationalized in some bauxite-producing nations, new mining projects were also initiated at an increasing rate by state enterprises. Bauxite production by major new mines – in Brazil, India, and Guinea – are or will be coming on-stream under state auspices. The case of Brazil, which hopes to become a major exporter by the mid-1980s, is instructive in this respect. By the early 1970s Alcan had discovered substantial bauxite deposits in the Trombetas region and was interested in developing them. The Brazilian government, however, demanded that Alcan find local partners that would have majority equity. The Brazilian state firm, Companhía Vale do Rio Doce (CVRD), together with local interests, acquired majority ownership of the company that was subsequently formed, and Alcan had to content itself with a minority equity of 19%. After three years and a cost of $365 million, the company, Mineracao Rio de Norte S.A., began exporting during mid-August 1979.[16]

The growing involvement of third-world states in alumina and primary metal production is motivated by the same combination of a desire for increased revenues from natural resources and a distrust of multinational companies. As bauxite mining provides only about 10% to 15% of the value added in aluminum production, the long-term objective of most bauxite producers has been to integrate downstream into alumina production and subsequently into smelting. By far the great majority of alumina refineries planned for the early 1980s in developing nations are state owned: During the next few years alumina SOEs in Brazil, Guinea, Indonesia, Jamaica, Surinam, and Venezuela will join those existing in Guinea, Guyana, India, Jamaica, Taiwan, and Turkey. Planned aluminum plants, on the other hand, are too numerous to list.[17] Suffice it to say that almost all the planned capacity in the third world will be at least majority owned by SOEs. A

Table 10.12. *Source of United States imports of bauxite, 1955, 1965, and 1975, in percent*

Source	1955	1965	1975
Country of source			
Guyana	7.9	4.0	7.4
Jamaica	46.6	56.9	44.8
Surinam	45.5	25.5	15.2
Dominican Republic	—	7.3	6.6
Haiti	—	2.5	3.5
Greece	—	0.3	0.2
Guinea	—	—	21.3
Australia	—	—	0.8
Other	—	3.5	0.2
Total	100.0	100.0	100.0
Type of source			
Subsidiaries	100.0	100.0	42.0
Subsidiaries in joint ventures with SOEs	—	—	50.0
SOEs	—	—	8.0

Note: Dash indicates no U.S. imports.
Source: UNCTAD, *The World Market for Bauxite: Characteristics and Trends,* TD/B/IPC/Bauxite/2, Feb. 10, 1978, pp. 39–41, 43–45; Metal Bulletin, *World Aluminum Survey;* U.S. Bureau of Mines, *Minerals Yearbook,* selected years; *IBA Quarterly Review* 3, No. 2 (Dec. 1977):18–21.

large part of the new investment in primary metal production is currently taking place in the Arab countries of the Middle East, exploiting the cheap energy sources of the area. All the new Arab smelters will be majority owned or fully owned by the state.

Given the increasingly visible role of third-world SOEs in all phases of the bauxite–aluminum industry, one would expect to see a growing dependence by the Western economies on ore imports from state firms rather than private multinationals. However, the statistics do not show any appreciable increase in the West's import dependence on SOEs. Tables 10.12 through 10.17 provide data on the suppliers' characteristics for the bauxite and alumina imports of the United States, Western Europe, and Japan. In each table imports are broken down on the basis of the ownership of sources. With the exception of Japan, where the private–SOE dichotomy in imports is quite clear-cut, a three-way classification has been used: imports from subsidiaries of MNCs; imports from subsidiaries involved in joint ventures with SOEs; and imports from SOEs. The first category includes imports from subsidiaries in joint ventures with other private firms as well as from fully owned captive sources. The second category denotes cases like Guinea and Jamaica where the MNCs are involved in joint ventures with state firms; the (quite

Table 10.13. *Source of United State imports of alumina, 1955, 1965, and 1975, in percent*

Source	1955	1965	1975
Country of source			
Guinea	—	17.6	—
Guyana	—	6.7	0.6
Jamaica	—	13.1	21.4
Surinam	—	3.8	13.4
EEC	—	0.1	1.2
Australia	—	—	59.2
Other	n.a.	58.7	4.2
Total	n.a.	100.0	100.0
Type of source			
Subsidiaries	n.a.	n.a.	84.0
Subsidiaries in joint ventures with SOEs	n.a.	18.0	15.0
SOEs	n.a.	n.a.	1.0

Note: Dash indicates no U.S. imports.
Source: See Sources Table 10.12.

Table 10.14. *Source of EEC imports of bauxite, 1955, 1965, and 1975, in percent*

Source	1955	1965	1975
Country of source			
Guinea	8.6	1.7	19.2
Guyana	1.1	6.1	3.5
Surinam	0.8	2.1	2.6
Yugoslavia	43.7	35.2	0.5
Greece	18.8	21.2	4.0
Indonesia	—	0.9	0.3
Australia	—	8.7	60.0
COMECON	—	1.1	—
Other	27.0	23.0	9.9
Total	100.0	100.0	100.0
Type of source			
Subsidiaries or affiliates	48.0	61.0	76.0
Subsidiaries in joint ventures with SOEs	8.0	2.0	19.0
SOEs	44.0	37.0	5.0

Note: Dash indicates no EEC imports.
Source: See Sources Table 10.12.

Table 10.15. *Source of EEC imports of alumina, 1955, 1965, and 1975, in percent*

Source	1955	1965	1975
Country of source			
EEC	100.0	26.2	30.8
Guinea	—	56.5	1.0
United States	—	12.1	0.7
Guyana	—	—	4.1
Jamaica	—	—	26.4
Surinam	—	—	19.1
Australia	—	—	10.6
Greece	—	—	7.0
Other	—	5.2	0.3
Total	100.0	100.0	100.0
Type of source			
Subsidiaries or affiliates	90.0	35.0	71.0
Subsidiaries in joint ventures with SOEs	n.a.	57.0	21.0
SOEs	n.a.	8.0	8.0

Note: Dash indicates no EEC imports.
Source: See Sources Table 10.12.

Table 10.16. *Source of Japanese imports of bauxite, 1955, 1965, and 1975, in percent*

Source	1955	1965	1975
Country of source			
Indonesia	72.8	31.7	18.3
Guyana	—	2.8	1.7
Surinam	—	2.6	0.2
Australia	—	27.7	68.2
Greece	—	—	0.1
Other	27.2	35.2	11.5
Total	100.0	100.0	100.0
Type of source			
Private companies	25.0	63.0	95.0
SOEs	75.0	37.0	5.0

Note: Dash indicates no Japanese imports.
Source: See Sources Table 10.12.

plausible) assumption here is that the importing country is supplied with the share of output apportioned to the MNCs according to their equity in the venture. The final category represents instances where imports actually originate from state firms.

Table 10.17. *Source of Japanese imports of alumina, 1965 and 1975, in percent*

Source	1965	1975
Country of source		
Australia	99.0	99.0
Other	1.0	1.0
Total	100.0	100.0
Type of source		
Private companies	100.0	100.0
SOEs	—	—

Note: Dash indicates no Japanese imports.
Source: See Sources Table 10.12.

As Tables 10.12 to 10.17 show, the import dependence of Western Europe and Japan on SOEs, if anything, has declined in the period 1955–75, whereas that of the United States has risen only by a small margin. In the case of the United States, roughly half of bauxite imports in 1975 came from subsidiaries of American multinationals involved in joint ventures with SOEs and only 8% directly from SOEs. The bulk of U.S. alumina imports came from captive sources and joint ventures with other private firms. West European imports of bauxite, on the other hand, came increasingly from private sources in the period 1955–75 as the relative role of Yugoslavia as an exporter declined. Similarly, in Japan's case, the importance of state-owned sources of bauxite declined as Japanese producers shifted from reliance on the Indonesian state-owned mines to the new Australian projects. The consequent conclusion is that vertical integration as a sourcing strategy in the bauxite–aluminum industry remains as prevalent as ever, if not even stronger. True, subsidiaries of American and European multinationals increasingly came into contact with SOEs in the form of joint ventures, a point that will be discussed in the following section, but the common pattern of reliance on upstream subsidiaries for secure ore supplies is far from being undermined. Moreover, the increasing propensity of Japanese firms to invest overseas is likely to increase the role of vertical integration even further.

The industrial economies of the West have been able to avoid dependence on state firms in developing nations mainly by switching at opportune moments to new ore deposits in places like Australia and Guinea. The growth of world bauxite production has been fast enough relative to the rise of demand in the industrialized countries to allow multinationals to increase their sources at the same time that state ownership spread by leaps and bounds. The West, therefore, has successfully limited the need to establish purchasing ties with state-owned bauxite or alumina producers.

But if Western imports from state firms have, if anything, declined relative to total imports at the same time that the number of SOEs multiplied, we are faced with the obvious question: How are the state-owned ore producers disposing of their exports? The answer, as we shall see in the following section, is that a growing number of SOEs are selling their ore to other state-owned entities downstream on the basis of a wide array of state-to-state deals, the long-term bulk-purchase contract being the most frequent strategy employed.

10.4   Emerging patterns of integration

Despite the new risks implied by widespread state ownership in the industry, the most important mode of integration for private firms continues to be foreign investment. As we saw, foreign investment was an important part of the industry almost from the very beginning of aluminum production. The typical pattern of foreign investment until the 1960s, especially in developing countries, was one of 100% ownership by a single multinational company. Almost all the Caribbean bauxite deposits were transformed into captive mines fully owned by one of the four North American aluminum majors. Increasingly since the 1960s, however, multinational firms have been participating in joint ventures with other MNCs, local private firms, or with SOEs such that the role of fully owned captive mines or alumina/aluminum plants has been steadily declining. An overwhelming number of the currently planned bauxite, alumina, or aluminum projects involve joint ventures of one kind or another. Indeed, the predominance of joint ventures in the industry has come to be one of its main identifying features.

Why are multinationals switching from full ownership to equity participation? The reason partly has to do with factors outside the control of the majors themselves. Most developing countries are nowadays intent on limiting the control of foreign firms in their economies and are insisting, therefore, that MNCs join local, private, or state capital in collaborative ventures. Even Australia requires that international firms find themselves local partners such that new projects are at least 50% locally owned. With such stringent requirements, the aluminum firms have frequently no choice but to limit their equity participation.

It would be misleading, however, to depict joint ventures as an integrative mechanism contrary to the interests of the majors. Direct foreign investment in collaborative ventures with other firms frequently provides benefits that full ownership cannot. For one thing, joint ventures serve to spread the risk inherent in foreign investment – a significant bonus for an industry that is nationalization prone. Second, they ease the capital-requirements burden on multinational companies in individual projects. As a result of rising costs of energy and materials, as well as higher interest rates, the construction of new aluminum capacity is becoming an increasingly expensive proposition. According to the calculations of the United Nations Conference on Trade and Development (UNCTAD), 1955 costs for primary capacity were roughly 40% of 1974 costs.[18] Even at the bauxite stage, the development of new mines characteristically runs into hundreds of millions of dollars; the exploitation of the Brazilian Trombetas deposits and the Boke deposits of Guinea have cost about $365 million and $400 million, respectively. Thus, by banding together in joint ventures, aluminum firms can make the best of limited financial resources.

A less appreciated factor is that the predominance of joint ventures can actually increase the control over the industry of the largest aluminum multinationals. Through equity participation in a multitude of projects around the globe, the majors are able to "magnify the influence of their investment ability" and have an input into the location and production decisions of more new capacity than they otherwise would have.[19] Moreover, MNCs frequently acquire a larger share of output than their equity would indicate when their partners (local firms or SOEs) have little use domestically for the ore or metal, as the case may be. Although Alcan owns only 8% of Dubal, the state-owned aluminum company of Dubai, for example, it has a right to 40% of the smelter's output. The Dubai government, on the other hand, gets only 20% of the output despite its 80% ownership.

As this last example indicates, MNCs are increasingly establishing partnerships with state firms from the third world. The preceding section showed that roughly half of U.S. imports of bauxite ore comes from subsidiaries of North American firms involved in joint ventures with third world states, mainly in Jamaica and Guinea. According to a rough classification of new aluminum projects expected to come on-stream during the 1980s, around half of these will be joint ventures between multinationals and state capital. As the Dubai example showed, the supply arrangements are usually quite favorable to the multinationals in such partnerships. To cite a different case, the government participation deals signed by U.S. multinationals in 1977 in Jamaica provide for continuous and adequate supplies for at least 40 years for the companies' plants in the United States, as well as a free hand in the management of the joint venture.

Aluminum majors continue to rely, therefore, on vertical integration to secure ore supplies and markets. Because of the many factors discussed earlier, vertical integration currently has the tendency to take the form of equity participation in joint ventures rather than full ownership. How do SOEs achieve security of supplies and customers in a highly concentrated and vertically integrated industry?[20]

An OECD report published in 1973[21] predicted that as most developing country firms did not have downstream connections they would be forced to sell a large part of their output in the open market. By and large, this prediction has failed to come true. The experiences of relatively early state-owned bauxite producers like Guyana's Guybau in the world market (or what exists of it) seem to have taught most other SOEs to avoid reliance on arm's-length or spot-market transactions. After the company's nationalization in 1971, Guybau faced considerable difficulties in marketing its noncalcined bauxite; during 1973 the company's alumina plant actually had to be closed down for a few weeks to allow the inventory to come down to normal levels. It is not hard to visualize the problems inherent in market participation in the case of a market as thin as that in the aluminum industry. An independent company can scarcely obtain security of supplies or guaranteed customers when the existing markets are little more than the residual production of a vertically integrated industry. Understandably, spot-market prices fluctuate more than list prices in periods of high demand as well as low demand. During "shortages," firms allocate existing supply to traditional customers, whereas those who depend on the spot market are left out in the cold.[22] The incentive for all firms, therefore, whether they are state owned or not, is to establish strong buyer–seller linkages.

If the shortcomings of the markets in the aluminum industry forced SOEs to search for more intimate forms of linkages than arm's-length transactions, the continued reliance of multinational firms on their subsidiaries both downstream and up meant that the state firms had few alternatives other than turning *to each other* for new modes of integration. The preponderance of state-to-state deals among SOEs in the bauxite–aluminum industry has less to do with ideology or third world solidarity than those two facts of the industry.

Among the state-to-state deals proposed so far, the most interesting have been a number of intergovernmental projects in the Caribbean, Latin America, and Africa. In 1974, for example, the governments of Jamaica, Guyana, and Trinidad-Tobago announced an agreement in principle for the joint construction and owner-ship of two aluminum smelters with an annual capacity of 200,000 tons to be supplied by Caribbean alumina. It was contemplated that the first smelter would be built in Trinidad-Tobago with 34% to be owned by the home government, and 33% each to be owned by the Jamaican and Guyanese governments. The second would be built in Guyana with Guyana owning 52% of the smelter and Jamaica and Trinidad-Tobago 24% each.

Probably the most ambitious intergovernmental project considered to date was the planned industrial complex involving the Jamaican and Mexican governments, as well as Kaiser and other private interests. This complex, the agreement for which was signed in 1974, was to be vertically integrated from bauxite mining to aluminum smelting. The project was to involve a new mining company, a 600,000-ton alumina plant in Jamaica (Javemex), and a 120,000-ton smelter in Mexico (Jalumex). The Jamaican government, according to the plan, would hold a 51% share in both the mining and alumina ventures. Kaiser would be a minority shareholder in both enterprises, and Mexico would hold the next largest share (29%) to Jamaica in the alumina plant. The Mexican government was to have the largest share in the aluminum smelter (71%), with the government holding 29%.

Eventually, these Caribbean-based schemes collapsed. The Mexican govern-ment has withdrawn from the Jalumex smelter project with the Jamaican govern-ment, ostensibly for reasons of the devaluation of the peso and cost inflation. Shortly after, the smelter's Jamaican counterpart, Javemex, was absorbed into the state-owned Jamaica Bauxite Mining, Ltd. In addition, part of the Jamaican–Guyana–Trinidad-Tobago joint venture has recently collapsed because of the withdrawal of the Jamaican and Guyanese governments in late 1976 from the smelter planned for Trinidad-Tobago. The smelter is now being considered as a one-nation endeavor at a much-reduced capacity.[23]

A similar project was announced in 1976 by the oil-rich Middle Eastern countries. The governments of Guinea, Egypt, Iraq, Kuwait, Libya, Saudi Arabia, and the United Arab Emirates were reported to have agreed to a joint venture to build a large bauxite–alumina complex in Guinea at a cost of $1 billion. Alusuisse, the Swiss giant, was commissioned to conduct feasibility studies and to undertake the preliminary design for the venture. The alumina plant is expected to come on-stream by 1982–3 and will have a capacity of 2 million tons. The construction of an aluminum smelter at a later stage is also envisaged. Recently, another bauxite–alumina project was announced in Guinea with the participation of the Algerian, Nigerian, and Guinean governments, as well as Reynolds. The total cost of the project is estimated to be $790 million.

In addition, there are a host of other, less complicated cases of actual and prospective joint ventures among state enterprises by which one SOE invests in a project principally owned by another state firm, getting part of the output in return. The Saudi Arabian government, for example, has a 20% ownership share in Aluminum Bahrain (Alba), a primary metal producer majority owned by the Bahrain government. Similarly, Venezuela's state-owned Corporación Venezolana de Guyana (CVG) was recently reported to have been considering purchase of a 5% share in Mineração Rio do Norte owned by Brazil's Campanhía Vale do Rio Doce (CVRD). The deal, if realized, would entitle CVG to receive 250,000 tons of bauxite per year and thus provide a breathing ground until Venezuela's own state-owned mines come on-stream.

Intergovernmental joint ventures of the sort described above are, by their very nature, hard to establish. A far easier and therefore more popular mode of quasi integration is the state-to-state long-term contract by which one SOE undertakes to supply another with an agreed amount of ore or metal for a set number of years at negotiated terms. Indeed, as we go into the 1980s a growing network of long-term contracts is encompassing SOEs from the most diverse areas.

Since the Jamaican government's take-over of U.S. multinationals, for example, that country has established a number of long-term contracts with state-owned refineries and smelters in other developing countries and socialist nations. The country is providing 1 million tons of alumina to a Venezuelan SOE (Venalum) under a seven-year contract and has also undertaken to ship an annual supply of 150,000 tons of alumina to an Algerian state-owned smelter expected to come on-stream in the early 1980s. The Jamaican and Nigerian governments have concluded preliminary talks on the possibilities of an exchange of Jamaican bauxite for a wide range of Nigerian commodities. Finally, in 1979 Jamaica concluded trade agreements with the USSR and Hungary for the annual sale of 50,000 tons of alumina to the USSR and 150,000 tons to Hungary. This output will be accommodated, reportedly, by using existing excess plant capacity.[24]

Resorting to long-term purchasing arrangements is a common pattern in all developing nations with state-owned capacity. Guyana's Bauxite Industry Development Company has been supplying socialist countries since Alcan's nationalization in 1971. The company has recently announced the conclusion of a four-year contract for the supply of alumina to Valesul Aluminio S.A. of Brazil – majority owned by CVRD – beginning in 1981 when Valesul's smelter is expected to start production. Similarly, the Indian state's share of the country's bauxite output finds its way to the USSR through long-term contracts. The Guinean government's share of the output of the mining consortia in the country (in which the state has 49% equity) is also shipped to socialist countries.

To be sure, state firms are not always the only partners involved in long-term contracts. Such contracts, at least on the surface, provide much-needed security and predictability to all sorts of independent firms in the industry. All Japanese smelters, being unintegrated, tend to rely on long-term purchasing arrangements with Australian private firms or the state-owned Indonesian producer for secure supplies of ore. The highly vertically integrated nature of the bauxite–aluminum industry, however, has precluded the existence of a large number of independent firms with the notable exception of state-owned producers whose raisons d'être are frequently less related to the structural conditions of the industry than those of private firms. Even the Japanese producers, as has been pointed out, have been increasingly interested in direct foreign investment and vertical integration as a way of assuring safe linkages with ore sources. This basically leaves state-owned enterprises as the main independent firms and, therefore, the prime candidates for integrative linkages more intimate than arm's-length transactions but less committing than direct foreign investment.

It is important to understand the integrative processes taking place in the industry as a result of the rise of SOEs from the third world. Vertical integration, albeit in a different form, continues to be the predominant integrative mechanism for private firms. In large part because of that, the new state enterprises are resorting to a variety of state-to-state deals ranging from intergovernmental complexes to long-term contracts. The pressures on the state firms to establish durable linkages with each other are causing the gradual but visible emergence of a distinctly different form of integration in the industry alongside the system favored so far by private firms. The state-owned sector of the industry, of course, is as yet definitely an adjunct to the multinationals; in fact, the share of SOEs in international trade is rising at a slower pace than their role in new projects would indicate, mainly because of increased local processing and domestic consumption. Nevertheless, the existence of a distinguishable subsystem of ownership and trade encompassing SOEs within the industry is becoming quite real.

The two subsystems of ownership and trade, one of private firms and the other of SOEs, do, of course, come into contact with each other in a growing number of instances of joint ventures between SOEs and multinational firms. The mechanisms through which the output is disposed of, however, tend to be different for the partners in such ventures: whereas the private firm tends to ship its share to affiliates or subsidiaries downstream, the state company typically disposes of its shares over and above local needs through the use of long-term contracts.

The state-owned subsystem of the bauxite–aluminum industry is potentially self-sufficient in the procurement of ore. Preliminary estimates for new capacity in the 1980s indicate that state-owned alumina refineries in the market economies will produce enough metal to feed all state-owned smelters in the nonsocialist world. This conclusion can be derived from the data in Table 10.10 on the basis of 2:1 conversion of alumina into aluminum. It is not clear whether the correspondence between planned capacity in alumina and aluminum is the result of linkages already established among SOEs or of sheer coincidence; there is probably some of both involved. Yet the availability of sufficient amounts of state-owned ore is likely to stimulate further the kind of state-to-state deals discussed here.

Nevertheless, the efforts of the state-owned sector to secure stability through joint state deals are plagued with considerable uncertainty. Some notable failures already have been noted in the discussion on integrated ventures. The instability inherent in the nature of state-to-state deals is even further accentuated in the case of long-term contracts. As global supply-and-demand conditions fluctuate throughout the period covered by the contract, the partners may be tempted to pull out of the deal, hoping for more lucrative arrangements generated by the temporary economic climate. During periods of glut, for example, buyers may seek lower cost sources, and sellers "may be tempted by potential windfalls" when supply is tight.

Of course parties seek long-term agreements precisely because *ex ante* they are willing to trade off potential short-term windfalls for long-term stability. But should either buyer or seller perceive market trends once thought cyclical actually to be secular, should either – for whatever reason – re-evaluate the rate at which it is willing to trade off the present against the future, the basis for the contract may be undermined.[25]

Those are precisely the reasons why private firms in the industry, and especially Japanese independents, have been moving away from long-term contracts toward more durable arrangements. There is potentially an added disadvantage to long-term contracts for state firms, and that involves the costs of politicization. As state enterprises continue to establish linkages among themselves, these linkages will tend to come increasingly into the realm of interstate political relations. Such politicization may result in unpredictable, but potentially quite undesirable, consequences.

State-to-state deals between third world producers and enterprises from socialist countries, a special category, pose different sets of problems. Among these problems financing difficulties are probably foremost: Long-term sales contracts to socialist countries are not generally accepted as collateral for project loans by private lenders. Moreover, such contracts frequently come at onerous terms: Hungary's commitment to buy Jamaican alumina, for example, was contingent upon the utilization of Hungarian technology and equipment for Jamaica's new state-owned refinery.[26]

The difficulties inherent in state-to-state deals aside, the worldwide increase in state-owned smelter capacity in the near future is likely to require different modes of integration at the aluminum end. As state ownership is much less widespread among fabricators, the proliferation of state-to-state deals in ingot will not be possible. Even so, the urge for cohesive linkages of one form or another will be all the stronger when a good number of new smelters come on-stream in oil-rich Arab countries with small domestic markets. At present, one can only speculate as to what shape these linkages will take. Long-term contracts with independent European and Japanese fabricators seem a probable outcome. Another possibility is the strengthening of aluminum trading at the London Metal Exchange as new smelters sell their output on the world market. Government-sponsored bilateral trading arrangements involving exchange of aluminum ingot for other commodities are also a likely eventuality.

Finally, a considerable slowing down of the growth rate of the bauxite-aluminum industry could upset altogether the existing patterns of integration. The relative insulation of the two subsystems of ownership and trade within the industry described earlier largely has been due to the high growth of global bauxite and aluminum production. Because of new discoveries of ore sources, as we have seen, aluminum majors have so far been successful in restricting their trade links with the SOEs to a minimum. But as multinational companies run out of the bauxite frontier and if state-to-state deals prove unsatisfactory for SOEs, the pressures on both types of enterprise to go further than joint ventures and establish trading links may intensify considerably. If that proves the case, we may eventually see the proliferation of integrative linkages among SOEs and multinational corporations. A very recent project in Jamaica provides an illustration of the integration possibilities for the future. In late 1979 the Jamaican government and Alcan established jointly a bauxite mining and alumina enterprise, owned 93% by Alcan and 7% by the state. The novelty of the project lies in the trading and marketing arrangements worked out between the two partners: The Jamaican government's share of the alumina output, which is equivalent to its equity, is to be bartered with Alcan for an agreed equivalent of aluminum metal, and Alcan is to act as agent for the marketing of this metal.[27]

A final word here about the impact of SOEs on bauxite prices may be necessary. The rise of state-owned bauxite producers during the 1970s has been accompanied by increased price militancy among third-world nations as evidenced by the creation of the International Bauxite Association (IBA) modeled after OPEC. This need not imply any causality between state ownership and increased prices, however; the ability to raise bauxite taxes is not necessarily contingent on state ownership, although that may help. The increasing incidence of joint ventures between state firms and multinational aluminum companies, in particular, could have a significant impact on pricing. Private partners in such joint ventures frequently do not possess the same amount of discretion in price policy as they would in a fully owned mine. They consequently may not have as much latitude in transfer pricing. However, what real influence this may have on unit costs of bauxite, considering the dearth of available evidence, is as yet impossible to say.

10.5 Conclusion

An implicit hypothesis of this chapter has been that the international behavior of state-owned enterprises can be better understood through an examination of the industry-wide pressures acting on them than through an analysis of how owner-ship per se affects behavior. In a less tightly structured industry than the bauxite industry the latter factor may predominate. Within the highly concentrated and vertically integrated context of the aluminum industry, state firms have had little choice but to seek stability via quasi-integrative arrangements among themselves. One wonders whether the outcome would have been much different had all the new entrants into the industry since the late 1960s been privately owned and unintegrated.

As we have seen, the prevalence of state-to-state deals among SOEs seems to be giving rise to a relatively insulated and self-sufficient subsystem of integration within the industry alongside the predominant vertical integration of private multi-nationals. The multinationals themselves, in no small part because of the increasing involvement of third-world states in the industry, have modified their foreign investment strategy from full ownership to equity participation in joint ventures with other multinationals, local private firms, or state entities. The continued prevalence of vertical integration has precluded increased dependence by Western economies on state-owned sources of ore. Similarly, the preference of SOEs for various integrative linkages has belied predictions that the role of the market would increase as state ownership spread.

As far as developing nations are concerned, the significance of state-to-state deals lies in the opportunities presented for market diversification and the expan-sion of trade within the third world. It is ironical that these horizontal ties among developing nations have resulted less from a desire on the part of SOEs to enter into partnership with each other than from the multinational firms' continued pref-erence for vertical integration and hence the limited room for trade between them and SOEs. The establishment of such horizontal linkages among state firms in developing nations is desirable whether one believes in disengagement from the international capitalist economy and the disruption of the ''vertical structures of imperialism'' (a la Galtung) or simply in the need for reducing dependence on concentrated markets in the industrialized nations. One should keep in mind, however, that if the behavior of state firms is heavily conditioned by the interna-tional structure of the industry, as I have argued earlier, SOEs may display considerable unresponsiveness to national goals.

It is important to appreciate the considerable impact SOEs have had on the industry, although so far this impact has been limited by the rapid growth of the industry and the wide availability of bauxite sources. The locus of decision making within the industry has increasingly been subject to centrifugal forces as state involvement has mushroomed in the developing world. And the limitations discussed in the last part of the preceding section notwithstanding, all of the trends delineated in this chapter are likely to crystallize even further in the near future as the overwhelming part of unexploited bauxite deposits and untapped energy sources are located in the developing world. The patterns will be reversed only if nonbauxitic sources become plentiful.

The findings of this chapter tend to dispel journalistic notions prevalent in many circles regarding the incompatibility of private and public enterprise. With the exception of a few specific instances, multinational firms seem to have suffered little from the rise of state ownership in the third world. Although the ownership share of the six majors has been declining, the cause for this has been the entry of new private multinationals as well as of SOEs. As I have argued, the prevalence of joint ventures among multinationals provides valuable opportunities for spreading risk and enhancing control. Moreover, the presence of state firms benefits international corporations in several ways: Joint ventures with SOEs in effect insure multinationals against political risk and help them raise capital in international capital markets and from multilateral institutions. Given the structurally weak position of SOEs, these unintended benefits to private firms could well increase further if state-to-state deals prove too fragile and if the need for trading links between SOEs and multinationals intensifies.

Given the novelty of widespread state ownership in the industry, these conclusions are perforce tentative. The instability inherent in state-to-state deals in particular, as discussed in the preceding section, may render such deals a temporary phenomenon. In any event, one would be well advised to concur with the cautious comments of an earlier observer of state involvement in the bauxite–aluminum industry.

One cannot yet say that the growing role of governments in the industry is in opposition to the role played by major transnational aluminum companies. So far there is no indication that the governments have either the capacity or the inclinations to attempt to challenge the dominant role of the aluminum companies in the international industry in production, processing, marketing, or technology.[28]

Notes

1 See John E. Tilton, *The Future of Nonfuel Minerals* (Washington, D.C.: Brookings Institution, 1977), Table 2-1.
2 See Norman Girvan, *Corporate Imperialism-Conflict and Expropriation* (New York and London: Monthly Review Press, 1976), pp. 103–7.
3 Merton J. Peck, *Competition in the Aluminum Industry, 1945–1958* (Cambridge: Harvard University Press, 1961).
4 See Girvan, *Corporate Imperialism-Conflict*.
5 Figures from Walter C. Labys, "The Role of State-Trading in Mineral Commodity Markets: Copper, Tin, Bauxite, and Iron Ore," Les Cahiers du CETAI, Ecole des Hautes Etudes Commerciales, Montreal, April 1979, p. 26b.

6 See International Bauxite Association, *IBA Quarterly Review* 4, Nos. 2 and 3:33.
7 See I. A. Litvak and C. J. Maule, "Transnational Corporations in the Bauxite-Aluminum Industry," Division of Economic Development, Economics Committee for Latin America (July 1977), p. 29.
8 In 1975 the COMECON producers pulled out of this agreement.
9 Members: Alusuisse, Pechiney, VAW, British Aluminum, Montecatini-Edison, Ranshofen-Berndorf, Holland Aluminum, Giulini. Reynolds is indirectly associated with Alufinance through its participation in British Aluminum Co., Ltd.
10 Members of the IPAI executive board: Pechiney, Alcoa, Alusuisse, Alcan, Reynolds, Kaiser, Ardal, Nippon Light Metals, VAW, British Aluminum, Comalco, and CVA.
11 On these bodies, see Zuhayr Mikdashi, "Aluminum," in *Big Business and the State,* ed: R. Vernon (Cambridge: Harvard University Press, 1974).
12 OECD, *Problems and Prospects of the Primary Aluminum Industry* (Paris: OECD, 1973), p. 42.
13 In 1975, e.g., the German Cartel Office prohibited VAW from establishing a jointly owned smelting and fabricating facility with Kaiser on the grounds that the deal would be detrimental to competition in the German aluminum industry. See *Wall Street Journal,* June 30, 1975, p. 4.
14 Sterling Brubaker, *Trends in the World Aluminum Industry* (Baltimore: Johns Hopkins University Press, 1967), p. 111.
15 OECD, *Industrial Adaptation in the Primary Aluminum Industry* (Paris: OECD, 1976).
16 See *Skillings Mining Review,* Sept. 22, 1979, and *Engineering and Mining Journal,* Apr. 1979.
17 Prospective state-owned aluminum enterprises will be established shortly in Abu Dhabi, Algeria, Brazil, Ghana, Guyana, India, Indonesia, Iraq, South Korea, Kuwait, Libya, Mexico, Qatar, South Arabia, Trinidad, Venezuela, and Zaire. Currently SOEs exist in Argentina, Bahrain, Egypt, India, Turkey, Venezuela, Taiwan, and Dubai.
18 UNCTAD, *The World Market for Bauxite: Characteristics and Trends,* TD/B/IPC/Bauxite/2, Feb. 10, 1978, p. 10.
19 Council on Wage and Price Stability, *Aluminum Prices 1974–75.* Staff Report, (Washington, D.C.: U.S. Government Printing Office, 1976), p. 230.
20 The increased levels of processing in developing nations and increasing absorption of the final product, of course, diminish the need for many SOEs to involve themselves with the international aspects of the industry.
21 OECD, *Problems and Prospects.*
22 Council on Wage and Price Stability, *Aluminum Prices 1974–75,* pp. 212–13.
23 Similarly, plans for an Indian smelter in Orissa to be financed by the Iranian government were given, in the words of *The Economist,* "quiet burial" following the Iranian revolution. *The Economist,* Nov. 10, 1979, p. 92.
24 U.S. Bureau of Mines, *Mineral Trade Notes* 76, No. 6 (June 1979):3
25 Brian Levy, "Market Integration and the Evolution of State Enterprise: The Case of Iron Ore," mimeographed Harvard University, Oct. 1979, p. 26.
26 Economic Commission for Latin America, *Negotiating Capacity of Latin American Governments vis-à-vis Transnational Corporations in Export Oriented Primary Commodities,* E/CEPAL/L.204, Sept. 21, 1979, p. 22.
27 *Skillings Mining Review,* Nov. 17, 1979.
28 Girvan, *Corporate Imperialism-Conflict,* pp. 152–3.

11 Public enterprise and manufactured exports in less-developed countries: institutional and market factors determining comparative advantage

Leroy P. Jones and Lawrence H. Wortzel

11.1 The issues

Many less-developed countries (LDCs) are shifting the emphasis of their industrialization strategies from import substitution to promotion of manufactured exports. To implement the new strategy the government has a variety of tools at its disposal. Some of these (including the exchange rate and tax and credit subsidies) are designed primarily to guide the behavior of private enterprises; others (including direct commands and bonus schemes) are designed primarily to alter the behavior of existing public enterprises. In addition, a government could create new public enterprises. Although the set of tools aimed at private enterprise has been extensively analyzed, the role of public enterprise in manufactured exports has been almost totally neglected. This chapter therefore asks what the role of the public-enterprise sector ought to be in promoting *manufactured* exports and how policy instruments might be manipulated to achieve this potential.

To help answer these questions we extend the list of determinants of comparative advantage to include *marketing* and *institutional* factors. The Heckscher–Ohlin theorem explains comparative advantage in terms of relative resource endowment and predicts labor-intensive manufactured exports from LDCs. This theory has been shown to have broad predictive ability, particularly when modified to recognize the human–capital component of skill-intensive manufactured exports and the natural-resource component of other manufactured exports.[1] Other factors that have been shown useful in explaining variance for particular products and countries include such commodity and national attributes as: scale economies (both static and dynamic), whether a good is for final

Work on this chapter was partially supported by a Ford Foundation grant to the Boston University Public Enterprise Program. We would like to thank Raymond Vernon, Donald Keesing, and Peter Cory for valuable comments on an earlier draft.

217

consumption or intermediate use, technological lag, product differentiation, price elasticity of demand, preference similarity, physical distance, and entrepreneurs' willingness to take risk.[2]

This chapter focuses on the role of marketing factors: the search for buyers, advertising, promotion, distribution, and the psychological and other non-economic aspects of pricing. Although largely ignored by economic theory, such variables are critical in practice. It is one thing to be able to produce a good cheaply for delivery at the factory gate and quite another to arrange its efficient, timely delivery to a foreign consumer. Comparative advantage in production need not correlate with comparative advantage in marketing. Cement is more capital intensive than high-fashion dresses, but as a standardized product, cement is far easier to market. Therefore, some LDCs may at times be in a position to export capital-intensive cement prior to labor-intensive high-fashion dresses, even though consideration of comparative advantage in production would predict the opposite.[3]

Economic outcomes are a function of both *market* factors (external to the enterprise) and *institutional* factors (internal to the enterprise). Market factors define opportunities and institutional factors determine the response. Economists typically assume that institutional factors are captured by a simple response rule, such as profit maximization, and focus on the impact of varying market price signals. Management scientists, on the other hand, typically take prices (except those within the control of the enterprise) as given and spend their careers trying to understand and alter institutional response functions. Although this may be a useful division of professional labor, we consider it essential to include *both* market and institutional factors in explaining the role of public enterprises in the export of manufactured goods from LDCs.

Whereas market factors determine potential comparative advantage, institutional factors determine the degree to which the potential is realized. At the institutional extremes, pure public and pure private enterprises may respond quite differently to the same export-market opportunity. For example, public enterprises may not cut their production costs sufficiently and private enterprises may not invest in export capacity if faced by major uncertainties as to the future course of economic and political events. To the extent that such differences in reaction to an opportunity exist, public enterprises will be more or less appropriate than private enterprises for certain types of manufactured export tasks. We thus do not aim at any single recommendation for a public-enterprise role in export development but rather at assessing the comparative advantage of one type over the other under different market conditions, that is, in marketing as opposed to production; in labor-intensive as opposed to capital-intensive production; and in "early" as opposed to "late" market entry.

We begin by examining the actual role of public enterprises in the manufactured exports of LDCs (Section 11.2). The Republic of Korea is first examined in some detail and the experience of selected other countries is then considered more briefly. The conclusion is that, historically, manufactured exports from the public-enterprise sector are generally negligible both as a share of public-enterprise output and as a share of total exports.

We then ask why this has occurred. Two sets of explanations are given. The first, based on market factors (Section 11.3), is simply that in LDCs public enterprises have a comparative *institutional* advantage over private enterprises in activities that are capital intensive, and LDCs have a comparative *production* advantage in manufacturing and exporting products that are labor intensive. Public enterprises exist largely in capital-intensive, import-substituting industries in which LDCs do not have a comparative advantage, and this in part explains their historically low level of manufactured exports.

The second set of explanations is institutional (Section 11.4). Even when public enterprises exist in industries where the country has a comparative export advantage, differences in the behavior of public and private decision makers may make it difficult for public enterprises to compete internationally. Institutional factors are discussed in three different contexts: consumer goods under "importer-pull" marketing; consumer goods under "exporter-push" marketing; and producers' goods. In each case we first sketch the behavioral requirements for successful export, then identify typical features of public and private institutions that encourage or discourage the requisite behavior, and conclude by examining policy implications.

11.2 The evidence: historical roles

Korea[4]

Korea has achieved a very high rate of economic growth while following a successful export promotion strategy and making large and increasing use of its public-enterprise sector.[5] Public enterprises, however, have played only a minor export role, directly exporting only 4.9% of their output[6] and thereby accounting for only 5.3% of total Korean exports of goods and services. Whereas the public-enterprise sector contributed a respectable share of total exports in two minor areas – raw materials (13%) and services (8%) – it had a very small share (2%) in manufacturing. *Indirect* exports (through sales of intermediate inputs ultimately embodied in exports) were substantially greater than direct exports, amounting to 8% of public-enterprise-sector output and thereby contributing an additional 8.6% of total Korean exports (mostly manufactures). In sum, the Korean public-enterprise sector accounted directly and indirectly for about 14% of total Korean exports of goods and services, with 61% of the total representing indirect exports.

The indirect exports had an importance well beyond that measured by their percentage share, as they consisted largely of critical intermediate inputs. The most obvious example is electricity, whose indirect exports were 2% of total exports (equivalent to total direct manufactured exports by all other public enterprises). Had the Korean Electricity Company *not* supplied electricity in a reasonably timely and consistent fashion, entire plants would have shut down periodically. The consequent net loss of exports would have been a substantial multiple of the 2% figure. The biggest contribution of Korean public enterprises to manufactured exports, therefore, has been through the reasonably efficient supply of intermediate inputs to private firms.

Brazil and other export success stories

Brazil also has combined rapid growth, an export orientation, and a large and rapidly growing public-enterprise sector. Although the public-enterprise role in exports has not to our knowledge been documented, the available literature,[7] plus discussion with scholars familiar with Brazil, suggests the following hypotheses. First, both the proportion of public-enterprise output that is exported and the public-enterprise share of total exports is far larger in Brazil than in Korea. Second, the difference is due primarily to export of raw or semiprocessed resources. Companhía Val do Rio Doce (iron ore and pellets) and its subsidiaries (mainly bauxite) are major public resource-based exporters. On the manufacturing side there is EMBRAER (aircraft), INTERBRAS (a trading company), and the new Companhía Siderurgica Tubaro (steel products), but these seem to be exceptions.

In general, then, it seems that Brazil differs from Korea not because the public-enterprise tool is used differently but because the material on which the tool operates is different. In both countries, public enterprises play a significant role in the export of raw materials (and services) but a negligible direct role in manufactured exports. The difference is that raw materials represent a minor share of Korea's exports but a major share of Brazil's. Comparative economic advantage differs between the two countries because of different factor proportions, but the public versus private institutional choice seems quite similar.

Taiwan, Singapore, and Hong Kong are the other major export success stories. The public-enterprise sector has not been studied in great detail in any of these countries, but the general pattern is clear from available surveys.[8] Taiwan and Singapore seem to parallel closely the Korean case with large public-enterprise sectors that do not play a significant role in direct manufactured exports, whereas Hong Kong is an exceptional case because it simply does not have many public enterprises.

India

India has pursued an autarchic, import-substituting strategy of development. It combines a small export sector (6% of GNP from 1972–3 to 1978–9)[9] with a large and growing public-enterprise sector (roughly the same size, growth, and structure as that in Korea).[10] In 1971–2 and 1972–3, direct exports by public enterprises constituted only 4% of total exports or less than 1% of public-enterprise production.[11] Two-thirds of these exports were mineral ores or petroleum products and another 23% consisted of pig iron and steel. The remaining 10% includes an impressive list of sophisticated manufactures (e.g., earth-moving equipment, electronic communication equipment, valves, boilers, aircraft components, machine tools, and wristwatches), but the total value of these exports has been negligible. Public-enterprise manufactured exports, including iron and steel, amounted to only about 3% of Indian manufactured exports.[12]

Other countries

Evidence on public-enterprise exports in other countries is scant; however, there is one multicountry survey that sheds light on the issues addressed here. A study by Raymond Vernon reports that of 175 Latin American manufacturing public enterprises surveyed, only 47 had substantial exports. Furthermore, of the 47 exporting countries, 38 were engaged in raw-materials processing and only 9 in manufacturing.[13]

Summary

Although we have systematic data for only Korea, incomplete figures from other countries seem to clearly support the Korean findings. Public enterprises do not in general directly export substantial quantities of manufactured products. There are certainly exceptions (which we will consider later), but so far as we can tell, these do not generally constitute either a large fraction of public-enterprise output or a large fraction of total exports, or even a large share of manufactured exports. The data suggest that private rather than public enterprises export manufactured goods, even when both the manufactured-export and the public-enterprise sectors are large.

11.3 Explanation one: market factors

How is the foregoing result to be explained? In answering this question, we must avoid the common fallacy in public-enterprise work of attributing differences in outcomes solely to the vagaries of public operation. For example, if it is observed that public enterprises are less cost conscious than their private counterparts, it is sometimes assumed that this is due entirely to bureaucratic control and the incentive system. This ignores the fact that public enterprises are often in a monopoly market position and that private or regulated enterprises operating in similar markets are often accused of similar deviations from cost-minimizing behavior. With ownership divorced from control, differences in the information available to the agent and the principal, and a "satisfactory" profit guaranteed by the market, there is less incentive for management to exert effort to control costs and avoid those expenditures that contribute to management's satisfaction at the expense of profit. Such market pressures affect behavior of both public and private managers.

Enterprise behavior is thus the product of two sets of environmental factors: first, market factors, including the product and factor markets in which the enterprise operates and the technological characteristics of production and marketing; and, second, institutional factors such as the control structure, incentive systems, and the existence of political, labor, and consumer pressure groups. In this section we consider the market explanation for the absence of public-enterprise manufactured exports and in the subsequent section we identify possible institutional factors as causes.

Capital intensity of public-enterprise production

Public enterprises are usually clustered in sectors with well-defined technical characteristics (Jones and Mason, Chapter 2). One such characteristic is germane: Public enterprises in LDCs are found in industries that are, on average, far more capital intensive than both the economy in general and the manufacturing sector in particular. This is most readily documented in the case of Korea, where on a direct basis the public-enterprise sector is more than three times as capital intensive as the economy as a whole, nearly three times as capital intensive as the nonagricultural economy, and more than twice as capital intensive as the manufacturing sector (measured in terms of the ratio of capital stock to total returns to labor).[14] On a direct plus indirect basis (allowing for the capital intensity of intermediate inputs), the public–private gap is reduced as the indirect ratios are near the economy mean. This reflects the dispersion of inputs across the interindustry system as a whole. Nonetheless, the public-enterprise sector still has a capital-to-labor ratio that is about two and one-half times as large as the economy as a whole, or one and two-thirds times that of the manufacturing sector. Not only are public enterprises capital intensive, but the capital-intensive industries are predominantly in the public-enterprise sector. Of the eleven most capital-intensive sectors (in a 117-sector input–output model), public enterprises produced almost all output in four and had a 10% to 50% market share in six others.[15] The public-enterprise average conceals high variance; there are highly capital-intensive nontradables (electricity, communications, and transport), on the one hand, and labor-intensive services (largely in the financial sector), on the other. Public-enterprise manufacturing enterprises, however, are still more than twice as capital intensive as Korean manufacturing as a whole (direct basis).

Less systematic data available for other LDCs suggest that the Korean case is not atypical. In India, over the period 1961 to 1973, public enterprises produced an average of 7% of GDP but absorbed 30% of gross fixed capital formation.[16] In Brazil, public enterprises account for 37.5% of net manufacturing assets but employ only 11.5% of the manufacturing labor force.[17] In Mexico, public-enterprise investment projects are reported to have been 2.4 times as capital intensive (as measured by the ratio of total fixed assets to labor) as "other" investments.[18] In Taiwan, industries that are either 100% or "overwhelmingly" public include electricity, gas, fertilizer, shipbuilding, aluminum, salt, cigarettes, liquor, petroleum, and coal. Industries that are 100% or "overwhelmingly" private include electrical equipment, garments, leather and rubber products, textiles, nonmetallic mineral products, and paper and paper products.[19] With the exception of the monopoly products (salt, cigarettes, and liquor), the markedly higher capital intensity of public enterprises is obvious. Sheahan reports:

> In Brazil and India it is almost as if industries were divided between private and public enterprises according to their capital intensity. In Algeria, public enterprise is focused on capital-intensive methods with little or no regard for chronically high rates of unemployment. A comparison between Indonesian public and private firms in the same industries showed systematically greater capital intensity for the public firms.[20]

These indicators are of course quite crude and even the more detailed Korean data were only appropriate at the most simple Heckscher–Ohlin level of explanation. They nonetheless are suggestive of a major characteristic of the public-enterprise sector that is relevant for exports of manufactures.

Exceptions

Three exceptions to the foregoing generalizations are worth noting. The first is that LDCs sometimes do export capital-intensive goods. Robert Boatler reports that the exports of the more industrialized Latin American nations (Argentina, Brazil, Mexico) are predominantly and increasingly capital intensive.[21] Part of the explanation for this may be his simple two-factor classification.[22] There are two other possible explanations, however.

One possibility is that these exports are socially irrational because of either market or institutional factors. Domestic price distortions (subsidized capital, cheap raw materials, and/or high industrial wages) can create a divergence between perceived and actual comparative advantage, leading to exports that are privately profitable but socially undesirable. On the institutional side, political intrusion may occur in the form of state-to-state bargaining (particularly when Eastern Europe is involved) and result in package deals involving some commodities whose trade might be irrational if viewed individually.

Even if the export decision is left to the public-enterprise manager, the incentive system may be such that exports can be valuable to the manager even though it is unprofitable in both private and social terms. This could occur, for example, if profit is not rewarded[23] but newspapers, politicians, or bureaucratic superiors applaud any export achievement, independent of its cost efficiency. Both market and institutional factors can strongly influence public enterprise's decision making. Therefore, careful evaluation of the social efficiency of exports is critical.

On the other hand, there are certainly legitimate reasons for some capital-intensive exports by public enterprises. Determination of comparative advantage is multicausal and the single-element Heckscher–Ohlin effect can be offset by other factors (see Section 11.1 and note 2). Two sets of such factors *might* create a valid role for capital-intensive public-enterprise exports. One such circumstance is where more industrialized LDCs trade with less-advanced LDCs and where their physical proximity and cultural and technological compatibility offset the endowment-based advantages of firms from more-developed countries (MDCs). A second case is where excess domestic capacity exists, resulting from either faulty investment decisions, changes in demand, or desire to take advantage of dynamic comparative advantage. In such circumstances, short-run exports of particular capital-intensive goods might be sensible.

Both of these export possibilities are enhanced where the product is standardized and undifferentiated (e.g., fertilizer or steel bars) and, therefore, where the marketing advantages enjoyed by MDCs are less important. There are thus legitimate reasons why one might find some exports of the capital-intensive products of public enterprises. Although we suspect that these factors are of only minor importance in explaining the Boatler findings, they are likely to play an increasing role in the future as more LDCs begin producing their own capital-intensive products.

A second exception is when public enterprises are found in labor-intensive sectors. Whereas most countries have a handful of small labor-intensive public enterprises (often as the result of take-overs of sick companies), there are some countries with significant labor-intensive manufacturing public enterprises. In Bangladesh, wholesale nationalization in 1972 brought such labor-intensive industries as textiles and jute within the public domain.[24] In Malaysia, many public enterprises have been established to develop ethnic Malay entrepreneurs and managers. In keeping with the budding capacity of this group, the public enterprises thus established are typically small and labor intensive (Mallon, Chapter 16). In Indonesia, an atypical and decidedly random pattern of public-enterprise-sector expansion has resulted in large numbers of small labor-intensive public enterprises.[25] In LDCs ranging from Nepal to Taiwan to Ghana, state monopolies produce demerit goods including cigarettes and liquor; the export potential of such commodities has been heavily exploited by the Swedish Tobacco Monopoly, and the LDC counterparts could do the same. More generally, where public enterprises are found in labor-intensive sectors, for whatever reason, the export potential is compatible with LDC comparative advantages.

State trading is a third exception. We have emphasized that exporting requires both production and marketing skills and that comparative advantage may differ between the two functions. This is true not only across countries but also across institutional forms. In some LDCs public enterprises may play a major role in export marketing through state trading organizations, even where their role in production for export is minimal. For example: In Peru, 84% of exports move through state trading organizations;[26] in Brazil, 10% of exports are via state trading organizations;[27] and in India, eight state trading organizations handled 15% of total merchandise exports in 1972–73, with 91% of this coming through two large organizations, the State Trading Corporation and the Minerals and Metals Trading Corporation.[28]

Summary

The low rate of manufactured exports from public enterprises is to a large extent "explained" at one level by market factors determining comparative advantage in production, namely, incompatibility between capital-intensive public enterprises and labor-intensive manufactured exports from LDCs. At a deeper level one must ask why public enterprises are found largely in capital-intensive industries. This question is treated in detail elsewhere (Jones and Mason, Chapter 2), but the following summary gives the flavor of the argument. The benefits from public enterprise are greater where market failures lead to suboptimal private response. One such situation occurs when domestic private entrepreneurs are unable to mobilize sufficient capital, provide the technological expertise, and absorb the risk associated with capital-intensive projects. These projects are often also large in scale, technologically complex, and characterized by long gestation periods. The costs of public enterprise are less where the organizational failures of public enterprise are lower as compared with the private sector. Public enterprises may have a comparative institutional advantage in mobilizing capital as opposed to managerial talent, in managing machine-paced as opposed to personnel-paced activities, and in large-scale as opposed to small-scale activities. Further, the apparent costs are less where output is sold in a noncompetitive market. Considerations such as these help to explain the relative capital intensity of the public-enterprise sector.

In sum, the export potential of LDC public enterprises can be viewed as being constrained indirectly by their capital intensity. There are nonetheless some institutional costs and benefits of the public-enterprise choice that directly affect export ability, a topic to which we now turn.

11.4 Explanation two: institutional factors and marketing

Institutional factors as explanatory and policy variables

Economic outcomes are determined not only by market forces *external* to the enterprise's decision-making hierarchy but also by *internal* organizational factors affecting the enterprise's behavioral response to these external factors. Because public enterprises systematically respond differently than private enterprises, public enterprises are more or less appropriate for particular jobs. Although these behavioral factors may explain some of the observed absence of public-enterprise

Table 11.1. *Stages of export marketing development*

	(Stage 1) Importer pull	Exporter push			
		(Stage 2) Basic production capacity marketing	(Stage 3) Advanced production capacity marketing	(Stage 4) Product marketing channel push	(Stage 5) Product marketing consumer pull
Product					
Internal design	†	††	††	††	††
External design	†	†	††	††	††
Package design		†	††	††	††
Quality control			†	††	††
Branding				†	††
Price					
First cost	††	††	††	††	††
Price to retailer				†	††
Price to consumer					†
Promotion					
To importer locally		††	††	††	
Destination			††	††	††
To retailer				†	††
To consumers					††
Physical distribution at destination					
To distributors				††	††
To retailer				†	††

Note: † = Partial responsibility taken by exporter. †† = Full responsibility taken by exporter.

manufactured exports, they are probably much less important than the market factors identified earlier. The institutional constraints are nonetheless important in suggesting reforms necessary to make public enterprises more effective in those cases where they *are*, or could be, used for manufactured exports. Institutional factors are policy variables as well as explanatory variables.

We will proceed in three steps. First, we define the export "job" in terms of the managerial and entrepreneurial behavior required for success. Second, we ask to what extent public-enterprise control systems encourage or discourage such behavior. Third, we examine the policy implications.

The answers to these questions will vary with the nature of the product being exported and the way in which marketing functions are split between exporter and importer. Accordingly, we address each of the three questions in three different contexts: (1) "early" consumer-goods exports under importer pull; (2) "late" consumer-goods exports under exporter push; and (3) producer-goods exports.

We begin with an overview of the theory and history of the role of marketing factors in the evolution of manufactured exports from LDCs.

The marketing cycle and LDC manufactured exports

Lawrence and Heidi Wortzel have identified five stages through which firms based in LDCs might move as they expand exports of manufactured consumer goods.[29] The stages are distinguished by the degree to which the exporter integrates forward in taking over product design and international marketing functions. These stages are summarized in Table 11.1, which shows the division of these functions between exporter and customer.

Empirical work has established that most successful LDC firms exporting manufactured consumer goods have started in stages 1 or 2. That is, exports were initiated not by sellers but by buyers looking for new sources of low-priced merchandise produced to their specifications and schedule. These purchases have been concentrated in clothing, athletic footwear, and consumer electronics.[30] Producers are selling production capacity only; all product decisions were made by the importer. Often, the buyer even dictated the choice of raw materials and the suppliers of packaging materials.

An exporter in stage 1 forgoes the profits associated with marketing, but this is not necessarily irrational. There are high costs associated with the search for customers as information is scarce and returns are uncertain. However, with experience, these costs are reduced, and it is sometimes possible to move to higher stages, performing more of the functions and appropriating more of the marketing markup. Once they have developed some export business, some exporters therefore begin to actively search for additional customers (stage 2 expansion). Some firms even enter as active searchers (stage 2 entry), though this is often the consequence of stage 1 experience by the entrepreneurs in another firm. The prospective exporter can now make a more rational determination of the costs and value of information. Some firms become increasingly able to produce merchandise that meets buyers' specifications, to perform more sophisticated manufacturing operations, and to provide a wider range of products. Their transaction costs decline as their store of information increases. As a result, many producers develop steady export customers and better procedures for finding new customers. This constitutes a movement into stage 3 of the cycle. To date, progress beyond stage 3 has been limited to only a small number of LDC firms, including four or five consumer electronics manufacturers from Taiwan and Korea and one or two producers of men's shirts in Korea. Each of these changes represents an internalization of transactions, vertical integration, and cost reduction.[31]

There are marked differences in the managerial requirements for success in the different stages of the marketing cycle. For present purposes, the most important qualitative differences occur between stage 1 – which we will call importer pull – and the subsequent stages – which we will call exporter push.

11.5   Consumer goods: importer pull

Requirements for success under importer pull

Under importer pull, buyers initiate customer contact, design the product, set product specifications, maintain quality control, and manage markets. The exporter must still demonstrate that it: has sufficient experience with relevant production processes to produce the required product; can manage efficiently enough to meet the contract price; has a sufficiently stable and cheap source of intermediate inputs, satisfactory labor relations and disciplined workers, capable management, and sufficient absence of government controls to meet contract deadlines; is sufficiently flexible to adjust quickly in response to changes requested by the buyer; is capable of maintaining quality control within contract guidelines; and is financially sound enough to complete the order.

The importance of these factors is emphasized by David Morawetz, who examines the determinants of the rise and fall of Colombian clothing exports and then attempts to explain why "Hong Kong, Korea and Taiwan have a combined population that is less than 2½ times that of Colombia, but the three nations' garment exports is 150 times that of Colombia."[32] His empirical work recognizes the importance of input prices but discounts such other traditional *external* explanations as cheap labor, heavy government subsidization, and cheap transport costs. Instead, he stresses the importance of factors *internal* to the firm such as labor productivity, purchasing efficiency, quality control, and punctuality.

Public-enterprise responses under importer pull

In principle, there is no reason why public enterprises should be any less able than private enterprises to solve the internal managerial requirements for exporting. In Western Europe this is evidenced by France's Renault, the Swedish Tobacco Monopoly, and British Petroleum (which is operating so much like a private firm that many consider it not to be a public enterprise despite 50% government equity). It is difficult to find similar manufacturing export success stories in the LDCs, but Brazil's aircraft producer (EMBAER) seems to qualify. Examples such as these show that there are no *necessary* reasons for public enterprises to be deficient in the requisite skills, but the paucity of such examples suggests there may be many *sufficient* reasons.

Identification of the behavioral–institutional factors inhibiting manufactured exports by public enterprises may thus be useful in partly explaining the historic absence of such exports and in identifying reforms necessary if public enterprises are to play a larger role in the future. As the specification of these constraints is difficult because of the absence of relevant case studies, we are forced to rely on indirect inference from observed public-enterprise behavior in other environments. What follows is thus only a set of informed hypotheses as to those institutional factors that may serve to inhibit exploitation of potential comparative advantage when public enterprises are found in industries appropriate to importer-pull activity.

First, public-enterprise control systems may inhibit exports. These are typically the offspring of bureaucratic systems that control processes rather than outcomes and that can require extensive lists of time-consuming approvals when new procedures are initiated. This is of less consequence in standardized operations, which can be planned well ahead of time and where one year is much like another. It can be deadly, however, in exporting where rapid responses to changing customer requirements are necessary and where short-term contracts dominate. A manager must be able to quickly react to an order; otherwise it will go elsewhere and not necessarily to the same country. Accepting an order might entail diverting facilities from domestic production, acquiring a new piece of machinery, hiring a technician with a particular skill, or instituting other changes that might require time-consuming bureaucratic approval. Even more important, the bureaucratic control systems may be an anathema to the entrepreneurially minded manager. Thus, the managers who gravitate to the public sector may be those who are least able to operate entrepreneurially.

Second, there may be a lack of competitive experience, as most public enterprises operate in the least competitive markets (Jones and Mason, Chapter 2). As a result, work habits may be formed that are not responsive to the requirements of international competition. There may be little pressure for cost consciousness, punctuality, quality control, task adaptation, and other characteristics demanded by international buyers.

Third, there may be a lack of motivation. Public-enterprise managers and workers seldom share to any significant extent in increases in enterprise surplus. Where such sharing does exist, it is often limited to a single year because of the subsequent adjustment of controlled domestic prices. There is thus little or no compensation for the extra effort and hours required to negotiate, adjust, monitor, and meet tight export contracts and therefore little reason to do so.

Fourth, there may be poor use of performance indicators. Where exporting is rewarded, a manager might be instructed to export some fixed target and may well respond with increased exports. However, if the target is simply set in quantity terms, he may ignore costs, exporting at a net social loss. There will be exports but at very high cost to the country. This is especially likely if the manager can cover export losses through cross-subsidization from price increases in a protected domestic market.

The alleviation of such problems is not a simple matter. For example, in recognition of the flexibility problems mentioned earlier, the managers of one LDC public enterprise were given formal authority to make a substantial range of decisions. They nonetheless continued to obtain the approval signatures of higher officials, explaining that otherwise they could get in trouble via future legislative inquiries where it was not always possible to fully document why a particular bid or contract was chosen over another or why a particular price was agreed upon. If, however, such postaudit procedures are eliminated, there is room for a manager (whose compensation is officially unrelated to marginal profits) to expropriate some profits for himself by side negotiations with foreign firms.

Whereas it is thus possible to ameliorate the problems associated with public control, their abolition is unlikely. This is hardly fatal, as public enterprises also have offsetting advantages. For example, in attracting managers, the problems of low compensation and frustration over constraints may in some countries be offset by higher status and the challenge of operating a large capital-intensive modern enterprise. If the private sector is typically smaller scale and labor intensive and if narrow family control precludes advancement to the highest ranks, smart young managers may opt for public enterprises.

The minimal direct role of public enterprises under importer pull

It seems that the bulk of the increase in LDC manufactured exports has combined production by the private sector with marketing by foreign buyers. The role of public enterprise in this process has been negligible thus far, and we see no compelling reason for this to change. If public enterprises suffer from a comparative disadvantage in production of small-scale, labor-intensive, differentiated products and if there are initially no marketing barriers to be overcome, these activities would seem best left to the private sector augmented by supporting government institutions.

This is not a trivial conclusion, for it is as important to know when to eschew use of the public-enterprise tool as to know when and how to employ it effectively. Government resources – capital and, even more important, administrative and managerial talents – are in markedly short supply and need to be allocated to the most productive users. Use of public enterprises in production or marketing under importer-pull conditions is thus likely to have high opportunity costs.

There is of course room for activity by public *institutions*.[33] One such function is information augmentation: for example, by an autonomous trade promotion board whose aim is to bring buyers and sellers together by informing foreigners of domestic suppliers and vice versa. Another function is to provide assistance in quality control and related production concerns. There is also a need for someone to play an advocacy role within government to cut through regulations and policies that inhibit trade. There is also a role for government involvement in sponsoring various bilateral trade negotiations and swap agreements. One public-enterprise role might be the provision of credit or credit insurance.

The fundamental indirect role

Nonetheless, by far the most important public-enterprise role under importer-pull conditions is the *indirect* supporting role of efficiently providing intermediate inputs. This role remains important under exporter-pull conditions, but, as we shall see, there then may be additional direct roles as well.

Public enterprises typically produce basic goods with high forward linkages,[34] so that efficient production and delivery of their output to private exporters is a major determinant of the ability of private-sector firms to realize *their* potential international competitiveness. The reliability factor is probably more important than the cost factor. If electricity, transportation, communications, steel, fuel, and petrochemicals cannot be predictably provided without interruption, the meeting of tight export contract deadlines becomes difficult, if not impossible. If these inputs are not produced with great efficiency, the downstream firms will not be cost competitive. The most important public-enterprise contribution to export promotion in mixed-economy LDCs will therefore result from policies designed to improve efficiency across the entire industrial sector and not merely in those public enterprises actually exporting.

The public enterprise's role as purveyor of intermediates suggests a second possible role in direct export promotion, that is, providing subsidies via pricing policies. Although there are compelling arguments for providing exporters with temporary subsidies in order to realize dynamic comparative advantage, there are also strong arguments against transmitting those subsidies via underpriced sales of publicly produced intermediate goods. Possible negative consequences of such a policy might include: (1) excessively capital-intensive production, as the inputs produced by public enterprises are likely to be more complementary to capital than to labor; (2) harm to the financial position of the public enterprise and thus to managerial motivation, levels of working capital, and national investment decisions (Gillis, Jenkins, and Lessard, Chapter 13),[35] (3) excessive subsidies that are hidden within the enterprise budget and thus less subject to public budgetary scrutiny; and (4) deterioration of income distribution as the same subsidies are likely to go to producers for the domestic market, to the benefit of either factory owners or the better-off consumers who buy intermediate–input–intensive commodities.

Although these arguments are strong, they are not definitive, as any subsidy transmission mechanism creates its own distortions. Nonetheless, such considerations should give serious pause to anyone considering use of public-enterprise prices as a transmission vehicle for export subsidies. The fundamental indirect role of public enterprises in providing low-priced inputs should be achieved by cost efficiency rather than by absorption of hidden subsidies.

11.6 Consumer goods: exporter push

An additional role for public enterprises emerges as countries move into exporter-push conditions. Recall that this entails vertical integration into marketing as the producer takes over more and more of the trading and distribution functions. The goal of the firm is to capture the trading margins as well as any quasi rents that accrue temporarily to the product in question. In this effort there is no change in the comparative disadvantage of public enterprise (the nature of the commodities being produced is unchanged), but a *marketing* role for public enterprises now becomes a serious possibility.

Requirements for success under exporter push

Under exporter push, along with improved production skills, major new marketing skills are now required. This constitutes a qualitative shift from more routine *production* activities to more innovative *entrepreneurial* ones. Recall that one of Schumpeter's examples of the "new combinations" that define entrepreneurial activity was "the opening of a new market, that is a market into which the particular branch of manufacture of the country in question has not previously entered, whether or not this market has existed before."[36] Fulfilling this entrepreneurial function requires: the motivation and ability to search for new customers; the demonstration of ability to produce a wider range of goods; the beginning of an ability to assist in product design and in the setting of product specifications; and a change of attitude from one of production service to one of product innovations.

The further one progresses, the greater the innovativeness required. The stage 4 firm is a marketer of products instead of production capacity. It takes responsibility for product design and for marketing at the destination. In doing so, it has shifted virtually all innovative activity from its customers to itself. Risk also increases at this stage as there is a shift from producing-to-order to selling-from-inventory and from finance via letter-of-credit to open-account transactions.

If public enterprises are sometimes constrained in applying efficient management techniques, they can be even more circumscribed in encouraging entrepreneurial ones. Foreign marketing is an innovative activity that can be readily discouraged under the constraints of public ownership and control, a phenomenon that has been well documented for the USSR.[37] Three reasons are worth mentioning.

First, under some sets of circumstances, the public manager may be risk averse and thus unwilling to expose himself to the vagaries of foreign markets (Tandon, Chapter 12).[38] Second, specialized personnel may be needed for marketing, design, and dealing with foreign buyers. If restricted government salaries or hiring practices preclude getting the best people, competitive foreign contracts may be lost. Similarly, certain expense-account items necessary in the international market may clash with government guidelines. Third, as the tenure of top management is often brief, there is little incentive for allocating time to developing extensive foreign-marketing networks, incurring research and development costs for new products, and absorbing current losses to generate long-term goodwill.

Potential roles for public enterprises under exporter push

Public enterprises have special opportunities as well as constraints. For one thing, there is a valid public role in overcoming private failures to respond in a socially optimal fashion where scale, risk, and information imperfections bulk large. Insofar as the technology of production of labor-intensive goods is small scale and the product line is limited, a single producer cannot afford to incur the substantial costs of establishing an overseas trading network. Fixed costs are high because of the facilities required to perform marketing and distribution and because of the learning required in adjusting to foreign markets. Variable costs are high because buyers are widely separated around the world, requiring a variety of regional offices and specialists to accomplish the marketing job, and because of the increased requirements for working capital. There are thus economies of scale in marketing that can be exploited by horizontal integration, both narrowly across producers in a single product line and more broadly across product lines. Where such differences in optimal scale between production and marketing exist, there may be a strong case for integrated general trading companies.

But should the choice be a public or private general trading company?[39] The revealed preference of successful manufacturing exporters comes down on the private side. Japan relied on private general trading companies when it began exporting, but the trading company role diminished as producers grew in size.[40] Taiwan, Hong Kong, and Singapore have not used such concerns at all. Although Korea has a number of general trading companies, there is room to question the extent to which they have played a true marketing and distribution role.[41] Many LDCs have public general trading corporations, but they have been notably unsuccessful in fostering manufactured exports (with the exception of Brazil's INTERBRAS).

There are, however, at least four reasons to believe that there may be a greater future role for state trading organizations in manufactured exports. One derives from the Gerschenkron hypothesis, arguing that there is a greater potential for a state role in late-coming nations where the task is imitation rather than innovation.

A second argument is that the precedents were largely set in East Asian nations with extensive international trading histories prior to their boom in manufacturing exports (Singapore and Hong Kong as entrepôts, Japan in its early colonizing role, and Taiwan and Korea as colonial subjects). Such experiences, perhaps enhanced by ethnic proclivities, created an export-oriented mind-set and pools of talent and information upon which the emergent private sector could draw. In the absence of such experience, there may be externalities creating greater need for functions that could be performed by state trading organizations but not by a private general trading company. Both premises of this argument are open to question. Was the stock of experience with international markets really greater in Taiwan or Korea in the 1960s than it is in India or Pakistan today? Are the externalities in question really nonpecuniary, requiring government intervention?

It may be that the relevant externalities are really pecuniary, but that they are capturable only with substantial scale, that is, the relevant market failure is not external effects but decreasing costs. This gives a third, and much more compelling, argument for state trading organizations in smaller LDCs where the optimal scale of a general trading company is beyond the entrepreneurial capacity of the private sector. This argument becomes more forceful when it is recognized that a general trading company is not confined to marketing manufactured exports but also can have a role in primary exports and in importing as well, thus substantially expanding the technologically optimal scale. If a state trading organization already exists as a prerequisite to trade with command economies, it may be cheaper to utilize its existing infrastructure rather than to create a new private general trading company.

A fourth possible argument is that the precedent does not hold because it may have represented suboptimal behavior in the first place. Recall that the bulk of LDC manufactured exports are in only a very narrow range of product categories; and few enterprises have progressed beyond stage 3 of the marketing cycle. Is this a natural result of comparative advantage or might there be some market failures involved that could have been overcome via a larger state role? The following factors may be relevant: the number of product lines in which there are active importers is limited; competing successfully in exporting some product lines requires skill in product design and quality control; success in some product lines requires prior experience with relevant production processes; risk is greater in the higher stages of the marketing cycle; the firm must form its own estimates; and rather than rely on buyers' judgments of changing consumer tastes, firms will have to design their own products and production processes.

For such reasons, moving to higher stages of the marketing cycle entails substantially more entrepreneurial risk, much more sophisticated research, development, and planning, as well as a larger marketing and distribution network. Accordingly, there may be a role for state trading organizations in spreading risk, realizing research and development externalities, providing inventory financing, and achieving economies of scale in distribution.

There are thus a number of legitimate arguments for a state trading organization to assist a country desiring to move up the marketing cycle. That the absence, or at least paucity, of really successful precedents in mixed-economy LDCs suggests great caution in acting on these prospects is hardly definitive. The lack of precedent may be due not to absence of potential benefits but to failure to create the institutional structures that allow the potential to be achieved.

11.7 Producers' goods

Requirements for success in exporting producers' goods

Producers' goods differ from consumer goods in two important ways. First, some producers' goods are capital intensive and therefore are in sectors where direct production by public enterprise is more likely. Second, on the marketing side, there is increased concern for stability, continuity, and long-term relationships. Although these concerns are demonstrated most strongly in the marketing of differentiated producers' goods, they are apparent in the marketing of undifferentiated goods as well.

Exports of producers' goods from LDCs have, so far, consisted primarily of labor-intensive products such as electronic components. They have been initiated primarily through exporter pull[42] or through exports from a multinational subsidiary that has been formed to take advantage of low wages.[43] In both cases, the exporter has been a private-sector firm. The limitation on these labor-intensive exports has been the inability of LDC firms to market their production capabilities rather than their inability to produce.

There also have been some exports of capital-intensive producers' goods. Most often these have been undifferentiated products such as iron and steel or textile fabrics. Here the factors limiting export growth have been production capacity as well as marketing ability. Finally, at least two countries – India and Hong Kong – have been exporting simple machinery, which is both capital intensive and differentiated. Here, the limitations to future exports are marketing ability rather than production capability or capacity.

Public-enterprise response

As already noted, public enterprises are likely to have a comparative institutional advantage in production of capital-intensive goods. On the marketing side, a critical distinction needs to be made between goods that are standardized and those that are differentiated. In the former case, the institutional constraints of public control are likely to be far less debilitating.

Compared to consumer goods, many producers' goods would seem to be relatively easy to market. Products such as iron and steel, fertilizer, petrochemicals, and aluminum are standardized and homogeneous so that the quality of any batch can be objectively determined. Unlike items such as clothing, footwear, textiles, and electronics, the specifications demanded by buyers change only slowly if at all; therefore, little product modification is required from batch to batch. International prices are widely known and exhibit less variance, reducing the need for sophisticated price negotiations. In sum, less innovation and less sophistication are required in marketing. Therefore, public enterprises are in a less disadvantageous position in marketing standardized producers' goods as compared with either the differentiated consumer goods considered earlier or with differentiated producers' goods such as engineering products.

This does not mean that entry into international markets is simple for either public- or private-sector firms producing standardized products. The quest by buyers for the stability of long-term relationships can manifest itself in vertical integration and barriers to entry. Supplier firms without long-term contracts must be able to respond quickly to opportunities in spot markets. Are public or private enterprises in LDCs better able to overcome these barriers?[44] The least that can be said is that public enterprises have some advantages in contract markets. If the foreign buyer is in Eastern Europe, the advantages of state organizations are clear. If the buyer is a private Western firm, ideological distaste might be thought to complicate matters, but in practice, private imports from public enterprises have reached immense proportions in the raw-materials markets,[45] and there has been a rapid increase in public–private joint ventures in manufacturing. In part this is due to absence of choice, but in part it also reflects a belief that governments may be the more stable long-run partners in politically unstable LDCs.

Where the sale is to other LDCs, public enterprises may also have certain advantages. Some recipient LDCs may be more open to government-to-government negotiations for ideological reasons, whereas others may find them congenial in a bureaucratic approval process. Still others may be susceptible to the initially favorable credit terms a government might be able to offer through swap transactions or concessionary financing terms. Public-sector firms may be more ready than private firms to accomplish such transactions.

These potential advantages of public over private enterprise may not hold with respect to spot markets. The successful marketer of spot products must be extremely agile and flexible. Such a firm must be able to respond quickly to inquiries and must develop, in addition, the means to uncover potential sales opportunities that occur in a wide variety of markets. The state-owned enterprise may be less likely than the private-sector firm to be able to react quickly to opportunity or to be able to develop a network that would allow it to identify opportunities. The public enterprise may therefore not be able to take advantage of all its spot sales opportunities.

None of the considerations just mentioned are definitive, but as a group they strongly suggest that public-enterprise marketing disadvantages are much less for standardized producers' goods than for consumer goods, at least where long-term contracts are involved.

For nonstandardized producers' goods the conclusion is different. The marketer of these goods faces all of the problems noted earlier for consumer goods. In addition, quality, continuity of supply, and the provision of ancillary services becomes even more critical. The prospective buyer often expects technical assistance before purchase, training at the time of purchase, and the provision of service after purchase. The buyer is therefore not likely to accept uncertainty about the performance of those tasks in return for a price cut. To date, few public or private enterprises in the LDCs have exhibited an ability to do the required marketing job themselves.

Unfortunately, networks of middlemen to take on these functions are not readily available. Where middlemen do exist, they are not accustomed to combing LDCs for new products, nor are they used to dealing with manufacturers who cannot provide support functions. The LDC firm wishing to break into markets for nonstandardized producers' goods often faces considerable up-front investment, with low returns expected during the first few years. Many private-sector firms are unwilling to make such investments, even if provided with the usual export incentives. This is simply because such firms are likely to have other investment choices offering better, more secure returns. The LDC firm that may be capable of competing in foreign markets for differentiated producers' goods can most probably find attractive possibilities for new products in its home market. The public enterprise may more readily forgo the short-term return in favor of the long-term gain and may be less concerned about the higher risk of overseas investment.

Potential roles for public enterprises

The foregoing list of obstacles can be overcome, however, even for nonstandardized producers' goods. For example, Brazil's EMBRAER has been successful in exporting highly sophisticated aircraft. To accomplish this, public enterprises need to be both encouraged via incentives and allowed via autonomy to seek out export business and to make use of their unique government connections. Although there are good reasons for public enterprises to behave differently from private firms in many *internal* markets, in *foreign* markets profit-oriented activity is precisely what is required to maximize the domestic interest. The primary goal is profits, and concern for the welfare of the foreign buyer (except as a long-term customer) is negligible.

The domestic interest requires that the long-term profit potential of the foreign market be exploited to its maximum. Public enterprises should behave in foreign markets like competent private enterprises. But they should be willing to take more risks than private enterprises will take and should be encouraged to do so. The public enterprise might be especially encouraged, for example, in those sectors where the magnitude of the required investment and a slower return might make a venture seem too risky for the private sector firm.

There is one caveat to this principle. Profits must be correctly measured so as to reflect social scarcity. Both public and private firms should export whenever marginal revenues exceed marginal costs[46]. The relevant marginal benefits and costs differ, however, between public and private firms. Taxes are private costs but public transfers. The recorded costs of labor and capital and foreign exchange may not reflect their true social opportunity costs[47]. Also, where the enterprise is a price setter rather than a price taker, the public enterprise should set a profit-maximizing, rather than a welfare-maximizing, price for export sales.

Whether conversion to a social calculus will make exports from public enterprises more or less likely cannot be predicted as there are generally offsetting distortions requiring empirical evaluation of relative magnitudes. Nonetheless, two hypotheses may be ventured. In the short run, where excess capacity exists, the social calculation is likely to make exports more attractive because the social value of labor is likely to be below the market price. In the long run (or in the short run where there is no excess capacity and the choice is between domestic and export production), the net benefits of export may be lower in social terms if underpriced credit more than offsets foreign-exchange gains. One clear policy prerequisite to public-enterprise exports therefore is that occasional checks should be run to ensure that marginal social benefits exceed marginal social costs and that the export decision is not misguided by the use of traditional private accounting practices.

With this exception, the closer public-enterprise behavior in foreign markets parallels best-practice private behavior, the better for domestic welfare. Accomplishing this requires specific attention to the standard requirements for improving public-enterprise efficiency, including clear goal specification and appropriate performance indicators, both monetary and nonmonetary incentives linked to the indicator, and sufficient managerial discretion to affect the indicator.

These reforms become all the more important as there are several reasons to expect that there could be increasing LDC exports of capital-intensive commodities of the sort presently produced by public enterprises. First, as industrialization and capital accumulation progress, wage rates increase and factor endowment shifts comparative production advantage towards capital-intensive goods. Moreover, expanding economies provide greater opportunity for realizing scale economies in these goods. Second, there is the likelihood of forward integration from raw-materials processing. Countries endowed with minerals can have a derivative comparative advantage in downstream industries that utilize these inputs, which are often capital-intensive. Third, a substantial portion of mineral export earnings (especially from oil) is being reinvested in capital-intensive local production. Often this takes the form of vertical integration, as, for example, when oil producers enter the petrochemical industry. Often the investments are in public enterprises. Fourth, some LDC investments in capital-intensive processes result in excess capacity, which provides a legitimate argument for capital-intensive exports of incremental production. This is independent of whether the excess capacity results from miscalculation of domestic demand or deliberate pursuit of dynamic comparative advantage. Fifth, many capital- and technology-intensive public enterprises were initially established in the name of dynamic comparative advantage, sometimes with exports in mind. The goal was to become efficient in protected domestic markets and then to move into international markets, emulating Japan's strategy. Insofar as these hopes are realized, capital-intensive exports from LDCs will increase. The rise in such sophisticated exports from India in the late 1970s may reflect this process.

11.8   Conclusion

We have identified not one but many roles (notably including no role at all) for public enterprises in different facets of the production and marketing of manufacturing exports in mixed-economy LDCs. This is as it should be, for public enterprise is simply one tool of government policy and the appropriate tool varies with the job. We have attempted to identify different jobs using a two-dimensional decomposition of the determinants of comparative advantage. First, we distinguished between opportunities arising from production conditions and those stemming from marketing activities. Second, we identified institutional factors that might make the realization of potential advantage more or less likely in public versus private enterprises. This framework allowed us to identify those problems in production and marketing that are more or less amenable to being solved by using public enterprise. Recognition of the particular institutional strengths and shortcomings of public enterprises further allows identification of those control areas that need to be modified to maximize benefits when public enterprises are in fact engaged in exporting manufactures.

In assessing the advantages and disadvantages of various institutional forms for promoting manufactured exports, we have raised what we believe to be interesting and important questions and have examined available evidence in an attempt to answer these questions. In a few cases there are enough data to support rather strong statements, but more often our "answers" are only hypotheses based on informed speculation. This results from a lack of previous research into the behavior of public enterprise in manufactured exports. We have therefore relied heavily on indirect evidence (e.g., the revealed preference of export success stories) and on a priori theorizing but to only a limited extent on direct observations of the export performance of LDC public enterprises. This lacuna suggests a profitable area for further research to confirm, modify, or deny the hypotheses tentatively proposed here.

Notes

1 See Bela Belassa, "A Strategic Approach to Comparative Advantage," World Bank, Staff Working Paper No. 256 (Washington, D.C., May 1977); Hal Lary, *Imports of Manufactures from Less Developed Countries* (New York: National Bureau of Economic Research, 1968).

2 See Raymond Vernon, "International Investment and International Trade in the Product Cycle," *Quarterly Journal of Economics* 80 (May 1966):190-207; G. C. Hufbauer, "The Impact of National Characteristics on the Commodity Composition of Trade in Manufactured Goods," in *The Technology Factor in International Trade,* ed. Raymond Vernon (New York: National Bureau of Economic Research, 1970), pp. 141-232; and William K. Gruber and Raymond Vernon, "The Technology Factor in a World Trade Matrix," ibid., pp. 233-72.

3 See Lawrence H. Wortzel and Heidi V. Wortzel, "Marketing Manufactured Exports from LDCs: Progress and Recommendations for Further Progress" (Paper presented at the Academy of International Business, Las Vegas, Nev., June 1979); and Donald B. Keesing, "Trade and Industrial Development: Relationships and Policies," World Bank, World Development Report Background Paper (Washington, D.C., Nov. 1978).

4 Data in this section are based on *Bank of Korea, Economic and Statistics Yearbook* (Seoul: Bank of Korea, various years) and Leroy P. Jones, *Public Enterprise and Economic Development: The Korean Case* (Seoul: Korean Development Institute, 1975).

5 Through the 1960s and 1970s real GNP increased at an annual rate of nearly 10%; exports increased from $41 million in 1961 to $13 billion in 1978; well over 90% of these exports were manufactured products; and public enterprises constituted a

leading sector in that they grew even more rapidly than the economy as a whole (expanding from less than 6% of GNP to more than 9%). In addition, there were high forward linkages that tied this expansion to growth elsewhere in the economy.

6 The source gives a higher figure, but this included sales of electricity, transport, and communications services to U.N. forces in Korea. These technical "exports" are excluded here.

7 Thomas J. Trebat, "An Evaluation of the Economic Performance of Public Enterprises in Brazil" (Ph.D. diss., Vanderbilt University, 1978); Werner Baer, Issac Kerstenetzky, and Annibal V. Villela, "The Changing Role of the State in the Brazilian Economy," *World Development* 1, No. 11 (Nov. 1973):23–34; Thomas J. Trebat, "The Role of Public Enterprise in the Brazilian Economy: An Evaluation," mimeographed (University of Texas, Houston, 1977); Werner Baer, Richard Neufarmer, and Thomas J. Trebat, "On State Capitalism in Brazil: Some New Ideas and Questions," *Inter-American Economic Affairs* 30, No. 3 (Winter 1976):69–91.

8 Frank Hsiao, "Dual Economic Structure and Factor Markets in Taiwan: The Role of Public Enterprise," Department of Economics Discussion Paper No. 114 (Boulder: University of Colorado, 1977).

9 Government of India, *Economic Survey: 1977–1978* (New Delhi: Government of India Press, 1978).

10 See N. S. Ramaswamy, U. J. Kesary, P. V. George, G. K. Nayan, V. G. Kamath, and P. D. Deenadayalu, *Performance of Indian Public Enterprise* (New Delhi: Standing Conference on Public Enterprises, 1978).

11 Government of India, Central Statistical Organization, *Statistical Abstract: 1975* (New Delhi: Government of India Press, 1976), p. 197; Vadilal Dagli, *Commerce Yearbook of the Public Sector: 1974–1975* (Bombay: Mahatme, 1974), pp. 56, 111–12; Documentation Centre for Corporate and Business Policy Research, *The Future of Public Sector in India* (New Delhi: DCCP, Mar. 1979). These data cover only central government enterprises.

12 Many informed Indians are surprised at this figure. This may be due to a rapid increase in public-enterprise exports by the late 1970s. Alternatively, it may be that the long and well-publicized list of sophisticated public-enterprise exports has created the impression of greater volume than actually exists. Many such exports are one-shot deals (note the marked annual discontinuities for many companies in Dagli, *Commerce Yearbook*, p. 111).

13 Raymond Vernon, "State-Owned Enterprises in Latin American Exports," manuscript (Cambridge University, Jan. 1980), p. 28.

14 Jones, *Public Enterprise and Economic Development*, pp. 123–5. If the more traditional man-year denominator was used, the relative capital intensity of the public enterprises would be still greater, as the sector makes a disproportionate claim on highly skilled, highly paid workers.

15 The exception is cement, which is capital-intensive but small scale.

16 Ramaswamy et al., *Performance of Indian Public Enterprise*, p. 139 and Appendix Tables 6 and 8. All figures are simple averages of annual figures.

17 Werner Baer and Adolfo Figueroa, "The Impact of Increased State Participation in the Economy on the Distribution of Income" (Paper presented at second BAPEG conference on Public Enterprise in Mixed Economy LDCs, Apr. 1980), p. 13.

18 Rocio de Villarreal and Rene Villarreal, "Public Enterprises in Mexican Development Under the Oil Perspective in the 1980s" (Paper presented at second BAPEG conference on Public Enterprise in Mixed Economy LDCs, Apr. 1980), p. 76.

19 Hsiao, "Dual Economic Structure," p. 4.

20 John Sheahan, "Public Enterprise in Developing Countries," in *Public Enterprise:*

Economic Analysis of Theory and Practice, ed. William Shepherd (Lexington, Mass.: Lexington Books, 1976). p. 211.

21 Robert W. Boatler, "Comparative Advantages: A Division Among Developing Countries," *Inter-American Economic Affairs* 32, No. 2 (Autumn 1978):59–66.

22 That is, Latin America's really abundant factor is natural resources and if the processing of such commodities requires relatively more capital than labor, then the apparent capital intensity is really hidden natural-resource intensity.

23 Either because there is no bonus system or because greater profit (or loss) is ultimately offset by a regulated pricing system, which wipes out any gain.

24 See Rehman Sobhan and Muzaffer Ahmad, *Public Enterprise in an Intermediate Regime: A Study of the Political Economy of Bangladesh* (Dacca: Bangladesh Institute of Development Studies, 1980).

25 See Malcolm Gillis and Ralph E. Beals, *Tax and Investment Policy for Hard Minerals: Public and Multinational Enterprise in Indonesia* (Cambridge, Mass.: Ballinger, 1980).

26 Alfred Saulniers, "State Trading Organizations: A Bias Decision Model" (Paper presented at second BAPEG conference on Public Enterprise in Mixed Economy LDCs, Apr. 1980), p. 24.

27 Ibid.

28 Dagli, *Commerce Yearbook*, pp. 111–12.

29 Wortzel and Wortzel, "Marketing Manufactured Exports."

30 Agnus Hone, "Multinational Corporations and Multinational Buying Groups: The Impact on the Growth by Asia's Exports of Manufactures – Myths and Realities," *World Development* 2, No. 2 (Feb. 1974):145–50.

31 P. Buckley and R. Casson, *The Future of Multinational Enterprise* (New York: Holmes and Meier, 1977).

32 David Morawetz, "Why the Emperor's New Clothes Are Not Made in Colombia: A Case Study in Latin American and East Asian Manufactured Exports," World Bank, Staff Working Paper No. 368 (Washington, D.C., Jan. 1980), p. 133.

33 Where institutions are distinguished from enterprises in that enterprises largely sell their services, whereas the former provide basically free public goods.

34 Jones and Mason, Chapter 2.

35 John Lintner, "Economic Theory and Financial Management," in *State Owned Enterprises in the Western Economies*, ed. Raymond Vernon and Yair Aharoni (New York: St. Martin's Press, 1981); and Kenneth Arrow, "On Finance and Decision Making," in Vernon and Aharoni, pp. 63–9.

36 Joseph A. Schumpeter, *The Theory of Economic Development* (Oxford University Press, 1961), p. 66.

37 For example, see Joseph Berliner, *The Innovation Decision in Soviet Industry* (Cambridge, Mass.: MIT Press, 1976).

38 For discussion of the critical question of the risk preference of public enterprise managers, see Zvi Adar and Yair Aharoni, "Risk Sharing by Managers of State-Owned Enterprises" (Paper presented at Second BAPEG conference on Public Enterprise in Mixed Economy LDCs, Apr. 1980).

39 The rich and growing literature on state trading organizations in LDCs has focused largely on their roles as importers and as exporters of raw materials and has surprisingly little to say about their role in manufactured exports. One exception, upon which we draw heavily, is Lawrence H. Wortzel, "Potential Role of State Trading in Marketing Manufactured Exports from Developing Countries," Boston University, Center for Asian Development Studies Discussion Paper No. 9 (Boston, Mass., Oct. 1977).

40 Hone, "Multinational Corporations and Multinational Buying Groups."
41 Michael Yoshino, *Japan's Multinational Enterprises* (Cambridge: Harvard University Press, 1976).
42 See Wortzel and Wortzel, "Marketing Manufactured Exports from LDCs."
43 Richard W. Moxon, "The Motivation for Investment in Offshore Plants: The Case of the U.S. Electronics Industry," *Journal of International Business Studies* 6, No. 1 (Spring, 1975):51–66.
44 As manufactured products become more standardized they become more like processed raw materials from the marketing point of view. See Vernon and Levy (Chapter 9 this volume) and Rodrik (Chapter 10 this volume).
45 See Vernon, "State-Owned Enterprises."
46 Where both marginal costs and benefits are correctly interpreted as changes in the net present values of streams of total costs and benefits. This allows for dynamic considerations.
47 The social calculus is also the correct one in domestic markets, but it is of decidedly less importance there than in foreign markets. It is correct because selling below social marginal cost entails both a relatively small deadweight welfare loss and a much larger transfer from the government (or the factors it employs) to consumers. Where the consumer is domestic, the transfer may well be a value neutral, but this is decidedly not the case when the beneficiary is foreign. For an estimate of the magnitude of such an external welfare transfer resulting from electricity pricing by a Canadian public enterprise, see Glenn Jenkins and Henry Lim, "Public Electricity and Economic Waste," mimeographed (Ottawa: Frazier Institute, 1977).

Part V

How does risk alter public-enterprise decisions?

12 Hierarchical structure and attitudes toward risk in state-owned enterprises

Pankaj Tandon

12.1 Public enterprises and risk behavior

Since the work of Arrow and Lind[1] first appeared, it has been widely agreed that the returns from a public investment should be evaluated using a risk-free rate of discount to the extent that such returns are uncorrelated with other sources of income. The implication is that managers of state-owned enterprises (SOEs) should behave in a risk-neutral manner as long as the risks associated with the enterprise are borne by the government.[2]

It is extremely difficult to clearly observe whether or not an enterprise is behaving in a risk-neutral manner. Nevertheless, few would dispute the observations that many SOEs do not in fact adopt a risk-neutral policy. SOEs are too vast and diverse a group of organizations to permit a simple generalization to be made on this matter; however, it seems safe to say that in many countries they exhibit an aversion to risk. This creates a problem, as normative theory would require them to be risk neutral.

Risk-averse behavior occurs because the manager of an enterprise may act to maximize not the net income (or profit) of the enterprise but rather his own utility. As Arrow and Lind note: "Their careers and income are intimately related to the firm's performance. From their point of view, variations in the outcome of some corporate action impose very real costs. In this case, given a degree of autonomy, the corporate managers, in considering prospective investments, may discount for risk."[3]

Although this observation is valid for any kind of large enterprise, public or private, it may be of particular relevance in the case of SOEs. Clearly, the fact that SOEs *should* be risk neutral makes risk averse behavior on the part of managers particularly problematic from a policy point of view. But further casual evidence

I gratefully acknowledge financial support of a Ford Foundation grant to the Public Enterprise Program at Boston University. I also wish to thank Leroy Jones and Michael Manove for helpful discussions.

seems to indicate that SOE managers as a class may tend to be more risk averse than private-enterprise managers. The latter must ultimately face the discipline of the marketplace, where the bottom line is measured, by and large, by their contribution to profits. Thus they are forced to take risks to achieve higher profits. SOE managers, on the other hand, cannot be evaluated so easily, as they face multiple objectives and profit maximization is not always one of them. Also, SOEs are likely to attract individuals who are more risk averse in the first place, as jobs are probably on average more secure, even though opportunities for quick advancement are probably more limited as well. It is quite possible, therefore, that the problem of manager risk aversion may be somewhat more severe in the case of SOEs than for private enterprises.

This analysis, as well as all the traditional analysis of enterprise behavior, is based on the stylized assumption that the enterprise has one manager who completely controls all decisions. In particular, it assumes that the manager possesses all the available information about options and that he is able to enforce completely all decisions that he makes. Typically, however, SOEs are large and are very often organized along hierarchical lines. As the manager does not possess all the relevant information, he is not able to enforce completely all his decisions. Thus the existence of a hierarchical structure may have a profound influence on the ability of an enterprise to operate efficiently. Again, this problem may be of particular importance to SOEs. Private enterprises are ultimately "controlled" by the market. But because SOEs frequently dominate their markets completely, their formal control mechanism may be their real control also. As Downs has pointed out, "co-ordination of large-scale activities without markets requires a hierarchical authority structure."[4]

This chapter seeks to examine the effect of hierarchical structure on the attitude of an enterprise toward risk. Two points are made. First, the problem of risk aversion among enterprise managers is exacerbated by the hierarchical structure of the typical SOE. There are two fundamental reasons for this: (1) The flow of communication both upward and downward in a hierarchy introduces new uncertainties regarding the information upon which each member of the organization must base decisions, and (2) risk aversion in officials at each level of the organization has a tendency to be cumulative, that is, unless an express effort is made to counteract its effects, risk aversion tends to be compounded, with the result that the organization as a whole tends to behave in a much more risk-averse manner than any of its individual members.

Second, and more striking, it is argued that the presence of a hierarchical structure can lead even a risk-neutral manager to behave as if he is risk averse if the transmission of information within the organization is subject to distortion. The information loss associated with this distortion hampers the ability of managers to make good decisions and therefore renders them less effective in uncertain situations.

12.2   The impact of hierarchical structure on risk

Much of the existing literature on the economics of information in hierarchies has concentrated on the question of monitoring job performance as a means to making optimal allocation of human resources in the organization.[5] In this chapter, hierarchies will be characterized somewhat differently. They will be viewed as structures for the gathering, organizing, and transmitting of information about an uncertain environment to aid the managers of the enterprise in making decisions. Such a view has been proposed, for example, by Arrow,[6] and serves to focus the discussion on those purposes of the organization most relevant in this context.

The assertion that the ability of an enterprise to deal with risk depends on its hierarchical structure is not a new one. Downs has argued that "the greater the degree of uncertainty regarding the bureau's activities, the flatter its hierarchy is likely to be."[7] His reasons, however, are quite different from those being proposed here. He points out that the elimination of hierarchical levels allows for a freer, less inhibited exchange of information and ideas and will be preferred by the more talented, creative individuals who are better able to cope with uncertainty.

At the same time, the importance of information flows between hierarchical levels and the limited capacity of such channels has not gone unnoticed either. Downs himself dealt extensively with this problem, as have Tullock[8] and Williamson.[9] However, the main implication of these analyses has been that limited channel capacity leads to the "control loss" phenomenon and imposes a limitation on the size to which a bureau or enterprise could expand. On the other hand, this chapter will argue that the problems relating to the flow of information between hierarchical levels hamper the ability of the enterprise to deal with risky situations and make the managers of the enterprise appear more risk averse than they are.

12.3   Communication problems in hierarchies

In a hierarchical structure, information flows both downward, from higher to lower levels, and upward, from lower to higher levels. Various authors have taken different views on which is the primary communication function. To the extent that lower levels attempt to transmit upward only that information they believe their superiors "want to hear," the principal direction in which "real" messages move is downward. This phenomenon will be ignored for the time being. It will be assumed that lower-level officials attempt to gather information and then transmit it upward. Based on the information he receives, the manager takes an action, which influences the payoff to the enterprise.

There are two kinds of informational flow problems that may occur: First, some random noise may enter the signal after it has been transmitted, so that the recipient of the signal receives a garbled version. This random noise may be interpreted as a genuine inability of the channel to carry the information in a distortion-free manner or as a result of the inadequacy of words and numbers to fully characterize an uncertain environment. Exactly the same message may mean slightly (or even radically) different things to different people. Thus some random distortion, or "misunderstanding," of signals cannot be prevented. This kind of distortion does not, however, alter the "average" value of the signal.

Second, signals may be intentionally distorted by the sender or misread by the receiver to serve his own interests. In this case, the expected value of the signal may well have changed.

With regard to each of these types of distortion, some attempt may be made to counteract its negative effects. There may be difficulties, however, in taking compensating action in situations involving uncertainty, as will be seen in the following discussion.

Consider first the effect of random distortion in the signal. Rothschild and Stiglitz have shown that if X and Y are two random variables with the same expected value, every risk averter prefers X to Y if Y is simply a distorted version of X. [10] In like manner, it may be argued in the context of SOEs that the addition of noise in the signal received by the manager will increase the uncertainty or riskiness of the situation. The manager would naturally prefer the less uncertain signal. If a message has to pass through several intermediary levels between the data source and the decision maker, the amount of noise entering the signal may be significant and the risk-averse manager is more likely to opt for a "safe" action. Each time the information is transmitted to the next higher level, it will undergo further distortion. Thus the existence of many hierarchical levels – and hence intermediaries – will render this problem more serious.

In the case of SOEs, the problems associated with signal distortions may be particularly acute not only because the typical number of hierarchical levels in a "bureaucratic" organization is high but also because the distance between some levels is great. In particular, there may be a great difference in perspective and perceptions between the central government (or ministry), on the one hand, and the SOE management, on the other. Thus there may be significant difficulties associated with defining the objective function of the enterprise as a whole. This may be especially problematic because there is considerable uncertainty about the objective function in the first place: It is multidimensional and some elements of it are unquantifiable.

The problem of distorted signals is further complicated by the possibility that officials may introduce intentional biases in the communication channels. As Downs has pointed out, all officials have a tendency to distort data by exaggerating those elements that reflect favorably on themselves, and downplaying (or even eliminating) data that has unfavorable connotations or is opposed to their interests and beliefs. [11] Thus managers may receive signals whose expected value may have undergone some "modification" in the process of transmission. If managers knew the biases of their subordinates, they could adjust the received signals for their distortion. However, if they do not know these biases, they face a situation of greater uncertainty and accordingly will suffer a lowering of their expected utility.

It may be argued that managers can prevent or at least counteract these intentional biases by attempting to monitor their subordinates. This may not be entirely possible in our current context for two important reasons: the fact that we are discussing SOEs and the fact that the situation is characterized by uncertainty. It will be difficult to monitor a subordinate's intentional biases in an SOE because of the multiple goals typical of such enterprises. In private firms, the profit-maximizing motive will readily reveal any extraordinary biases of particular officials. In an SOE, on the other hand, a bias may be explained away more easily as an effort to further some other (perhaps perfectly legitimate) goal of the enterprise. In this sense, officials may in fact be less accountable in an SOE. Further, if an enterprise experiences a higher rate of turnover, so that officials have less time to familiarize themselves with each other and thereby develop informal, more reliable networks of communication, there will be less opportunity for such informal ties to serve as monitoring devices.

Monitoring becomes even more difficult because of the uncertainty that is under discussion. A biased signal may look much more plausibly true in an uncertain environment than in a certain one. Under certainty, the manager can more easily check on the truthfulness of a given official by occasionally sampling the signals directly. In particular, to the extent that a situation is less uncertain mainly because it occurs frequently, managers may have a very good understanding of the situation and will immediately notice a signal that is unusual. In situations of uncertainty, however, and in situations that occur infrequently, the manager's experience may be less of an aid, and even a spot check may not help him gain much information on the overall trustworthiness of a particular official.

12.4 The cumulation effect

So far, it has been assumed implicitly that only the manager or decision maker in the enterprise is risk averse. The next point is somewhat different. Quite independent of random and deliberate noise in the information channels of a hierarchical structure, it is argued that the presence of risk aversion at each level of the structure tends to cumulate and therefore cause the hierarchy to appear even more risk averse than any of its members. In this context it is important to recognize that the enterprise has a management and that this management has goals of its own. Thus it is unrealistic to assume that the "enterprise" can be made to do what it is told to do; rather, the managers may be maximizing their own utility functions.

The logical extension of this argument is that every official in the hierarchy is attempting to maximize his own utility function. This phenomenon has been touched upon implicitly in the earlier discussion on intentional distortion. Officials, it was argued, distort information to serve their own interests. The "interests" of the official might refer merely to the fact that he is risk averse. A risk-averse official may distort information for precisely the reason that he is risk averse. If successive levels of a hierarchy are characterized by risk aversion, a systematic, cumulative distortion is built into the signals, and consequently, the organization (or decision maker) tends to discriminate more heavily against more uncertain projects.

This result depends on a key behavioral assumption that the higher-level officials are unable to (or, for whatever reason, do not) counteract this systematic bias. It may be argued that managers ought to be able to correct for such biases if they know they exist. There are two types of difficulty, however. First, even if the manager knows that his subordinates are risk averse, he may find it quite difficult to estimate the extent of this risk aversion. Thus he is faced with at least one new type of uncertainty. Second, and perhaps more important, it may be difficult to even observe or deduce in situations of uncertainty that a subordinate is risk averse. It will probably be quite costly to attempt to monitor the subordinate's behavior, especially if the situations under consideration do not often recur. In fact, it may not be unrealistic to characterize uncertain situations as ones that are not recurrent, in which case this point may assume some importance.

12.5   The effect of distorted signals on risk-neutral managers

In this section, a somewhat more striking result is presented: An organization may behave in a risk-averse manner even when the managers and officials are all risk neutral. To demonstrate this point, a more formal model is presented and it becomes necessary to introduce some cumbersome notation. The basic argument, however, may be summarized as follows. To the extent that the decisions of a manager affect the performance of the enterprise, and to the extent a manager has to base his decisions on information obtained from lower levels in the organization's hierarchy, the performance of the enterprise may be fairly sensitive to the efficiency of its information channels. If information from lower levels is subject to random (or nonrandom) noise in the process of transmission, there is a loss of information attributable to the hierarchical structure. Thus the manager of a hierarchical organization must base his decisions on information that is more imperfect than one who gathers information himself. The loss of information results therefore in lower expected payoffs to the manager and creates a bias against projects that appear to the manager to be uncertain.

A formal model may help clarify this argument. Suppose there are n possible states of nature $\theta_1, \theta_2, \ldots, \theta_n$, and m possible actions that the enterprise manager can take. We could then think of a payoff matrix $R = [r_{ij}]$ where r_{ij} would represent the payoff to the enterprise if action i were taken and θ_j turned out to be the state of the world. The ith row of R, r_i, could be thought of as describing the ith action. Suppose the manager has prior subjective probabilities on the states of the world $p(\theta_1), \ldots, p(\theta_n)$, and let P be a diagonal matrix whose diagonal is this vector of prior probabilities. If the manager had no further information, he would choose the action r_i to maximize

$$E(r) = \sum_j p(\theta_j) \, r_{ij}$$

On the other hand, the manager might well be able to raise the expected payoff to the enterprise by observing a signal s, in order to improve his information on the probabilities of the states of the world. Suppose s can take on any of k values $s_1, s_2, \ldots, s_k$. The manager is assumed to know the likelihood of each value, that is, he knows the matrix $L = [\ell_{ij}]$ where $\ell_{ij} = p(s_j | \theta_i)$. Note that each element of L is nonnegative and each row sums to unity, thus L is a Markov matrix. Having observed s, the manager will pick the action r_i to maximize the expected payoff. Thus with each observed value of s we may associate an action (and hence a vector of payoffs) by which the expected payoff is maximized. These vectors may be arranged in a decision matrix, $D = [d_{s\theta}]$, where the ith row of D represents the vector of payoffs that accrue when $s = s_i$ is observed and the optimal action is chosen. We may write $d_{ij} = r(s_i, \theta_j)$, that is, the payoff when s_i is observed, and the optimal action is chosen when θ_j turns out to be the state of the world.

Consider the matrix PLD. It is easily seen that the expected payoff upon observing s is simply the trace of PLD. It may also easily be shown that the trace of PLD is no less than the expected payoff prior to observing s. Thus observation of the signal can lead only to an improvement in the expected payoff.

It is now possible to examine the effect of a hierarchical structure on the expected payoff. Suppose the manager cannot himself observe s but rather has a lower-level official do that and transmit to him the information collected. However, as argued earlier, the message may not be received unaltered by the manager. Rather, some random error may enter the message. Thus, suppose the manager receives a message s', with v possible values, $s'_1, s'_2, \ldots, s'_v$, represented by a likelihood matrix L'. The signal s' is said to be a *garbling* of s if

$$L' = LM$$

where M is a Markov matrix whose typical element is

$$m_{ij} = p(s' = s_i \mid s = s_j)$$

This is a simple way to model the introduction of purely random error or even of intentional distortion in the transmission of the signal.

Suppose the decision matrix upon observing s' is D'. Then the expected payoff from observing s' is tr $PL'D'$. However, by Blackwell's theorem,[12] the following statements are equivalent:

$$L' = LM \quad \text{where } M \text{ is Markov} \tag{1}$$

$$\text{tr } PL'D' \leq \text{tr } PLD \quad \text{for all possible } P \tag{2}$$

Thus the expected payoff to the enterprise when the manager observes the distorted signal s' rather than the "true" signal s is certainly no greater and in general may be lower. In other words, in situations involving uncertainty, the expected payoff is lower when information has to travel up a hierarchy.

As the manager in fact observes s', the expected payoff from the "project" under consideration will be lower than if he had observed s. Thus he will be less likely to adopt such uncertain projects and will prefer situations characterized by certainty.

A numerical example

As the proof of Blackwell's theorem is fairly complicated, and this result itself is not intuitively obvious, a simple numerical example may help to illustrate the point. Suppose there are two possible states of the world, θ_1 and θ_2, and two possible actions a_1 and a_2. Suppose the payoff vectors associated with the two actions are $(1,0)$ and $(0,1)$. That is, if action a_1 is taken, the enterprise receives a payoff of 1 in state θ_1 and 0 in θ_2; if a_2 is taken, the payoffs are 0 in θ_1 and 1 in θ_2. Suppose the manager's prior belief is that the probability of θ_1 is 2/5 and $p(\theta_2) = 3/5$. In the absence of any further information, the optimal action is clearly a_2, and the expected payoff is 3/5.

Now suppose a signal s may be observed. Suppose that if θ_1 is the true state, there is a 50% chance that s will take on the value s_1, and a 50% chance that $s = s_2$. However, if θ_2 is the true state, suppose there is only a 25% chance that $s = s_1$ and a 75% chance that $s = s_2$. Depending on what we observe (s_1 or s_2), we would revise our opinion on the probabilities of θ_1 and θ_2. Specifically, if s_1 is actually observed, the likelihood that the true state is θ_1 will be greater than $p(\theta_2)$; and so the optimal action will be a_1. If s_2 is observed, the optimal action will remain a_2. The signal allows the manager to improve his information and to select the appropriate action. The expected payoff may be shown to be 13/20.[13] Thus the expected payoff has gone up by 1/20; observing the signal is indeed worthwhile.

If the manager did not observe the signal s but rather a garbled version of it, s', the expected payoff might be different. Suppose s' can take on two values, s_1' and s_2', and that the probabilities of these obtaining depend only on s_1 and s_2. Suppose $p(s_1' \mid s_1) = x$ and $p(s_1' \mid s_2) = y$. Calculations similar to the earlier ones show that the maximum payoff will be

$$\frac{3}{5} + \frac{1}{20}x - \frac{5}{20}y$$

or

$$\frac{2}{5} - \frac{1}{20}x + \frac{5}{20}y$$

If there is any distortion, that is, if x, $y < 1$, then it is easily seen that this maximum is always less than 13/20. For example, if $x = 0.8$ and $y = 0.1$, the maximum expected payoff is 12.3/20.

12.6   Possible extensions of the analysis

The possible distortion of information in the process of transmission from one level to another in an organization such as an SOE has been shown to create problems in decision making. Distortion introduced by the presence of risk aversion tends to be compounded. More significantly, however, it has been shown that random noise tends to increase the probability of rejecting uncertain projects, thereby making the enterprise appear more averse to risk than are its managers. This has been shown to be the case even when managers are risk neutral. It has long been known that managers may exhibit risk-averse behavior if they maximize their own utility functions rather than the payoffs to the enterprise; the striking result in Section 12.5 indicates that the appearance of such behavior can result even if the managers are doing what they are supposed to do, that is, maximize expected payoffs. The normative implication of this is that SOEs that are involved in risky activities should try to minimize the length of communication channels. What appears as risk-averse behavior in large SOEs might simply be a reflection of poor information flow.

Some possible extensions of this analysis come to mind. I will mention three. First, there has been no discussion here of possible solutions to this problem. Naturally it would be desirable to install more efficient information channels that tended to reduce the amount of noise introduced into messages. It might also be interesting to attempt to design incentive schemes that would eliminate tendencies for intentional distortion. Second, and of more interest to the specific case of SOEs, it would be instructive to model the problem of multiple objectives, which is so characteristic of the public sector. Here it has been assumed that the enterprise is maximizing a single quantifiable objective. The problem becomes considerably more complex when the existence of multiple goals is acknowledged. Third, a very simple notion of risk has been used in this chapter. In fact, SOEs face some very special kinds of risks that are perhaps not amenable to the kind of analysis performed here. Most important, they face various kinds of political risks – perhaps the most dramatic being the possibility that a government may not be reelected and therefore the policy of the enterprise may be subject to sudden changes. Another important kind of risk may be what Prakash Tandon called the "risk of success" – the fact that successful enterprises tend to receive special attention and perhaps become subject to more control. Risk aversion in the traditional sense (i.e., with respect to short-run profits) may therefore in fact turn out to be long-run risk neutrality.

My last observation is a purely speculative one. If the model in Section 12.5 contains an element of truth, it may be that hierarchical organizations such as SOEs in fact end up with lower expected profits than do nonhierarchical ones. The "information loss" phenomenon must of course be weighed against the fact that a larger (hierarchical) organization may actually be able to process more information and hence may "discover" a larger number of potentially high-payoff projects. Also, this cannot be taken as an argument to explain why SOEs tend to perform more poorly than private enterprises, as the latter also are often organized along hierarchical lines. Nevertheless, the possibility that large, "bureaucratized" organizations may perform more poorly because their managers receive garbled information remains a provocative suggestion.

Notes

1 K. J. Arrow and R. C. Lind, "Uncertainty and the Evaluation of Public Investments," *American Economic Review* 60, No.3 (June 1970):364–78.
2 A. Bergson, "Managerial Risks and Rewards in Public Enterprises," *Journal of Comparative Economics* 2, No. 3 (Sept. 1978):211–25.
3 Arrow and Lind, "Uncertainty and the Evaluation of Public Investments."
4 A. Downs, *Inside Bureaucracy* (Boston: Little, Brown, 1967), p. 52
5 A. M. Spence, "The Economics of Internal Organization: An Introduction," *Bell Journal of Economics* 6, No. 1 (Spring 1975):163–72
6 K. J. Arrow, *Essays in the Theory of Risk-Bearing* (Amsterdam: North-Holland, 1971).
7 Downs, *Inside Bureaucracy*, p. 57.
8 G. Tullock, *The Politics of Bureaucracy* (Washington, D.C.: Public Affairs Press, 1965).
9 O. Williamson, "Hierarchical Control and Optimal Firm Size," *Journal of Political Economy* 75, No. 2 (April 1967):123–38.
10 M. Rothschild and J. E. Stiglitz, "Increasing Risk: I. A Definition," *Journal of Economic Theory* 2, No. 3 (Sept. 1970):225–43.
11 Downs, *Inside Bureaucracy*.
12 D. Blackwell and M. A. Girshick, *Theory of Games and Statistical Decisions* (New York: Wiley, 1954), Chap. 12.
13 The calculation proceeds as follows: The expected profit $E(\pi)$ is given by

$$E(\pi) = P(s_1) \cdot E(\pi|s_1) + P(s_2)E(\pi|s_2)$$

Now

$$P(s_1) = P(s_1|\theta_1) P(\theta_1) + P(s_1|\theta_2) P(\theta_2)$$

$$= \left(\frac{1}{2}\right)\left(\frac{2}{5}\right) + \left(\frac{1}{4}\right)\left(\frac{3}{5}\right) = \frac{7}{20}$$

Similarly,

$$p(s_2) = \frac{13}{20}$$

How do $p(\theta_1)$ and $p(\theta_2)$ get updated by the signal? We need to calculate these probabilities conditional on s_1 and s_2. Suppose s_1 was observed. Then

$$p(\theta_1|s_1) = \frac{P(s_1|\theta_1) p(\theta_1)}{p(s_1)}$$

$$= \left(\frac{1}{2}\right)\left(\frac{2}{5}\right) / \frac{7}{20} = \frac{4}{7}$$

Similarly,

$$p(\theta_2|s_1) = \frac{3}{7}$$

That is, if s_1 is observed, the updated $p(\theta_1)$ is 4/7 and the updated $p(\theta_2)$ is 3/7. In this event it is clearly optimal to pick the action a_1. The expected profit, $E(\pi|s_1)$, is 4/7.

By similar calculations, it may be shown that if s_2 is observed, the updated $P(\theta_1)$ is 4/13, and $P(\theta_2 \mid s_2) = 9/13$. In this case a_2 is adopted and the expected payoff is 9/13. Thus

$$E(\pi) = \left(\frac{7}{20}\right)\left(\frac{4}{7}\right) + \left(\frac{13}{20}\right)\left(\frac{9}{13}\right)$$

$$= \frac{13}{20}$$

13 Public-enterprise finance: toward a synthesis

Malcolm Gillis, Glenn P. Jenkins, and Donald R. Lessard

Public-enterprise finance, broadly defined, encompasses mechanisms for raising funds, distributing profits, and absorbing losses. Although these functions are shared with private finance, public-enterprise finance typically differs in one important respect. When private firms raise capital on a commercial basis, they incur explicit obligations to repay specific amounts or shares of their profits in the future. These obligations reflect the opportunity cost of funds for claims of similar riskiness. Thus, in raising funds, they also specify the distribution of future profits and losses. In contrast, when public enterprises raise funds, they often do so without incurring such explicit obligations. Even when public enterprises borrow from commercial sources, they often do so with governmental guarantees, implicit or otherwise. As a result, public enterprises incur explicit financing costs that do not reflect the private opportunity cost of funds employed in the enterprises, let alone their social opportunity costs.

In this chapter we argue that the typical pattern of public-enterprise finance yields a distorted picture of the opportunity cost of funds employed and, hence, of the profitability and efficiency of public enterprise. Although this should have no real effect in an idealized setting where all public-enterprise decisions are made in light of the full set of social costs and benefits – including the social-opportunity cost of funds employed – we believe that in practice the way public enterprises are financed often contributes to inappropriate investment and operating decisions. In our view, the structure of management incentives is the primary link between financing and the strategic and operating decisions of a public enterprise. Although the social opportunity cost of funds employed in a public enterprise depends on their use and not on how they are labeled, the explicit cost of these funds does depend on how the public enterprise is financed. This explicit financial cost – reflecting the nature of the financial obligations incurred by the public enterprise when it raises funds – is an important factor in its financial profitability and capacity to generate cash flows.

Financial assistance from the International Division of the Ford Foundation for the completion of this study has been greatly appreciated. This study has benefited from the very helpful comments of Ralph Beals, Leroy Jones, Richard Mallon, Charles McLure, John Sheahan, Raymond Vernon, Donald Warwick, and other participants of the Boston Area Public Enterprise Group seminars. All errors that remain are the responsibility of the authors.

257

In many cases, public enterprises are judged at least in part on the basis of their financial profitability. Even when they are not, their ability to generate and control cash flows will be an important determinant of enterprise autonomy and, hence, of the power and prestige of the managers.

This chapter is organized into four sections. In Section 13.1, we consider the impact of both investment risk and the pattern of financing on the social opportunity cost of funds employed by public enterprises and their implications for pricing of capital in public-enterprise decision making. In Section 13.2, we examine existing patterns of public-enterprise finance in order to infer how capital is explicitly or implicitly priced in practice. In Section 13.3, we discuss the likely impact of divergence between the social opportunity cost of funds and their apparent cost on decision making in public enterprises, via effects on management incentives. Finally, in Section 13.4, we provide suggestions for future research on public-enterprise financing.

13.1   The social opportunity cost of public-enterprise capital

From the perspective of mainstream social cost–benefit analysis, the way public enterprises are financed by the state should be irrelevant, as all advances from the state are viewed as coming from a single pool of social resources with a single opportunity cost, and all taxes, interest payments, dividends, and reinvested profits are considered to be returns to the state and, hence, economically indistinguishable. Although this view is correct in some tautological sense, it is potentially misleading for two reasons. First, it ignores the fact that public enterprises are decentralized social organizations whose managers have limited information and do not necessarily seek to optimize overall social goals, even in the rare cases where these are clearly articulated by the government. To the extent that funds provided to public enterprises are not "priced" at their social opportunity costs, public enterprises are likely to make inappropriate real decisions. Second, there is no single social opportunity cost of capital. Rather, there is a schedule of opportunity costs of funds, depending on the social risk of the activities in which they are employed. Although the social opportunity cost of funds utilized in a public enterprise is independent of the way it is financed, unless foreign financing is employed, that this cost varies across uses increases the likelihood that the explicit pricing of finance may not provide appropriate signals to public-enterprise managers regarding the use of social resources and may therefore lead to particular biases in decision making.

In this section, following a brief discussion of the concept of the social opportunity cost of capital, we describe the implications of investment risk, financial structure, and foreign financing for this cost.

The concept

The social opportunity cost of capital reflects the total rate of return forgone by society when funds are drawn from capital markets and applied to a particular project. In one widely used formulation of this concept introduced by Harberger, this cost is, in a closed economy, equal to the required rate of return in the capital market *plus* a figure reflecting net forgone tax revenues from investments displaced and savings induced by the increase in this required return resulting from the additional demand for capital.[1] In a partially open economy, a fraction of the additional funds raised is drawn from displaced investment, but to the extent that the country faces an upward-sloping supply schedule of foreign capital because of the costs of enforcement and compliance associated with cross-border financing, the social opportunity cost becomes a weighted average of the domestic market rate adjusted for displaced taxes and the marginal cost of foreign borrowing.

An important implication of this definition of the discount rate is: Consider a project with an after-tax private net present value of zero that pays average taxes per unit of capital employed and contributes as well an average amount per unit of capital employed to the country's access to foreign financing. Such a project will have a social net present value, including tax payments, of zero if it creates no other net externalities. Thus, it is appropriate only for a public enterprise that pays normal taxes per unit of capital employed to judge new ventures by discounting the net-of-tax cash flows at the appropriate private market rate *or* gross-of-tax flows at the appropriate social rate.

Risk and the social opportunity cost of capital

In the literature the social opportunity cost of capital is typically characterized as a single rate for an entire economy. However, it is now generally accepted that the return in the private market is dependent on the risk of the activity being financed. There are compelling reasons for believing the same is true for the social rate. The rationale for a schedule of opportunity costs that depends on risk is that individuals (and society as their collective agent) are risk averse and, consequently, demand a premium in the form of a higher expected return for bearing risk. However, as they can diversify their claims against risky ventures, in equilibrium only those risks that cannot be averaged out in the total market or social portfolio will command a premium. The resulting relationship between systematic risk and expected rate of return required by private investors is shown in Figure 13.1a.[2] As already noted, the social opportunity cost exceeds the private opportunity rate by an adjustment for financial externalities, and it is likely that this adjustment increases with the risk of the activity.[3] The resulting schedule of social opportunity costs of capital is depicted in Figure 13.1b. This schedule applies to specific projects undertaken by a public enterprise rather than to the public enterprise as a whole. In other words, a public enterprise has no cost of capital, only its individual undertakings have a cost of capital.

The view that the social opportunity cost of capital for a public enterprise (or for a specific undertaking of a public enterprise) may include a risk premium deserves some comment, as it is contrary to much of received wisdom.[4] If risks facing

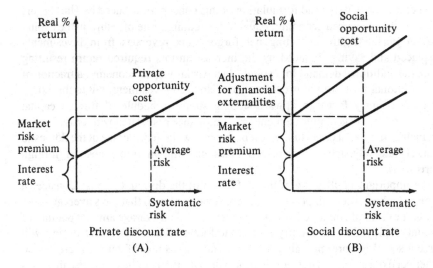

Figure 13.1. Private and social risk–return relationships: (A) schedule of private required rates of return; and (B) schedule of public required rates of return.

public-enterprise investment are fully diversifiable within the economy, no risk premium should be charged. However, for many less-developed countries (LDCs), public-enterprise investment involves significant nondiversifiable risk. That is, the impact of a particular public-enterprise investment on the variability of national income cannot be totally offset by counteracting risks of other activities in the country. If this is the case, capital-market theory holds that on such investments a risk premium should be charged in addition to the basic interest rate.

This risk premium will be small only if, as in some LDCs, the sector of the economy facing the same risks as those facing the public enterprise is small, *and* if the risks to which it is exposed are not common to significant sectors of the economy, a situation not common for LDCs. Where large-scale public enterprises dominate a sector such as manufacturing, mining, or agriculture, particularly when these are export oriented, operate on a world scale, and comprise a large proportion of domestic output, the risk is largely systematic,[5] and hence, a public-enterprise investment should be charged a risk premium if finance is to give correct signals.[6]

Although there are no direct measures of the appropriate risk premiums for public enterprises in developing countries, empirical evidence for the United States suggests that the risk premium for the typical industrial investment is on the order of 6% to 7% a year, much larger than the 1% to 2% *ex post* real rate of interest.[7] Risk premiums for public enterprises in developing countries from the parent state's perspective are likely to be higher than for investment in the United States, especially in strategic sectors, because of limited local diversification potential.[8] In the case of copper mining, for example, Lessard found that a much smaller fraction of the risk associated with copper production was diversifiable within the major producing countries' economies than within the world economy.[9]

Financial structure and the cost of capital

As long as all financial claims against the public enterprise are held by the state, the opportunity cost of funds employed in the public enterprise is independent of whether they are labeled as debt, equity, or subsidy capital (see section 13.2). Regardless of the division of future cash flows into interest, dividends, taxes, and so on, the expected value and variance of the composite will be unaffected. This implies that if a riskless component of the future uncertain return is valued as debt, the remaining component will be riskier than the whole and will command a proportionately higher risk premium.[10] However, if third parties and, in particular, foreign lenders or investors hold some claims and if these claims bear proportionately more or less risk than those of the state, the discount rate that the state as public-enterprise owner should use for evaluating its share will differ from that appropriate to the profit as a whole. For example, if foreign financing takes the form of credit – a fixed payoff regardless of the enterprise's profits – the state holds levered equity with enhanced risk and, hence, requires a larger risk premium. Conversely, if the state preempts a fixed return and grants a residual share to foreign investors, the risk premium applicable to the state's share will be less than that applicable to the project as a whole.

Foreign financing and the cost of capital

In addition to its impact on the relative riskiness of the state's financial claims on a public enterprise, foreign financing for a public enterprise also raises the question of whether it displaces other foreign financial flows. One reason for this is that external perceptions of political risk might depend on the total outstanding financial claims against a country relative to some measure of national wealth, that is, so called country-risk.[11] As a result, the cost of foreign funds and hence the social opportunity cost of capital will be an increasing function of the ratio of foreign obligations to a nation's capacity to meet these obligations.

As long as the foreign borrowing of a public enterprise does not exceed its contribution to the country's "debt capacity"[12] it is appropriate to discount the country's share of net foreign cash flows at a rate reflecting the riskiness of its share of the proceeds using the analysis outlined. However, if the foreign borrowing of a public enterprise exceeds its contributions to the country's access to foreign funds, and thus increases the cost of foreign borrowing, additional adjustments must be made to reflect the returns (including taxes) forgone from projects displaced by the resulting higher social discount rates. As it may be difficult to determine the project's impact on a country's access to external finances, it is generally preferable to value the project in terms of its total cash flows.

A further point of interest, beyond the scope of this chapter, is that the risk premium appropriate to a given enterprise or venture may be lower for foreign investors than for the capital-importing country even after country risk is taken into account. This will be true whenever the risks involved are more diversifiable in a broader capital-market context within the local economy.

13.2   Patterns of public-enterprise finance

In this section, we briefly characterize existing patterns of public-enterprise finance. Our primary interest is in determining the "pricing" of capital implicit in the terms on which it is provided to the public enterprise. Finance can be broken down into broad types, depending on the type of repayment obligation involved:

1.   Credit, where the expected cost (return to the lender) is equal to the promised interest rate less the anticipated default losses
2.   Risk capital, where the expected cost (return to the investor) is a specified share of future expected profits
3.   Subsidy capital, where no future financial obligation is incurred

To the extent that the expected cost of credit or risk capital is less than the market rate, the resulting finance is actually a combination of one of these forms of commercial financing and subsidy capital.

Although public enterprises vary substantially across countries, and even within countries, we believe that certain generalizations are possible. The following generalizations are drawn both from our experience in several countries (Bolivia, Brazil, Colombia, Ghana, Indonesia, Malaysia, and Sri Lanka) and from secondary sources. Although some observations may be disputed, they represent our best effort to summarize the scanty evidence available on this topic. We hope they will be received in that same spirit.

The discussion is divided into three sections: (1) sources of finance, (2) rules for distributing surpluses, and (3) rules for absorbing losses.

Sources of finance

Sources of public-enterprise finance may be grouped into five major categories: (1) private foreign finance (external borrowing); (2) local private finance from banks; (3) direct government finance in the form of equity, credit, or subsidy capital; (4) reinvested cash flows from operations; and (5) indirect transfers from the government, either via tax concessions, taxes earmarked for state-owned enterprises, or the subsidization of prices of factor inputs.

External borrowing. There is growing concern over the international indebtedness of public enterprises in developing countries. This concern is well placed. Flows of external commercial debt contracted by public enterprises in

LDCs rose by nearly 350% in the period 1975–8. Growth in public-enterprise external borrowing was particularly marked in the Eurocurrency market, where new loan commitments to LDC state-owned firms reached $12.2 billion in 1978. This amounted to nearly one-third of total LDC commercial borrowings for all purposes for that year and fully 12% of international borrowing of all types by all debtors, including firms and governments from industrial countries.[13] The expanded flows of international debt capital to public enterprises has been a prime factor in the buildup of large and potentially troublesome stocks of external debt in such countries as Brazil, Peru, Zaire, and Zambia through 1979 and Indonesia from 1972 to 1976.

The overwhelming majority of foreign loans to public enterprises carry explicit or implicit guarantees from public-enterprise owners: LDC governments. Because of these guarantees, public-enterprise debt tends to be treated as sovereign debt, backed by the full faith and credit of the issuing country. Consequently, the explicit cost of this finance reflects the risk to the nation as a whole and not the risk to the enterprise.

Domestic borrowing. Nonfinancial public enterprises often enjoy preferential access to domestic sources of credit as well, not only because of the presence of governmental guarantees normally unavailable (except in Korea) to private firms but because in many countries a substantial share of institutions in the financial system are also state owned (Indonesia, Mexico, Pakistan, Bolivia) and susceptible to governmental blandishments to extend credit to its own progeny. Because financial controls, primarily in the form of interest-rate ceilings, are pervasive in most LDCs, preferential access to domestic credit is often tantamount to concessional credit.

Owing to both influences already noted, public enterprises typically enjoy high leverage relative to comparable private firms. The degree of leverage often exceeds the commercial debt capacity of the enterprises. For private enterprises, the operational consequences of high leverage are well known. Except where lending institutions enjoy extraordinarily close relationships with borrowing enterprises, as in Japan and, to some extent, Korea (where debt-equity ratios of 5:1 and higher are not uncommon), high leverage materially increases a firm's vulnerability to fluctuations in business conditions and therefore involves greater risk of bankruptcy. High leverage in public enterprises also matters, but given the reluctance of parent governments to allow public enterprises to go out of business, bankruptcy risks are not the reason. Rather, as we point out in Section 13.3, high leverage becomes a significant problem for public enterprises because of its implications both for incentives facing managers and for the disposition of enterprise surpluses.

Direct government finance. Public enterprises commonly receive direct subventions from the public treasury. These subventions take a variety of forms, including injections of true risk capital (equity), direct loans from the budget, subventions labeled as equity participation (but which in actuality represent write-offs of direct loans or government assumption of enterprise debt with third parties), explicit or implicit operating subsidies, and other less obvious methods of transfer.

In most LDCs with large public-enterprise sectors, governments have displayed considerable reluctance to furnish their progeny with true risk capital where the expected repayment is sufficient to compensate for the risk involved of the type discussed earlier in this section. This reluctance is due to a variety of factors, but four in particular seem to stand out from experience across countries.

First, there is a pervasive tendency in LDCs to equate finance with credit and to assume that any project that is worthwhile can be financed with credit. Second, governments that must continually cope with fiscal "tightness" in the form of shortfalls of tax collections relative to expenditures (a category that excludes only the major oil exporters) often find it easier, both politically and procedurally, to channel direct loans, rather than equity finance, to public enterprises, as equity injections are ordinarily classed as government expenditure, whereas direct loans often escape this label, wholly or partially. Third, government agencies seeking to maintain control over enterprise activities often prefer loans over equity transfers as a way of keeping firms more closely beholden to the granting agency, as loans carry explicit repayment obligations.

Finally, the nature of many multilateral foreign-aid programs predisposes governments to emphasize direct loans over equity transfers to public enterprises. Since 1967, much of multilateral project aid (as from, e.g., the World Bank) has been channeled to activities undertaken by public enterprises. This has been particularly true for Colombia, Indonesia, Bolivia, and Bangladesh.[14] Under such aid programs, the donor extends the loans to the parent government, which then transfers the funds to public enterprises in the form of credit, which bears specific terms as to interest rate and repayment period. In some cases, as in Indonesian and Bolivian railways, Indonesian agricultural estates and fertilizer enterprises, and Colombian development finance institutions, government loans of this type have in some periods accounted for the majority of public-enterprise debt obligations.

Preferences and pressures for loan finance notwithstanding, government equity participation in public enterprises has not been unimportant in all countries. Indeed, this method of finance has become increasingly more common in major oil-exporting LDCs since 1973, when rapidly rising export earnings from crude oil began to ease fiscal tightness for this group of countries. Venezuela and Indonesia are perhaps the two best examples of this genre; in Indonesia government capital participation in public enterprises has averaged about 10% of total annual government nonrecurrent ("development") expenditures since 1974. Even in Brazil, not an oil-exporting country, direct participation by government accounted for about one-fifth of external financing of public enterprises in 1974–5.[15]

However, not all of what is recorded as government capital participation in public enterprises represents *bona fide* transfers of equity. Rather, much of what is labeled "equity" in public enterprises represents, in many countries, little more than government assumption of public-enterprise debt (whether direct loans from government or from domestic and foreign financial institutions) that the enterprises were either unwilling or unable to service (or government assumption of other liabilities of enterprises) and does not carry with it an explicit rate of return or dividend target. Examples of the former include shipping enterprises in Indonesia, a number of manufacturing enterprises in Ghana, Turkey, and Malaysia, and state mineral enterprises in Bolivia. Examples of the latter include state-owned financial institutions in Indonesia, Bolivia, and Colombia.

Although governments may prefer debt to equity finance for public enterprises, the opposite is normally true for public-enterprise managers, who tend to view equity as having no cost to the firm. This perception is reinforced by the failure of governments to "price" equity, either in the form of shadow prices communicated to public-enterprise managers or in the form of specific dividend obligations (see later discussion).

Reinvested cash flows from operations. This source of finance has at times been significant in several countries, including Korea from 1961 to 1972,[16] Brazil in 1966–75,[17] Uruguay in 1975–6, India in 1970–72, Taiwan in 1960–74, and Sri Lanka.[18] In all these countries, the public-enterprise sector generated more than 10% of total national savings in the periods cited. Reliance on reinvested cash flows has perhaps been most striking in Brazil. During the period 1966–75, a group of 40-odd of the largest public enterprises surveyed by Trebat were able to internally finance from 40% to 60% of their gross investment, a share of internal finance that just about matches that for private Brazilian firms.[19] The share of internal finance in Korean public enterprises, although relatively high when compared with most LDCs, was apparently much lower than in Brazil. Jones reports that during the period 1961–72, the public-enterprise sector generated slightly more than 10% of national savings and absorbed something like 30% of investment.[20]

The experience of Brazil and, to a lesser extent, Korea contrasts sharply with that of public-enterprise sectors elsewhere. In some instances, public enterprises not only have been unable to internally generate funds for self-finance but have persistently run deficits that had to be financed from the national treasury. At times one or two enterprises alone have accumulated losses and external debt obligations of such size as to severely hamstring developmental efforts in general, as, for example, the state-owned minerals enterprise Corporacion de Minería de Bolivia (COMIBOL) from 1957 to 1972; the state-owned Indonesia National Oil Company, Pertamina, from 1972 to 1976, and state mining enterprises in both Zaire and Zambia from 1974 through 1978. In many countries, such as Argentina, Egypt, Guyana, and Panama, the net savings of the consolidated public-enterprise sector from 1970 to 1973 was typically negative. In several others, enterprise self-finance has been minimal, and state enterprises as a group have contributed only marginally to national savings efforts. In the early seventies, these countries included Bangladesh, Thailand, Bolivia, Chile, and Uruguay (all with large public-enterprise sectors) and Somalia, Jamaica, and Colombia (all with relatively small public-enterprise sectors). In all these nations, the savings of public enterprises accounted for less than 5% of total investment finance over the period 1970–3.[21]

Indirect transfers from governments. These sources of public-enterprise finance assume a variety of forms ranging from tax concessions through assignment of earmarked taxes to public enterprises and loan guarantees.

Tax concessions to public enterprises, clearly a form of concessional transfer of public resources, are of two basic types: full or partial exemption of public enterprises from generally applicable taxes, as in Algeria, Iran, Bolivia, and El Salvador,[22] and governmental cancellation or "forgiveness" of delinquent taxes due from taxable enterprises, as in Bolivian mineral enterprises[23] and the Indonesian state petroleum enterprise in 1975–6.

Channeling of earmarked government taxes to public enterprises is fairly common and has been particularly important in Colombia, Ghana, and Brazil. In the latter country, earmarked taxes accounted for fully 12% of public-enterprise investment finance in 1974–5.[24]

Rules for extracting and distributing profits

In developed countries, managers of widely held private-sector firms face conflicting incentives both for underreporting and for full reporting of pretax profits. The presence of income taxes provides the incentive to underreport or conceal profits; the need to tap capital in equity markets provides an incentive to show substantial profits or prospects for same. Capital markets are considerably less well developed in LDCs, and many large private firms are closely held. Thus, although private firms still face the same incentive to conceal profits as in developed countries (income taxes), the incentive for full disclosure is far weaker.

Public enterprises may understate profits as well, not only to minimize income-tax obligations (where public enterprises are in fact taxable), but to enhance managerial efforts aimed at ensuring enterprise growth and independence. This can be done by disguising profits as expenses incurred for enterprise performance of social or "equity" functions prescribed by government (or, as is sometimes the case, chosen unilaterally by the enterprise), thereby retaining more funds within the enterprise and enhancing enterprise autonomy. That is to say, quite apart from any tendency of public enterprises to generate low (or negative) profits, owing either to poor cost control or to imposition by parent governments of multiple social objectives or requirements to sell output at less than full costs, public enterprises may also understate actual profits to much the same degree as their counterparts in the private sector.

Given a certain amount of reported profits per period, two legitimate instruments are available for extracting profits from the public enterprise and distributing them to claimants. The first is much less commonly employed than the second.

Dividend payout. Dividend payments from public enterprises to the parent government are uncommon in LDCs. This is due partly to an absence, in many countries, of any well-defined policy on this score. A few countries, notably Indonesia, Pakistan, and, since 1977, Sri Lanka, have adopted formal policies toward the obligations of public enterprises to transfer a portion of after-tax income to the shareholder in the form of dividends. In both Indonesia and Pakistan, dividend payments by public enterprises have for some enterprises in some years rivaled in size income-tax payments by the firms. But, in general, government policies toward dividends from public enterprises are vague and informal, where they exist at all, and determination of the government's share of after-tax surpluses typically involves delicate and protracted negotiations between the parent and the public enterprise on an ad hoc basis that shifts from year to year.

Many governments have viewed dividend policy toward public enterprises as immaterial in any case, as recorded profits of large portions of their public-enterprise sectors have been insignificant in any case. In some cases, public enterprises are so highly leveraged that large cash outflows are required to repay the principal of their loans, so that sufficient cash to pay dividends is less likely to be available in public enterprises than in their private-sector counterparts.

Taxation. Many LDCs, unlike the United States, do (nominally at least) subject public enterprises to much the same taxes (especially income taxes) as those applicable to private firms. Examples include Colombia (since 1974), India, Pakistan, Indonesia, Tanzania, the Philippines, and Syria. But a larger group of countries exempt, fully or partially, public enterprises from virtually all taxes, especially income taxes.[25] Among countries where public enterprises are wholly or largely exempt from income taxes are Brazil, Bolivia, El Salvador, Iran, and Colombia before 1974.[26]

Thus, practice on taxation of public enterprises varies substantially. In general, however, public enterprises in LDCs pay considerably lower taxes than do comparable private firms. Although in a few cases (as noted earlier) this is due to explicit tax exemptions for public enterprises as a group, in many other cases public enterprises are nominally subject to all taxes but are de facto exempt, owing to accommodations between public-enterprise managers and tax administrators. For example, even though Colombian public enterprises have been nominally subject to income taxes since 1974, virtually no income taxes had been paid by such firms through 1980. Even when taxed, public enterprises often face lower effective tax rates than private firms because of the high proportion of their investment financed by debt, as interest payments are almost everywhere allowed as a tax deduction.

Rules for absorbing losses

High leverage in public enterprises increases the prospect that cash flows of the firm will fall short of meeting operating and investment requirements. As a result, the sponsoring government often must intervene in the form of providing additional funds either through direct subsidies, the rolling-over of debt, the guaranteeing of additional external debt, or related methods. Such bailouts are typically ad hoc in nature, with governments assuming public-enterprise bank debt or conversion of these claims to public-enterprise "equity." In many cases, this recapitalization of public enterprises does not result in an exchange of future financial obligations for the current ones but merely "wipes the slate clean."

In summary, we can caricature the financial linkages, rules for the distribution of profits, and rules for covering losses as: Public enterprises have access to many sources of finance for which explicit costs are artificially low relative to their social costs. After the fact, if operations result in substantial surpluses, the public enterprise is often able to retain control over virtually all these flows. In contrast, if the "profits" of the public enterprise are insufficient to meet the formal commitments associated with the initial financing terms, the government, in one fashion or another, will typically assume its liabilities. Of course, in this latter case, the government may intervene in the enterprise and penalize its managers, possibly even by dismissing them, as in several cases in Indonesian oil and banking public enterprises. However, even this link may be broken if the public enterprise can gain access to additional financing by arguing that the losses were due to factors beyond its control and that it has met its mission in supplying or in meeting the multiple social objectives thrust upon it.

13.3   Impact of financing patterns on public-enterprise decisions

Behavioral assumptions

There is no generally accepted theory of how public-enterprise managers react to changes in the variables that can be altered by the financial structure of the organization. However, the pattern and outcomes of financial linkages suggest that they both influence and are influenced by managerial motives within public enterprises. This possibility has seldom been recognized in the economic literature dealing with the evaluation of public-sector projects.

When differences between the information and objective sets of managers and the state are taken into account, the role of finance in public-enterprise decision making becomes much more like the role of finance in private enterprises. In the case of private enterprises, financial structure matters primarily because it affects enterprise vulnerability to bankruptcy and because it alters the distribution of profits going to shareholders (and other private financial claimants) and to the government through taxes. In the case of public enterprises, financial structure, and the return required by the state on different types of financing that it extends to the public enterprise, will alter the distribution between the surpluses returned directly to the state and those controlled by the public enterprise and, hence, relevant to the public-enterprise manager.

The views of public-enterprise managers examined here might be characterized as (1) the broadly rational maximizer of net social benefits and (2) the narrowly rational seeker of autonomy and stability.

The maximizer of net social benefits. Implicit in most economic literature on social cost–benefit analysis as applied to public enterprises are two assumptions: First, that public-enterprise managers have perfect information and, second, that they are motivated solely by a desire to maximize some clearly defined measure of social welfare. If public-enterprise managers were really omniscient social maximizers, the way public enterprises are financed and the way their performance is evaluated, as asserted earlier, would have little impact on their decisions regarding resource allocation, output and pricing, and reinvestment or distribution of operating profits. Rules for investment and operating decisions derived in a neoclassical framework involving future, uncertain costs or benefits would apply, assuming, of course, that social costs and benefits were properly valued and included in the relevant cash flows. These rules, however, would be invariant with respect to the nature of the state's financial claims against the public enterprise. It would not matter whether these claims were in the form of debt, equity, value-added taxes, or income taxes, as the broadly rational manager will take all these returns into account.

There are many reasons for believing that managers, whether public or private, operate with much less than full information and pursue objectives that do not correspond precisely to those of the state. The "behavioral theory of the firm," as developed by Simon,[27] March and Simon,[28] Cyert and March,[29] and others, suggests that the organizational decision making is "narrowly rational," as characterized by localized and incomplete search, bounded rationality, a reliance on long-term memory, strong influence of tastes, imitation, acceptance of ambiguity, and "satisficing" with respect to organizational objectives. If this is true for private managers, it may be even more applicable for public-enterprise managers, as the state's objectives are usually less well articulated than is the case in private undertakings.[30] The state's objectives as communicated to public-enterprise management tend to be a complex, confusing, changing set of often contradictory goals, representing the view of various interested parties, including the public-enterprise managers themselves as well as their suppliers, buyers, employees, and other constituencies.

The seeker of autonomy and stability. Some analysts have outlined an alternative rival objective function, one in which a major goal of the public-enterprise manager is that of maintaining independence vis-á-vis the government to assure continuity and stability of both employment and public-service programs (cf. Bolivia, Colombia, Indonesia, Ghana, most of Europe, Sri Lanka).[31] That is, managers seek to avoid the need to appeal to the government for handouts or for new equity to cover losses or new investments, as this invites unwanted and often troublesome scrutiny or intervention. Consequently, the impact of alternative financing arrangements on enterprise autonomy, independence, and stability will be of central concern to public-enterprise managers.

In financial terms, this desire for autonomy implies that managers will strongly seek to maintain positive cash flows. It may also lead such managers to accept more risks than the broadly rational maximizer of social benefits, as acceptance of more risks may increase the likelihood of sustained organization growth and autonomy. This notion stands in sharp contrast to a view of public-enterprise finance that might arise from purely economic considerations, assuming idealized information and coordination within the public sector.

The assumption that public-enterprise managers are narrowly rational is evidenced by the following implications.

Implications for public-enterprise behavior

Capital intensity. To the extent that the explicit cost of funds is understated relative to their social opportunity costs or treated as zero, narrowly rational public-enterprise managers will tend to overinvest in capital to reduce recurring expenditures that will have to be covered by future operating revenues or government appropriations.[32] This effect will be exaggerated when public-enterprise access to credit is conditional on the purchase of (foreign-sourced) capital goods, as with tied-in foreign aid or credits from suppliers. It also will be exaggerated if public enterprises are exempted from import restrictions and customs duties (as in Mexico, in Colombia before 1974, and in state oil firms in Indonesia and Bolivia), especially if these measures support an overvalued exchange rate. Although it is difficult to measure the relative cost of capital goods, even in the face of a substantial labor surplus, a variety of studies have found that public enterprises tend to adopt far more capital-intensive processes than their private-sector counterparts, quite apart from the fact that public enterprises tend in any case to be concentrated in capital-intensive sectors. Many studies of pre-1978 vintage are summarized in Gillis.[33] Other, more recent, evidence adds further weight to the argument. A 1979 Indonesian study for the World Bank indicates that public enterprises in the industrial sector had very low rates of labor use compared with both agricultural activities and private-sector industry. Trebat finds that partly as a result of their privileged access to capital, capital intensity increased markedly in major Brazilian public enterprises over the period 1966–75, as the average capital-output ratio for these firms rose from about 2.8 to 5.0, versus a gross capital-output ratio for the economy as a whole of less than 1.5 in 1968–73.[34]

Public-enterprise financing and risk taking. Public enterprises are often created explicitly to take on risky ventures for which the private sector has neither the appetite nor the capacity. Nevertheless, many observers of public enterprises note that public-enterprise managers are more risk averse than their private counterparts. However, it is difficult to generalize on this point, as there are also cases in which public-enterprise managers appear to be relatively risk prone (Pertamina in Indonesia prior to 1976, Malaysian International Shipping prior to 1978, Petro Canada). In fact, any general statement regarding the risk aversion of public-enterprise decision makers is likely to be misleading. A more appropriate statement is that public-enterprise managers' responses to risk differ from those of private managers facing similar objective circumstances because of the pattern of public-enterprise finance and control. As has also been pointed out by Adar and Aharoni, public- and private-enterprise managers who may have identical attitudes toward risk as individuals are likely to respond differently to the same type of risky situation because of the structure of incentives they face.[35]

In public enterprises subject to close bureaucratic control where losses or errors regardless of size are given great weight and where little or no direct credit or organizational autonomy is obtained by economic success, public-enterprise managers will tend to avoid risks at virtually any cost. For example, public-enterprise managers of COMIBOL in Bolivia and many of Sri Lanka's nationalized sectors appear to have been placed in this type of operating environment. Also, most Canadian public electric utilities would also fall within this category.

In contrast, in more entrepreneurial public enterprises, managers may perceive relatively few penalties for economic losses as long as they continue to satisfy politically important constituencies by providing desired services and, perhaps more important, as long as these penalties may not increase proportionately with the magnitude of the loss. These same managers may perceive substantial benefits from economic success, as success will increase organizational autonomy and enhance the chances of satisfying politically relevant constituencies, as well as provide the psychological and material rewards of a growing empire. The near-catastrophic recent history of Pertamina in Indonesia, the state economic development corporations in Malaysia, and the present development of Petro Canada illustrate this type of behavior.

For any business organization there is some explicit or implicit mechanism whereby the returns to the enterprise are transformed into returns that are relevant for determining managerial rewards or punishments. In Figure 13.2 we illustrate an owner-managed enterprise where the relevant return for the management's success or failure rating is identical to that of the firm. Therefore, given a return of R for the firm, the managerially relevant return (not necessarily his own personal income) is also R. In this case the entire set of returns to the enterprise, when transformed into the returns relevant for managers, falls along the 45-degree line OC.

An alternative is shown in Figure 13.3, which we submit is illustrative of some public-enterprise situations. Here managers suffer relatively high costs when the enterprise generates a low return (below L), receive an above normal return when the enterprise's returns are normal (L to H), and only have their returns increased

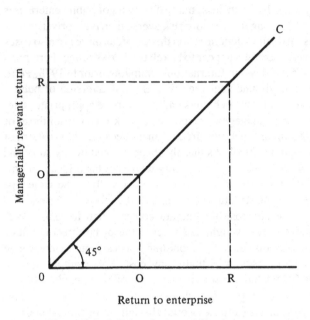

Figure 13.2. Relation of managerially relevant return and return to enterprise in private, owner-managed enterprise. See text for explanation.

modestly when the enterprise's returns are high (above H). This mapping of the enterprise returns into managerially relevant returns is shown by the curve DB. These managerially relevant returns need not comprise only the manager's salary or other personal financial returns. They will include all the returns the managers view as yielding positive benefits to them. These include financial gains, working environment, status, future job security, and power. However, these managerial relevant returns are likely to be a complex function of the resources that remain in the command of the enterprise.

Suppose a return of R to the enterprise falls in the normal range. In this case this would be translated into an R''' return as far as the manager is concerned, where $R''' > R$. However, for an enterprise rate of return below L or above H (e.g., B and K, respectively), the relevant managerial rates of return (B''' and K''') are less than the enterprise returns. Hence, these managers would strive to obtain a return within the normal range (L to H) where their relative "rewards" would be greatest. Conversely, they would avoid risky projects with the prospect of yielding high and low enterprise returns, which would in turn lead to managerially lower rates of return relative to those of the enterprise.

This mapping of enterprise returns does not mean that the public-enterprise manager is any more or less risk averse as an individual than are private-sector managers. The transformation between these two returns depends on the financial

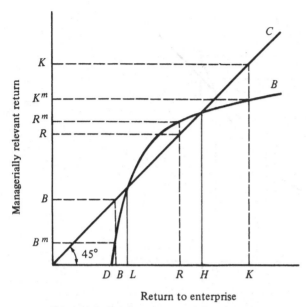

Figure 13.3. Relation of managerially relevant return and return to enterprise in bureaucratic public enterprise. See text for explanation.

environment in which they work. The financial environment in turn will be an important component of the incentive system facing the management. A key determinant of this environment is the financial structure of the enterprise and the financial commitments undertaken to obtain this financing. In contrast, Figure 13.4 illustrates the case of the entrepreneurial public enterprise where the manager is not penalized as much for abnormally low rates of return as in private enterprise (below L) but is rewarded more than normal for high rates of return (above H). In this case the financing arrangements and the institutional control of the enterprise are such as to make the prospect of rates of return within the normal range of L to H less attractive to the managers of the public enterprise than to their private-sector counterparts. Hence, an incentive is created that will cause managers of public enterprises to want to undertake more risky projects. It is important to note that it is not the basic attitude of the public-enterprise manager toward risk that is different. Rather it is the financial structure and ultimately the incentive structure that is different in these two cases.

In the existing literature on private- and public-sector managerial behavior the emphasis has often been on the presence or absence of risk aversion for these groups without making a clear distinction between the determinants of the "managerially relevant" payoffs as illustrated by Figures 13.2 to 13.4 and the risk tolerance of the individuals. It is likely that the differences in perceived payoffs will swamp differences in managerial risk tolerance. The particular financing

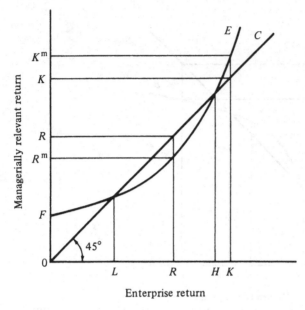

Figure 13.4. Relation of managerially relevant return and enterprise return in entrepreneurial enterprise. See text for explanation.

arrangement provided the public enterprise will in turn play a major role in determining the managerially relevant returns for the various returns generated by the enterprise.

Finance and social obligations. It is typically assumed that public-enterprise managers would prefer to minimize their social obligations or responsibilities. But it is entirely possible that managers of successful public enterprises may tend to seek to expand the social scope of their operations, possibly even by expanding the set of multiple public (social) objectives. The reason for this is to justify their control of the existing flow of funds and to maintain financial independence from the central government. Otherwise, if they appear to generate substantial surpluses, the funds are likely to be recaptured by the central treasury. In contrast, when public enterprises are thrust into ventures whose market structures, cost situations, or service requirements lead them to be unprofitable, they will try to reduce their public-service load (social obligation) to obtain that level of profitability that allows them stability and independence.

13.4   Issues for further research

Development of an operational framework to analyze the role that financing plays in public-enterprise activities requires an understanding of the way in which particular financial arrangements for public enterprises alter the incentives faced by managers and controllers.

Coupled with a more explicit methodology for measuring the opportunity costs of funds committed to public enterprises, this should suggest ways for incorporating these costs into the decision-making process of public enterprises. In turn, this may mean that nonconventional financial instruments need to be designed so that both public-enterprise managers and governments will have an incentive to minimize the distortions created by financial illusion.

Given the patterns of incentives created by alternative financial environments, it would be useful to develop theoretical models to help explain the behavior of public enterprises under various existing financial environments as well as to indicate what changes in operating patterns are likely to arise when changes are made in the rules governing public-enterprise finance.

An important aspect requiring further study is the impact of foreign financing on public-enterprise operation and the economic welfare of the country. Evaluation of the economic cost of such financing will require both an assessment of the opportunity cost of employing these funds by the public enterprises instead of in other uses and a determination of the distribution of the undiversifiable risk associated with such foreign-financed activities. Hence, issues concerning the comparative level of taxation and changes in the tax revenues of governments resulting from the foreign financing of public enterprises need also to be examined.

Notes

1 Arnold C. Harberger, "On Measuring the Social Opportunity Cost of Public Funds," in *Project Evaluation: Collected Papers.* (Chicago University of Chicago Press, 1972).
2 The simplest model yielding these results is the Capital-Asset Pricing Model (CAPM) of William F. Sharpe, "Capital Asset Prices: A Theory of Market Equilibrium Under Conditions of Risk," *Journal of Finance* 19 (Sept. 1964):425–42; John Lintner, "Security Prices, Risk, and Maximal Gains from Diversification," *Journal of Finance* 20 (Dec. 1965):587–615, and John Lintner, "The Valuation of Risk Assets and the Selection of Risky Investments in Stock Portfolios and Capital Budgets," *Review of Economics and Statistics,* 47 (Feb. 1965):13–37 and Jan Mossin, "Equilibrium in a Capital Asset Market," *Econometrica* 34 (Oct. 1966):768–88. The most important assumptions are that individuals (or the state) are risk averse but agree on outcomes and that return distributions can be characterized by only their means and variance. The Capital-Asset Pricing Model states that the required rate of return on an asset is a linear function of its systematic or non-diversifiable risk

$$\hat{R}_j = r + B_j (\hat{R}_m - r)$$

where $\hat{R}_j$ is the required expected return on asset j, r is the interest rate on a riskless security, B_j is asset j's coefficient of systematic risk defined as covariance j_m / variance$_m$, and $\hat{R}_m$ is the expected return on the market or social portfolio of risky assets. Please note throughout that the terms *opportunity cost of capital, cost of capital,* and *required rate of return* are used interchangeably.

3 See Carliss Baldwin, Donald Lessard, and Scott Mason, "Financial Incentives for Employment Creation" (Report to Labor Market Task Force, Canada, May 1981) for a fuller statement of the relationship between the two variables.

4 For opposing views on this point see Kenneth J. Arrow and Robert C. Lind, "Uncertainty and the Evaluation of Public Investment Decisions," *American Economic Review* 40 (June 1970):364–78, and Martin J. Bailey and Michael C. Jensen, "Risk and the Discount Rate for Public Investment," in *Studies in the Theory of Capital Markets*, ed. M. C. Jensen (New York: Praeger, 1972).

5 Systematic risk (as opposed to total risk or enterprise-specific risk) is related to general levels of economic activity and general financial development, e.g., changes in fiscal or monetary policy, a fall in world prices of tin, rubber, etc.

6 See John Lintner, "Finance in Enterprises Under State Ownership: Theoretical Perspectives" (Paper presented to Conference on Public Sector Enterprises, Harvard University, 1979), for a discussion of the applicability of the CAPM to public enterprises.

7 Roger Ibbotson and Rex Sinquefield, "Stocks, Bonds, Bills and Inflation: Historical Returns" (Charlottesville, Va.: Financial Analysts Research Foundation, 1979).

8 Tamir Agmon and Donald Lessard, "Financial Factors and the Expansion of Small Country Firms," in *Multinationals from Small Countries*, ed. Tamir Agmon and Charles Kindleberger (Cambridge, Mass.: MIT Press, 1977).

9 Donald Lessard, "Risk Efficient External Financing for Commodity-Producing LDCs," manuscript (Massachusetts Institute of Technology, 1977).

10 These statements parallel Franco Modigliani and Merton H. Miller's Propositions I and II, that the value of all claims against an enterprise is unaffected by the way in which those claims are partitioned and, consequently, that if claims are partitioned into riskless debt and equity, the risk premium in the cost of equity must increase to reflect its greater proportionate risk. In general, these propositions depend on arbitrage in financial markets but are tautologically true if one invester (the state) holds all claims; see "The Cost of Capital, Corporation Finance, and the Theory of Investment," *American Economic Review* 48 (June 1958):261–97.

11 Arnold C. Harberger, "On Country Risk and the Social Cost of Foreign Borrowing by Developing Countries," mimeographed (University of Chicago, 1976); Arnold C. Harberger, "On the Determinants of Country Risk," mimeographed (University of Chicago, 1976).

12 A more precise statement is that if the combination of the public enterprise's foreign borrowing (movement *along* the supply schedule of foreign funds) and its contribution to the country's access to foreign finance (*shift* of the supply schedule) do not result in increased costs of foreign borrowing, the partial analysis is appropriate.

13 Figures on borrowing by LDC-based public enterprises are computed on the basis of data presented in the World Bank, Financial Studies Division, *Borrowing in International Capital Markets* EC-181 (Washington, D.C.: World Bank, 1978).

14 Malcolm Gillis, "The Role of Public Enterprises in Economic Development," *Social Research* 47 (Summer 1980):248–89.

15 Thomas Trebat, "An Evaluation of the Economic Performance of Large Public Enterprises in Brazil, 1965–1975," Technical Papers, Series 24 (University of Texas at Austin, 1980).

16 Leroy F. Jones, *Public Enterprise and Economic Development: The Korean Case* (Seoul: Korea Development Institute, 1975), pp. 83, 123, 190–4, 200, 236–44; Table B.

17 Trebat, "Evaluation of Economic Performance."
18 Gillis, "Role of Public Enterprises."
19 Trebat, "Evaluation of Economic Performance."
20 Jones, *Public Enterprise and Economic Development.*
21 Gillis, "Role of Public Enterprises."
22 Robert H. Floyd, "Some Aspects of Income Taxation of Public Enterprises," *International Monetary Fund Staff Papers,* Vol. 25, No. 4 (1978).
23 E.g., in the mid-1970s the Bolivian-government state-owned minerals enterprises, COMIBOL, reported a debt–equity ratio of almost 1:1. However, virtually all the "equity" in the enterprise was little more than the combined result of past government cancellations of overdue taxes due from the enterprise and government assumption of past enterprise debts. See Malcolm Gillis, Meyer W. Bucovetsky, Glenn P. Jenkins, Ulrich Petersen, Louis T. Wells, and Brian D. Wright, *Taxation and Mining: Non-Fuel Minerals in Bolivia and Other Countries* (Cambridge, Mass.: Ballinger, 1978), Chaps. 2 and 6.
24 Trebat, "Evaluation of Economic Performance."
25 In many countries, public enterprises are also exempt from customs duties on their imports, e.g., Indonesian and Bolivian oil enterprises and all public enterprises in Mexico. Imports of public enterprises are generally taxable in Colombia, and all non-oil enterprises are taxable in Indonesia and Bolivia.
26 Floyd, "Some Aspects of Income Taxation."
27 Herbert A. Simon, "Theories of Decision-Making in Economics and Behavioral Science," *American Economic Review* 48 (June 1959):253–83.
28 James G. March and Herbert Simon, *Organizations* (New York: Wiley, 1958).
29 Richard M. Cyert and James G. March, *The Behavioral Theory of the Firm* (Englewood Cliffs, N.J.: Prentice-Hall, 1963).
30 Yair Aharoni and Raymond Vernon, "Public Enterprises: Theory, Fact, and Speculation" (Paper presented to Conference on Public Sector Enterprises, Harvard University, 1979).
31 Yair Aharoni and Raymond Vernon, "Public Enterprises: Theory, Fact, and Speculation," and Yair Aharoni, Chapter 4, this volume; George C. Manistis, "Managerial Autonomy in Public Enterprises: Fact and Anti-Fact," *Annals of Public and Co-operative Economy* 39 (1968).
32 Glenn P. Jenkins, "Public Utility Finance and Economic Waste," manuscript (Cambridge: Harvard Institute of International Development, 1980).
33 Gillis, "Role of Public Enterprises."
34 Malcolm Gillis, Dwight Perkins, Michael Roemer, and Donald Snodgrass, *Economic Development* (New York: Norton, forthcoming).
35 Z. Adar and Yair Aharoni, "Risk Sharing by Managers of State-Owned Enterprises" (Paper presented at second BAPEG conference on Public Enterprise in Mixed Economy LDCs, Boston, Apr. 1980).

Part VI

How are incentive structures to be designed?

14   Performance indices for public enterprises

J. Finsinger and I. Vogelsang

14.1   Alternative devices for efficient pricing in multiproduct monopoly situations

Two rules for the efficient pricing of monopoly firms have been widely discussed in the literature. The marginal-cost rule was the center of controversy in the 1940s and 1950s, and the Ramsey rule[1] was the fashionable topic of the last decade. Both rules require substantial information for their implementation. Mainly because outside regulators lack such information, the marginal-cost rule has lost its popularity. Information to implement the Ramsey rule may be even harder to come by. However, as this chapter shows, the information requirement to implement both rules can be lowered substantially by setting appropriate performance indices for public-enterprise managers.

A combination of two features distinguishes the public enterprise from other economic institutions: (1) it is mainly financed by the revenues derived from the sale of its products in markets, which makes it differ from ordinary public administration, and (2) it differs from private capitalistic enterprises by virtue of public (state) ownership. This hybrid position of public enterprises gives rise to two natural starting points for a normative analysis. First, what can be gained by decentralizing part of the administration via public enterprises? Second, what advantages can public enterprises hold over private firms? If there are such advantages, they must have a restricted domain, because otherwise the hybrid would dominate its parents.

To be the superior institutional setup, public enterprises first have to be feasible. This is of major relevance for the decision to turn a government administration into a public enterprise. If the administration's output consists of pure public goods with no possibility to exclude, a public enterprise simply is not feasible. To give a complete set of conditions for the optimality of public enterprises is beyond the capacity of this chapter. Instead, plausibility arguments will be used to delineate a class of unsolved problems with other institutional arrangements.

Our starting point is the set of situations where public enterprises are feasible and where the prevalence of economies of scale yields nonoptimal private market solutions. Financing the outputs in question by taxes and offering them through public administration may, under these circumstances, have desirable distributional features. The allocative outcome, however, is likely to be unattractive, because under a tax financing system well-known public-goods problems appear. No use is made of the fact that the good in question is private. This setup can be justified only if preferences for the goods are obvious, for example, the same for everyone and unrelated to income. It is hard to imagine examples where this is true. Merit wants could be classified here. In all other cases the market seems to be a particularly attractive institution for preference revelation on private goods. Consequently, the situation described by economies of scale in the production of private output leads to undesirable results with respect to both the pure public administration and the pure private market solution. Several other solutions to this problem have been proposed and are being used. They include antitrust measures, bidding processes, and government regulation of private firms as well as the use of public enterprises.

The smaller the number of firms that are cost minimizing for the industry, the less satisfactory antitrust measures tend to be. Under the economies-of-scale assumption, chances for reaching an efficient state with antitrust measures only are minuscule. Markets would have to fulfill the idealized market and sustainability conditions described by Willig.[2]

Bidding mechanisms as proposed by Demsetz[3] have been further developed by von Weizsäcker.[4] Their feasibility has been convincingly criticized by Williamson[5] and V. P. Goldberg.[6] These criticisms rest on the presence of intertemporal cost effects and changes in the environment. But even in the absence of intertemporal cost effects and in a stationary environment there is an important limitation to bidding mechanisms: They work only when many potential suppliers know the relevant cost and demand functions. If such knowledge can be acquired only in a lengthy and costly learning-by-doing fashion, competitive bidding needs substantial time to develop its desired properties.

Government regulation has to cope with similar information problems, especially in multiproduct monopoly situations. If the price structure for these products is not directly regulated, one expects output distortions to go along with input distortions possibly caused by regulation. Efficient, direct price-structure regulation could be extremely difficult to achieve for at least two reasons. First, the specific micro type of information on product-specific demands and costs necessary to pursue this goal is hard to come by. Only the management of a regulated firm can be expected to acquire this information in the trial-and-error process of decision making. Most of this information cannot be revealed by regulatory auditing. Second, changes in the price structure of the regulated firm potentially hit the individual consumer or consumer groups harder than changes in the price level. Their relative position (competitiveness) is altered. Structure is a better lever for redistributive action than level. Pressure groups may have both the incentive and the means to influence price-structure regulation in their favor. A regulatory rule aimed at the price structure could help overcome these tendencies and improve informational requirements. Vogelsang and Finsinger have recently suggested such a regulatory price adjustment process for multiproduct monopolies.[7] Its core is a constraint, which the regulatory agency applies iteratively, that for time period $i + 1$ constrains the firm to choose a positive price vector p in the set

$$R_{i+1} = \{p \mid px_i - C(x_i) \leq 0\}$$

Under the appropriate assumptions, the process described by this constraint reaches a steady state with Ramsey prices. Thus, the mechanism is a good device to solve the price-structure problem. It can also be shown to induce the firm to use peak-load pricing and other more sophisticated pricing techniques, which improve welfare.[8] However, its usefulness hinges on the requirement of decreasing ray-average costs, a special kind of increasing returns to scale. This technological condition is empirically hard to demonstrate and may be restricted to rather few industries. Being aware of this, we have suggested an extension of the mechanism, which, however, requires myopic profit maximization by the firm as a behavioral assumption. Strategic behavior matters even if the decreasing ray-average cost condition is met. The process will eventually converge to a constrained welfare optimum. As Sappington has shown, however, misrepresentation can occur on the way to this optimum.[9] The special form that misrepresentation may take here is as a waste of inputs. Furthermore, misrepresentation may lead to the introduction of unprofitable new products and to wasteful innovative activities. Rate-of-return regulation, with the allowed rate of returns exceeding the cost of capital r, could reduce problems of strategic misrepresentation.[10] Finsinger demonstrates that with $s > r$ the process converges.[11] However, overcapitalization tendencies of the Averch–Johnson kind and nonoptimal pricing will occur.[12]

The mechanism developed in Vogelsang and Finsinger is based on the behavioral assumption of profit maximization, which presupposes that the internal incentive problem of translating the regulatory scheme into the desired behavior has been solved successfully between the shareholders and managers of the regulated firm.[13] It is doubtful whether a regulatory adjustment process can be sensitive enough to solve these two types of incentive problems simultaneously. This is especially relevant if firm ownership is widely dispersed. Incentives directly applying to the management of the firm might be a shortcut provided by the existence of a public enterprise.

Economists have a clear picture of efficient performance by public enterprises. Public enterprises should produce at minimum costs and sell at marginal-cost prices. However, economists have only vague ideas of how to implement the prescribed optimality conditions. Clearly, it is not enough to tell public-enterprise managers to go ahead and do so. By producing off the production function, such managers could easily make their performance look optimal. Their true performance, however, can be optimized with some reliability only if the existing incentive structures are taken into account. This interaction between incentive structures and state intervention is a central theme of the theory of regulation. Economists have tried to understand the performance of regulated industries under various assumptions about managerial goals such as profit maximization, revenue maximization, managerial utility maximization, and so on. They predict deviations from efficient performance under all these managerial theories. Thus it becomes necessary to design and install the appropriate incentive structure directly.

We now make a small step in this direction by suggesting performance indices to guide the managers of public enterprises to produce efficiently and to charge welfare optimal prices. The performance indices are embedded in the incentive structure of the public enterprise, that is, its management. Our main informational assumption is that the management, compared to the government and the public, has by far superior knowledge on demand and cost conditions. Thus, we require the management to be able to learn about the local behavior of the cost and demand functions, whereas the welfare maximizing government needs only to know book-keeping data on prices, quantities, and profits. The first performance index proposed will be shown to lead to marginal-cost prices. It will then be modified to take into account institutional constraints such as a balanced budget.

14.2   A performance index leading to marginal-cost prices

The partial-analytic framework commonly applied in public-utility economics allows us to measure welfare by the sum of consumers' surplus and profits. Furthermore, the technology can be represented by the minimum-cost function. In this environment the following four assumptions form the basis of our main results.

Assumption 1: consumers

Consumers' welfare is given by consumers' surplus, $V(p)$, with $p \in B \subset \mathbf{R}_+^n$ being the price vector charged by the public enterprise. B is supposed to be compact, which conforms to the intuition that there exists a price, $\bar{p}^j$, for each good j such that demand for this good at any higher price is zero. $V(p)$ shall be twice differentiable. Income effects are assumed to be absent. Then the following relationship (Roy's identity[14]) holds between the demand function $x(p)$ and $V(p)$:

$$\frac{\partial V(p)}{\partial p} = -x(p) \tag{1}$$

Assumption 2: the public enterprise

$\pi(p)$ represents the profit function of the firm with

$$\pi(p) = px(p) - C[x(p)] \tag{2}$$

The minimum-cost function, $C[x(p)]$, is assumed to be continuously differentiable. There are no intertemporal cost effects. At announced prices, p, all demand has to be served. We now characterize the management incentive structure.

Assumption 3: management performance index

The managers of the public enterprise maximize their discounted flow of income. They receive the following payment, Y_i, at the end of period $i + 1 \epsilon N$,

$$Y_i = A + I_i \tag{3}$$

where A is a fixed income component determined by competitive management salaries and where the performance index I_i stands for

$$I_i = x_i(p_i - p_{i+1}) + \pi_{i+1} - \pi_i \tag{4}$$

This performance index contains only bookkeeping data. I_i measures the performance improvement between period i and period $i + 1$. For simplicity, the incentive payment is supposed to coincide with the performance index, but the incentives and the index may be linked in other ways. The incentive payment would have to be paid out of tax revenues or profits, whereas income A is a fixed cost to the firm. I_i, however, shall not be included in calculating π_{i+1} or π_i. I_i is allowed to become negative in case of performance deterioration.

Assumption 4: social welfare

Social welfare is measured by the sum of consumers' surplus and profits:

$$S(p) = V(p) + \pi(p) \tag{5}$$

The performance index provides managers with an incentive always to produce firm output at minimum cost. Any cost savings can be directly translated into earnings. Therefore, we may write:

$$I_i = I(p_i, p_{i+1}) = x(p_i)(p_i - p_{i+1}) + \pi(p_{i+1}) - \pi(p_i)$$
$$= p_{i+1}[x(p_{i+1}) - x(p_i)] - (C_{i+1} - C_i) \tag{6}$$

Now because

$$C_{i+1} - C_i = \int_{x_i}^{x_{i+1}} C'(x)\,dx$$

we can see from Figure 14.1 that I_i is just the shaded area between p_{i+1} and $C'(x)$ over the quantity change $x_{i+1} - x_i$.

In the appendix to this chapter we prove that under the four stated assumptions the performance index will lead managers to successfully improve the pricing conduct

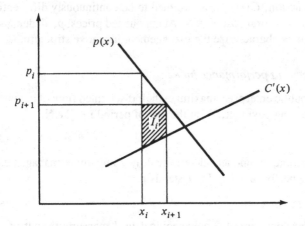

Figure 14.1. The size of the performance index I_i.

of the firm so that in the limit marginal-cost prices will be reached. We also show that these prices will represent at least a local welfare maximum. Furthermore, there are good reasons to believe that the process will end only at global welfare maxima.

Why does this performance index lead the managers of public enterprises to pursue marginal-cost prices in the limit? Marginal-cost prices maximize the sum of consumers' surplus and profits. This is a property that has already been used by Loeb and Magat to construct a mechanism leading to marginal-cost prices.[15] They simply require the state to pay a subsidy to the firm that equals consumers' surplus. It is easily verified then that the profit-maximizing firm has all the incentives to charge marginal-cost prices. Loeb and Magat, however, have no suggestion as to the method for measuring consumers' surplus. Our mechanism provides such a revelation technique: The sum $x_i(p_i - p_{i+1}) + \pi_{i+1} - \pi_i$ is a linear approximation of the total surplus increments gained through changes in management behavior. In the absence of income effects, consumers' surplus will generally be convex.[16] Therefore, the total welfare increment is always larger than the performance index. Management, under our assumption, can increase its income by increasing total surplus, that is, by moving in the direction of marginal-cost prices. If it moves in other directions, its income will be reduced. By moving in cycles, these reductions can never be more than offset as shown in lemma III of the appendix. Thus, management has an incentive to end up at marginal-cost prices.

The convergence speed of the process depends very much on the discount rate applied by management to its future income. At zero r, the smaller the price changes from one period to the next, the closer management income approximates consumers' surplus. Thus, the sum of management incomes of all periods is maximized by moving in infinitely small steps (lemma II). On the other hand, if managers apply a positive discount rate, the stream of future gains is worth less to

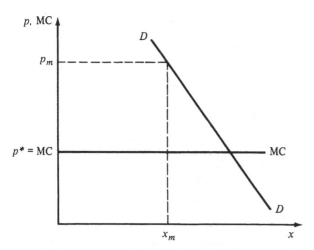

Figure 14.2. Behavior of performance index under constant marginal cost.

them. Within some interval, the larger the steps are, the larger the income increment will be for the current period. Thus, there is an incentive to start off the process with large steps in order to have high income early. This is true only within a certain interval because lowering prices down to marginal costs in a single period may leave management without any gain (if marginal costs are constant) or even with a loss (if marginal costs are falling).

For the one-product case this is easily demonstrated in Figures 14.2 and 14.3. In Figure 14.2 we have constant marginal costs. If the firm starts at a price p_m and lowers it down in one step to $p^* = MC$, profits decrease by $x_m(p_m - p^*)$ and thus $I(p_m, p^*) = 0$. In Figure 14.3 we have decreasing marginal costs. If in this case the firm starts at a price p_m and lowers it down to $p^* = MC$ in one step, profits decrease by $x_m(p_m - p^*) + B$ where B denotes the shaded area. Thus $I(p_m, p^*) < 0$.

Under the described process, management will want to minimize costs for the given output at every period during which the process runs. This is a feature by which the performance index differs from the regulatory adjustment process described in Vogelsang and Finsinger.[17] Under the latter process, production costs of the previous period directly enter the constraint of the current period, whereas under the process described in this chapter, costs have no such bearing. However, the management could have an incentive to raise prices and costs before the process starts. With a zero discount rate, management would want to start with infinite production cost and at a price where demand approaches zero so that losses are infinitely large and consumers' surplus approaches zero. This would give management a possibility to make large income gains in the following periods. Given the stationarity assumption, however, government could easily prove the cheating involved in such behavior.

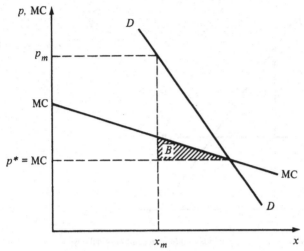

Figure 14.3. Behavior of performance index under decreasing marginal cost.

In a changing environment the performance index holds some other advantages over the regulatory adjustment process. Management will want to introduce cost-reducing innovations because, at least for some time, it can reap all profits and also consumers' surplus increases from such innovations. The same is potentially true for product innovations. The management has an incentive to introduce new products whenever they offer new income opportunities. Here again, the arguments by Sappington against the regulatory adjustment process do not carry over.[18] The management has no incentive to engage in unprofitable activities. It is, however, not guaranteed that management pursues the optimal rate of innovation.

Rate-of-return regulation and other regulatory schemes have to be supplemented by adjustment clauses in times of rapid inflation. Then, problems with strategic management behavior arise. The proposed incentive scheme does not need a special provision for inflationary cost increases. Of course, the performance index may become negative for some time and management would then have to pay for these losses out of the fixed income A. If inflation is persistent, A has to be chosen sufficiently large to compensate the management.

The described performance index can be applied to public enterprises having different types of cost curves. Under decreasing returns to scale, the firm will make a profit in the steady state. Under increasing returns to scale, it will suffer a loss. This loss has to be covered by subsidies. General arguments against such subsidies were raised in the marginal-cost pricing controversy initiated by Coase.[19] One argument states that there is no natural limit to the amount of subsidies. Coverage of deficits resulting from marginal-cost pricing may thus enhance cost inefficiency. As shown earlier, guided by the performance index, management will want to produce at minimum cost. The subsidy then is the result not of vague calculations of costs and consumers' surplus but of optimizing behavior by management and consumers.

14.3   A performance index leading to Ramsey prices

The suggested performance index I_i solves some major incentive problems associated with marginal-cost pricing and subsidies. However, other problems remain unsolved. If the process described by the performance index never reaches a point where the firm makes positive profits, whether consumers are willing to pay the total costs of providing such products remains questionable. Furthermore, if taxes themselves involve distortions, which increase with the total amount of taxes collected by the state, raising additional taxes to cover deficits of public enterprises may be more distortive than deviating from marginal-cost prices. A balanced-budget constraint for the enterprise avoids this type of tax-induced distortion.

With this concern in mind we suggest that managers receive an income at the end of period $i + 1$ of

$$y_i = A + x_i(p_i - p_{i+1})$$

subject to $\pi(p_{i+1}) \geq 0$ as a binding constraint. This constraint could be enforced drastically by dismissing management whenever losses are experienced. Alternatively, one could set management income at

$$y_i = A + \pi(p_{i+1}) \quad \text{if} \quad \pi(p_{i+1}) < 0 \quad \text{and} \quad x_i(p_i - p_{i+1}) > 0$$

and

$$y_i = A + x_i(p_i - p_{i+1}) + \pi(p_{i+1}) \quad \text{if} \quad \pi(p_{i+1}) < 0 \quad \text{and}$$
$$x_i(p_i - p_{i+1}) \leq 0$$

This would also ensure that management tries to avoid losses for the firm.

The basic reason for the functioning of this second mechanism is similar to that given for the first. It depends on the similarity of interest between the managers and the consumers, which this incentive device creates and which lasts as long as profits are nonnegative. The convexity of $V(p)$ again ensures that every income increase of the public-enterprise management resulting from $x_i(p_i - p_{i+1}) > 0$ will make consumers better off by $\Delta V(p) \geq x_i(p_i - p_{i+1})$. Coming from a negative-profit situation, $x_i(p_i - p_{i+1})$ will generally be negative and thus consumers will end up worse off when the firm starts the process with losses. This, however, is the price to be paid for fulfilling the balanced-budget constraint. Except for meeting the balanced-budget constraint, this incentive mechanism is indifferent with respect to profits. That is why under this process management will end up maximizing consumers' surplus, $V(p)$, subject to the balanced-budget constraint, $\pi(p) \geq 0$, and will not maximize social surplus, $S(p)$.

The balanced-budget performance index discussed in this section is related more closely to the regulatory adjustment process described in Vogelsang and

Finsinger[20] than to the marginal-cost pricing index proposed in the preceding section. The balanced-budget performance index, however, has some highly desirable features when compared to the regulatory adjustment process. All the advantages of the marginal-cost-pricing performance index carry over. However, no subsidies are required.

Both incentive mechanisms can be applied to public enterprises only; they leave no room for profit maximization. Thus, they suggest that there may be certain areas where public enterprises hold a distinct advantage over other modes of organizing markets.

14.4   Extensions

We have proposed performance indices for managers of public monopoly firms. However, the balanced-budget mechanism could be usefully applied as well to oligopolistic situations. In West Germany there is an ongoing discussion of the role of public enterprises as a means for introducing competition into narrow oligopolistic markets.[21] The public enterprise is seen in the role of a leader driving down oligopolistic prices to their competitive level. The problem is to find success indicators for such a policy. How can the management of a public enterprise be induced to behave competitively if its success cannot be measured?

Our balanced-budget performance index could provide such an indicator. It may be applied to the price and quantity data pertaining to the public enterprise only. Or, if prices and quantities of the competing firms can be measured without difficulty, the performance index could depend on the prices and quantities relating to the total industry. This extension would help to overcome tendencies of the public enterprise to try to monopolize the industry.

Thus, the described performance indices can be adapted quite flexibly to different types of environments. This is an important prerequisite for their ultimate practical application. Our analysis suggests that welfare theoretic improvements of public-enterprise management behavior can be achieved by incentive schemes based on profits *and* prices, where prices are weighted by quantities sold in the last period.

14.5   Appendix: Proof of propositions

The main propositions are proved below using Assumptions 1 through 4 in the text. First, we establish some properties of the performance index to show the convergence of the sequence of welfare levels $\{S(p_i)\}_{i=1}^{\infty}$. Then the optimality properties of the limit will be discussed.

Lemma I

For any $l, m \in \mathbf{N}, m \geq l$, we have

$$S(p_{m+1}) - S(p_l) \geq \sum_{i=1}^{m} I_i \tag{7}$$

Proof. $V(p)$ can be shown to be convex by a revealed preference argument. Hence,

$$V(p_{i+1}) - V(p_i) \geq x(p_i)(p_i - p_{i+1}) \tag{8}$$

or

$$S(p_{i+1}) - S(p_i) \geq I_i \tag{9}$$

for any p_i, p_{i+1}. Summation yields

$$S(p_{m+1}) - S(p_l) = \sum_{i=1}^{m} [S(p_{i+1}) - S(p_i)] \geq \sum_{i=1}^{m} I_i \quad \text{q.e.d.} \tag{10}$$

Lemma I establishes an upper bound for the performance index and the incentive payments if the discount rate, r, is assumed to be zero. The welfare gains always exceed the performance index. The following lemma shows that positive welfare gains can be translated into positive incentive payments. For zero discount rate r, the incentives exactly reflect the welfare gains.

Lemma II

Suppose there is a differentiable path, $p(t)$, $t \in [0,1]$, such that $S[p(t)]$ is strictly increasing. Then the management can find a sequence of prices – $\{p_i\}_{i=1}^{n}$, $p_1 = p(0)$, $p_n = p(1)$ – that yields positive income. In particular, for $r = 0$, all static welfare gains can be appropriated in infinitely small steps.

Proof. Clearly, we have

$$V[p(1)] - V[p(0)] = \int_0^1 - x[p(t)]\dot{p}(t)\,dt \tag{11}$$

From the definition of this line integral and from (7), we infer the existence of a partition p_ϵ such that for any finer partition, $[t_i, t_{i+1}]$, $i = 0, 1, \ldots, N-1$, with $t_o = 0$ and $t_N = 1$.

$$0 < S[p(1)] - S[p(0)] \leq \sum_{i=0}^{N-1} I_i + \epsilon \tag{12}$$

For a sufficiently fine sequence, $\{p_i\}_{i=1}^{n}$ on $p(t)$, the performance indices I_i will all be positive because of the monotonicity of $S[p(t)]$. Hence, we must also have

$$\sum_{i=0}^{N-1} \frac{1}{(1+r)^i} I_i > 0 \quad \text{q.e.d.} \tag{13}$$

For positive discount rate r, upper and lower bounds on the incentives can be given in terms of the welfare gains.

Lemma III

For any sequence $\{S(p_i)\}_{i=l}^{m+1}$ with $S(p_i) \leq S(p_l) \, i = l, \ldots, m, \ldots, n$ we have

$$0 \geq \frac{1}{(1+r)^m} [S(p_{m+1}) - S(p_l)] \geq \frac{1}{(1+r)^m} \sum_{i=l}^{m} I_i \geq \sum_{i=l}^{m} \frac{1}{(1+r)^m} \, I_i$$

(14)

Proof. For $m = l$, (14) is equivalent to (7). Now suppose (14) holds for $m > l$. Then (7) implies

$$\frac{1}{(1+r)^{m+1}} [S(p_{m+2}) - S(p_l)] \geq \frac{1}{(1+r)^{m+1}} \sum_{i=l}^{m} I_i + \frac{1}{(1+r)^{m+1}} \, I_{m+1}$$

(15)

As $\sum_{i=l}^{m} I_i \leq 0$ from the assumptions and from (7), we have

$$\frac{1}{(1+r)^{m+1}} [S(p_{m+2}) - S(p_l)] \geq \frac{1}{(1+r)^{m+1}} \sum_{i=l}^{m+1} I_i$$

$$\geq \frac{1}{(1+r)^m} \sum_{i=l}^{m} I_i + \frac{1}{(1+r)^{m+1}} \, I_{m+1}$$

(16)

By the induction hypothesis (14) we obtain

$$\frac{1}{(1+r)^{m+1}} [S(p_{m+2}) - S(p_l)] \geq \frac{1}{(1+r)^{m+1}} \sum_{i=l}^{m+1} I_i$$

$$\geq \sum_{i=l}^{m+1} \frac{1}{(1+r)^i} \, I_i \qquad \text{q.e.d.}$$

(17)

Hence, (14) holds for any m, $l \leq m < n$.

Lemma IV

For any increasing sequence of welfare levels $\{S(p_i)\}_{i=l}^{m+1}$, we have

$$\frac{1}{(1+r)^i} [S(p_{m+1}) - S(p_l)] \geq \sum_{i=l}^{m} \frac{1}{(1+r)^i} \, I_i$$

(18)

Proof. First, sum over all $I_i \geq 0$. Then

$$\frac{1}{(1 + r)^i} \Sigma [S(p_{i+1}) - S(p_i)] \geq \frac{1}{(1 + r)^i} \Sigma I_i \geq \Sigma \frac{1}{(1 + r)^i} I_i \qquad (19)$$

For the $I_i < 0$ we trivially have

$$\frac{1}{(1 + r)^i} [S(p_{i+1}) - S(p_i)] \geq \frac{1}{(1 + r)^i} I_i \qquad (20)$$

Summation of (19) and of all (20) for $I_i < 0$ yields (18). q.e.d.

Lemmas III and IV allow us to split the sequence of welfare levels $\{S(p_i)\}_{i=1}^{\infty}$, into steps with increasing welfare and sequences with decreasing welfare. As a consequence of lemma III, the management will let welfare decrease only if later on welfare can be raised above its previous level. Equivalently, there must be a strictly monotonic subsequence of welfare levels, $[S(p_{i_j})]_{j=1}^{\infty}$, leaving out only those levels below or equal to some previous level. The limit exists and is denoted by $S^* = \overline{\lim}_{i \to \infty} S(p_i)$. We now proceed to show the convergence of $\{S(p_i)\}_{i=1}^{\infty}$.

Lemma V

> $\{S(p_i)\}_{i=1}^{\infty}$ converges to S^*.

Proof. Suppose $\{S(p_i)\}_{i=1}^{\infty}$ does not converge. Then there exists some $\epsilon > 0$ such that for all $n \in N$ there exists $t \in N$, $t \geq n$ with

$$S^* - S(p_t) > \epsilon \qquad (21)$$

Also, there must be some price p_{i_s} with

$$S^* - S(p_{i_s}) < r \frac{\epsilon}{1 + r} \qquad (22)$$

and such that

$$S(p_{i_s}) \geq S(p_l) \qquad (23)$$

for $l = i_s, \ldots , t$ and with

$$S^* - S(p_t) > \epsilon \qquad (24)$$

In other words, welfare decreases from $S(p_{i_s})$ down to $S(p_t)$. By moving down to p_t, the management loses at least $L = 1/(1 + r)^{t-1} [S(p_{i_s}) - S(p_t)]$ by lemma III. But from lemmas III and IV we can see that the gain in later periods is bounded by $G = 1/(1 + r)^t [S^* - S(p_t)]$. Because (22) and (24) imply $L > G$, the management has no incentive to leave p_{i_s} and to move "down" to p_t.

To show that (22) and (24) imply $L > G$, we note

$$L = \frac{1}{(1 + r)^{t-1}} [S(p_{i_s}) - S* + S* - S(p_i)]$$

$$\geq - \frac{1}{(1 + r)^t} r\epsilon + \frac{1}{(1 + r)^{t-1}} [S* - S(p_i)]$$

But $L - G > 0$ follows from

$$- \frac{1}{(1 + r)^t} r\epsilon + \frac{1}{(1 + r)^{t-1}} [S* - S(p_i)] - \frac{1}{(r + 1)^t} [S* - S(p_i)] > 0$$

or

$$- \frac{1}{(1 + r)^t} r\epsilon + \left[\frac{1}{(1 + r)^{t-1}} - \frac{1}{(1 + r)^t} \right] [S* - S(p_i)] > 0$$

or

$$- \frac{r}{(1 + r)^t} \epsilon + \frac{r}{(1 + r)^t} [S* - S(p_i)] > 0$$

But this holds from $S* - S(p_i) > \epsilon$.   q.e.d.

It is good to know that the performance index guides the public enterprise to a welfare level $S*$. But we would also like $S*$ to be as high as possible.

Theorem

$S*$ is a local welfare maximum.

    Proof. As $p_i \in B$, which is compact, there is a subsequence $\{p_{i_s}\}_{s=1}^{\infty}$ converging to $p*$. By continuity $S(p*) = S*$.

    If $p*$ was not a local maximum, there would exist a differentiable path $p(t)$, $t \in [0,1]$, $p(0) = p*$, such that $S[p(t)]$ is strictly increasing. Then lemma II would contradict the limit property of $S*$.   q.e.d.

    In fact, we expect $S*$ to be a global welfare maximum. At least for small discount rates or in the presence of large potential welfare gains, the incentive mechanism leads away from inferior local maxima (lemma II). This is why we do not suggest more stringent incentives and do not require the nonnegativity of the performance index in each period. If we required $I_i \geq 0$ for all periods i, welfare would always be increasing (7). The sequence $\{S(p_i)\}_{i=1}^{\infty}$ would be monotonic on a compact set and thus would converge to a local welfare maximum by lemma II. However, this local maximum could be far from the global optimum and there may be no feasible path away from this inferior outcome.

Although welfare converges, the prices p_i need not converge. Welfare may be flat in the relevant region, and the management may be indifferent between these prices with identical welfare levels. Except for such implausible mathematical oddities, we expect the sequence p_i to converge to $p*$ with $S(p*) = S*$. Then we have the following result.

Corollary

If det $[\partial^2 V(p*)/\partial p^2] \neq 0$, the sequence of prices converges to marginal cost prices.

Proof. At $p*$ we must have

$$\frac{\partial S(p*)}{\partial p} = 0$$

or equivalently

$$\left(p* - \frac{\partial C}{\partial x} \right) \frac{\partial x}{\partial p} = 0$$

Now,

$$\frac{\partial^2 V}{\partial p^2} = - \frac{\partial x}{\partial p} \quad \text{implies} \quad p* = \frac{\partial C}{\partial x} \quad \text{q.e.d.}$$

Notes

1 F. Ramsey, "A Contribution to the Theory of Taxation," *Economic Journal* 37 (1927):4–61.
2 R. D. Willig, "What Can Markets Control?" in *Perspectives on Postal Service Issues*, ed. R. Sherman (Washington, D.C.: American Enterprise Institute for Public Policy Research, 1980), pp. 137–60.
3 H. Demsetz, "Why Regulate Utilities?" *Journal of Law and Economics* 11 (1968):55–66.
4 C. C. von Weizsäcker, *Barriers to Entry, A Theoretical Treatment* (Berlin, Heidelberg, New York: Springer Verlag, 1980).
5 O. E. Williamson, "Franchise Bidding for Natural Monopolies in General and with Respect to CATV," *Bell Journal of Economics* 7 (1976):73–104.
6 V. P. Goldberg, "Competitive Bidding and the Production of Precontract Information," *Bell Journal of Economics* 8 (1977):250–61.
7 I. Vogelsang and J. Finsinger, "A Regulatory Adjustment Process for Optimal Pricing by Multiproduct Monopoly Firms," *Bell Journal of Economics* 10 (1979):157–71.
8 J. Finsinger, "Wohlfahrtsoptimale Preisstrukturen von Unternehmen unter staatlicher Regulierung" (Ph.D. diss., University of Bonn, 1979).
9 D. Sappington, "Strategic Firm Behavior Under a Dynamic Regulatory Adjustment Process," *Bell Journal of Economics* 11 (1980):360–72.

10 Ibid.
11 Finsinger, "Wohlfahrtsoptimale Preisstrukturen."
12 H. Averch and L. L. Johnson, "Behavior of the Firm Under Regulatory Constraint," *American Economic Review* 52 (1962):1052–69.
13 Vogelsang and Finsinger, "Regulatory Adjustment Process."
14 R. Roy, *De l'utilité* (Paris: Hermann, 1942).
15 M. Loeb and W. A. Magat, "A Decentralized Method for Utility Regulation," *Journal of Law and Economics* 22 (1979):399–404.
16 Vogelsang and Finsinger, "Regulatory Adjustment Process."
17 Ibid.
18 Sappington, "Strategic Firm Behavior."
19 R. H. Coase, "The Marginal Cost Controversy," *Economica* 13 (1946):169–82.
20 Vogelsang and Finsinger, "Regulatory Adjustment Process."
21 B. Röper, "Die Wettbewerbsfunktion gemeinwirtschaftlicher Unternehmen in Theorie und Praxis," in *Gemeinwirtschaft im Wandel der Gesellschaft*, ed. G. Rittig and H. B. Ortlieb (Berlin: Duncker & Humblot, 1972), and B. Röper, *Theorie und Praxis der gemeinwirtschaftlichen Konzeption* (Göttingen: Schwartz, 1976); C. A. Andreae and W. Glahe, *Das Gegengewichtsprinzip in der Wettbewerbsordnung*, Vol. 1, *Wirtschaftliche Macht und Wettbewerb* (Cologne, 1966); K. Kühne, "Das Gemeinwirtschaftliche Unternehmen als Wettbewerbsfaktor," *Schriftenreihe Gemeinwirtschaft*, Nr. 6, Europa-Verlag, Frankfurt, 1971; and J. Goldberg, "Gemeinwirtschaft als Gegenmacht," *Gewerkschaftliche Monatshefte* 13 (1972).

15 Public enterprise versus regulation when costs are uncertain

Michael Manove

Public control of economic activity takes two major institutional forms: public ownership and economic regulation. Of these, public ownership is the more profound. In principle, the government has direct control over the entire range of managerial instruments of a publicly owned enterprise. The institution of economically regulated private enterprise, by comparison, provides the government with only indirect influence on enterprise behavior.

One potential advantage of public ownership and management is the ability of managers to react in the public interest to new information developed at the enterprise level. Although economic regulators can influence the managers of a private enterprise with a system of economic rewards and punishments, the objective of those managers must be in part to serve the interests of the private owners. Of course, large economic enterprises, whether public or private, share the problem that managers may act in their own self-interest rather than in the interest of the owners. However, to the extent that managers, given the information they have, do act in the interest of the owners, public enterprise can be expected to have an advantage over regulated private enterprise in achieving public objectives. In this chapter, I attempt to analyze the factors that determine the size of this advantage for the special case of a publicly owned or regulated industry with uncertain costs. My primary objective is to gain some insight into the value of the information that may be available to the management of a publicly owned enterprise but not available to the public regulators of a privately owned enterprise.

15.1 The setting

Consider an industry composed of several enterprises, all producing the same homogeneous good for a closed domestic market. Suppose that each enterprise faces uncertain and possibly different costs. These costs vary stochastically over time, and there may be a number of sources of this variation. We shall analyze the case in which the entire marginal-cost function of each enterprise can shift up or down because of a change in one or more random variables.

This research was supported by the Economics Program of the U.S. National Science Foundation, grant no. SES 7523287.

297

As an example, consider an industry in which several enterprises are producing a basic industrial good, say electric motors. The marginal-cost curve for motors produced by each enterprise can shift up or down for a number of reasons. A high incidence of labor absenteeism could develop. Unexpected breakdowns of major capital equipment could occur. Shortages of important inputs like copper wire could appear. Some of these problems are specific to our enterprise; others are industry-wide.

The total social value of the output of each enterprise depends on the total quantity of output produced by all the enterprises. To achieve the most efficient allocation of production among the enterprises, the marginal cost to each producing enterprise at its own level of production must be equated to the marginal social benefits of aggregate production. We will analyze the extent to which this goal can be achieved under different forms of ownership and control.

15.2   Information availability

The optimal level of production for a given enterprise depends not only on its own cost function but on the cost functions of all other enterprises producing the same good. Optimal production levels also depend on the social-benefits function – the function that describes the relationship between the social value of aggregate output and the quantity of that output. Because of the uncertain and varying nature of enterprise cost functions, it is normally impossible for one agency to have all this information in one place at the time production decisions must be made. This precludes the possibility of achieving an optimal production pattern. The extent to which this optimum can be approximated in different institutional settings depends on the hierarchical structure of the industry and the information available at each level of that structure.

Suppose that the industrial hierarchy has two levels: a central-administration level and an enterprise-management level. Each enterprise has its own enterprise management. In the regulatory scenario, the center acts as regulator and specifies the parameters that determine the revenue function of each enterprise. In the public-enterprise scenario, the center issues instructions to the enterprise managers that are contingent on outcomes of future cost variations. For purposes of comparison, we will also discuss a "competitive" scenario in which the center is replaced by a free market.

The center is assumed to have complete information about the social-benefits function. The center also knows the statistical parameters of the cost variations at the enterprise level, but it does not know, nor can it find out, the actual outcomes of those cost variations. The center is informed, after the fact, of specific enterprise production levels, however, so that, as an economic regulator, the center can specify enterprise revenue functions, which depend on the production levels.

Enterprise management, both public and private, is assumed to have complete information about the outcome of cost variations within its own enterprise before production decisions are made. Moreover, management knows the source of these variations. As we shall see, this latter information can be of considerable value. However, the management of one enterprise has no knowledge of cost variations within another enterprise.

15.3 The model

The framework used for my analysis is in part a generalization and in part a simplification of models developed by Martin L. Weitzman,[1] and much of my inspiration was derived from his work.

Suppose there are n identical enterprises with uncertain costs, as described above. Let $(x_1, \ldots, x_n)$ be the vector of output levels of the n enterprises, with x_i denoting the output of enterprise i. The marginal-cost function of enterprise i is assumed to be constant with respect to output x_i and to have an expected value given by the constant c, invariant over i. There are two types of stochastic cost variations given by the random variables ϵ_i and ϕ, respectively. The first type, ϵ_i, is specific to enterprise i and may be a result of such factors as the local weather, the health of workers, and the condition of plant and equipment. The second type, ϕ, is common to all enterprises; this variation may result from input price changes or shortages of inputs. We assume that the ϵ's and ϕ have an expected value of zero and are uncorrelated. Hence, for all i,

$$E\epsilon_i = E\phi = 0 \text{ and for } i \neq j, E\epsilon_i\epsilon_j = E\epsilon_i\phi = 0$$

Furthermore, the variance of all the ϵ's is assumed to be the same, so that for all i, $\sigma^2(\epsilon_i) = \sigma_\epsilon^2$.

We can now specify the marginal-cost function for enterprise i as:

$$C_i'(x_i \,|\, \epsilon_i, \phi) = c + \epsilon_i + \phi \tag{1}$$

It is best to picture (1) as a flat marginal-cost curve that moves up and down randomly, as illustrated in Figure 15.1.

A marginal social-benefits function is also specified. There is a nonmarket analog of demand. We assume that marginal benefits is a linearly decreasing function of total industry output. This function is given by

$$B'(X) = \alpha - \beta X \tag{2}$$

where $X = \Sigma_i x_i$ is industry output, and $\alpha, \beta > 0$ are constants. This function is also illustrated in Figure 15.1.

Assuming that there are no fixed costs or fixed benefits, we obtain the following total cost and benefit functions:

$$C_i(x_i) = (c + \phi + \epsilon_i) x_i \tag{3}$$

$$B(X) = \alpha X - \frac{\beta}{2} X^2 \tag{4}$$

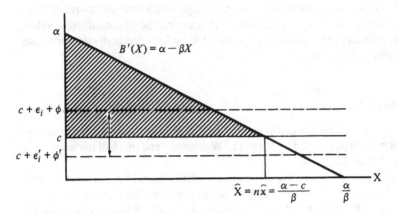

Figure 15.1. Production and welfare with uncertain costs in the no-information scenario.

We define social surplus S to be total benefits minus the sum of total costs. S will depend on the allocation of production among the enterprises and on the outcome of all the variations in cost. Therefore, we have

$$S(x_i, \ldots, x_n \mid \epsilon_i, \ldots, \epsilon_n, \phi) = B(\Sigma_i x_i) - \Sigma_i C_i(x_i \mid \epsilon_i, \phi) \qquad (5)$$

We now proceed to establish two benchmark levels of efficiency, one corresponding to production plans made with no *ex post* information about the ϵ_i's and ϕ, and the other corresponding to production plans made with full *ex post* information about all ϵ_i's and ϕ.

15.4   The no-information scenario

Suppose now that the center must set output targets with no knowledge of the actual outcome of the ϵ_i's and ϕ. If the center is risk neutral and maximizes expected social surplus, it will derive a production target for the entire industry but will be indifferent to the allocation of that target among the enterprises. This is because the enterprises are identical *ex ante* and have constant marginal costs.

The value of $\hat{X}$ is determined as follows. Recalling that

$$E\epsilon_i = E\phi = 0$$

we have

$$ES = B(X) - \Sigma c x_i$$

Appropriate substitutions yield

$$ES = \alpha X - \frac{\beta}{2} X^2 - cX \qquad (6)$$

Thus, if $X = \hat{X}$ maximizes ES, we have

$$0 = \alpha - \beta\hat{X} - c$$

so that

$$\hat{X} = \frac{\alpha - c}{\beta} \tag{7}$$

If the center chooses to divide the production allocation equally among the enterprises, each enterprise will receive the target

$$\hat{x} = \frac{\alpha - c}{n\beta} \tag{8}$$

The intuitive explanation of this result is apparent from Figure 15.1. The expected value of social surplus corresponding to (7) is obtained by substituting (7) into (6). We have

$$E\hat{S} = \frac{(\alpha - c)^2}{2\beta} \tag{9}$$

This is the area of the shaded triangle in Figure 15.1. Later we will compare the welfare implications of this no-information scenario with that of other scenarios.

15.5 The full-information scenario

Suppose now that the center has complete information about the actual values of the ϵ's and ϕ at the time production targets must be set. How should the center determine these targets? Because we have constant costs, the answer in this model is especially simple: All production should be carried on by the firm with the lowest cost, and all other firms should temporarily shut down. If $\epsilon_m = \min_i\{\epsilon_i\}$, the production target for the firm with minimum costs should be

$$X_f = \frac{\alpha - c - \epsilon_m - \phi}{\beta} \tag{10}$$

and the expected value of social surplus as defined by (5) in the full-information scenario is

$$ES_f = E\left[\frac{(\alpha - c - \epsilon_m - \phi)^2}{2\beta}\right] \tag{11}$$

The value of ES_f depends on the frequency distribution of ϵ_m, the minimum of the ϵ_i's. Later in the chapter, we will compute ES_f for a specific distribution of the ϵ_i's and ϕ. Clearly, ES_f is greater than $E\hat{S}$, and the expected value of social surplus associated with other scenarios will always lie between these two values.

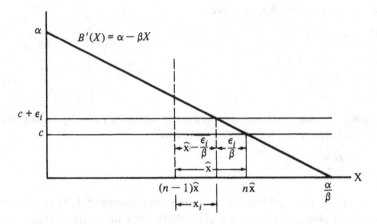

Figure 15.2. Optimal response to enterprise-specific cost variations in the public-enterprise scenario.

15.6 Public enterprise

In the public-enterprise scenario, the center is assumed to know only the benefits function and the statistical parameters of the cost function. The center must instruct the enterprise managers on how to react to cost variations. The managers will make the ultimate production decisions after observing the outcome of their own cost variations.

In what form should the managers be instructed? The center can specify a number of alternative production levels contingent on the outcomes of the stochastic cost variations. Mathematically stated, a function of the form $x_i = x_i(\epsilon_i, \phi)$ can be specified for enterprise i. After Weitzman, we shall call this function a response function.

The center's problem is to find the optimal response function for the purpose of maximizing social surplus. The optimal response function will achieve a higher level of expected welfare than could be achieved under the no-information regime, because managers now can use their knowledge of actual costs in making their production decisions. However, expected surplus will be lower than the full-information level, because managers do not know the actual costs to other producers.

We will show presently that the optimal response function $x_i^*(\epsilon_i, \phi)$ has the following form (provided that the right-hand side is nonnegative)

$$x_i^*(\epsilon_i, \phi) = \hat{x} - \frac{1}{\beta}\epsilon_i - \frac{1}{n\beta}\phi \tag{12}$$

Intuitively, this function is easy to justify. Recall that ϵ_i affects and is known only to enterprise i, so that the expected value of production for other enterprises is

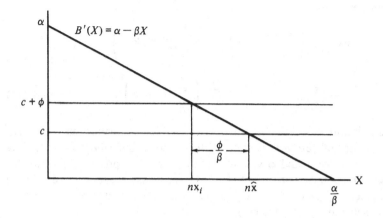

Figure 15.3. Optimal response to industry-wide cost variations in the public-enterprise scenario.

independent of ϵ_i. Therefore, if ϵ_i is different from 0, enterprise i should count on absorbing the entire change in production by itself. Because $-\beta$ is the slope of the marginal-benefits function, and because it is optimal to keep marginal costs equal to marginal benefits, an increase of ϵ_i in marginal cost requires a decrease of $(1/\beta)\epsilon_i$ in output. This line of reasoning is illustrated in Figure 15.2.

The variable ϕ, however, affects all enterprises equally, so that each enterprise should absorb only $1/n$ of the reduction of output indicated by an increase in cost of size ϕ. That is why the coefficient of ϕ in (12) is $1/n\phi$. This argument is illustrated in Figure 15.3.

We now proceed to demonstrate that (12) gives the solution of the following problem:

$$\max_{\{x(.,.)\}} \quad ES[x_1(\epsilon_1, \phi), \ldots, x_n(\epsilon_n, \phi)]$$

where $\{x(.,.)\}$ is the set of response functions.

We show that (12) satisfies the ith first-order condition. We have

$$S(x_1, \ldots, x_j, \ldots, x_n) = B\left(\sum_{j \neq i} x_j + x_i\right)$$

$$- \sum_{j \neq i} (c + \epsilon_j + \phi)x_j - (c + \epsilon_i + \phi)x_i \qquad (13)$$

Substituting, we have

$$S = (\alpha - c)\left(\sum_{j \neq i} x_j + x_i\right) - \phi\left(\sum_{j \neq i} x_j + x_i\right)$$

$$- \sum_{j \neq i} x_j \epsilon_j - x_i \epsilon_i - \frac{\beta}{2}\left(\sum_{j \neq i} x_j + x_i\right)^2 \tag{14}$$

At this point, to make our demonstration tractable, we assume that the probability distribution of ϵ_i and ϕ is discrete, with $f(\epsilon_i, \phi)$ denoting the joint probability that given values of ϵ_i and ϕ will materialize. We now proceed to verify the first-order condition for particular values of ϵ_i and ϕ, say $\bar{\epsilon}_i$ and $\bar{\phi}$. To do this we calculate the expected value of S and differentiate it with respect to $x_i(\bar{\epsilon}_i, \bar{\phi})$. Substituting (12) for x_j, $j \neq i$ yields

$$\frac{\partial ES}{\partial x_i(\bar{\epsilon}_i, \bar{\phi})} = f(\bar{\epsilon}_i, \bar{\phi})\{\alpha - c - \bar{\phi} - \bar{\epsilon}_i$$

$$- \beta\left[(n-1)\hat{x} - \frac{n-1}{n\beta}\bar{\phi}\right] - \beta x_i(\bar{\epsilon}_i, \bar{\phi})\} \tag{15}$$

Setting $\partial ES/\partial x_i(\bar{\epsilon}_i, \bar{\phi}) = 0$ and solving for $x_i(\bar{\epsilon}_i, \bar{\phi})$ yields the function given in (12). The quadratic nature of the benefits function guarantees that the solution of this first-order condition maximizes social surplus.

We conclude that in the public-enterprise scenario, the managers of enterprises should be instructed to react to cost variations according to (12). Keep in mind that under our informational assumptions, cost variations cannot be verified by the center. Whether or not public-enterprise managers actually follow (12) would be a matter of trust.

15.7   Economic regulation

Suppose now that all the enterprises are privately owned and the center acts as an economic regulator. Enterprise managers maximize profits, given the incentive structure specified by the center. Any incentive structure that the center provides to the enterprises can depend only on information that the center can obtain, and the center can obtain information about only the social-benefits function, the production levels of enterprises, and the statistical parameters of enterprise cost functions. In addition, we assume that an incentive structure specified for an enterprise must be sufficiently well defined in advance so that the management can precisely determine the outcome of that structure contingent only on its own behavior.

The most general incentive structure that conforms to those conditions is a revenue function whose only variable is enterprise output. The parameters of this revenue function may depend on the social-benefits function and the statistical characteristics of the cost functions. Therefore, in the regulatory scenario, the problem of the regulator is to choose the best of all such revenue functions.

Suppose the center specifies the revenue function $R_i = R_i(x_i)$ for enterprise i. Then the enterprise management will set x_i so that marginal cost equals marginal revenue, or

$$R'(x_i) = c + \epsilon_i + \phi \qquad (16)$$

Because c is a constant, we may solve (16) for x_i to obtain a solution of the form:

$$x_i = g(\epsilon_i + \phi) \qquad (17)$$

where g is a function obtained from the inverse function of R'.

The function g is a response function. This function yields the reaction of the enterprise to cost variations, given a particular revenue function specified by the center. We shall say that the function g is the response function *elicited* by the revenue function R.

Note that g, and any response function elicited by a revenue function, has a very special form. The general response function can be a function with each different cost variation as an independent argument, whereas the value of g is completely determined by the *sum* of the cost variations. This makes sense, because with a revenue function that depends only on output and a goal of profit maximization, there is no reason for the source of a cost to be relevant to the decision-making process. Put differently, there is no way the center can use a revenue function to induce a response function in which costs from different sources are treated differently. Clearly, therefore, the optimal response function given by (12) cannot be elicited in the regulatory scenario.

What is the best response function that can be elicited by the regulators? So far we have shown that response functions only in the form $x_i = g(\epsilon_i + \phi)$ can be elicited. We should point out, however, that all such functions can be elicited. If $g(\epsilon_i + \phi)$ is any desired response function, the center need only define the revenue function as:

$$R(\bar{x}_i) = \int_0^{\bar{x}_i} [c + g^{-1}(x_i)] \, dx_i \qquad (18)$$

This means that the "best" response function that can be elicited by regulation is the function of the form $x_i = g(\epsilon_i + \phi)$ that maximizes social surplus. Suppose $\tilde{x}_i = \tilde{g}(\epsilon_i + \phi)$ is that surplus-maximizing response function. Then, as can be shown by a demonstration similar to the derivation of (12), g must be defined by the following function (provided that the right-hand side is nonnegative):

$$\hat{x}_i = \hat{x} - \frac{1}{\nu}(\epsilon_i + \phi) \tag{19}$$

where

$$\nu = \frac{\sigma_\epsilon^2}{\sigma_\epsilon^2 + \sigma_\phi^2}\beta + \frac{\sigma_\phi^2}{\sigma_\epsilon^2 + \sigma_\phi^2}n\beta \tag{20}$$

Expression (20) has a useful heuristic interpretation. In the otpimal response function (12), ϵ_i has the coefficient $1/\beta$ and ϕ has the coefficient $1/n\beta$. In the regulatory situation both ϵ_i and ϕ must have the same coefficient, denoted by $1/\nu$. It should not be surprising therefore that in the best such response function, ν is a weighted average of β and $n\beta$. The weights are the fractions of the total variance of costs caused by ϵ_i and ϕ, respectively.

15.8   Welfare implications

It should be clear that under our information assumptions, full information provides the most expected social surplus, followed by public enterprise, regulation, and no information, in that order.

Expected surplus in the no-information regime is given by (9), and expected surplus in the full-information regime is given by (11). By evaluating the right-hand side of (11), we obtain

$$ES_f = \frac{(\alpha - c)^2}{2\beta} + \frac{\sigma_\epsilon^2 + \mu_{\epsilon m}^2}{2\beta} - \frac{(\alpha - c)}{\beta}\mu_{\epsilon m} + \frac{\sigma_\phi^2}{2\beta} \tag{21}$$

where $\mu_{\epsilon m}$ and $\sigma_{\epsilon m}^2$ are the mean and variance, respectively, of the random variable ϵ_m (the minimum of the ϵ's). We define Δ_f to be the fractional increment of ES_f over $E\hat{S}$, that is,

$$\Delta_f = \frac{ES_f - E\hat{S}}{E\hat{S}}$$

From (21) and (9), we get

$$\Delta_f = \frac{\sigma_{\epsilon m}^2 + \mu_{\epsilon m}^2}{(\alpha - c)^2} - \frac{2\mu_{\epsilon m}}{(\alpha - c)} + \frac{\sigma_\phi^2}{(\alpha - c)^2} \tag{22}$$

We shall interpret (22) below.

Be substituting (12) into (3) and (4) and the results into (5) we obtain the following expected surplus for the public-enterprise scenario:

$$ES^* = \frac{(\alpha - c)^2}{\beta} + \frac{1}{2\beta}\{n\sigma_\epsilon^2 + \sigma_\phi^2\} \tag{23}$$

The fractional increment of ES^* over $E\hat{S}$ is given by

$$\Delta^* = \frac{n\sigma_\epsilon^2}{(\alpha - c)^2} + \frac{\sigma_\phi^2}{(\alpha - c)^2} \tag{24}$$

By using equation (19), we can obtain analogous results for the economic-regulation scenario. We have

$$E\tilde{S} = \frac{(\alpha - c)^2}{2\beta} + \frac{n}{2\beta} \frac{(\sigma_\epsilon^2 + \sigma_\phi^2)^2}{\sigma_\epsilon^2 + n\sigma_\phi^2} \tag{25}$$

and

$$\tilde{\Delta} = \frac{n}{(\alpha - c)^2} \frac{(\sigma_\epsilon^2 + \sigma_\phi^2)^2}{\sigma_\epsilon^2 + n\sigma_\phi^2} \tag{26}$$

It is apparent that both Δ^* and $\tilde{\Delta}$ increase as the number of firms, n, increases. This means that compared with the no-information scenario, the relative advantage of both the public-enterprise scenario and the regulation scenario increases as the number of firms increases. Furthermore both Δ^* and $\tilde{\Delta}$ increase as σ_ϵ^2 and σ_ϕ^2 increase. This is because information about ϵ and ϕ is worth more, the greater is their potential variation.

What about the comparison of regulation and public enterprise? Using (26) and (24) we obtain the ratio $\tilde{\Delta}:\Delta^*$

$$\frac{\tilde{\Delta}}{\Delta^*} = \frac{n(\sigma_\epsilon^2 + \sigma_\phi^2)^2}{(\sigma_\epsilon^2 + n\sigma_\phi^2)(n\sigma_\epsilon^2 + \sigma_\phi^2)}$$

Consider $\tilde{\Delta}:\Delta^*$ to be a ratio of the efficiency of regulation as compared to the efficiency of public enterprise.

If either σ_ϵ^2 or σ_ϕ^2 is 0, then $\tilde{\Delta}:\Delta^* = 1$. This means that regulation performs as well as public enterprise if there is only one true source of cost variation. If, on the contrary, $\sigma_\epsilon^2 = \sigma_\phi^2$, so that the degree of cost variation from both sources is the same, then $\tilde{\Delta}:\Delta^*$ is minimized. This outcome results from an advantage enjoyed by public enterprises in this informational setting, namely, that publicly employed managers can be instructed to treat different costs differently, whereas privately employed managers cannot be induced to do so.

If $\sigma_\epsilon^2 = \sigma_\phi^2$, then we have

$$\frac{\tilde{\Delta}}{\Delta^*} = \frac{4n}{(n + 1)^2}$$

This means that in the equal-variation case, regulation yields about 89% of the social-surplus increment accruing from public enterprise if there are 2 enterprises in the industry, 75% if there are 3 enterprises, 55% for 5, and 33% for 10. This is because the more enterprises there are, the more important it is for each enterprise to distinguish between cost variations peculiar to itself and cost variations that affect the entire industry. Indeed, with a very large number of enterprises in the industry, any enterprise that encounters a cost increase of the former type should curtail production drastically, whereas increases of the latter type can be practically ignored.

It now remains to compare public enterprise to the full-information regime. At the outset, we can conclude that even under the most favorable circumstances, the public-enterprise rule, (12), must result in considerably less surplus than the full-information rule of producing all output in the firm with the lowest cost. The public-enterprise rule has two problems. First, production at an enterprise is increased or decreased depending on whether its own realized ϵ is less or greater than the true (population) mean, regardless of the realized ϵ's of other firms. Thus, if all firms have positive ϵ's, the production level of all firms will decrease, even though far more social surplus could normally be created by increasing the output of the relatively low-cost firms. This problem is far more likely to be important when there are only a few firms than where there are many. This is because with few firms the true statistical distribution of costs may differ substantially from the sample distribution of those actually realized.

Second, the public-enterprise rule increases the output of all firms whose costs are below normal, whereas the full-information rule increases the output only of the least costly firm. The public-enterprise rule cannot be improved in this regard, because the assumed informational environment of public enterprise precludes the direct comparison of the realized ϵ's of the different firms.

The expected public-enterprise surplus can be compared mathematically with the expected full-information surplus, but this comparison is a tricky one. If the distribution of ϵ and ϕ is not specified carefully, the level of public-enterprise output as given by (12) will become negative and be invalid. Therefore, we now make the added assumption that ϵ and ϕ are distributed uniformly about 0, and the upper limits of their distributions are sufficiently low so as to guarantee that the right-hand side of (12) will be positive.

More precisely, let us assume that the ϵ's are distributed uniformly on the interval $[-r_\epsilon/2, r_\epsilon/2]$ and that ϕ is distributed uniformly on the interval $[-r_\phi/2, r_\phi/2]$. By requiring that

$$r_\epsilon < \frac{\alpha - c}{n}$$

and

$$r_\phi < \frac{\alpha - c}{2}$$

we ensure that (12) will always yield a positive result.

For a uniform distribution, $r_\epsilon = \sqrt{12}\ \sigma_\epsilon$, so that

$$\sigma_\epsilon < \frac{\alpha - c}{4\sqrt{3}\ n} \tag{27}$$

Furthermore, given a uniform distribution, it becomes possible to evaluate the parameters $\mu_{\epsilon m}$ and $\sigma_{\epsilon m}^2$ for the minimum ϵ sampled in equation (22). One can derive the following relationships

$$\mu_{\epsilon m} = -\frac{n-1}{n+1}\ \sqrt{3}\ \sigma_\epsilon \tag{28}$$

and

$$\mu_{\epsilon m}^2 + \sigma_{\epsilon m}^2 = 3\ \frac{n^3 + n + 2}{(n+2)(n+1)^2}\ \sigma_\epsilon^2 \tag{29}$$

Forming the ratio $\Delta^*{:}\Delta_f$ from (22) and (24) and substituting in (28) and (29), we obtain

$$\frac{\Delta^*}{\Delta_f} = \frac{n\sigma_\epsilon^2 + \sigma_\phi^2}{3A_n\sigma_\epsilon^2 + 2\sqrt{3}\ B_n\ (\alpha - c)\ \sigma_\epsilon + \sigma_\phi^2} \tag{30}$$

where A_n and B_n are functions of n that converge to 1 from below. The inequality in (27) implies that the first term of the numerator of (30) is less than the second term of the denominator. Thus $\Delta^*{:}\Delta_f < 1$, a fact we knew all along. Less obvious, however, is that $\Delta^*{:}\Delta_f$ increases as n increases. This means that in our model, the efficiency of public enterprise improves in comparison with full information as the number of firms gets large. This comes about because statistical knowledge is a good proxy for hard information when the sample is large.

15.9 Conclusion

We have analyzed the problem of properly allocating production between enterprises when costs are uncertain and information is limited. We have shown that in a situation where cost variations can be monitored only at an enterprise level, public enterprise has an advantage over economic regulation in the creation of social surplus. Furthermore, both these institutions can perform better than a hierarchical regime in which strict quantity targets are set without accurate knowledge of costs. This hierarchical regime is inefficient because once targets are set the enterprise management is no longer in a position to use new information about costs as it materializes.

We have placed all cost variations into two classes: those that are peculiar to a single enterprise and those that are common to the entire industry. We have shown that the advantage of public enterprise is greatest when the variations of these two types are most equal in magnitude. Furthermore, the advantage of public enterprise increases as the number of enterprises increases.

These results follow directly from the informational assumptions we have made and cannot be easily generalized to apply to cases with different informational availability. If there is a lesson to be learned from this chapter, it is that in deciding between different modes of public control of enterprises, information is an important factor and should be carefully modeled.

In regard to the efficiency of pure competition in the allocation of production between enterprises, it should be noted that the efficiency of the competitive mode will turn on the amount of information available to the proprietor of each firm. We must ask: What did the proprietor know and when did he know it? If at the time production decisions must be made, each proprietor knows his own costs and the costs to every other enterprise as well, then every proprietor will be able to predict future prices of his output, and the full-information level of efficiency can be reached. If future markets exist, the traders on these markets may be able to obtain relevant information about the costs of many enterprises and thereby promote efficiency. If each proprietor knows only about his own costs but can distinguish between local and industry-wide cost increases and make the appropriate inferences about future output prices, then a level of efficiency equal to that of the public-enterprise mode can be obtained. However, if each proprietor knows only about his own cost variations and cannot make useful inferences about cost variations in other firms, the level of efficiency will be lower than that achieved by economic regulation.

Our comparison of the efficiency of various forms of ownership and control was derived from the informational environment we associated with each of those forms. Information is all important to the goal of economic efficiency. It is by no means axiomatic that competitive institutions produce more information than public institutions do. In fact, to the extent that information is a public good, they may produce even less.

Note

1 See Martin L. Weitzman, "Prices vs. Quantities," *Review of Economic Studies* (Oct. 1974):477–91; and Martin L. Weitzman, "Optimal Rewards for Economic Regulation," *American Economic Review* (Sept. 1978):683–91.

Part VII

How does public enterprise compare with other intervention mechanisms in overcoming particular problems?

16 Public enterprise versus other methods of state intervention as instruments of redistribution policy: the Malaysian experience

Richard D. Mallon

Malaysia provides a fascinating case study of the explicit use of public enterprise for the purpose of redistributing asset ownership and employment in favor of disadvantaged, indigenous citizens of the country. This policy was adopted after it was decided that less direct methods of state intervention in the economy could not achieve desired results rapidly enough. This experience therefore offers the opportunity of comparing the effectiveness of alternative policy strategies and tools for achieving common objectives, although, as will be seen, the new strategy has been implemented in ways that make comparisons extremely difficult, if not impossible, to make in practice.

At the time of independence in 1957, participation in economic activity was highly specialized along ethnic lines. The indigenous Malay, or *bumiputra,* community was engaged mainly in nonplantation agriculture, whereas other ethnic groups, notably the Chinese, were dominant in the so-called modern sectors: industry, commerce, plantations, and mines. On the other hand, the Malay community, which accounted for about half the total population, was dominant politically. The government was therefore naturally concerned about redressing economic imbalances.

During the following decade government redistribution policy focused on four areas. First, it developed programs to promote Malay participation in business. The Rural and Industrial Development Authority (RIDA, renamed MARA in 1965) provided small-business loans and technical assistance to Malay entrepreneurs, and Bank Bumiputra was founded to extend credit to Malays by accepting land from Malay reservations as collateral. Similarly, Malaysian Industrial Development Finance (MIDF) provided financial assistance and through two subsidiaries, MIDA and MIEL, prepared feasibility and market studies for bumiputra businessmen and sold or rented factory building units under favorable terms.

Second, the government set up institutions to encourage the indigenous community to save and invest. An effort was made to reserve shares in local capital issues for Malays, and the Mara Unit Trust, established in 1967, mobilized and invested small savings in modern business activities. Three years later a stock exchange was organized exclusively for Malay security trading.

313

Third, the government designed programs to improve the quality of indigenous human resources. The Mara Institute of Technology provided vocational and technical training for Malays at the intermediate level, and places were reserved in higher educational institutions for Malays under special scholarship programs.

Fourth, to stimulate increased demand for bumiputra employees, the government undertook an affirmative-action program. The Public Works Department (PWD) gave preference to bumiputra firms in bidding on contracts, and indigenous people received preferential treatment in the allocation of truck and taxi licenses. Pioneer industries that received special tax incentives were also pressured to hire Malays in their work forces.

These policies did not, however, achieve rapid results. By 1969 Malays still owned a mere 1.5% of the share capital of limited companies, and they were still grossly underrepresented in modern business employment. According to the Socio-Economic Survey of Households in 1967–68, only 22% of administrative, executive, and managerial positions in the country were held by Malays, and their participation in clerical, secretarial, and sales employment was only slightly higher. In manufacturing as a whole a disappointing 24% of the work force was Malay, mostly employed in less skilled jobs, and even in small-scale industry, which presumably benefited from the government's special promotion programs, less than 8% of the chief executive officers were Malay.[1]

A decade is of course a very short period of time in which to restructure a society without strong, direct state intervention in the ownership and operation of economic activity. Indirect state intervention policies were easier to evade. Numerous "Ali-Baba" firms, ostensibly operated by Malays but in fact owned and controlled by other ethnic groups, cropped up to take advantage of bumiputra promotion programs and preferences. Even government agencies established to run the new programs tended to divert their attention to more commercially profitable activities, as they were at the same time under strong pressure to be "efficient" and businesslike and to become financially self-sustaining. As late as 1971–5 bumiputra individuals and firms accounted for only 17% of MIDF's loans, and Bank Bumiputra was almost as conservative. An exception was MARA, which dealt exclusively with Malay clientele.

As MARA was not expected to become financially self-sustaining, it turned into a kind of social-welfare organization. Almost all its staff was bumiputra, most of whom had little or no previous experience in business or finance. They apparently viewed their objectives as maximizing the flow of credit to borrowers and the movement of students through special training programs. A group of outside experts hired to evaluate MARA's performance reported that

there has been too much emphasis on the amount of loans and not enough emphasis on ensuring that the project financed is viable... Targets should be the number and value of successful projects and the number of bumiputras attaining gainful employment, rather than the number of [loans made and of] students completing training programs.[2]

The default rate on loans was exceedingly high, and tangible results from both credit and training programs were limited, except for the Mara Institute of Technology.

Affirmative-action programs also proved difficult to enforce. Preferences granted to Malays in licensing trucking firms, for example, were circumvented through the formation of Ali-Baba enterprises, and the new firms also had to face stiff competition from trucks owned by other enterprises supposedly to serve their own needs. These "C"-licensed trucks, which were of course not subject to bumiputra preferences, found a very lucrative business in transporting occasional cargoes of other firms instead of returning home empty. Even in the public sector, agencies under tight budgetary constraints or obliged to meet strict deadlines were loath to give preference to Malay contractors, whom they considered less efficient or more risky. Even after the Treasury issued circulars 16/76 and 11/78 reducing prior deposit requirements and providing monthly advances on small contracts, government contracts awarded to bumiputra firms did not increase noticeably.

The Malaysian government, committed as it was to maintaining a competitive free-enterprise system and to promoting a rapid rate of overall economic growth, might not have considered changing its redistributional policy had it not been for the traumatic events of 1969. The party in power came very close to losing the election in May of that year, and shortly afterward ethnic violence exploded in the capital city, Kuala Lumpur. The main cause of these events was diagnosed as unsatisfactory progress toward redistributing assets and employment. The government therefore decided to launch a New Economic Policy (NEP) whose main objectives were: (1) by 1990, 30% of the equity in Malaysian business should be owned by the bumiputra community, and (2) the distribution of employment by occupational categories should reflect by the same year the overall ethnic distribution of the population.[3]

Most important from the point of our special interest in public enterprise, the Malaysian government decided that to achieve these objectives it would be necessary to increase greatly direct state intervention in the ownership and operation of business enterprise. At the same time it decided that public enterprises would not be created by expropriating or nationalizing existing businesses but by starting new ventures to compete with the private sector. Malaysia's commitment to maintaining a free-enterprise system and to creating a development strategy based on a relatively open, competitive, export-led economy did not change.

16.1 Public enterprise as an instrument of redistribution policy

Prior to adoption of the NEP, the overwhelming share of direct government investment, aside from that made in economic and social infrastructure, was in agricultural land development to improve bumiputra income and employment opportunities in traditional occupations. After 1970 the share of government development expenditure on industry and commerce quintupled, and during the Second Malaysian Plan period, 1971–5, public enterprises absorbed about half of government development expenditures, an amount equal to almost 4% of GDP. Government contributions to public enterprises reached a peak of approximately 6.5% of GDP in 1977, after which their relative importance declined, presumably because the enterprises were better able to finance their investment requirements from retained earnings.

The chief new initiatives undertaken under the NEP were, first, the establishment of the National Corporation (PERNAS) as a public-enterprise holding company to set up wholly owned subsidiaries, joint ventures with private investors, and associated companies with minority government investment. PERNAS was instructed to operate as a commercially profitable enterprise and was given considerable operational autonomy under the direct supervision of the prime minister's office. Second, State Economic Development Corporations (SEDCs), a few of which existed prior to the NEP, spread to all 13 states to build industrial estates, promote small bumiputra businesses, and set up wholly owned and joint ventures on a larger scale. Finally, the central government formed the Urban Development Authority (UDA) in 1971 to carry out programs at the national level similar to those implemented at the state level by the SEDCs.

In addition to these new initiatives, efforts were made to strengthen the Malay business-promotion, savings-and-investment, human-resource-development, and affirmative-action programs begun in the previous period. In 1972 the Credit Guarantee Corporation started to underwrite bumiputra business loans from commercial banks, which were obliged to fix quotas for such loans, initially at 20% of their total credit operations. The government greatly increased budgetary allocations to already existing agencies responsible for carrying out redistribution policies. Development fund appropriations for MARA, for example, rose from $50 million (Malaysian dollars) in 1966–70 to $215 million in 1971–5, and to over $600 million in 1976–80. Most significant, many government statutory authorities and enterprises that had not been set up for the purpose began to organize their own commercial subsidiaries. From a relatively small base prior to 1969, the number of public enterprises (including joint ventures) escalated to more than 700 by the mid-1970s, and their exact number today is unknown.

The shift in redistribution policy from relying on indirect measures to promote greater bumiputra participation in the modern sectors of the economy to more emphasis on direct state intervention appears to have produced desired results with respect to ownership. As can be seen in Table 16.1, Malay ownership of share capital in limited companies increased from 1.5% of the total value of such shares in 1969 to 10.3% in 1978. State-owned enterprises held two-thirds of these shares in trust for the bumiputra community. These enterprises have been earmarked for eventual transfer to individual bumiputra owners and therefore represent potential participation of Malays in actual ownership. However, the par value of shares bears little relation to the real net worth of enterprises with cumulative losses approximately equal to, or exceeding the value of, paid-up capital, of firms with exceedingly high leverage ratios (a common occurrence among

Table 16.1. *Ownership of share capital in limited companies, by ethnic groups*

Owner	1969		1978	
	Millions of Malay dollars	Percent	Millions of Malay dollars	Percent
Malays	70.6	1.5	2,156	10.3
Non-Malays	1,697.1	22.1	9,214	43.7
Foreigners	2,909.8	62.1	9,695	46.0

Source: Figures for 1969, Economic Planning Unit, *Second Malaysia Plan* (Kuala Lumpur: Government of Malaysia, 1970), p. 40; for 1978, Economic Planning Unit, *Mid-Term Review of the Third Malaysia Plan* (Kuala Lumpur: Government of Malaysia, 1979), p. 49.

state-owned enterprises), or of financially successful firms that have reinvested a substantial share of profits without any changes in the number or value of shares (a less common occurrence so far in Malaysia).[5]

The statistical contribution of public enterprises toward achieving NEP targets for redressing imbalances in employment is summarized in Table 16.2. Although the sample of enterprises is incomplete and although employment in government statutory authorities acting as public-enterprise holding companies is not reflected in the table, the general conclusion that seems justified by these figures is that the overall, direct contribution of public enterprise to increasing Malay employment was rather marginal up to 1975, the latest year for which data are available. Furthermore, an increase in the number of Malays employed by public enterprises in certain occupations does not necessarily indicate skill upgrading or improved employment opportunities. Given the relative shortage of experienced and skilled bumiputra professionals and workers, many of them are simply moving from one firm to another in response to the highest bidder; and information gathered on employment in Malaysia does not distinguish clearly between full- and part-time work, nor do occupational classifications reflect accurately differences in professional qualifications.

It must be recognized, however, that the aggregate data in Table 16.2 do not indicate what may be going on in individual sectors. Two-thirds of public enterprises, as measured by paid-up capital or value of sales, were located in service activities in the mid-1970s (banking, insurance, wholesale and retail trade, hotels and restaurants, transportation, real estate, and others), sectors in which Malays have traditionally been especially underrepresented in employment. It is therefore quite possible that bumiputra employment preferences, such as those incorporated in the PERNAS joint venture agreement with the Kuala Lumpur Hilton Hotel,[6] have significantly improved the share of Malays in certain occupations from which they were previously virtually excluded without this fact showing up in a comparison of overall national participation rates. Considerable bumiputra employment is also provided by public enterprises indirectly. Because of

Table 16.2. *Employment of Malays, by occupational categories*

	Public enterprises (1976)		National total (1967–8)		National total (1975)		National total (change)	
	Number (thousands)	Percent of total	Number (thousands)	Percent	Number (thousands)	Percent	Number (thousands)	Percent
Professional, technical, administrative, managerial								
100% government owned	2.2	63.1						
50–99% government owned	1.2	40.7						
0–49% government owned	0.6	29.9						
Total	4.1	47.3	63.5	40.6	99.0	43.4	35.5	49.5
Other occupations								
100% government owned	15.7	91.2						
50–99% government owned	7.5	68.1						
0–49% government owned	7.9	60.5						
Total	31.1	75.3	1,114.1	50.4	1,674.4	52.7	560.3	57.9

Source: Figures for public enterprises computed from responses to questionnaires submitted to the Implementation Coordination Unit of the prime minister's office. National figures from Socio-Economic Survey of Households for 1967–8; figures for 1975 are from Economic Planning Unit, *Mid-Term Review of the Third Malaysia Plan* (Kula Lumpur: Government of Malaysia, 1979).

Table 16.3. *Financial performance of the public-enterprise sector in 1976*
(millions of Malay dollars)

% of government ownership	Total paid-up capital			Total net income/loss	
	Government	Non-government	Total	1976	Cumulative
100%	681.5	—	681.5	653.4	− 133.0
50–99%	242.7	170.4	413.1	0.7	− 48.2
0–49%	81.3	289.3	370.6	46.4	53.3
Total	1,005.5	459.7	1,465.2	700.5	− 127.9

Note: Dash indicates nil.
Source: See Source Note Table 16.2.

government limitations on salaries and other restrictions, state-owned firms frequently find it more advantageous to contract out certain activities rather than to perform them with direct-hire personnel. The logging industry in the state of Perak is a good example: Most public-enterprise logging firms there have only about five employees and carry out the bulk of their operations via contracts with private firms in which Malay employees are likely to predominate.

It is therefore exceedingly difficult to quantify the effective contribution of public enterprises to redistributing ownership and employment in Malaysia. But what can be said about the opportunity cost of public enterprises as an instrument of redistribution policy? Measurement of the opportunity cost of government contributions of equity capital and loans to public enterprises is conceptually straightforward. The return that otherwise could be realized from these resources in the best alternative use is at least equal to the cost of raising government funds in the money market. The difference between this cost and the rate of return earned from investing these resources in public enterprises indicates the order of magnitude of the opportunity cost we are looking for. Available data for 1976 on the financial performance of the public-enterprise sector by share of government ownership is presented in Table 16.3. The rate of return on government equity investment appears negligible in this year for all but minority joint ventures, once the profits of the State Petroleum Corporation (PETRONAS), which amounted to approximately $650 million (Malaysian dollars), are deducted from the total. Since 1976, the profitability of the public-enterprise sector seems to have improved, but there are many reasons why valid conclusions cannot be drawn from this kind of aggregate data.[7]

The government not only provides funds to public enterprises in the form of capital grants and loans but also guarantees commercial borrowings of a number of public authorities that operate as public-enterprise holding companies, and it may permit such authorities to guarantee commercial bank loans to their subsidiaries. As the capital structure of most state-owned enterprises in Malaysia is highly leveraged, the direct capital subsidies (via preferential terms) and the indirect subsidies (via guarantees of commercial borrowings) represent an important component of their financial cost to society. A further complication is that government loans are normally granted for specific projects or programs that often form part of the activities of more than one public enterprise, and the terms of the loans seldom bear any relationship to project payback periods. Thus, it is extremely difficult to track down the ultimate beneficiaries of the loan subsidies.

A dramatic example of what can happen when concessionary government loans do not coincide with projected enterprise cash flow is provided by the Federal Land Development Authority (FELDA), which is also a public-enterprise holding company. Project development costs are repayable to FELDA by settlers over a 15-year period once production begins, which in the case of oil palms (an important user of land) is about 4 years after planting. Even after the time required to clear the land, develop infrastructure, and house the settlers is taken into account, the total time elapsed between initiating the project and beginning to receive repayments is much shorter than the 11-year grace period granted by the Treasury on loans for such projects. FELDA itself, in fact, expects that settler repayments will continue to exceed loan payments to the Treasury until the 1990s. In the meantime FELDA is in a position to cover its administrative costs very amply, to invest substantial sums in securities (thereby earning interest arbitrage income), and to finance the expansion or subsidize the losses of its subsidiaries. The incidence of initial Treasury loan subsidies is difficult to measure under these circumstances.

A second major problem of evaluating the real opportunity cost of capital to public enterprises in Malaysia is created by ad hoc subsidization of project inputs. Some public enterprises engaged in land-intensive activities such as agricultural, regional, and housing development, for example, pay little or nothing for land, whereas others pay close to market prices. As land falls under jurisdiction of the states and is the source of roughly half of their fiscal revenue, the states have a strong incentive to assure that the land they alienate increases their revenue base, which they have increasingly endeavored to do by entering into commercial plantation, timber, and urban development projects, often in collaboration with their SEDCs. A common way for SEDCs to finance their equity participation in projects of this kind, often in joint-venture arrangements, is by contributing the land, whereas their private partners put up the cash. Any analysis of the rate of return of these projects would have to take into account imputed land rent as well as the return to financial capital.

Figures on the rate of return to public enterprises are not meaningful if profits are determined to a significant extent by government monopoly privileges. This problem is not as common in Malaysia as it is in many other less developed countries, but it crops up quite frequently, sometimes in rather subtle ways. For example, most of the financially profitable commercial and industrial public enterprises analyzed by R. Thillainathan in a recent study enjoy some kind of monopoly privilege.[8] Competitive imports of steel products are regulated in accordance with the size of stocks held by domestic producers, the most important of which is Malayawata, a public-enterprise joint venture in which PERNAS has a 30% equity interest. On the other hand, PERNAS Trading (a 100% owned subsidiary) has been given the exclusive concession to import steel for government projects, and it has also been granted a monopoly over the profitable China import trade. Kontena Nasional, a joint-venture trucking company owned 50% by PERNAS, has been given the exclusive right, along with the National Railways, to transport containers, which has become an increasingly lucrative business.

The granting of special privileges to public enterprises is a double-edged sword, because in some cases they undermine the profitability of other public enterprises. For example, the special concession granted Kontena Nasional has worked to the disadvantage of Malaysia Lori, a wholly owned MARA trucking subsidiary, which has suffered from a chronic deficit until very recently. Another example is the ban on imports of white cloth used in the manufacture of batik. The ban was very advantageous to the Kima Textile Company, a joint venture 70% owned by MARA, which enjoyed substantial profits before taxation and depreciation charges in 1976, but it was detrimental to the profitability of Batek Malaysia, another MARA subsidiary in perennial financial difficulties.

The prevalence of captive markets and cross-subsidization within public-enterprise holding groups constitutes another important obstacle to evaluating the opportunity cost of individual public-enterprise contributions to redressing economic imbalances. For example, an SEDC on the east coast of Malaysia subsidizes cash advances made by a trading company subsidiary to bumiputra contractors with the profits earned by a trucking subsidiary that receives preferential treatment in transporting cement, fertilizers, and other materials for SEDC projects under an exclusive franchise. Another SEDC has established a management services department that provides assistance to subsidiaries for a variable fee adjusted to keep taxable subsidiary profits low (SEDC profits are not taxable). Under the elaborate holding-company system that exists in Malaysia, opportunities for these kinds of arrangements are pervasive. PERNAS, for example, had 19 subsidiaries as of January 1979, 8 of which owned or held shares in 40 more companies, 5 of which owned or held shares in 8 additional firms, 2 of which owned or had equity interests in 24 enterprises, and at least one of which was a holding company in its own right.

Finally, public enterprises are frequently given multiple social objectives, so that it is very difficult to determine in practice which part of their costs is attributable to carrying out redistribution policies and which should be charged against fulfilling other social purposes. For example, the Pertima fish cannery, a wholly owned subsidiary of the Trengganu SEDC, was established not only to promote bumiputra participation in business but to develop a natural-resource–based industry of regional importance. Its failure to become commercially viable to date is due mainly to the delay in completing the new fishing port, which is necessary to solve the severe shortage in the cannery's supply of raw materials. Similarly, the Syarikat Gula Negeri Sembilan sugar mill, a joint venture of another SEDC, was set up for regional development as well as for redistributional reasons. After investing $110 million (Malaysian dollars) in the project and subsidizing $47 million in cumulative losses up to 1979, the government reached the conclusion that the mill was not economically viable and closed it down. What part of this cost is attributable to public enterprise as an instrument of redistribution policy?

16.2   Comparison of alternative redistribution policies

From what has been said it should be clear by now that there is no practical way of comparing the cost effectiveness of alternative redistributional policies in Malaysia, given current limitations of available statistical information and the way policies have been implemented. Little concern has been shown by Malaysian authorities, at least until very recently, with motivating their agents to become cost effective in carrying out redistribution policies, and so quite naturally systems for evaluating agency performance in this policy area were inadequate from the start. As was seen, a basic flaw in implementing earlier redistributional policies was the assignment of responsibility largely to agencies that were under pressure at the same time to operate in a businesslike manner and to become financially self-sustaining, without providing them with special compensation or incentives to carry out less remunerative or more risky social obligations. Faced with a choice between receiving tangible rewards from following more conventional policies and doubtful recognition for fulfilling social obligations, these agencies leaned in the former direction.

At the same time, responsibility for implementing important segments of the small-business promotion program was entrusted to an organization without previous experience in the field and with no guidelines to measure the cost effectiveness of its efforts. If this organization had followed the approach later developed by the Extension Service Unit of PERNAS Edar, more tangible results might have been achieved. The Extension Service provides a broad range of assistance to small-trades men, including shop renovations, advice on inventory control, seminars, and training visits. Fourteen criteria have been devised for measuring the performance of tradesmen participating in the program, which is broken down into several stages. Participants are required to achieve minimum performance levels in one stage before continuing to the next stage, and if successful, they become eligible for additional assistance to upgrade their businesses. In this way participants are motivated to use the Extension Service's assistance effectively and are discouraged from considering it simply as a giveaway program.

The shift in emphasis in redistribution policy toward more direct state intervention in the economy through the formation of public enterprises was made with equally little concern about facilitating appraisal of their cost effectiveness.

Criteria conceived for judging their contribution to redressing economic imbalances were incomplete, inaccurate, and biased, and the information system set up to monitor performance was very deficient. Government policy toward public enterprises has been confusing and at times contradictory, and the organization of the public-enterprise sector was permitted to become so complex that it is almost impossible to determine how many enterprises the government holds equity in and even more difficult to estimate their real cost to society.

The multiple layering of public enterprises under holding companies with wholly owned subsidiaries, joint ventures, and associated companies further complicates evaluation of the performance of individual firms. Arbitrary transfer pricing and cross-subsidization are common among members of holding-company groups, which frequently protect their weaker members by providing them with captive markets. Opportunities for these forms of noncompetitive behavior are facilitated by the vertical integration of most holding companies.

Appraisal of the cost effectiveness of public enterprises in carrying out public policy in Malaysia would in most cases require laborious research. Yet the stakes are high in Malaysia: If ill-conceived and ineffective public enterprises are allowed to proliferate under the shelter of the New Economic Policy, the government's development strategy could founder. As this strategy depends on redistributing *increments* in the value of assets and in employment, any slowdown in the rate of overall growth will make it increasingly difficult to achieve policy targets by 1990. It is therefore worthwhile to consider what practical steps the government might take to reduce the danger of this threat by facilitating sound decisions.

One of the most helpful steps that could be taken would be to divide public enterprises into two groups: those charged primarily with carrying out socio-economic programs and natural monopolies on the one hand, and those set up with shares held in trust for eventual transfer to individual members of the bumiputra community. Performance of the first group of enterprises, which are expected to remain in the public sector, can best be evaluated according to social cost–benefit criteria. Enterprises in the second group, which account for about half of government equity in wholly owned firms and more than 80% of government equity in firms with majority private ownership, should be required to meet the market test if they are to become commercially profitable in competitive markets. If they are not so required, experience demonstrates that they will try to justify their performance in terms of social contributions that are difficult to measure and will try to organize themselves in ways that impede holding them accountable for results.

Adoption of the following rules would greatly facilitate applying the market test in evaluating the performance of enterprises held in trust:

1. The enterprises should be obliged to conduct their relationships with other public enterprises at arm's length so as to reduce opportunities for arbitrary transfer pricing and indiscriminate cross-subsidization. This measure would necessitate changing some public-enterprise

holding arrangements and perhaps consolidating other enterprises too
weak to stand separately on their own feet.

2. No special privileges or protection would be given them, nor any special
    social obligations imposed on them, that do not affect private enter-
    prises competing in the same activities.

3. All subsidies, both direct and indirect, would be consolidated under a
    unified system and administered by a single government authority.

The most expedient solution would be to design a single subsidy based on the estimated value added by bumiputra factors of production and then oblige the same
enterprises to pay market prices for any service they receive from the government. Ideally, the subsidy would be of limited duration, say about 10 years, and
would be paid also to qualifying private enterprises.

At the same time, it would be desirable to provide explicit compensation to
enterprises, both public and private, to help implement bumiputra business
promotion programs so that social "burdens" of this kind cannot be used as
an excuse for not becoming financially self-sustaining. Also, if the level of compensation were determined through competitive bidding, a better idea could
be obtained about the cost of these programs in comparison with the cost of
alternative redistributional policies.

Notes

1 See Donald R. Snodgrass, "Summary Evaluation of Policies Used to Promote
  Bumiputra Participation in the Modern Sector in Malaysia," Harvard Institute for
  International Development Discussion Paper No. 38 (Feb. 1978), and *Economic
  Inequality and Development in Malaysia* (Kuala Lumpur: 1980), Oxford University
  Press, esp. Chap. 8.
2 SGV Consultants, *Organization and Systems Study of MARA*. Vol. I, (Kuala Lumpur:
  SGV Consultants, Jan. 1977), p. 20.
3 Economic Planning Unit, *Second Malaysian Development Plan, 1971–75*, (Kuala
  Lumpur: Government of Malaysia, 1970), pp. 41–2.
4 Economic Planning Unit, *Mid-Term Review of the Third Malaysia Plan* (Kuala
  Lumpur: Government of Malaysia, 1979), pp. 46 and 47.
5 It should be noted in this regard that no conjecture can be made at this time about the
  likely difference between the net worth and the nominal value of shares of enterprises
  held in trust. The consolidated balance sheet of the PERNAS group of companies for
  Jan. 31, 1979, shows a net worth of $191 million (Malaysian dollars), compared with
  $116 million for the value of shares. Because of incomplete reporting and obvious
  errors in the data submitted by public enterprises to the Implementation Coordination
  Unit of the prime minister's office, it was not possible to draw any conclusions from a
  larger sample.
6 As a 50% owner of the Kuala Lumpur Hilton Hotel, PERNAS insisted in the terms
  of agreement that 60% of the staff at all levels should be of Malay origin. See R.
  Thillainathan, "The Public Enterprise as an Instrument for Restructuring Society:
  the Malaysian Case," in *Malaysian Economic Development and Policies*, ed. Stephen
  Chee and S. M. Khoo (Kuala Lumpur, 1975).

7 Distortions created by accounting conventions and valuation problems, which are among the most important reasons, will not be discussed in this chapter. For a thorough treatment of this subject, see Leroy Jones, *Public Enterprise and Economic Development: The Korean Case* (Seoul: Korean Development Institute, 1975).
8 R. Thillainathan, *Public Enterprise Policy on Investment, Prices and Rates of Return in Malaysia* (Kuala Lumpur: Asian and Pacific Development Administration Centre, Jan. 1978).

17 Mixed enterprises and risk sharing in industrial development

J. M. Mintz

One of the more frequently used and interesting forms of public enterprise experienced in many developed and less-developed countries is the "mixed public–private enterprise." Such special forms of public enterprise have both public and private joint ownership of the equity shares issued by a commercial corporation.[1] Although public ownership is often more than 50% of the common stock, it is not uncommon for a government to take only a minority position in the mixed enterprise.

There are three reasons for a government to choose to enter into a joint venture agreement with private interests. First, the partial ownership of the voting common stock of a firm enables the government to control, or at least influence, decisions made by the management, without removing altogether private interests who may provide efficient management skills or superior technologies. Second, through partial ownership of the capital, the government has a claim to a portion of the profits of a firm; often the revenue can be used for distributional purposes or to finance the production of public goods. Third, by investing capital in the form of equity, the government shares with the private sector the risk inherent in many capital projects and thus encourages entrepreneurs to invest in projects that have uncertain future profitability.

This chapter will concentrate on the third reason for the creation of mixed public–private enterprises, namely, the desire of the government to share risks with the private sector. This risk-sharing role of the government in mixed enterprises entertains many important issues that, to the best of my knowledge, have not been considered in public-finance theory. In particular, the following will be considered:

First, when is government risk sharing desirable?[2] Leaving aside issues related to equity and the redistribution of profits, whether a government should intervene in the market economy by acquiring a portion of the equity in mixed enterprises will be examined. In Section 17.1 the conditions under which government risk sharing with private interests is desirable are discussed. One proposition is that in

I wish to thank A. B. Atkinson, P. Hammond, M. King, R. Arnott, R. Harris, and L. Jones for comments on earlier drafts of this chapter. Errors remain the responsibility of the author.

327

economies without well-developed financial markets, such as in less-developed countries, government risk sharing would be desirable in that the government, acting essentially as a mutual fund, invests savings of households in equities issued by firms.

Although this chapter emphasizes government ownership of equities, many of the results to be developed later apply as well to government ownership of risky bonds. A firm that does not honor its obligations when losses are incurred will declare bankruptcy. The owners of debt will not receive full payment of interest and principal when the firm's assets are of insufficient value to cover the value of debt owed. Hence, the owners of debt share the riskiness that faces a firm. From this follows the question, is it desirable for the government to own risky debt?[3] In the last section, the appropriateness of government intervention via debt, rather than equity, financing is considered.

Second, if the government undertakes a risk-sharing role, is partial or complete public ownership of each firm's equity capital more desirable? Again, leaving aside issues related to equity, it could be argued that under certain conditions the government should not incorporate risk in its investment decisions (this is the well-known Arrow–Lind argument).[4] If the private sector wishes to avoid risk with respect to investment in any particular project, the government, because of its large number of shareholders (taxpayers) and because of its ability to diversify its investments in uncorrelated projects, would be willing to supply capital at a lower cost than risk-avoiding private entrepreneurs. Section 17.2 considers a "farm" economy composed of many competitive firms owned by entrepreneurs who are unable to sell equity to others in capital markets. The only agent, excluding private entrepreneurs, that is able to own the equity of firms is the government, which in turn acquires capital funds from households in the economy. In this section the optimal share of public ownership and the cost of capital for investment is determined for each firm. Moreover, it will be demonstrated that mixed enterprises are, in general, desirable and that wholly nationalized firms are desirable when projects' returns are stochastically independent of each other and when individuals have the same expectations and endowments (these are the Arrow–Lind conditions).

Third, will public and private interests unanimously support decisions taken by the firm? If a mixed enterprise is the most desirable form of public enterprise with respect to risk sharing, it will be of interest to ask whether policies undertaken by a firm (such as with respect to its investment decisions) are supported by both public and private interests. It is shown that such an agreement is possible when the government and a private individual are both interested in maximizing the profits of the firm. However, there are many, perhaps obvious, reasons for governments to believe that entrepreneurs, who maximize profits, often make decisions deleterious to social welfare. Such decisions may result from: (1) inaccurate expectations generated by misinformation about the future, and (2) a conflict between the government's goal of achieving an equitable distribution of wealth and the efficiency of using resources arising from a competitive firm maximizing profits. Conflicts such as these may be resolved by assessing interest rate subsidies or taxes imposed by the government as a complementary policy to equity financing, thus ensuring entrepreneurial decisions are in accordance with the government's desire to pursue nonprofit maximizing investment plans. Partial state ownership of equity would continue to be desired by both private and public interest as a means of sharing risk.[5]

In the final section, policy implications drawn from the model are outlined in nontechnical terms. In particular, the results are applied to less-developed countries where capital markets may be at early stages of development.

17.1 Stock-market economies and mixed public–private enterprises

In this section, the economies of two firms owned by entrepreneurs are considered to illustrate how the direct trading of the shares of the firms' profits in stock markets can allow entrepreneurs to share risks (and to improve their position). Then the government is allowed to acquire shares of a firm and redistribute the profits back to each individual. The model shows that when stock markets exist, such government risk sharing fails to make an improvement in an economy such that individual entrepreneurs can achieve more if the definition of welfare is based on the expected utility levels of individuals (see note 2). Thus, government equity financing to encourage greater risk taking would not be needed.

The theorem is illustrated in Figure 17.1 (the results will be derived in a theoretical framework in later sections). Each entrepreneur consumes a single type of a commodity (corn) from output produced by each firm where consumption and corn production depend on two states of the world (rain and sun). Individuals maximize expected utility, which depends upon their own expectations and the utility gained from consuming corn of uncertain supply. The vectors labeled 1 and 2 represent the output produced by each respective firm in each state of the world. Assume initially that individual A owns Firm 1 and individual B owns Firm 2. Indifference curves are used for a specified level of expected utility, which depends on consumption available in each state of the world (indifference curves are labeled $E^A U^A$ and $E^B U^B$ for each respective individual).

Now suppose that individuals, who do not know which state of the world is to occur, decide to trade shares of output directly with each other. Suppose individual A trades with individual B a portion of Firm 1's output for a portion of Firm 2's output. Let the output of each firm obtained by each individual be denoted as follows (Table 17.1).

A stock-market equilibrium occurs when each individual maximizes his expected utility. For individual A, this is Point A and for individual B, Point B. Each individual trades shares of output of firms until their marginal rates of substitution between consumption-if-it-rains and consumption-if-the-sun-shines is

Table 17.1. *Output of each firm obtained by each individual*

Individual	Firm 1 output obtained	Firm 2 output obtained
A	Oa	Oa'
B	Ob'	Ob

Note: $Oa + Ob' = O1$ and $Ob + Oa' = O2$.

equal to the relative price ratio. The prices of consumption in each state of the world are defined by the prices of shares of output of the two firms exchanged between the two entrepreneurs.[6] As can be seen, such risk sharing improves the positions of both individuals.

Note in Figure 17.1 that individuals have not traded shares of firms such that an individual owns the same share of each firm. Such an equilibrium, where points A and B would lie on the same vector emanating from the origin, would require the following restrictions. First, individuals would be required to have the same expectations and tastes. Second, preferences would need to be homothetic (constant relative risk aversion) where marginal rates of substitution are independent of wealth, or the initial endowments of each individual would need to be the same (with the same endowments, lines $1A$ and $2B$ would join each other in the figure).

Suppose the government acquires a portion of each firm's output (i.e., creates a mixed enterprise), indicated by Oc for Firm 1 and Od for Firm 2. Individual A owns directly the output Oc' (where $Oc' + Oc = O1$) of Firm 1 (which can be less than in the case of direct trading in stock markets). Individual B owns directly the output Od' (where $Od + Od' = O2$) of Firm 2 (which can be less than before). The government, after acquiring a share of output of each firm, has obtained output indicated by the vector Og (which is the sum of $Oc + Od$). If individual A has a share, Oe/Og, and B has a share, Of/Og, of the government's output vector (where $Oe + Of = Og$), then individuals A and B would be able to obtain Point A and B, respectively, where at these points each respective expected utility is maximized.

There are several interesting points that can be drawn from the figure.

First, as claimed at the beginning of this section, the government, acting in essence as a financial intermediary (or as a mutual fund between consumers and firms), cannot improve upon an allocation achieved by individuals who are trading shares of firms directly among themselves in stock markets. Thus, with the existence of stock markets, state ownership of mixed enterprises as a means of diversifying entrepreneurial risk is entirely unnecessary.

Figure 17.1 assumed that there were two linearly independent vectors of firms and two states of the world. By trading shares of outputs produced by firms in stock markets, both individuals were able to span their consumption space. If spanning were not possible (i.e., fewer firms than states of the world), could

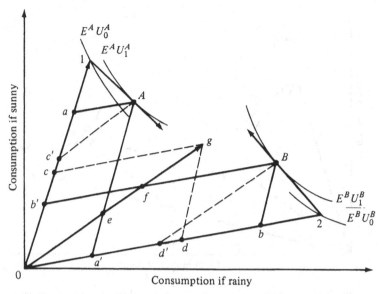

Figure 17.1. Stock-market equilibrium and the effect of mixed-enterprise ownership by the government on equilibrium.

the creation of mixed enterprises by the state improve the stock-market equilibrium? The answer is no! The government creates a vector of output available to individuals that is in itself contained in the space spanned by firms. No new linearly independent vector is created, thus no improvement is made in the original stock-market equilibrium.

Second, if stock-market trading is not possible (because of prohibitively high transaction costs), the creation of mixed public–private enterprises and subsequent risk diversification can improve the welfare of individuals in the economy. This can be seen in Figure 17.1 where both individuals A and B are better off with the creation of mixed enterprises rather than owning only their own firm's vector. Note, however, that if the government chooses both the government's share of each enterprise as well as the shares of the government's output that each individual receives, the final point of consumption may not be at points A and B as illustrated in Figure 17.2. In this figure the government acquires a smaller share of each firm's equity as compared to Figure 17.1. After allocating a portion of the government's vector, Og, to each individual, the position of each individual is improved (points A' and B', respectively) but not to the extent as in the preceding figure where points A and B were attained. To achieve points A and B, the government needs to acquire a greater share of equity of each firm (and lower points c' and d' along the rays 01 and 02, respectively), which would extend the vector $0g$. After increasing its ownership of output, the government would allocate public output to each individual and move both points e and f to the right. Thus, even if the government makes "mistakes," the positions of both individuals may be

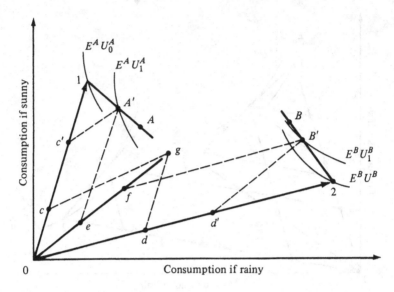

Figure 17.2. Government makes "mistakes" when there is no stock-market equilibrium.

improved with government ownership of enterprises; however, even more improvement would be expected in stock-market economies. To avoid "mistakes," a government can allow individuals to trade shares of a government-controlled financial intermediary if transaction costs are not prohibitive (in some countries the government has allowed a portion of the shares of a government-controlled intermediary to be sold to the public).

Third, it can be shown also that it may be preferable to partially, not wholly, nationalize firms. Although complete nationalization might improve the position of both individuals, more improvement is derived in a mixed-enterprise economy. Figure 17.3 illustrates this result.

If the government wholly nationalizes both firms, it creates a vector $0g'$. It can then give a portion of the government's output to each individual such as $0A''$ to individual A and $0B''$ to individual B where $0A'' + 0B'' = 0g'$. Although the positions of both individuals are improved after complete nationalization, they are not at points A and B where they would maximize their respective expected utilities. For $0g'$ to be the vector that maximizes the expected utility of both individuals, it is required that (1) individuals have the same expectations and the same homothetic tastes or (2) individuals have the same expectations and the projects are stochastically independent of each other such that $0g'$ lies on the vector of which consumption is the same in both states of the world ($c_R = c_S$). These two conditions are important to the argument that the government does not require the incorporation of risk in its discount rate arising from risk pooling. In Figure 17.3, government nationalization of both projects results in certain consumption that would dissipate risks for both individuals ($0g'$, A'', and B'' would lie on the line

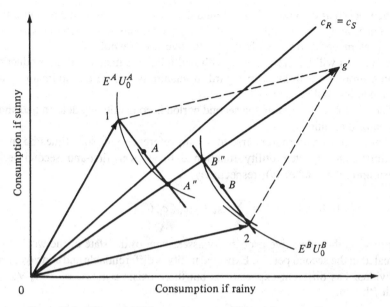

Figure 17.3. Effects of 100% government ownership of firm on welfare.

$c_R = c_S$). Given the same expectations, individuals would have the same marginal rate of substitution when $c_R = c_S$. It can be noted also that a stock-market equilibrium would result in the same equilibrium.[7]

The preceding figures explain many of the results obtained by using the mathematics presented in the following section. Readers who do not wish to read the following technical section may continue on to the final section.

17.2 A centralized planning model

Technology and consumer preferences

The model used is similar to that developed by Sandmo.[8] Consider a one-commodity economy of $i = 1, \ldots, n$ consumers and $j = 1, \ldots, m$ firms where $m \leq n$. Production involves real capital, y_j, invested in the jth firm in the first period. The production of output in the second period is characterized by a function, $f_j(y_j)$, exhibiting decreasing marginal productivity of capital. Furthermore, production of output is affected by technological uncertainty, assumed to be separable from investment decisions: $f_j(y_j) \, \phi_j(\theta)$, where $\phi_j(\theta)$ is a value-of-distribution parameter depending on the state of the world, $\theta = 1, \ldots, T$.

The assumption of multiplicative uncertainty is a simplifying assumption, which implies that the ratio of output in one state of the world to output in another state is independent of the scale of the firm, thus further implying that real capital invested in a firm does not affect the pattern of returns across states of the world.[9]

In the stock-market model, it was found that under the assumption of multiplicative uncertainty, shareholders of firms are unanimous in decision making, and decisions made by firms with respect to investment would be pareto optimal.[10] However, as will be shown, even with multiplicative uncertainty in production, certain problems will arise in regard to unanimity and pareto optimality when stock markets fail to exist.

The price of the output in the second period is competitively determined and is normalized to unity.

Consumers (or entrepreneurs, to whom reference will sometimes be made) maximize an expected utility function defined over first-and second-period consumption, c_{1i} and $c_{2i}(\theta)$, respectively:

$$E^i U^i [c_{1i}, c_{2i}(\theta)] = \sum_\theta \pi_\theta^i U^i [c_{1i}, c_{2i}(\theta)]$$

where π_θ^i is the subjective probability assessment of the state of the world to be revealed in the second period. Expected utility is differentiable and concave. Each individual has different expectations but there exists a norm, $\phi_j = 1$, $\forall\theta$, for each jth firm.

Imperfect capital markets and the role of the government

To capture the notion of the imperfectness of stock markets, the following assumptions are made. The state takes a share of each jth firm's output according to the fraction α_j. Each consumer owns a portion of one and only one firm (at the maximum) $(1 - \alpha_i)$ where α_i is the share of output acquired by the state with respect to the ith firm owned directly by the ith consumer. Short sales are disallowed to ensure boundedness: Hence, $0 \le \alpha_i \le 1$.

The state distributes its share of output earned on public investments to the ith consumer according to the weight γ_i, where $\Sigma_i \gamma_i = 1$ and, for simplicity, $0 < \gamma_i < 1$ is assumed.[11] In the model the central planner determines γ_i endogenously as well as α_j.

A resource constraint exists in the first period such that total resources, W^1, are allocated to individuals as first-period consumption and firms as real capital:

$$W^1 = \sum_i c_{1i} + \sum_j y_j$$

In the second period, the social planner allocates resources available in each state of the world to each consumer according to the transfer d_i, where $\Sigma_i d_i = W^2$, W^2 being the total amount of wealth available in the second period. (If state-contingent transfers of wealth were allowed in the second period $[d_i(\theta)]$, it can be easily shown that unconstrained pareto optimality would occur and, moreover, mixed enterprises would be unnecessary.)

Second-period consumption of each individual is represented by

$$c_{2i}(\theta) = (1 - \alpha_i) f_i(y_i) \phi_i(\theta) + \gamma_i \sum_j \alpha_j f_j(y_j) \phi_j(\theta) + d_i$$

which is assumed to hold with equality.

The social planner maximizes an ex ante social-welfare function recognizing both the expectations and utility functions of all consumers in the economy: $W(E^1 U^1, \dots, E^n U^n)$. This specific form of social-welfare function will be discussed later.

The programming problem and first-order conditions

The programming problem for the social planner is

$$L = W(E^1 U^1, \dots, E^n U^n) + \lambda_1 \left(W^1 - \sum_i c_{1i} - \sum_j y_j \right)$$

$$+ \lambda_2 \left(W^2 - \sum_i d_i \right) - \lambda_3 \left(\sum_i \gamma_i - 1 \right) + \sum_j \lambda_{3j} \alpha_j$$

$$+ \sum_j \lambda_{4j} (1 - \alpha_j) \tag{1}$$

where $c_{2i}(\theta)$ is defined as before and interior solutions are assumed for γ_i.

Before analyzing the programming model, certain important properties associated with the concept of pareto optimality in stock-market economies will be outlined.[12] First, unconstrained pareto optimality occurs when linearly independent securities span a T-dimensional consumption set of consumers. This means that the first-order conditions can be used to solve for a global maximum, as Arrow–Debreu prices for state-contingent commodities are defined. Second, constrained pareto optimality occurs, as in the Diamond model (see note 9), when linearly independent securities span an m-dimensional space spanned by firms (where $m < T$). With multiplicative uncertainty in production, first-order conditions may be used to solve for a global maximum as well. Third, if there are fewer linearly independent securities than states of the world or, under multiplicative uncertainty, fewer linearly independent securities than firms, the above programming problem is not concave, as the constraint in (1) is not convex.[13] As Drèze had shown (see note 10), the existence of nonconvex constraints results in solutions for α_j, y_j and in the above case, γ_i, solving for both local and global maxima. This means that, because each individual has only two securities available with more than two states, there can be a multiple number of solutions for the choice variables obtained from the necessary conditions.

The necessary conditions for the preceding programming problem are:

$$L_{c_{1i}} = W_i E^i U_1^i - \lambda_1 = 0 \qquad\qquad \forall i \quad (2a)$$

$$L_{d_i} = W_i E^i U_2^i - \lambda_2 = 0 \qquad\qquad \forall i \quad (2b)$$

$$L_{\gamma_i} = W_i E^i U_2^i \left(\sum_j \alpha_j f_j \phi_j \right) - \lambda_3 = 0 \qquad\qquad \forall i \quad (2c)$$

$$L_{\alpha_j} = \sum_i W_i E^i U_2^i \gamma_i f_j \phi_j - W_j E^j U_2^j f_j \phi_j + \lambda_{3j} - \lambda_{4j} = 0 \qquad \forall j \quad (2d)$$

$$L_{y_j} = \sum_i W_i E^i U_2^i \gamma_i \alpha_j f_j' \phi_j + W_j E^j U_2^j (1 - \alpha_j) f_j \phi_j - \lambda_1 = 0 \qquad \forall j \quad (2e)$$

$$\lambda_{3j} \alpha_j = 0, \lambda_{3j} \geq 0 \qquad\qquad \forall j \quad (2f)$$

$$\lambda_{4j} (1 - \alpha_j) = 0, \lambda_{4j} \geq 0 \qquad\qquad \forall j \quad (2g)$$

Note that W_i is the partial derivative of the social-welfare function with respect to the expected utility of the ith individual and that $f_j'(y_j)$ is the marginal productivity of capital of the jth firm.

The first-order conditions may be rearranged and interpreted as follows, assuming that $\lambda_{3j} = \lambda_{4j} = 0$, $\forall j$; corner solutions will be discussed later.

1. Equations (2a) and (2b) yield

$$MRS = \frac{E^i U_1^i}{E^i U_2^i} = \frac{\lambda_1}{\lambda_2} \qquad\qquad \forall i \quad (3)$$

The marginal rate of substitution between first- and second-period consumption is the same for all individuals.

2. Equations (2a) and (2b) also yield the following distribution rule:

$$W_i E^i U_1^i = W_k E^k U_1^k \qquad\qquad \forall i, k \neq i$$

$$W_i E^i U_2^i = W_k E^k U_2^k \qquad\qquad \forall i, k \neq i \quad (4)$$

The state administers lump-sum transfers of wealth to equalize the *social expected marginal utility* of consumption in each period for all consumers. This distribution rule is derived from an ex ante social-welfare function maximized by a social planner who adjusts the wealth of consumers to achieve an ex ante optimum. It is important to note that once the state of the world is known, the ex post social marginal utility of individuals need not be equalized, $W_i U_2^i \neq W_k U_2^k$. The ex post distribution rule could be realized if, for example, expectations were the same $\forall i$ and the social-welfare function weights are not state-contingent.

3. Equations (2c) and (2d) yield:

$$\delta_i (g) = \sum_j \alpha_j f_j \delta_{ij} = \frac{\lambda_3}{\lambda_2} \qquad\qquad \forall i \quad (5)$$

where $\delta_{ij} = \mu_{ij} \rho_{ij}$, $\mu_{ij} = E^i \phi_j$ and $\rho_{ij} = E^i U_2^i \phi_j / E^i U_2^i E^i \phi_j$

The risk-discount factor, δ_{ij}, incorporates a measure of expectations (if $\mu_{ij} < 1$, the ith individual is relatively pessimistic, and if $\mu_{ij} > 1$, relatively optimistic, with respect to the jth firm) and a measure of risk aversion (if the ith individual is risk averse and the jth firm's output is nonnegatively correlated with the ith individual's portfolio, then $\rho_{ij} \le 1$; see Appendix A).

From (5), the risk-discount factor with respect to the government's portfolio of assets $[\delta_i\,(g)]$ is the weighted sum of the risk-discount factors of m firms (δ_{ij}), where the weights depend on the output of the jth firm (f_j) and the share of the jth firm's equity held by the government (α_j). Although $\delta_i\,(g)$ is the same $\forall i$, it cannot be assumed that δ_{ij} is the same $\forall i$ as long as there are fewer linearly independent securities than firms.

4. Equations (2b) and (2d) yield:

$$\delta_{gj} = \sum_i \gamma_i\, \delta_{ij} = \delta_{jj} \qquad\qquad \forall j \quad (6)$$

The social planner selects the level of ownership in each firm such that the risk-discount factor of the individual owner is equal to the weighted mean risk-discount factor used by the state (δ_{gj}).

5. Equations (2a), (2b), (2d), and (2e) yield:

$$f_j' = MRS \times \delta_{jj}^{-1} = MRS \times \left(\sum_i \gamma_i\, \delta_{ij} \right)^{-1} = MRS \times \delta_{gj}^{-1} \qquad (7)$$

The optimal investment rule for the mixed enterprise is that marginal productivity of capital be equal to the product of the marginal rate of substitution between first- and second-period consumption and the inverse of the risk-discount factor used by the jth individual owning directly the jth firm or that used by the government (δ_{gj}).

The equilibrium condition of equation (7) is related to that derived by Sandmo[14] in his discussion of public-investment discount rates when capital markets are imperfect. The difference between Sandmo's result and (7) is that Sandmo assumed that there existed either public or private firms, the corner solutions of the model in this chapter. However, the state need not invest in nationalized firms only. If the government is attempting to simply share risks, the state may own the equity only in part.

Corner solutions

With either $\lambda_{3j} > 0$ (full private ownership where $\alpha_j = 0$) or $\lambda_{4j} > 0$ (full nationalization where $\alpha_j = 1$), either one of the following conditions holds:

$$\sum_i \gamma_i\, \delta_{ij} < \delta_{jj} \qquad\qquad (6a)$$

$$\sum_i \gamma_i \delta_{ij} > \delta_{jj} \tag{6b}$$

First consider (6a). If the individual's risk-discount factor is higher in value than that used by the government, the individual will own the firm wholly. This condition holds because the individual is more optimistic as measured by μ_{ij} than most other individuals in the economy or less risk averse (ρ_{ij} is closer to 1 than for most other individuals).

In (6b), the individual sells the whole of the firm to the government if his risk-discount factor is lower in value than that used by the government. Full nationalization is the solution if the individual is relatively pessimistic or risk averse in comparison to the rest of the economy.

The condition expressed in (6b) is especially relevant to the debate concerning the incorporation of risk in the social discount rate of nationalized firms. Hirshleifer has contended that the discount factor for public investment should be equal to that used by private firms where the return to capital is perfectly correlated with that of the public firm.[15] Arrow and Lind have shown that, given wholly nationalized projects, the state should ignore risk in discount rates when three conditions hold: (1) the project's returns are (stochastically) independent of the returns of other firms in the economy, (2) individuals have the same expectations and endowments, and (3) there are a large number of taxpayers (tending to infinity).[16] Sandmo demonstrated that public investments should include risk in the discount rate when stock markets exist and the returns of private and nationalized firms are perfectly correlated.[17] If capital markets are imperfect in that each individual owns directly the maximum of one firm, Sandmo argued that the discount rate for public investment should be different from that used by private firms of the same risk class. Mayshar demonstrated that, under the Arrow–Lind conditions, nationalized firms could disregard risk when evaluating projects in the presence of imperfect equity capital markets.[18] If the government wholly nationalized all firms and eliminated risk, the preceding arguments would suggest that mixed enterprises would not be an equilibrium. In Appendix B, it is demonstrated that complete nationalization is desirable when the Arrow–Lind conditions hold, namely when the projects' returns are distributed independently of each other, individuals have the same expectations, and there are a large number of individuals. However, as shown in Figure 17.3, where the first two Arrow–Lind conditions do not hold, partial, rather than complete government ownership of firms improves the position of individuals because of the individuals' different patterns of consumption (owing to differences in expectations, preferences for risk, i.e., relative risk aversion, and endowments).

17.3 Consumer and firm behavior in a mixed-enterprise economy

This section will examine a "decentralized" economy to determine whether the behavior of entrepreneurs is compatible with the (constrained) pareto optimum defined in Section 17.1. In the mixed-enterprise economy each ith entrepreneur chooses his savings plan and the amount of capital to be invested in his ith firm and the government chooses the optimal share of profits and equity of firms and distributes profits earned on state investments to individuals according to the individual's shares as calculated in the programming problem of Section 17.2.

Individuals may trade bonds in a market where the return earned on a bond is $(1 + r)$ and independent of the state of the world. These bonds do not default because personal bankruptcy is ruled out – individuals will not desire to take action that may result in negative consumption in any state of the world. Allowing for bankruptcy and the existence of risky bonds would not appreciably affect the conclusions.

The consumer has an exogenously determined amount of wealth, w_i, in the first period. With his wealth and for a given share of capital of the ith firm financed by the government, $\alpha_i y_i$, less a tax imposed on the individual to finance government investments, $\gamma_i \sum_j \alpha_j y_j$, the consumer purchases his quantity of the consumption good in the first period, c_{1i}, and bonds, b_i. The consumer's wealth constraint is binding so that

$$w_i = c_{1i} + b_i + (1 - \alpha_i) y_i + \gamma_i \sum_j \alpha_j y_j \tag{8}$$

In the second period, the ith consumer's consumption depends on income earned from the following three sources: (1) his share of profits earned by the ith firm owned directly by him, $(1 - \alpha_i) f_i (y_i) \phi_i (\theta)$, (2) the return earned on bonds held by him, $(1 + r) b_i$, and (3) his share of profits earned by the government, $\gamma_i \sum_j \alpha_j f_j (y_j) \phi_j (\theta)$. It is assumed that the second-period income constraint is binding such that

$$c_{2i} (\theta) = (1 - \alpha_i) \Pi_i (\theta) + \gamma_i \sum_j \alpha_j \Pi_j (\theta) + (1 + r) b_i \tag{9}$$

where $\Pi_j = f_j (y_j) \phi_j (\theta)$.

The individual maximizes an expected utility function $E^i U^i [c_{1i}, c_{2i} (\theta)]$ where $c_{2i} (\theta)$ is defined by solving equation (8) for b_i and substituting b_i into equation (9). Choosing c_{1i} and y_i, the respective first-order conditions are

$$E^i U_1^i - (1 + r) E^i U_2^i = 0 \tag{10a}$$

$$(1 - \alpha_i + \gamma_i \alpha_i) E^i U_2^i [f_i' \phi_j - (1 + r)] = 0 \tag{10b}$$

Equation (10a) yields the condition that the marginal rate of substitution between first- and second-period consumption is equal to one plus the bond rate (where r is determined independent of i). Equation (10b) yields the condition that the entrepreneur will choose a level of investment in a firm such that marginal productivity of capital is equal to the bond rate times the inverse of the risk-discount factor, δ_{ii}.

The question central to this section is: Would the conditions under which a government was maximizing social welfare be in agreement with the investment decision made by the entrepreneur? The following theorem proves that such unanimity is possible.

Theorem 1

Given the government controls γ_i, w_i, α_j, and r, assuming y_j and c_{1i} are fixed, a change in ex ante social welfare resulting from an increase in y_j will be of the same sign as a change in the expected utility of the jth entrepreneur.

Proof. Define an indirect social-welfare function where the optimal choices γ_i^* and w_i^* for all i, α_j^* for all j, and r are made by the government as in programming problem (1). The indirect social-welfare function is defined over the indirect expected utility levels of individuals, which depend on the choice of the government with respect to γ_i^*, w_i^*, α_j^*, and r^*, which in turn depend on capital decisions of each firm: $V = V(y_1, \ldots, y_m)$. Assuming that the jth entrepreneur revision of y_j has no effect on the decisions made by the other entrepreneurs and using the envelope thoerem, the effect of y_j on social welfare can be determined as

$$\frac{dV}{dy_j} = \sum_{i \neq j} \frac{\partial V}{\partial E^i U^i} E^i U_2^i \gamma_i^* \alpha_j^* [f_j' \phi_j(\theta) - (1 + r^*)]$$

$$+ \frac{\partial V}{\partial E^j U^j} E^j U_2^j (1 - \alpha_j^* + \alpha_j^* \gamma_j^*) [f_j' \phi_j(\theta) - (1 + r^*)]$$

$$(11a)$$

As the government chooses w_i^* optimally, dividing by $(\partial V / \partial E^i U_2^i = \lambda, \forall i)$,

$$\frac{dV}{dy_j} \cdot \frac{1}{\lambda} = \left[\alpha_i^* \sum_i \gamma_i^* \delta_{ij} + (1 - \alpha_j^*) \delta_{jj} \right] f_j' - (1 + r^*) \quad (11b)$$

As both α_j^* and γ_i^* are chosen optimally by the government, $\Sigma_i \gamma_i^* \delta_{ij} = \delta_{jj}$ and

$$\frac{dV}{dy_j} \cdot \frac{1}{\lambda} = f_j' \sum_i \gamma_i^* \delta_{ij} - (1 + r) = f_j' \delta_{jj} - (1 + r^*) \quad (12)$$

From the entrepreneur's problem (10b)

$$\frac{1}{E^i U_2^i} \frac{dE^j U^j}{dy_j} = f_j' \delta_{jj} - (1 + r)$$

which is in agreement with (12). Thus both the government and the entrepreneur would increase y_j if

$$f_j' \delta_{jj} > (1 + r) \qquad \text{q.e.d.}$$

Several important assumptions in the preceding theorem guaranteed unanimity. First, the assumption that the government controlled w_i and γ_i for all i and α_j for all j, whereas entrepreneurs controlled y_j only, allowed the government to ensure that an individual would trade his bonds for investments of equity in his own firm such that risk-discounted returns are the same for the two investments. With expected social marginal utilities of individuals being equated with lump-sum transfers w_i, certain consumption streams are evaluated at the same rate for all individuals. If entrepreneurs controlled, in addition to y_j, γ_i or α_j, unanimity would not be possible. This problem arises from the nonconvex constraints in the programming problem (see note 2) where some of the several local solutions existing would be pareto inefficient. If the government is allowed to optimally control both γ_i for all i and α_j for all j then the entrepreneur's program is concave in y_j and the government would agree with the decision of the entrepreneur that maximizes his expected utility. (Thus selling the equity issued by a government-controlled financial intermediary may not be desirable.)

This unanimity theorem was also possible because the government controlled w_i^*. If the state could not administer wealth transfers to achieve equity, the government would not agree with the investment plan of the entrepreneur that maximizes his expected utility but not social welfare. However, the government could adjust α_j for all j and γ_i for all i to take into account equity considerations and still agree with the investment plan of the entrepreneur. This can be seen with the following argument.

If the government cannot distribute wealth perfectly, equation (4) should be disregarded as a condition for optimality. Equations (6) and (7) would have to be corrected as follows:

$$\delta_{gj}^* \equiv \sum_i B_i \, \gamma_i \, \delta_{ij} = B_j \, \delta_{jj} \tag{6c}$$

$$f_j' = (1 + r) \, \delta_{gj}^{*^{-1}} = (1 + r) \, (B_j \, \delta_{jj})^{-1} \tag{7a}$$

where $B_i = W_i \, E^i \, U_2^i$.

In (6c) the socially evaluated risk-discount factor of the jth individual owning the jth firm (the social weight being B_j) should equal the government's risk-discount factor, which is now a weighting of socially evaluated risk-discount factors for all i. Note that (6c) is similar to Meade's weighting of market prices to accommodate a change in a welfare policy adopted by the government when there are no distortions in the economy.[19]

It may be immediately noticed that (6c) and (7a) are not in agreement with (11b). If, however, the government solves for an optimal α_j and γ_i such that

$$\hat{\delta}_{gj} = \sum_i \frac{B_i}{B_j} \, \gamma_i^* \, \delta_{ij} = \delta_{jj} \quad \text{and} \quad f_j' = (1 + r) \, \hat{\delta}_{gj}^{-1} = (1 + r) \, \delta_{jj}^{-1}$$

the entrepreneur will choose a level of investment compatible with maximizing social welfare. On the other hand, entrepreneurs would like to have the government choose the shares γ_i for all i and α_j for all j differently, but as with any taxes, individuals may have no choice but to accept them.

A third reason for unanimity between the government and the entrepreneur is that the interesting possible market failures, which may give rise to a conflict between the objectives of public and private sectors (e.g., the existence of unemployed labor, imperfectly competitive firms, and externalities) have not been included in the model. From a long list of market failures, the following example will suffice.

Suppose the government believes individuals have inaccurate expectations resulting from a lack of knowledge about future events, and that with this knowledge, individuals would revise their probability estimates of future states. The planner maximizes an ex post social welfare function (where the tastes, not the expectations, of individuals are recognized). Social probability estimates of future states of the world π_θ^s, $\theta = 1, \ldots, T$, vary from those of the individual, π_θ^i. For convenience, it is assumed that social expectations are of the norm such that $E\phi_j = 1$ for all j firms. The ex post social-welfare function may be represented by: $E\,W\,(U^1, \ldots, U^n, \theta) = \Sigma_{\theta=1}\,\pi_\theta^s\,W\,(U^1, \ldots, U^n, \theta)$. The ex post social-welfare function can be shown to be equivalent to an ex ante social-welfare function (in Section 17.2) under three conditions: (1) expectations of all individuals and social expectations are the same, (2) the social-welfare function is not state-contingent, and (3) utility functions of consumers are weighted linearly.

If the government maximized an ex post social-welfare function with state-contingent transfers of wealth, all conditions (3) to (7) would be amended. For example, (6) and (7) become:

$$S_{ij} = \sum_i \gamma_i S_{ij} \tag{6d}$$

and

$$f_j'(y_j) = SMRS \times \left(\sum_i \gamma_i \delta_{ij} \right)^{-1} \tag{7b}$$

where

$$S_{ij} = \frac{E\,W_{i\theta}\,U_2^i\,\phi_j(\theta)}{E\,W_{i\theta}\,U_2^i} \quad \text{and} \quad SMRS = \frac{E\,W_{i\theta}\,U_1^i}{W_{i\theta}\,U_2^i}$$

Should the jth entrepreneur choose c_{1j} and y_j, it can be seen, by comparing (10a) and (10b) with (6) and (7), that consumer behavior would not be ex post socially optimal. Note however, mixed enterprises would remain desirable in the equilibrium.

The state does have an option to assure that consumer behavior is consistent with the social optimum. Assuming that individual expectations are not altered, the state may impose a personalized Pigovian tax rate, t_j,[20] on the equity capital invested by the jth individual in the jth firm owned directly by him such that

$$t_j = SMRS \times S_{jj}^{-1} (1 - B) \quad \text{where } B = \frac{MRS \times \delta_{jj}^{-1}}{SMRS \times S_{jj}^{-1}}$$

If the individual's risk-adjusted discount rate, $MRS \times \delta_{jj}^{-1}$, is lower than that of the social optimum, the state would impose an interest-rate tax to reduce the investment in the individual's firm. Conversely, an individual who uses a higher risk-adjusted discount rate than that of the social optimum would need to receive an interest-rate subsidy to stimulate the individual to accept more risk in investing in the jth firm. However, the personalized tax rate, t_j, depends on the state having sufficient knowledge with regard to consumer preferences and expectations. Otherwise, the state would be constrained to imposing taxes and subsidies on individuals assumed to have common expectations and utility functions but perhaps differing in characteristics such as wealth or skill.

17.4 Conclusions and policy implications

The intent of the model developed in Sections 17.1, 17.2 and 17.3 was to analyze the risk-sharing role of the government as a reason for the creation of mixed enterprises. It was determined that risk sharing by the government can be effective in economies with poorly developed capital markets (especially those in less-developed countries). If an entrepreneur cannot avoid risk by selling to others a share of the profits earned by his own firm in exchange for shares of profits earned by other firms, the government can enable entrepreneurs to indirectly exchange shares by acquiring partial state ownership in mixed enterprises and redistributing the profits earned on government investments back to individuals.

This conclusion has many interesting policy implications. First, if the government were to invest in firm shares for the purpose of risk sharing, it is well possible that only a minority interest will be desired. The optimal share of government ownership depends on the preference of individuals for risk, their expectations, and uncertain income streams. The government's share of ownership will be greater to the extent that individuals desire to reduce variability in their income streams. In regard to the management role in which the government may be interested, there is no reason to suppose that the government would desire to nationalize or acquire a controlling interest in a mixed enterprise. Thus the existence of mixed enterprises with partial state ownership of less than 50% can be explained by the model.

Second, if government were to invest in mixed enterprises solely to share risks, one would presume that such investment would take place in small firms that do not have easy access to capital markets. Indeed, a sample of 100 mixed enterprises in Turkey (1966) suggested that the average capital size of mixed enterprises with minority government participation was 13.3 million Turkish lira (TL) and those with majority government participation was 55.2 million TL.[21] Although it is possible that there are many reasons why the government acquired a minority share in small enterprises and a majority share in large enterprises (such as the need to convert debt to equity capital to forestall bankruptcy), one possible explanation is that small firms need risk capital from the government because of the lack of well-developed capital markets, whereas large mixed enterprises exist for other reasons. Large firms that have access not only to domestic, but also to international, credit markets do not need risk capital from a government. Majority government ownership in large enterprises may result from the government's desire to control and manage the firm.

Finally, it might be suggested that equity participation by the government in a particular mixed enterprise is not the only means for the government to share risks. Mintz has investigated the profit tax with a full-loss offset,[22] which allows the entrepreneur to write off either (1) the interest cost of both debt and equity financing and the true cost of depreciation from taxable income or (2) the immediate investment expenditure (with no allowance for depreciation or the interest cost of financing).[23] It was shown that such a profit-tax scheme would enable the government to share risks with entrepreneurs, as would equity financing if no pure profits are earned (i.e., profits over and above that required to compensate individuals for risk). However, when pure profits are being earned (as with production functions with decreasing returns to scale), a full-loss offset tax, unlike equity financing, can reduce risk taking. This results because a tax expropriates the profits and the wealth of the entrepreneur, whereas with equity financing, profits are not necessarily expropriated if compensation is paid. Moreover, with taxation, the government does not acquire a controlling interest. Entrepreneurs might take advantage of subsidies and invest in projects that reduce profits but lead to nonpecuniary gains to entrepreneurs, such as less work (i.e., a moral hazard problem). Should the government desire to assist in managing firms to reduce costs arising from moral hazard, equity participation may be necessary if the government cannot appoint without equity ownership public representatives on the board of directors to monitor the firm.

A second substitute for equity financing is the direct lending of debt by the government to firms. If firms or the owners of firms can bankrupt themselves, such debt becomes risky. Where credit markets are poorly developed, governments can share risk by providing direct loans to businesses at interest rates less than those charged by private lenders. The government provision of debt rather than equity provides the government with a higher claim to the assets of the firm should the firm go bankrupt. When moral hazard problems are especially severe, in that entrepreneurs may increase the likelihood of bankruptcy when the government owns equity, debt financing may be better from the point of view of the government.

On the other hand, equity financing by the government reduces the likelihood of bankruptcy as interest on debt is a fixed charge incurred by the equity owners of the firm. A decrease in leverage (the debt–equity ratio) would reduce the firm's cost of credit, as the firm is less likely to go bankrupt (leaving aside moral hazard issues). Thus there can be a clear trade-off between debt and equity financing as a form of state intervention.

17.5 Appendix A: Evaluation of the risk-discount factor

Under risk aversion and ϕ_j being nonnegatively correlated with second-period consumption,

$$\rho_{ij} = \frac{E^i U_2^i \phi_j}{E^i U_2^i E^i \phi_j} \leq 1 \tag{A1}$$

Let $U_2^i [*]$ be the marginal utility of consumption in the second period when all the value-of-distribution parameters are equal to their mean, μ_{ij}. The result is proved by contradiction.

Suppose $\rho_{ij} > 1$

$$\Longrightarrow E^i U_2^i \phi_j > E^i U_2^i \mu_{ij}$$
$$\Longrightarrow E^i (U_2^i - U_2^i [*]) \cdot (\phi_j - \mu_{ij}) > 0 \tag{A2}$$

(since $U_2^i [*] E^i [\phi_j - \mu_{ij}] = 0$)

Under the assumption of risk aversion and the nonnegative correlation of the individual's second-period consumption with ϕ_j, $U_2^i \overset{>}{_<} U_2^i (*)$ when $\phi_j \overset{>}{_<} \mu_{ij}$. This contradicts (A2), thus proving (A1) to be true.

17.6 Appendix B: The Arrow–Lind conditions and nationalization

The following proves that the government would own all firms wholly if the Arrow–Lind conditions hold.[24]

Suppose the government chooses α, the extent to which it owns the private sector. Each individual's consumption can be written as:

$$c_{2i} (\theta) = (1 - \alpha) f_i (y_i) \phi_i + \gamma_i \alpha \sum_j f_j(y_j) \phi_j$$

The first-order condition for an interior solution is

$$E^i U_2^i \left[\gamma_i \sum_j f_j (y_j) \phi_j - f_i (y_i) \phi_i \right] \qquad \forall i$$

Let expectations of individuals be the same. Moreover, assume that the sizes of firms are the same and $\gamma_i = 1/N$ where N is the number of taxpayers. This implies

$$E U_2^i \left[\frac{1}{N} \sum_j \phi_j - \phi_i \right] = 0 \qquad \forall i$$

Let N be sufficiently large and ϕ_j be independently distributed. With $\Sigma_j \phi_j$ being determinate, $(1/N) \Sigma_j \phi_j = E \phi_i$. Thus

$$E U_2^i [E \phi_i - \phi_i] = 0 \qquad \forall i$$

For the conditions to hold for all individuals, U_2^i must be independent of ϕ_i. When the solution is $\alpha = 1$, U_2^i is independent of θ and the first-order equation is satisfied for all individuals.

Notes

1 L. Musolf defines a mixed enterprise as a corporation with either (1) joint public and private ownership of equity shares or (2) joint control of the management whereby both private and public sectors appoint members on the board of directors; see *Mixed Enterprise and Developmental Perspective* (Lexington, Mass.: Lexington Books, 1972).

2 There are two notions of desirability (or in economic jargon, social-welfare optimality). The first notion holds that the situations of some individuals can be improved without undermining the situations of others by making suitable compensating transfers of wealth from those who gain to those who lose from a policy change (efficiency criterion). The second notion of desirability, which is applied when suitable transfers of wealth cannot be made, holds that the government is concerned not only with the efficiency of a particular policy but also with its impact on equity (i.e., distribution of wealth). It is also important to this subject whether the welfare level of individuals is considered before or after states of the world occur. In a formal sense, the government may be concerned about ex ante welfare of individuals where the measure of welfare is based on expected utility levels achieved before the future is known. However, such a normative rule can lead to the experiencing of much different welfare levels once the future is known. If the government is concerned about ex post welfare, the action taken may be much different. This will be relevant to later discussion. For a discussion on welfare with uncertainty, see P. Hammond, "Ex-ante and Ex-post Optimality Under Uncertainty," University of Essex, Discussion Paper No. 83 (Colchester, Essex, 1976).

3 If such bonds are not risky in that the firm honors its obligation with certainty, the government can share risks only through the ownership of equity, not bonds. See J. Mintz, "State Equity of Industry: A Theoretical Appraisal of Public–Private Mixed Enterprises" (Ph.D. diss., University of Essex, 1980).

4 K. J. Arrow and R. C. Lind, "Uncertainty and the Evaluation of Public Investment Decisions," *American Economic Review* 60 (1970):364–78.

5 As will be pointed out in the last section, other alternative policies such as corporate taxation with a full-loss offset can substitute, although imperfectly, for equity financing as a means for the government to share risks with entrepreneurs.

6 In Figure 17.1 there are two firms and two states of the world. Securities span the consumption sets of individuals, enabling prices of state-contingent commodities to be well defined. If there were only one firm and two states, a stock-market

equilibrium would be possible, but marginal rates of substitution between state-contingent commodities would not be the same for both individuals. Even if riskless bonds were introduced, spanning would not be achieved, as no new linearly independent security is introduced. See P. Diamond, "The Role of the Stock Market in a General Equilibrium Model with Technological Uncertainty," *American Economic Review* 57 (1967):759–76, and L. Gevers, "Competitive Equilibrium of the Stock Exchange and Pareto Efficiency," in *Allocation Under Uncertainty*, ed. J. H. Drèze (London: Macmillan, 1974).

7 For a formal proof of the latter point, see E. Malinvaud, "The Allocation of Individual Risks in Large Markets," *Journal of Economic Theory* 9 (1972):312–28, and E. Malinvaud, "Markets for an Exchange Economy with Individual Risks," *Econometrica* 41 (1973):383–410.

8 A. Sandmo, "Discount Rates for Public Investment Under Uncertainty," *International Economic Review* 13 (1972):287–302.

9 Diamond, "Role of the Stock Market," p. 759–76, and R. Wilson and S. Ekern, "On the Theory of the Firm in an Economy with Incomplete Markets," *Bell Journal of Economics* 5 (1974):171–80.

10 J. Drèze, "Investment Under Private Ownership: Optimality, Equilibrium and Stability," in *Allocation Under Uncertainty*, ed. J. Drèze (London: Macmillan, 1974).

11 γ_i is considered fixed in Sandmo, "Discount Rates for Public Investment," pp. 287–302, and J. Mayshar, "Should Government Subsidize Risky Projects?" *American Economic Review* 67 (1977):20–8.

12 Drèze, "Investment Under Private Ownership," pp. 130–66.

13 If $c_{2i}(\theta) = \gamma_i\,\alpha_j\,f_j$, then for $c_{2i} \neq \bar{c}_{2i}$, $f_j\,\phi_j$ constant and $0 < \lambda < 1$, $\lambda\,c_{2i}(\theta)$ $+ (1 - \lambda)\,\bar{c}_{2i}(\theta) = [\lambda\,\gamma_i + (1 - \lambda)\,\bar{\gamma}_i]\,[\lambda\,\alpha_j + (1 - \lambda)\bar{\alpha}_j]\,f_j\,\phi_j = \lambda\,\gamma_i\,\alpha_j\,f_j\,\phi_j$ $+ (1 - \lambda)\,\bar{\gamma}_i\,\bar{\alpha}_j\,f_j\,\phi_j + \lambda(1 - \lambda)\,f_j\,\phi_j\,(\gamma_i - \bar{\gamma}_i)\,(\alpha_j - \bar{\alpha}_j)$. The third term on the right-hand side is not zero, since $\gamma_i \neq \bar{\gamma}_i$ and $\alpha_j = \bar{\alpha}_j$.

14 Sandmo, "Discount Rates for Public Investment," pp. 287–302.

15 J. Hirshleifer, "Investment Under Uncertainty: Applications of the State Preference Approach," *Quarterly Journal of Economics* 80 (1966):252–77.

16 Arrow and Lind, "Uncertainty and the Evaluation of Public Investment Decisions," pp. 364–78. This is a "risk-spreading" argument in that the cost of risk is spread over individual taxpayers. As the number of taxpayers grows, the cost of risk to each taxpayer reduces more quickly than the return. This argument differs from the "risk-pooling" argument, which states that when a large number of projects are small and independently distributed, the risks of each tend to offset each other. See E. James, "A Note on Uncertainty and the Evaluation of Public Investment Decisions," *American Economic Review* 65 (1975):200–5. Note that the condition of stochastic independence is still important in the risk-spreading argument.

17 Sandmo, "Discount Rates for Public Investment," pp. 287–302.

18 Mayshar, "Should Government Subsidize Risky Projects?" pp 20–2. L. P. Foldes and R. Rees have suggested that the Arrow–Lind conditions do not apply if the returns on public investments are correlated with the tax revenue earned by governments or the funds expended on public programs; see "A Note on the Arrow–Lind Theorem," *American Economic Review* 67 (1977):188–93.

19 J. E. Meade, *The Theory of International Economic Policy*, Vol. 2, *Trade and Welfare* (London: Oxford University Press, 1955).

20 This point is developed by A. Sandmo in "Merit Goods and Ex Post Welfare Optimality" (Bergen, Norway, 1981), unpublished.

21 W. Friedman, *Public and Private Enterprise in Mixed Economies* (New York: Columbia University Press, 1974), p. 152.
22 A full-loss offset arises when the government shares all the losses incurred by a firm at the same rate that profits are taxed.
23 J. Mintz, "Some Additional Results on Investment, Risk Taking and Full Loss Offset Corporate Taxation with Interest Deductibility," *Quarterly Journal of Economics*, Nov. 1981.
24 I want to thank A. B. Atkinson who suggested this proof.